# COMMANDMENTS AND CONCERNS
## Jewish Religious Education in Secular Society

# COMMANDMENTS
# AND CONCERNS

## Jewish Religious Education in Secular Society

# MICHAEL ROSENAK

The Jewish Publication Society
*Philadelphia • New York • Jerusalem   5747 / 1987*

Rosenak, Michael.

   Commandments and concerns.

   Bibliography: p. 274.
   Includes index.
   1. Jewish religious education—Philosophy.   I.  Title.
BM103.R63   1987        296'.07        86–27667
ISBN 0–8276–0279–0

FRONTISPIECE: Photo by Debbi Cooper. Used by permission of Debbi Cooper and the
Pardes Institute, Jerusalem.



Designed by Adrianne Onderdonk Dudden

# Contents

*Preface    vii*

*Introduction    3*


PART ONE: RELIGION AND PHILOSOPHY OF EDUCATION

1    *Jewish Religious Education: Two Philosophical Schools    15*

2    *Aspects of Normative Religious Education    27*

3    *Secular Diagnoses of Educational Crisis    48*

4    *Religious Responses to Secular Solutions    64*

5    *The Scholar, the Believer, and the Educator    83*

6    *Explicit and Implicit Religious Life and Teaching    108*


PART TWO: THEOLOGY OF JEWISH EDUCATION

7    *Norms Despite Modernity: Explicit Educational Theology    129*

8    *Encounter and Deliberation:
     Implicit Educational Theology    151*

9    *Standards and Spontaneity: A Theology
     of Jewish Education    170*

## PART THREE: A THEORY OF RELIGIOUS JEWISH EDUCATION

10   *From Theology to Theory of Religious Education   191*

11   *Educating the Loyal Jew: Theory of Explicit Teaching   207*

12   *Cultivating the Authentic Jewish Individual:
Theory of Implicit Teaching   228*

13   *The Elements of Religious Jewish Education   250*


*Conclusion   270*

*Notes   274*

*Acknowledgments   303*

*Index   305*

# Preface

There are some people who deserve explanation about this book, and others who deserve thanks.

To those who expected a completely detached treatment of Jewish religious education, I must explain that I find it hard to be detached. But I have tried to be fair and honest. To readers who expected solutions to all problems of religious education and recipes for "making them more religious," I must apologize by saying that the disciplines I have integrated in my work are not attuned to that. From these disciplines I have learned that what we need before recipes is reflection and that, after reflection, we may decide to forgo recipes altogether and simply think, talk, and teach with more intelligence, competence, and conviction. I shall go into this matter at length, so there is no point in dwelling upon it here. So much for apologies.

My thanks go to my teachers and friends, to all those who helped me in various ways with the book, and to my family.

First, I should like to mention my teacher, colleague, and friend, Professor Seymour Fox of the Hebrew University, from whom I learned how to read and "do" philosophy of education. His influence on my educational thinking extends far beyond the footnotes that cite him, and the educational conversation that we have conducted between us for many years is reflected in many ideas developed here. I also owe a debt of gratitude to Professor Ernst Akiva Simon, professor emeritus at the Hebrew University, whose religious-educational thought has enriched my life and thinking. He was not formally my teacher, but in many respects he is certainly a mentor. And then there are the many people at the Hebrew University's Melton Centre for Jewish Education and beyond who have commented, encouraged, and generally helped by being knowledgeable and being friends. Professor Arnold Eisen of Stanford University deserves special thanks for encouraging me to expand on an article that was the springboard for this book. Dr. Barry Chazan and Mr. Alan Hoffman, directors of the Hebrew University's Melton Centre for Jewish Education in the Diaspora, made important comments, gave much appreciated advice, and were helpful in many ways. The members of the Curriculum Project on the Teaching of Jewish Values in the Diaspora of the Hebrew University's Melton Centre, a project I was privileged to head, enriched my thinking on my subject immensely, and I am grateful to all of them. Also, I wish to thank Drs. Barry Holtz and Eduardo Rauch of the Jewish Theological Seminary's Melton Center for Jewish Education and Dr. Avraham Shapiro of Tel Aviv University for their interest, which blurred, with Rosenzweigian finesse, the distinction between the professional and the personal. And, of course, the superb typing of Ms. Barbara Piperno and Ms. Terri Picow is especially appreciated. They not only turned untidy pages into a tidy manuscript but also commented when ideas seemed unclear or sentences obscure.

Very special thanks are due to Ms. Barbara Spector, my editor at The Jewish Publication Society. Ms. Spector and I conducted very illuminating postal conversations that led me to re-examine many sentences, words, and ideas. I am grateful to her for her patience and insight.

Last but not least, thanks are due to Dr. David Patterson and his staff at the Oxford Centre for Post-Graduate Hebrew Studies in Yarnton, England. The wonderful summer of 1983 that I spent as a visiting scholar at the Centre I did much revising and some rethinking, and it was there that I put the finishing touches on this book.

There are many others I wish to thank, people with whom I have thrashed out educational ideas, particularly in our Jerusalem community of Jewish educators, but mentioning additional names may be more offensive to those not included than gratifying to those noted. Thanks to all of you!

That religious affirmations should be comprehensive yet critical I learned from my parents. I was taught by my father, of blessed memory, and by my mother, that one can be anchored firmly in religious community without sacrifice of individual sensibility or loss of spiritual freedom. Their lives and teaching exemplify what I have come to see as the creative tension between explicit and implicit religiosity—between what is accepted as self-understood and what invites search and reverent openness.

My children, I suppose, deserve both apologies and thanks. They have been victims of my groping toward a viable theory of religious education in the situation of modernity, and I know that they were often confused and even aggravated. Yet I thank them for often setting me straight, as for their kindness in entering into discussions with me when there were more interesting things to do.

As for my dear wife and friend, Geulah, explanations are useless and thanks, at least in public, are gratuitous. We have been educating together for a long time and are fortunate in sharing a religious view of how to do it. Certainly, we have learned a good deal about the precarious relationship between theory and practice. Where we have fallen short, may God set it right. As for that which we seem to have done well, may we accept it with gratitude.

M.R.

None of . . . (the nations) knows at birth just what it is to be; their faces are not molded while they are still in nature's lap.

But our people, the only one that did not originate from the womb of nature that bears nations, but—and this is unheard of!—was led forth "a nation from the midst of another nation" (Deut. 4:34)—our people was decreed a different fate. Its very birth became the great moment of its life, its mere being already harbored its destiny. Even "before it was formed," it was "known," like Jeremiah its prophet. And so only he who remembers this determining origin can belong to it; while he who no longer can or will utter the new word he has to say "in the name of the original speaker," who refuses to be a link in the golden chain, no longer belongs to his people. And that is why this people must learn what is knowable as a condition for learning what is unknown, for making it his own.

Franz Rosenzweig
"The Builders: Concerning the Law"

Reprinted by permission of Schocken Books Inc. from *On Jewish Learning* by F. Rosenzweig, ed. N. N. Glatzer. Copyright © 1955 by Schocken Books Inc.

# Introduction

This book deals with the problem of religion in contemporary Jewish education. It grew out of my thinking and teaching about Jewish education, which made me realize that religion is always on the agenda of Jewish education, that for many it is *the* agenda, and that is seen as a *problem*. "Religion" and "religious education" are nebulous and controversial terms in this secular and pluralistic age, and *Jewish* "religion" raises special problems of definition, legitimacy, and relevance. The nature of this subject and the rhetoric that envelops it is such that any attempt to clarify the meanings, problems, and possibilities surrounding Jewish religious education in a "non-religious" world arouses suspicion and occasions polemics.

The suspicions and the polemics are not necessarily confined to those who, in Israel, are called the "non-believers" or to professed secularists anywhere. They are to be found also among those Jews in Israel and in the Diaspora who are concerned with the content and who are involved, as parents or educators, in one of the frameworks of religious Jewish education, and who espouse one of several religious ideologies.

For example, members of the Orthodox educational community ask whether the term "religious" as used in a study such as this one encompasses Reform and Conservative Jewish education—and, if so, by what right. On the other end of the spectrum, those radically Reform Jews who persevere in their adherence to the post-Emancipation definition of Jewry as a purely and exclusively religious community insist that "religion" be defined in theological and existential terms that render the cultural forms of the past (i.e., the traditional Jewish law—the halakhah—and its way of thinking) archaic and irrelevant.

Some religious educators are certain that religious Jewish education must be understood as initiation into the observance of the commandments. For some, religious education is bestowing upon the young familiarity with the cultural (and textual) tradition that may spark commitment; others define it as the cultivation of existential awareness, theological concern, and "encounter." Nor may we neglect to mention those religious educators, especially in Israel, who believe that religious education must incorporate a strong commitment to the shaping of the Jewish national renaissance in line with some religious interpretations of Jewish nationhood: mystical, normative, or both.

To write about religious Jewish education is to invite shrugs or frowns also from those who believe that Jewish education in the modern world should be non-religious, or "worldly." The adherents of "general" educational systems—especially in Israel, but also in Jewish communities with a predominantly secular tradition and orientation, such as Argentina—believe that religious education is a distorted or sectarian way of dealing with the Jewish cultural tradition. They are likely to agree that this tradition, given its cultural wealth, its historical circumstances, and its scope necessarily includes religious aspects, but will argue that it can be made meaningful to contemporary Jewish children only if these "religious" features are placed in broader historical and cultural perspectives. In their eyes, specifically religious education will be congenial only to those who desire—or have not outgrown—a truncated ("religious-liberal") or an archaic ("Orthodox") Jewish identity. For secular educators of this persuasion, dealing with Judaism as "religion" and teaching it "religiously" is symptomatic of assimilation into non-Jewish patterns of thinking or testifies to a refusal to move beyond a traditionalist-pietistic stage in the development of Jewish national culture.

As for those Jews whom others often call "ultra-traditionalists," their opinion of theoretical discourse on "religious education" that incorporates not only sacred sources but also the tools and conceptual constructions of social science and educational theory is well known. Such discussion they consider irrelevant except where it makes available useful technologies and tactics. They argue, in this echoing the professedly non-religious, that Judaism is not a "religion." In their eyes, the revealed truth of Torah requires no clarifications provided by—or contexts borrowed from—humanities, philosophy, or science. Like many of the modern Orthodox, the ultra-traditionalists wish to share neither categories nor theories with heretics. They wish to keep their distance from discussions in which they will be described or analyzed scientifically, for in such discussions, they will find themselves grouped together with virtual non-believers. True, such theoretical discourse may contribute clarity to their educational formulations and evaluations. But the price, objective comparison with religious "deviants," is too high.

The preceding paragraphs merely illustrate, in broad and perhaps simplistic strokes, how difficult it is to engage those who are committed to Jewish education in principled discourse on *religious* Jewish education. For, although discussions of Jewish identity and identification can evoke large agreement and even cooperation between Jews of very diverse theological, social, and political convictions (and the Zionist enterprise is both a pioneer and a paradigm of this in the modern world!), discourse on religious education, like that on religion itself, is diverse in the contemporary world. The Jews who call themselves religious not only are not religious in any agreed-upon sense but also are bitterly at odds—often to the extent that they will not deign to talk to one another about their disagreement. Moreover, many Jews who dislike the term "religious"—or even vehemently disclaim it—have characteristics that may plausibly be termed "religious" and will even admit to these orientations (although one person's notion of plausibility in this realm may be another's conception of devious semantics).

The almost complete absence of consensus and common language of discourse about *Jewish* education and *religious* education for Jews (except, ironically, in Israel, where all education that is not Orthodox is officially "non-religious") raises serious problems for one who wishes to treat the subject systematically. For even if it were granted that there are prominent normative and existential dimensions of Jewish world view, culture, and community that can best, even today, be defined in religious terms (and this is *not* granted!), it may still be asked whether any conception of the Jewish religious tradition is both historically authentic and at the same time existentially "present" enough to serve as a relevant basis for educational discourse by the general community of Jewish educators. This tradition has been so massively undermined by science and secularism, by the subjectification of religion and its privatization, that most Jews will be suspicious of any theoretical treatment of Jewish religious education that takes traditional assumptions and data as indispensable elements of educational deliberation. Such a treatment will be dismissed by many as apologetic, as narrow and biased. The very claim that a theoretical investigation of religious Jewish education, or of religion as a factor in Jewish education, is justified and even necessary can be interpreted as testifying to the eccentric or sectarian beliefs of theoreticians and their urge to defend them, rather than to the real needs of Jews who desire to transmit a Jewish identity to their children.

Yet, I believe that the search for theoretical guidelines that will clarify the status and meanings of Judaism as a religious phenomenon for the purposes of educational activity and evaluation is both justified and necessary. It is *justified* because there are institutions, communities, textbooks, curricula, and teachers with articulate or implicit religious assumptions, ideals, and aims; it is *necessary* because there is obscurity or confusion with regard to these assumptions, ideals, and aims.

Let us briefly elaborate on some representative assumptions and give several examples of prevalent confusions:

a. There are many Jewish communities that, for reasons historically related to their desire to gain acceptance in modern liberal societies, have publicly defined themselves—and to a large extent have learned to see themselves—as religious confessional groups. For such communities, conveying a distinctly Jewish message and identity to their children is conceivable and acceptable only through the religious medium, however they understand it. Though the "religious" self-definition is less rigorous in contemporary Jewries in the Western Diaspora than it was in the pre-Holocaust period, largely because of the influence of Israel (and perhaps, of the Holocaust itself) on consciousness, it still dictates much of the organizational structure, image, and self-perception of Jews in these communities. Consequently, it also shapes their view of Judaism and Jewish education.

b. Even among those who rejected this "religious" self-definition and who responded to modernity by defining themselves Jewishly as a national community (specifically, in our contemporary discussion, the Zionists) there have been men and women with a religious, even a religiously Orthodox, conception of Jewish nationality. The Orthodox religious Zionists established a religious school system and a network of youth movements and institutions of their own in which the conception of Judaism taught was national *and* Orthodox; the Orthodox Zionist "school trend" co-existed with "non-religious" Labor and General Zionist "trends" as well as with Orthodox schools that were non-Zionist. Nor should one forget that in the Labor and General Zionist "trends" there were notable religious but non-Orthodox educators who sought to foster a "religious dimension" in *all* Israeli education. Even now, the question of religion in general Jewish culture is constantly on the agenda of the "state-general" school in Israel (which replaced the Labor and General Zionist "trends"); this question has been expressed in an interesting and complex fashion by the controversy concerning "Jewish consciousness" in the Israeli school.

c. The discussion of "religion" in Israeli "non-religious" education points to an inherent feature of Jewish education as such. No Jewish educational system, no matter how "untraditional" in definition and goals, can evade dealing with issues arising out of the individual's search for meaning and consciousness of commitment—*as these issues arise in the national heritage of the Jewish people*. Some will argue that the quest for meaning and the foundations of obligations are "religious" whenever and wherever people become conscious of the "ultimacy" of the pertinent questions. Blatantly secular educators may consider this existential line of reasoning devious. However, the secular Jewish educator, before dismissing it out of hand, will have to keep two particular characteristics of Jewish culture and history in mind.

First, it must be remembered that all non-religious Jewish educators, even when they insist that Judaism is not essentially or only a religious affair, do agree that the religious factor was very important to Jewish culture in the pre-secular age and, thus, that an understanding of the national history and literature requires a sense of historical Jewish sensibility. Part of the meaning of this heritage is allegedly its ability to call forth or demand some "understanding" on the part of the pupil; to the extent that the teacher and the pupil perceive the Jewish tradition as incapable of evoking such an understanding or making spiritual demands, the heritage is viewed as problematic.

Second, it must be remembered that the "secular" national educational ideologies of Jews in Israel and in the Diaspora (with few and marginal exceptions) maintain a traditional view of the relationship of the national Jewish culture to the specific religious heritage of Judaism, insofar as it is generally agreed that non-Jewish religion is incompatible with Jewish national identity. Consistent secularists may consider Jewish religiosity benighted; yet most of them would agree that non-Jewish religiosity is apostasy. This means that the Jewish educator must either deny the significance of "religion" in principle or must seek a way to cultivate spiritual and religious values that can be justified as a reshaping and a partial rediscovery of the Jewish religious tradition.

d. Contemporary successes in religious Jewish education, even in such consistent and thoughtful systems as, for example, the Israeli Yeshiva High School or the Conservative Ramah camps in the United States, create model "products" who embody only partially the wide-ranging religious ideal formulated by the educators concerned. Not only is success often unclearly defined, but also the price of success (say, in the first case, the cultivation of halakhically observant and "learning" Jews) seems to involve a corresponding failure (for example, hostility to humanistic "general" culture) that is all-too-readily disposed of by the argument that these failures are perhaps not failures at all, or that they are insignificant, or that they are inevitable. It is noteworthy, in the instances of educational enterprise just cited, that the most "successful" graduates of Yeshiva High Schools go on to study at higher yeshivot that are ideologically antagonistic to or ambivalent about the ideology of the Yeshiva High School, and that many of the more "creative" graduates of the Ramah camps have "rebelliously" moved to the religious right or left of the camps' theological and halakhic position. Therefore, success and failure, as well as the relationship between them, are areas that deserve definition and examination.

e. Some, if not most, of the disinclination of secular educators to incorporate religious dimensions into Jewish education thoughtfully and articulately flows from conventional, often stereotyped conceptions of religion and religious education or from negative views of what is presented (in the literature of our age, in the mass media, in unpleasant encounters) by groups and individuals who bear the symbols or stigma of "religiosity." This is, of course, particularly true in Israel, where everyone "knows" what to understand by— and expect from—*datiim* ("the religious"); it is also, though perhaps more diffusely, true in certain countries of the Diaspora where Jewish "religion" is at least generically related to what is "known" regarding (non-Jewish) clerical forces of theological benightedness and political reaction.

As a result, the available options with regard to theoretical understandings of religious education usually remain unexamined, philosophically as well as theologically and educationally. What is done in practice, when the occasion indicates the propriety of a bow to "tradition," is heavily folkloric, romanticized, or reductionistic. That is, it is marked by a failure or perhaps an inability to confront the religious tradition seriously. An examination of the diverse meanings, applications, and contexts of religion is thus likely to be useful.

To summarize these points: Those who have a commitment to religious Jewish education should be seeking defensible criteria of success as well as foundations for plausible curricula. As for those who make no claim to such a commitment, they might be well served by a more comprehensive idea of "Jewish education" that will help them deal with their Jewish subject matter in terms acceptable to them and give them Jewish cultural frames of reference for their existential concerns. This too invites an investigation of possible understandings and uses of "religion" in the Jewish school, youth group, camp, community center, and Israeli army base.

In the chapters to follow, I shall be making two assumptions, one substantive and one methodological, that do not enjoy universal consent.

My first assumption is that Jewish religion and all Jewish education are in serious trouble. My claim is that modernity, in both its vulgar and its sophisticated manifestations, has overwhelmed most Jews and, conversely, that most of the Jews who refuse to be overwhelmed have not adequately confronted modernity. One finds Jewish educators speaking warmly of the integration of the Torah and general wisdom, yet much Jewish education neglects or evades Jewish knowledge or is indifferent or antagonistic to universal forms of inquiry. Our educational practice is usually unclear, indicating that we do not know what we want; it is often dishonest, that is, we know what we want but do not believe in it, or we have decided that in present circumstances no one who knows what we know will believe it. Consequently, we lack theories of religious Jewish education (or, in the case of non-religious schools, theories of the status and significance of religious elements in the Jewish tradition). When we have theories, they are as partial as the theologies or ideologies that nourish them. And this, as we shall see, leads to educational distortions.

This substantive assumption will annoy, first of all, secular educators, at least to the extent that they trace the crisis of religion in the modern world and in "religious" Judaism to its alleged pretensions and untruth. But it will also annoy those religious educators who are convinced that confrontation is either unnecessary or undignified, either because they believe that in their camp there has been successful and adequate confrontation or because they are embarrassed by their vulnerability.

By confrontation with modernity I do not mean simplistic accommodation or relevance at any price. I am not arguing for a reduction of religious and traditionally Jewish categories to scientific ones. "Inadequate confrontation" should thus not be understood to signify "insufficient compromise," for reasoned rejection of aspects of modernity is certainly legitimate. Conversely, one can hardly even discuss the issue of religious education in the modern world if one rejects *all* contemporary culture or considers it meaningless. In the enterprise of cultivating persons who are both reasonably sophisticated and able to deal with the world as it is and who are in some comprehensive sense loyal and pious, guidelines are obviously needed; if these guidelines are to strengthen the tradition and make it as all-embracing in the present as it claims to be perennially, then it will certainly have to be seen *also* (but not *only*) through the prism of contemporary knowledge, experience, and insight.

My second, methodological assumption is that the discussion of religious education is most communicative, fruitful, and honest if it strives to be, in a large and generous sense, academic. The task is to clarify an educational problem: that of the place of "religion"—its ideas and inherent educational assumptions, its texts and their capacity to foster initiation into community and personal growth, and the contexts in which "Judaism" speaks and is spoken to and about. Here, this will be accomplished by examination of recorded statements of relevant experience, chosen according to defensible criteria, and systematic reflection and analysis of such experiences as we find them in historical, social-scientific, and philosophical research and scholarship. That is, I shall speak of religious phenomena as they affect educational theory and practice, not only as men of God relate their experiences but also as theologians ponder what saints have said, as social scientists analyze the contents of their words, and as philosophers of religion draw ground rules for wide-ranging conversations about religion. I shall also attempt to draw that discussion into the realm of educational theory. This discussion, guided by the philosopher of education, sifts through the inter-disciplinary discourse, seeking a better understanding of the nature of the "religious subject matter" and a way to perceive and prescribe more accurately how children, teachers, and society may use it—and learn from it.

This does not, of course, imply that academicians and educational theorists may not have beliefs and aims with regard to the transmission of what they believe to be true and normative. Nor is it being suggested that so-called objective inquiry is not predicated on a particular kind of belief, based on particular experiences and axioms. It means only that the discussion should be comprehensible and "inviting" to those who do not share a particular immediate experience of religion and that detached study, despite its limitations, can be illuminating and can nourish discourse. Ignoring modern scholarship, in the context of the contemporary world, is a gateway to obscurantism; taking this scholarship to be "all there is to know about it" can readily lead to idolatrous systems, illusions, educational manipulations, and ultimate disillusionment. I do not wish this book to be mysterious to agnostics, nor to bring "strange fires" to those who hear or await the word of the living God.

The concept underlying this book is that two fundamental orientations to educational theory, the normative-ideational and the deliberative-inductive, are in many respects analogous to two basic religious ways of understanding. The religious orientation correlative to normative-ideational educational theory I shall term *explicit religion;* it concerns itself with what is imposed on the learner (and the teacher) by tradition and authority. The converse religious orientation I shall call *implicit religion;* this concerns itself with subjective spirituality and individual discovery.

My thesis is that educational theory, at least in our age, must be both normative and deliberative and that a theology of education that does not incorporate both explicit *and* implicit religiosity will lead to partial—dogmatic or vacuous—understandings of religious tradition. Moreover, I suggest that theology of education must be translated into religious educational theory and that this translation today requires the insights to be gained from social scientific understandings of "norms" and "development," lest the theory of education be simply preached at teachers and become a frill or a sham in the educational enterprise.

I make no claim to have discovered or coined the concepts, nor am I proposing new philosophies of religion. My aim is to clarify ideas that are ''out there'' but that sometimes are blurred. In the process, I shall attempt to expand on them and to put them together in a way that may make sense to teachers. If this effort succeeds, I shall be grateful and, presumptuously, a little bit more hopeful.

# Part One

# RELIGION AND PHILOSOPHY OF EDUCATION

# 1 Jewish Religious Education: Two Philosophical Schools

## MOVEMENTS AND PHILOSOPHIES IN MODERN EDUCATION

Our century, like other eras of great crisis, has been blessed with an abundance of educational schools of thought. Both the crisis and the schools are rooted in the philosophical and social movements toward modernity of the preceding centuries. These movements reshuffled religious beliefs and at times discarded or rejected them as they sought to interpret and direct the economic, political, and scientific revolutions of the age. The developments were swift and complex. Though attempts were sometimes made to see them as a gradual and rational unfolding of human potential or of historical necessity, this detached and serene view of things was difficult to maintain in the face of social upheavals and political instability. Thought and ideology alternated between utopian expectation and romantic yearning, between rationalistic optimism and a sense of insecurity and foreboding.

Given the traumas of the twentieth century, the forebodings were well-founded. For, after Freud and Einstein, in the wake of "the guns of August" of 1914 and the cloud of Hiroshima in 1945, the revolutions and innovations could no longer be seen as only innovative and expansive; they were perceived by most as complicated, if not terrifying. Once this perception was established, it was inevitable that the sense of "great events" should also bring an air of crisis. Thus educational theories and schools of thought proliferated, engendered by revolutionary hope and existential fears.

Anyone who has taken one or two undergraduate courses in philosophy of education knows about the abundance of educational schools of thought in modern society. The liberal arts "tradition" defended "great books" from an overemphasis on prosaic science; progressive education "reconstructed" the school in order to defend the child against the text. Since the Second World War, all practitioners of education have read—or read about—theorists and curricula based on "the structure of the disciplines," which sought to teach central concepts and methods of diverse fields, enabling modern pupils to gain the creative competence needed in the world of tomorrow. Teachers have also encountered the tools, if not the theory, of neo-behaviorism, which claimed that our society most urgently required not culture, nor creativity, but skill and technical mastery. And, of course, most teachers, especially if they are interested in religion and the humanities, have followed the development of "humanistic psychology," whose proponents have attacked the alleged lack of soul in "structure-of-the-disciplines" teaching and the mechanistic programming of knowledge in neo-behaviorism. These writers have demanded a reemphasis on "personality" in educational endeavor.[1]

Philosophers of education have organized and typed these varied educational movements according to basic conceptions of reality, human nature, knowledge, and, consequently, instruction. For example, Scheffler refers to three fundamental views of knowledge and to three "philosophical models of instruction," whereas Lamm distinguishes among the imitative, molding, and developmental "logics in teaching."[2] In the various contemporary educational movements, the fundamental philosophical orientations toward reality, value, human endowment, and knowledge find distinctive programmatic embodiments. The movements are numerous and, in principle, almost innumerable, for they arise in response to new challenges and situations, whether the Industrial Revolution or the Russian Sputnik. The philosophies, on the other hand, are in a sense perennial, although they are periodically invigorated and enlarged by new thought and knowledge. For the philosophies, as already noted, are systematic statements of fundamental orientations: to humanity and the world, to truth and value, to criteria of what is trivial and what deserves devotion. They bespeak different temperaments; they speak to different sentiments. In our civilization, these visions, implicitly or explicitly, date back to the prophet and talmudic sage on the one hand and to the Greek philosopher and dramatist on the other.

For the purposes of our discussion on religious Jewish education, we shall examine these fundamental views through the prism of two models of educational thinking. One we shall call the *normative-ideational* model; the other, the *deliberative-inductive* one.[3] I believe that an examination of these two orientations will help us to focus our discussion of Jewish religious education; I am hopeful that it will make us more sensitive to the central issues of religious education, help us to distinguish among diverse religious inclinations and ideologies, and make us better equipped to identify central questions that must be asked and analyzed. Indeed, in later chapters, we shall attempt to find these normative and deliberative approaches on the map of religious experience and theology.

Here, we shall be looking at these orientations as alluded to, implied, or interpreted by contemporary educational thinkers whose intent is curricular and analytical rather than unequivocally partisan with regard to a specific movement, for our aim is to illustrate philosophical orientations rather than to review ideological schools of thought. The reason for this is two-fold: (1) Educational movements are numerous (there are certainly more than two), and they interpret the basic ''visions'' in specific directions, since they are not only ''orientations'' but also explicit responses to perceived challenges. (2) Most comprehensive educational movements, while leaning to one orientation and claiming to spell out aspects of it, are also indebted to insights and assumptions of the other orientation.

## *The Normative-Ideational Orientation*

The normative-ideational point of view begins educational discourse (which prescribes and evaluates educational practice) with the defense of ideal goals, based on or linked to the exposition of true ideas. These true ideas may be declared eternally valid by a philosopher who expounds a vision; or they may, with or without metaphysical buttressing, articulate a society's fundamental convictions and insights.[4] In either case, the normative-ideational viewpoint posits that certain understandings correspond to some objective or external (to the knowing subject) truth; certain attitudes and actions are good and certain knowledge is valuable. The major principle of this orientation is either that ideas that are true and good must be embodied in ideal ways of understanding or action, or, when the orientation is less scholastic and metaphysical, that norms and operative ideals can be expressed—and justified— in terms of abstract and comprehensive ideas that reflect the heights of human understanding or cultural achievement. In either case, the ideals posited for model human behavior and wisdom are the philosophical ground of educational endeavor, determining what human beings, individually and collectively, should optimally be helped to become. These ideals, properly related to one another and coherently linked to general concepts by thinkers, constitute the philosophy of education.[5]

Only after the ''true ideas'' have been located and brought down into the human world in the form of ideals or, conversely, after society's ideals have been clarified and defended by conceptual analysis, does the educational discussion move to an examination of concrete and specific realities "out there"—in society and in the particular child. This examination is necessary in order to determine how the ideal goals may best—or most nearly—be achieved under the less-than-ideal conditions that characterize all *practical* (i.e., empirical) situations. For all education takes place in a specific environment, with specific pupils, variously endowed and motivated. The practical educational problem, therefore, is how to transmit a desirable corpus of knowledge, commitment, and competence under the given (prosaic) circumstances. The educational discussion is concerned with recognizing the obstacles to ideal achievement and partially overcoming them.

Thus, in the normative-ideational approach, the particular circumstances— social, psychological, economic, or ideological—are significant mainly because they constitute the soil in which *a priori* principles or norms, as expressed in a "philosophy of education," must be planted. The assumption of the "normatively" inclined educator is either that his or her fundamental objectives are (theoretically) true and good for all times and all people or that they adequately embody the wisdom of a historical society that will be true to itself only if it continues its cumulative tradition. But because education deals with human beings and not angels, with real rather than theoretical conditions, we require practical deliberation on plausible strategies in education. Without knowledge of particular conditions, normative philosophies cannot be translated into concrete educational objectives. As Tyler expresses it, this knowledge provides the educator with "certain kinds of information and knowledge [that] provide a more intelligent basis for applying the philosophy (of the educator) in making decisions about objectives."[6] Objectives are the result of a negotiation between a *philosophy* and the elements in the given human reality that must be taken into account. The philosophy "screens" possible objectives in terms of its definition of the nature of a good life and a good society, even as psychology of learning, a second "screen," gives us realistic expectations of possible achievement. But philosophy, the first "screen," is the normative one, for "in the final analysis objectives are matters of choice, and they must therefore be the considered value judgments of those responsible for the school."[7] We begin educational discourse, therefore, with guiding principles.

Hirst, using analytical tools for establishing bases of educational philosophy, maintains that "for curriculum planning to be rational, it must start with clear and specific objectives, and then, and only then, address itself to discovering the plan of means, the content and method in terms of which these objectives are to be obtained." Hirst, in his analysis, is not concerned with the truth or value of a given set of objectives. He wishes merely to clarify *what we mean* by them. His argument is that the educator is one who teaches in order to achieve a set of objectives.[8] A *good* educator does this *well,* under specific circumstances. Hirst's concept of an educational theory is normative; he suggests that educational theories, unlike descriptive ones identified with scientific inquiry, are prescriptive. They help the educator to decide what should be done, under given conditions, to achieve philosophically conceived objectives.[9]

Those educators who view the issues of religious education in general, and Jewish religious education in particular, in terms congenial to this normative-ideational approach are likely to think of educational theory in an overtly theological fashion.[10] They will posit, on the basis of normative-theological ideals and commitments as garnered from the tradition, what religion "means," what it says "to" and "about" education, and what it envisions as ideal outcomes of religious education. This does not mean that they will not be influenced by what they have learned about the history of their religion, by the anthropologist's view of religious development, by the sociologist's theories of society and religious authority, and by psychological research into the varieties of religious experience. But these influences on their educational theory are either theological, and thus indirect, or instrumental, and thus normatively trivial. In the former case, new normative religious educational philosophy is really (and primarily) new theology; in the latter case, new knowledge is seen as providing the ability to use new tactics in education.

Jewish educators whose view is based on this approach know (or believe that, in principle, they could know if they had the necessary diligence or insight) what Judaism is in its "essence." When they say that historically "it has always meant" observance of the *mitzvot* (commandments) or monotheistic faith or prophetic morality, they are not primarily arguing a historical issue but offering a declaration of normative conviction. They are saying what loyalty and continuity require; what a good Jew must do and what (perennial) meanings Judaism offers. They are convinced that all that is wrong in Jewish life and Jewish education arises from the corrosion and corruption of the religious bases of educational philosophy. In this way they understand the community's lack of interest in inculcating religious commitment, the dearth of serious students willing to consider Jewish education as a career, the inability of even good schools, staffed by good teachers, to achieve what formerly, in perhaps "better" times, was done routinely (so they believe) by the teacher and the book, in cooperation with the home and the street.

Consequently, normative-ideational educators feel that the apathy and ignorance that characterize "the world out there" make "real" Jewish education a difficult task, so that perhaps only an elite can be *really* educated under present circumstances. Yet, educational discussion should search for ways to supply everyone with fundamentals and an appreciation of normative Judaism (as represented by the elite). These ways, based on a thorough analysis of the concrete realities, will include better selection and packaging of materials, greater awareness of negative factors in the environment and more diligence in neutralizing them, and more effective teacher training.

For normative-ideational educators, therefore, the basic problem is always and *a priori* known and evident. Likewise, a solution is (in principle, at least) clear. The problem is "not enough (or no) Judaism" as represented by a cumulative tradition and defined and interpreted by theologians who speak for a given normative understanding of the tradition; the solution is in achieving more "real" Jewish belief, life, community.

The central educational issue is how to diminish the problem by broadening the scope of the solution and how to make given circumstances more congenial to known religious objectives. Orthodox normative educators, when they argue that children should be taught to be "more religious," generally mean that youngsters should be more effectively initiated into a community of Orthodox belief and halakhic practice.[11] When Reform educators say that religious teaching ought to make children "really religious," they are more likely to be thinking of an ideal spiritual orientation as understood by Reform Jews, one linked to symbolic acts that are meaningful to the Jewish people as well as to a moral commitment associated with Jewish spiritual traditions. Both educators, Orthodox and Reform, are aware that "out there" most people neither understand nor care about "real Judaism"; in both cases, religious education is meant to bring about some change in that situation. Both of them are glum about the gap between "ideal" Jewish education and the realities, between Judaism and the Jews. They take comfort from "model social situations" that are, they believe, at least partially a consequence of successful education, certainly a partial embodiment of what they mean by "real" Jewish life (such as Boro Park in Brooklyn as an Orthodox community, Kibbutz Yahel in the Negev as a Reform one).[12] Both educators also "do the best they can" in generally grim circumstances with people to whom they are *a priori* committed by their "philosophy."

In concrete terms, the normative educator sees the solution to the problem of Jewish education in the successful molding of pupils by Jewish subject matter that is represented and adequately transmitted by good teachers. It is assumed that "success" is ultimately judged by categories supplied by the normative tradition itself, even as "Jewish subject matter" is defined and selected on the basis of the tradition. The problem the normative educator faces is that the children who must be shaped by the subject matter belong to communities that are Jewishly in a state of disorder and live in environments that are obstacles to proper molding.

However, although children and communities are both "problematic" for the contemporary normative-ideational educator, in principle they do not represent the same kind of problem. The educational problem of children is perennial and inherent, since education is molding and initiation. All children, at all times, are born without culture and must be nurtured. The problem of community is historical: It is the result of Enlightenment, Emancipation, and other developments that engendered the modern secular society, which, in turn, undermines religious Jewish norms. If the community were more congenial, children could be more readily molded.[13]

## *The Deliberative-Inductive Orientation*

The second approach to educational discourse and practice, the deliberative-inductive one, is located in a different world of concepts. The point of departure for educational deliberation in this school of thought is not what is demanded of people as they stand under a roof of imposed values, but how they will interact with the world and other people, how they will understand themselves and solve the problems that obstruct proper "creative" functioning and well-being. Educated individuals are not those who correspond to some pre-established and imposed pattern of wisdom and virtue, but those who can understand reality, relate themselves meaningfully and effectively to it, change themselves when necessary, and shape the environment when feasible and desirable. In short, the educated person is one who is equipped to solve problems. Achievement in education is to locate a problem, to find a tentative solution to it, and to have both the ability to implement the solution and the courage to abandon it when it loses its relevance or effectiveness. Ideas are not to be equated with a vision of truth far above or deep within earthly reality, but, in the words of Dewey, are to be seen

as anticipations of possible solutions. They are anticipations of some continuity or connection of an activity and a consequence which has not as yet shown itself. They are therefore tested by the operation of acting upon them. They are to guide and organize further observations, recollections, and experiments. They are intermediate in learning, not final.[14]

However, before there are solutions, however tentative, and problems, however carefully discovered, there are *problematic situations,* which Schwab has described as a consciousness of "conditions which we wish were otherwise,"[15] a feeling of unease. The root of the unease is to be found in a sense of imbalance, of malfunctioning that may be traced to psychological, or even biological, sources, but the uneasy feeling is to be understood within a broad context of society and environment. The problematic situation is analogous to a symptom immediately perceived by the sufferer before he discovers with the aid of medical experts the nature and source of the disease. The relationship of the problematic situation to the problem is therefore comparable with that of symptom to diagnosed disease. Because we have become aware of an uncomfortable symptom, we know that *something* is wrong, and we attempt to discover by intelligent probing and research ("deliberation") exactly what is amiss (i.e., the actual disease).[16] That is, we discover the *problem*. Only then does it become plausible to weigh varying and alternative courses of action in an attempt to accomplish what Dewey describes as "the rectifying of present troubles, the harmonizing of present incompatibilities, by projecting a course of action which gathers into itself the meaning of them all."[17] In brief: The problems that must be dealt with arise and become the agenda for deliberation only because of a consciousness of unease and a desire to find out "what to do about it." This is accompanied by a realization that prior patterns of thought and conduct do not dissolve the problematic situation and that one may, in this situation, be faced with a new problem. However, the problems are never obvious, exactly as, to use Fox's illustration, a headache is never "obviously" symptomatic of either indigestion or cancer.[18] Thus, problems are properly located only by experts. Furthermore, the problems are not to be determined by *a priori* principles, either ontological or moral; we know of their existence because of experienced discomfort, not because of indignation at the destruction of objective norms.

Just as there are no permanent solutions in the deliberative-inductive approach, so are there no perennial formulations of problems. Reality is too plastic for such finality; moreover, the way that the problem is stated is a significant factor in the determination of proposed solutions. As a result, it may become necessary, in the course of "spelling out" or testing a solution, to revise the formulation of the problem if this will eliminate difficulties in the agreed-upon solution or expose more congenial—or simpler—alternatives. Obviously, this conception of "problems" and "solutions" is heavily indebted to scientific method and philosophy.

Fox has pointed out that the educational orientations, which we have called the normative-ideational and the deliberative-inductive approaches, and the theorists one may marshal in support of them, should not be viewed as diametrically opposed.[19] Tyler and Hirst, for example, agree that deliberation is necessary to determine the rightful role or weight of the diverse elements "out there" and their predictable interactions with normative "screening" philosophies. Conversely, Schwab agrees that a normative philosophy may be a legitimate constituent element of deliberation. Therefore, the "unease" that initiates deliberation may be that of very "normative" Jewish educators (whether Zionist, Hasidic, or Classic Reform) whose "problematic situation" is that their traditional or accustomed ways of transmitting enthusiasm for aliyah, devotion, or prophetic ethics are not "functioning" well. Indeed, we shall argue that both approaches must be used in religious Jewish education, and brought into confrontation, on both theological and pedagogical grounds.

Yet, it may be posited that religious Jewish educators who feel an affinity for the deliberative-inductive approach will tend to analyze, implement, and evaluate differently from their colleagues whose inclinations are normative-ideational. Whereas the latter insist that aims are arbitrary unless based on principles drawn from the world of true ideas or normative values, the former will consider such principles "meaningful" only if the context can be shown to be congenial to the premises. For the deliberative-inductive mode is uncomfortable with perennial truths out of the context of given particulars.[20]

Normative-ideational educators find deliberation unsettling and unfocused unless the discussants understand and can say "what they want," namely, which problem they are trying to solve. Deliberative-inductive teachers, on the other hand, are distressed with articulated principles or "absolutes" because these absolutes set potentially stifling pre-conditions on deliberation and *finding* the problem. Deliberative-inductive concepts of tradition and culture will usually be more heavily indebted to social sciences than to theology, and these educators will incline to the "liberal" temperament, which sees the past as a resource, selectively invoked, rather than a repository of binding norms.

The deliberation process characterizing the second school of thought is experimental in its fundamental methodological assumptions; its rhetoric is down to earth and its modes of research are rational. Yet, at the same time, this deliberative process calls for the consideration of so many factors and is so complex that, in all but trivial cases, "the appropriateness of a particular choice" of action ultimately corresponds and testifies to the experience of the individual, and it is the individual who must weigh—and decide.[21] The deliberative-inductive approach is thus congenial to those who value scientific thinking and yet think of moral and existential decision making in a very personal and subjective manner. Teachers with this orientation are likely to see themselves as being more open, curious, and rational than their "dogmatic" (normative-ideational) colleagues; they are likely to feel that moral vision must correspond to *their* insights as well as to the prophet's. Rules, in this conception, are more like regulative paths to insight than normative prescriptions.

The deliberative-inductive model would seem, therefore, to appeal to a different kind of religious sentiment from the normative-ideational one. This sentiment would be religiously more inclined to the indwelling spirit than to God's transcendent majesty, more supicious of religious authority than worried about the spiritual misuses of autonomy, more devoted to the sanctity of the child's soul than reverent toward the communal and historical wisdom represented by the teacher.

The Jewish educator who favors the deliberative-inductive approach, like the proponent of the normative-ideational orientation, is uneasy and concerned about what is happening in the Jewish school, but the concern will be evoked and expressed in a different way. The deliberative-inductive educator will focus dismay not on the fact that people are not practicing Judaism sufficiently but on the apparent "irrelevance" of the tradition and its failure to "speak" to people or to deal with their "real" problems. This teacher will wish to examine what has gone wrong in the "power" of the tradition; the boredom of children and the subtle sabotage of parents inform the deliberative-inductive educator that the community is not *related* to the religious tradition. The teacher wishes to examine how the child's questions (and that of parents *and teachers*) can be located in the tradition so that the "answers" indicated within the Jewish heritage can be seen to make sense and can be applied or used as valuable resources. The deliberative-inductive educator is not certain that it can be stated, in advance of deliberation, what "a good Jew" is in the twentieth century, for yesteryear's "normative" Jew may seem spiritually inadequate in the present.

All that the deliberative-inductive educator knows in advance is that *something* is wrong: with the state of Judaism, with the strength of Jewish identity, with the spiritual nourishment given the individual by the religious tradition of the Jews. The religious educator of this school of thought may surmise that such *problematic situations* as anomie and assimilation are caused by the loss of "the religious dimension" (which is put forward as the conjectured *problem*) and by the philosophies of secularism (which are seen as unsatisfactory solutions). In line with *this* formulation of the problem, Judaism will be relevant if (a) it can be shown to address itself to such problems (i.e., it offers avenues of restoring men and women to the religious dimension of experience), and (b) it can be seen to be a vital framework for dealing with unpredictable and variegated problematic situations (i.e., it has innovative and creative capacities).

But, of course, other Jewish educators, on the basis of deliberation-following-unease, may decide that the traditional "religious" way of apprehending Judaism is unproductive and useless (i.e., false) for the modern Jew, and that the religious way has been—or should be—outgrown and discarded. In their eyes, the problem may be considered the normative religious definition of "Judaism" itself, which, it can be charged, alienates modern secular-minded people. Normative-ideational educators who are religious know in advance "what to answer" to such secular colleagues; deliberative-inductive educators must take these colleagues more seriously because they admit to sharing a *problematic situation* with them.

## THE TWO ORIENTATIONS AND JEWISH TRADITION

We may summarize as follows: Normative-ideational educators begin their educational discourse with a conviction of what is right; deliberative-inductive educators begin with a feeling that something is wrong. The first group, as Jewish educators, wish to derive a comprehensive "philosophy of education" from the Jewish tradition and to apply it under given circumstances; the second seek to disclose the reasons for contemporary Jewish unease, to locate the questions that Jews are asking in their socio-cultural situation, and to examine the accessibility of religious answers supplied by the tradition. They are somewhat intimidated by conceptions of "philosophy of education" in the classic sense, which seem (to them) more attuned to system and detached thought than to ongoing discussion and to the flow of experience. Normative-ideational teachers or theorists frown on "flow of experience" as a vacuous notion bespeaking subjectivism and individual idiosyncrasy. They affirm that educated people live within a tradition that shapes their understanding of reality and invites them to responsibility; to which deliberative-inductive–oriented teachers will retort that people will refuse to live within a tradition unless the tradition is alive. And "life" denotes the capacity to deal with what are perceived as real problems, distilled out of genuine discontent with previous ways of thinking, acting, and reacting.

We intend to relate seriously to both schools of thought in analyzing the problem of religious Jewish education; we hope to learn from both. The first is obviously the "classic" model of educational thought. It overtly proposes a structure and substance for a normative philosophy of religious Jewish education, standing guard over the integrity and authentic "presence" of the tradition in the educational enterprise that is termed "religious." The second offers us a process that suggests "what to do next"—other than capitulation—when "classic" normative conceptions break down and fail, in new situations, to mobilize allegiance. The normative tradition must always remain visible, even in times of crisis, if Jewish religious education is to refer to a historical and cultural entity; the deliberative tradition must be called upon if Judaism is to remain in the world. Or, to paraphrase Abraham J. Heschel, the Torah must be *from* Heaven and yet not *in* Heaven.[22]

What is meant by a ''classic'' model of educational thought? What, in this model, are seen to be the tasks to be addressed in education? How is it—or can it be—related to religious tradition? And when does normative-ideational education, in which all problems are well defined, itself become problematic?

We now turn to these questions.

# 2   Aspects of Normative Religious Education

There are three questions, according to Frankena, that concern every normative educational thinker.[1] (1) Which "dispositions" are to be considered good? (2) Why are these attributes or dispositions considered to be good and worthy of cultivation, and which criteria and principles led to the choice of these rather than others? (3) How and by what means or processes can these chosen attributes be cultivated in the learner?

Although the third question, which deals with means and processes, is also related to normative-ideational educational thought because it concerns itself with the nature of knowledge and the meaning of "teaching" and "learning," it will not play a central role in our discussion in this chapter, since it is heavily dependent on the "screen" of psychology as well as practical pedagogy. Here, our interest is primarily in deciding what is good and worthy of being taught and the establishment of criteria for what is "known" to be good and worthy.

Educational thinkers, even when they are not dealing overtly with educational questions but with such issues as individual happiness, social reconstruction, and the characteristics of virtue and truth, deal with the normative questions: *What is good to teach and how do we know that it is good?* in three ways. Often, they address themselves to the affirmation and clarification of a world view in which true ideas—somehow "above" prosaic human realities— are related to operative human ideals "within" the real world. At other times, they are primarily concerned with the issue of culture and cultural continuity, basing themselves on the dual assumption that (a) the educating society wishes to be continued, and (b) individuals must live the cultural heritage in ways somehow congenial to them as persons. And usually, educational thinkers, whether their approach is philosophical or cultural, will address themselves to the existential issue of "the educated individual" as a whole person, who not only lives by ideals and cultural "goods" but also through whom the pristine qualities of a world view and a heritage are illuminated and shown to be worthy and noble.

These philosophical, cultural, and existential approaches to normative educational theory are not, of course, really distinct, but they are distinguishable. They allow us to approach our problem from differing perspectives and, as we shall see, they pinpoint different aspects of the contemporary crisis of normative-ideational education.

## THE PHILOSOPHICAL APPROACH: VALUES AND THE WORLD VIEW

The first approach to education in the normative-ideational orientation concerns itself with society's (and the educator's) *Weltanschauung:* basic beliefs about reality, knowledge, and value that are embodied in a comprehensive system of ideas and ideal patterns of behavior.[2] In this context, all the primary ontological, epistemological, and axiological questions of reality, knowledge, and value may be relevantly posed. For example: What is the nature of the world and of humanity? What can be known and what is worth knowing? What is virtue and how do we know that it is virtuous? Can human beings, given their "nature," be virtuous? Does reality, as known to us through sense and theory, or feeling and will, have any connection with the good as morally experienced? Can one assume any reliability in the reports conveyed to us by our senses, our theory, and our moral experiences? Are people "naturally" good? If so, how can they be saved from corruption? If not, how can they be cultivated?

What is believed to be real, knowable, and virtuous will determine, on a philosophical level, how an educational vision approaches a concrete human reality. The basic principles or beliefs, drawn from "primary forms of understanding and awareness," provide theoretical criteria for curricular selectivity: what to include and what to exclude, what to stress and what to consider superfluous, how to approach what is deemed important and how to build intelligence and morality. The vision, articulated in ontological, epistemological, and axiological ideas, will offer guidelines for educators who wish to understand such conceptions as "experience"; it will tell them what is admissible in thinking about experience and "reality" and "worth." On the basis of the theory, one may maintain that "knowing" is "really" insight, or an internal-

ized moral code, or sensual contact, or technical competence; armed with beliefs, one may decide whether, *in principle,* chemistry or Talmud is deserving
of more time, or whether both are equally worthy—or equally insignificant.[3]

The educational normative vision will vary, depending on the asserted relationship between the real, the knowable, and the good. If, for example, the
good can be known—whether through revelation, intellect, action, insight,
feeling, or some combination of these and perhaps other factors—and the
"real" and the "good" have a common "providential" origin, one may expect a large measure of optimism and cultural self-confidence in the educational ideals that "flow" from this belief. Conversely, if it is held that the
"real" is morally senseless and that the "good" is heroically attained and pre-
cariously and "absurdly" maintained, the derived educational ideals are likely
to be pessimistic, individualistic, "existential."

But because all of the foregoing is only *ideationally* constructed, this is not
*necessarily* the case. One may believe in a senseless world that yet accords the
hope of salvation through the anchor of mind or fellowship; one may be radically individualistic yet believe in a God Who created the world and gave human beings knowledge of His moral will. The reason for these seeming
discrepancies is that principles (basic beliefs and ideas) are never unambiguous, and they are never educationally sufficient, for they take on actual meaning from the mode of their interpretation and translation into *norms* of social
and individual life. In other words, educational world view is no less concerned with the translation of beliefs into "ideal" embodiments in the lives of
real people than it is with the affirmation of the principles themselves. Indeed,
with respect to the Jewish tradition, it may be agreed that the ideal embodiments precede in experience and consciousness the ideas that systematically
buttress them; commandments come before theology, and "listening" to God
is a more primary form of understanding than is "seeing" Him.[4] But in all
cases and cultures, the theoretical-normative sage or thinker cannot be said to
be addressing education unless he or she indicates what given principles would
"ideally" look like in a social, cultural, and moral context. Thus, the fact that
two thinkers both believe in, say, atheistic existentialism is not likely to make
them educational allies, if the one translates this "belief about" reality, knowledge, and virtue into a normative pattern of humanistic liberalism and the other
gives his ideas concrete ideological shape through fascism. Both of them can
demonstrate how their norms (liberal and fascistic) flow from their atheistic
existential belief, but beliefs that are disembodied, not "brought down" into
the world, have not yet revealed their educational significance and intentions.

A good example of the relationship between basic principles (ideas) and
ideal patterns (norms) in human life is that between *faith* and *religion.* The

former, when used in the sense of "belief," is a philosophical view of reality, knowledge, and value, even when it bases itself on the primary form of mystical, rather than intellectual, experience; the latter consists of discrete ways of translating this view into human life through norms. A Catholic and a Jew may share many principles, such as belief in a created world, revealed truth, and ultimate redemption, but they share few religious norms, or ideal embodiments of these principles. Therefore, they cannot agree about what kind of world God created, in the normative sense of how one should relate to it religiously; they differ about what He revealed and thus do not share the same commandments, and they disagree about the nature of His redemption and therefore do not share an ideal of a perfected world and how (or even *if*) to "work" toward it. As a result, they cannot "do" religious education together.

Most specifically, thoughtful parents would like their children to study at schools in which their cherished norms are taught on the basis of their principles. But, as a result of the unambiguous nature of norms and the amorphous character of the beliefs to which these norms are linked, most parents, if they must choose between their principles and their norms, between their "faith" and their "religion," will choose the school that more closely approximates their norms, their social and personal ideal. Thus, one may be an Orthodox Jew who shares a common theological language with certain Reform friends more than with certain Conservative ones—at least if the former speak of Torah in theological terms and the latter prefer cultural-historical ones. Yet if the community has no Orthodox school, the children of this Orthodox Jew will probably be sent to a Conservative school and not to a Reform one. The reason is that in the Conservative school there is more of what the Orthodox Jew considers Torah study and a closer approximation to what he or she deems proper Sabbath observance, and the atmosphere seems to be more (what the Orthodox parent recognizes as) religious. Conversely, a "liberal" Conservative Jew who has come to settle in Israel and consequently must choose between a "general" and a "religious" (i.e. Orthodox) school may well decide on the Orthodox school because it *is* "religious" and "children learn more Torah" there; on the other hand, if the liberal Jew decides on the general school, it is because it represents an ideal that is more congenial to the parent, such as an "open" attitude toward the Jewish tradition. Indeed, such a school claims not to be religious, but, having chosen that school, the newcomers will not readily accept this "secular" self-definition, since that would mean that the parents see no necessary connection between their norms and their stated beliefs. The newly settled parents are apt, in this case, to assert that in the "general" school the educators are much more "religious" than they themselves realize.

In short, principles ("beliefs") take on meaning in a cultural context that education is designed to perpetuate. This meaning is spelled out in norms, and in patterns of life that are perceived as significant. This does not mean that fundamental beliefs are mere metaphysical ornamentation; normative ideals without an anchor in belief readily become arbitrary, indefensible, "unprincipled," and the belief that metaphysics is superfluous and meaningless is itself a certain kind of basic conviction. But it does mean that abstract principled ideas, in the absence of normative ideals, are mere slogans. Thus, "philosophy" alone is never adequate for educational decision making, even theoretically, without a program of ideals, which tell us how to live by the principles.

To illustrate: For many religious people, moral norms designed to deal with people in a manner that safeguards and enhances human dignity are based on the belief that people are created in God's image. However, the mere doctrinal assertion that "people are created in God's image" is inconsequential, unless we uncover its normative aspect. This requires the following: (a) a statement with valuative implications, such as " 'God's image' means that people are dignified"; (b) a prescriptive statement, such as "dignity requires that people relate to one another in certain ways in specific situations"; (c) a social conception to protect and further the norms, such as "a good framework for assuring human dignity is socialism, or rugged individualism, Hasidism, or Kibbutz." Ultimately, we also require (d) a programmatic educational statement, such as, "therefore we should educate children to treat others with dignity, to understand why they should do so, and to defend the social framework and system that are congenial to it."

Indeed, if someone asserts a belief in a certain principle, such as "a belief in God," but does not favor the ideals associated with it (for example, Judaism) and refuses to specify what, in concrete reality, he or she *does* identify normatively with the principles, that person is ignored, or suspected of hypocrisy, or charged with attempted sabotage. When such a person is ignored, it is because he or she is not "serious" and does not understand that principle alone is vacuous. If the person is suspected of hypocrisy, it is because he or she seems to be unwilling to live up to some ideals that flow from the alleged principle; the suspected hypocrite wants to be credited for belief without paying for it. As for the saboteur, he or she can be charged with undermining the significance of the principle by implying that no ideals flow from it—or with missionizing. In the last case, the person subverts an (accepted) ideal by arguing for the primacy of the principle in order to "move" people, unawares, from one ideal embodiment to another.

Those who speak in the name of the same principles but who obviously do not share the same norms not only cannot educate the young together but also are often the bitterest enemies. In order to live in peace, they must at least state how they translate their (common) principles into the norms that really articulate their loyalties and priorities; they must clarify how these ideal norms are similar and where they are different, and what the implications of the similarities and differences are. Then they can begin to argue in a friendly manner.

## THE CULTURAL APPROACH: INITIATION AND INDIVIDUALITY

A second approach to the normative philosophy of education places the nature of initiation into a historical-cultural social framework. Essentially, the issue is: How can the young be introduced into *our* world and taught to identify with it and to continue it? For we live in a cultural cosmos that we wish to continue, that we consider valuable, but that, as mortals, we are precluded from continuing ourselves.[5]

Perry has suggested that education be defined as the enterprise wherein children are brought into a culture and are taught how to be creative within it. In his words, "The purpose of education is . . . inheritance, participation, and contribution."[6] This formulation, which emphasizes the need for continuity and loyalty on the one hand and for spontaneity and self-expression on the other, exposes a tension and raises numerous problems: What should be the relationship between *the society* and its demands for loyalty and conformity and *the individual* and his or her desire for self-expression? To what extent does a culture require reliability and standard "normative" behavior from its "educated" participants, and to what degree does it itself require creativity in order to be saved from decay and ultimate irrelevance? What distinguishes a loyal member of society from a dull and "uncreative" one? When may a creative and innovative member of society be termed apostate? That is, when does one cross the line between being a gadfly within the community and deserting or betraying it?

In concrete instructional categories, one must raise the following questions: What counts as success in maintaining "the chain of tradition"? Must *educated* pupils, who of course are the disciples of *successful* teachers, do what their elders and mentors have done, and is their *successful* education therefore evaluated in terms of their willingness and competence to "carry on" the heritage? Or, perhaps, pupils should be considered to have been successfully initiated into the culture if they do as they choose or what they consider adequate to the situation but do so on the basis of received and appropriated principles and value ideals. Or should teaching be viewed as successful if the learners have acquired the competence and confidence to live by their freely chosen values and beliefs?

Lamm, as previously mentioned, has termed these categories the *imitation, molding,* and *development* "logics of instruction" and has explored their ramifications in depth.[7] Although progressive educators have argued forcefully for the third of these "logics"—the development model—it must be kept in mind that the conception of free and existentially "responsible" choice of principle and ideal reflects a specific ideological desideratum in the educating community and is based on an available ideal, usually (but not always) derived from the belief that a person is and must be a "value-maker."[8] Moreover, the development model, as is also true of the imitation and molding ones, rests upon a corpus of educational theory, on a tradition. Thus, although the third approach seems to be tangential to normative-ideational philosophy of education, for it argues against education as imposition of *a priori* cultural values and norms, it is not "against" all cultural initiation as such, but against what are considered rigid, unreasonable, and stultifying forms of socialization.[9] Conversely, no theory of initiation, of education as cultural socialization, can dispense with individuality and self-expression.

Socialization and initiation require some individuality and selfhood on the part of the child and not only for the psycho-sociological reason that socialization is never "perfected." We can see clearly why this is so, if we compare the question of what we mean by *initiation into culture* with the question of what we mean by *principles*. Just as we cannot know what a principle means unless we see it embodied in specified ideals and norms, so we cannot know what loyalty is unless we see it embodied in a particular individual, who expresses it "in his or her own way." As Green has pointed out,[10] a person who is *well-behaved* should never be confused with one who *acts* well; there is a clear and crucial distinction between an automaton who goes through the right motions and a person who, through the workings of a distinctive personality with its sense of autonomy and individual responsibility, acts well. The one who acts well is in tune not only with a *tradition* but also with a *situation*. This person has absorbed not only the behavior patterns but also the fundamental assumptions of his culture; he or she knows the difference between aping the past and continuing its tradition. Rabbi Akiva was not the same as Moses, but he was conscious of continuing his teachings; sophisticated pious Jews of this century know that they are different from Rabbi Akiva but hope that their way of life and beliefs would be considered legitimate and pleasing to Rabbi Akiva if Akiva were alive today.[11]

We return, therefore, to the fundamental dilemma of the cultural issue in normative-ideational educational thinking: If maintaining a culture requires creativity as well as loyalty, when is "creatively maintaining" a culture in fact a form of undermining it? When are criticism of the culture and innovation within it the best way of maintaining it? The Talmud states that the building up of the young (i.e., the foolish) is to be considered destruction, whereas the tearing down of the old (i.e., the wise) is called building.[12] But how does one distinguish between the old and wise and the young and foolish?

For example, if, as a result of Zionist ideology and active participation in the life of the State of Israel, a Jew stops speaking Yiddish or Ladino as his parents did and shares in the revival of a spoken Hebrew culture, is his act foolish and destructive or wise and constructive? If my son or daughter practices my ideal but scorns my principle (for example, by observing the Sabbath but denying its commanded and revealed character), should I consider his or her initiation more or less successful than that of my (other) child, who is committed to my principle but does not acknowledge my ideal? In the latter case, the non-observed child may affirm a belief in God and His revelation to Israel but may think that the pattern of Sabbath observance as codified is an archaic way of "expressing" God's commandment. Both children claim to be loyal and to be continuous with the tradition; each of them argues that he or she has been successfully educated and initiated and is able to continue it creatively. Neither does so in the exact manner I do. Should I agree that their education "succeeded"? Should I have a preference?

The question arises because we wish to transmit the *language* of our culture; namely, that which bespeaks loyalty and continuity to it—"at-home-ness" in its basic assumptions, rhetoric, forms of inquiry, patterns of community, and symbolic expression. At the same time, we wish for all individuals to express *themselves* in this *language*, to speak their own *literature*; that is, to be themselves—to use the culture's syntax, but to make their own sentences. If they are gifted, we hope they will creatively interpret and add, if possible, to the cultural heritage; we certainly wish each "educated person" to gravitate toward the options within the tradition that are congenial to him or her.[13] We want individuals to find their own way within the tradition. And yet, normative-ideational educational theory expects individuals to be shaped by a tradition that is *a priori,* that is imposed, and that, in its very objectivity, is said to offer the necessary cultural framework for individual self-realization.

## THE EXISTENTIAL APPROACH: THE "WHOLE" PERSON

The third way of approaching issues that concern the normative-ideational philosopher of education can be seen as flowing from the philosophical and the cultural discussions summarized previously, from the realms of *Weltanschauung* and *initiation,* but it is focused on the person and the personality rather than on ideas or traditions. Here, the emphasis is on the relationship of the sentiments to the accomplishments, of the soul to the competences of the educated person; we are called upon to consider what constitutes an integrated and outstanding personality. For ideals suggest ideal persons, "heroes" worthy of admiration and emulation. In terms of specific beliefs and norms, within a given culture, we wish to know what a good person is like. Is he or she necessarily wise or pious, rational, contemplative, active? Is he or she necessarily happy, and is this happiness occasioned by his or her moral attributes? And, if so, how?

We have noted that this approach is heavily indebted to metaphysical discourse and to historical models of culture. The question, "What kind of person has realized his or her potential?" cannot be isolated from the query, "What is humanity?" Obviously, ideal relationships between self-realization and socialization, between freedom and authority, are concerned both with problems of cultural transmission and with existential issues of authenticity; the courage to be alone and the capacity to love and to share are not only external questions of principle and of culture but also intrinsic ones—of human "becoming" and inner nobility.

The project of education, in this approach, involves the personality in all its facets. The educator seeks to cultivate the intellect, to educate sentiments, to strengthen and direct the will, and to make action subservient to will, open to sentiment, and evaluated intelligently.

Accordingly, there is concern here with the education enterprise as comprehending all constituent elements of the personality. Analytical philosophers of education as well as admittedly normative thinkers have therefore insisted that educational theory cannot define success in narrow or one-dimensional terms. The educator is warned not to cultivate merely "brainy" people or paragons of sentimentality or docile conformists—although he or she will be working to foster intelligence, to cultivate sentiment, and to enable pupils to engage in normative action. Indeed, the very pejoratives, "brainy," "sentimental," and "conformist" indicate that "educating" the mind, the emotions, or the ability to act, without integrating the thinking, feeling, and acting personality is not really education. Thought, it is held, must be responsible to the whole person, actions must be thoughtfully examined, and feeling that is not thoughtfully evaluated and then translated into action is often irresponsible. Cultivating only one aspect of the personality, analytical thinkers have argued, may properly be called instruction, drilling, conditioning, or indoctrination, but hardly education.[14] Thus, were a theory of education to insist on concern with less than "a whole person" as commonly understood, it would have to either present a rationale for such a limited conception of personality or supply philosophical, psychological, or ideological reasons for ignoring or suppressing a given facet of personality, in principle or under particular circumstances.

## THE UNDERLYING ASSUMPTION OF NORMATIVE-IDEATIONAL EDUCATIONAL THEORY

All three approaches to the issues described previously fall within the domain of normative-ideational philosophy of education. The basic ideas and ideals, the "language" of the cultural tradition, and the valued "images of humanity" either are considered objectively or perennially true or are believed to represent the cumulative wisdom of a civilization. This means that these truths do not now, or in principle will not even in the future, depend in their essence on the learning individual for their validity. Thus, they may—and, indeed, should—be imposed on the learner by agents or representatives of the adult world and its norms; these agents and representatives, moreover, are presented as models of adult wisdom, morality, and wholeness, worthy of emulation and respect.

Deliberative-inductive educators are not devoid of ideals, cultural treasures, or conceptions of noble personality. They are, however, committed to the legitimacy of changing ideals in line with new situations, and they are ready to rethink fundamental ideas. They view heritage as a non-normative reservoir of potentially valuable cultural goods, and they believe that "ideal personalities" are not shaped primarily by metaphysical assumptions or cultural expectations but rather by individuality and natural development and by perceived needs. They do not attempt to impose these needs, except to the extent that empirical knowledge of psychological development and minimal social stability require tactical—and temporary, if possible—guidance or coercion.[15]

This does not imply that the classic normative-ideational theory of education is necessarily rigid and authoritarian. The ideals that are imposed in normative education may be broad as well as narrow; the living space given the individual within a culture may be minimal, and "creativity within culture" may enjoy no more than lip service. But the opposite is also possible, and a culture may be pluralistically understood without being "unprincipled."[16] Furthermore, the realm of ideals and the concept of cultural loyalty may be broad enough to allow for many and variegated types of "ideal" or "educated" personalities, just as these "images of humanity" may be dogmatically and ungenerously conceived. But if the orientation is normative, the teacher knows in principle what is right before asking the pupil and recognizes the problems to be solved—at least in principle—before confronting the varying discomforts, experiences, and expectations of the learners. To "teach them right" is to change their perspectives, enrich their experience through cultural goods, and educate their expectations. And to begin with, the teacher and the society know how to do this better than the pupil. For the latter is inexperienced in norms, ignorant of culture, and not yet a hero. The teacher, who knows what norms demand and what culture is and who is, it is hoped, closer to self-realization, imposes himself or herself on the pupil and selects normative subject matter "by right" and for the youngster's "own good."

## RELIGION AND NORMATIVE-IDEATIONAL EDUCATION

On the basis of our brief descriptions of the realms of normative-ideational discourse, we can readily grasp what the religious educator would mean by declaring that religion is a primary source of the normative philosophy of education. The educator can easily point to the religious basis of "world view," of cultural traditions, of conceptions of ideal personality.[17]

On the level of principles and ideals, what we have called the *Weltanschauung*, the religious educator would insist that religion provides the basis of doctrine and conviction about reality, knowledge, and value, in the form of *belief*. Religion demands, so this educator would argue, that these beliefs be translated into ideal embodiments: values and norms. It is the latter that the religious person calls "God's will" or "His commandments." As religious belief gives the "highest" and "most profound" and "most comprehensive" knowledge of reality, so it provides a "teaching" for the application of *what is known* to the sphere of *what must be done* so that society and humanity may be "pleasing to God." And the question of whether the religious person knows principles or *beliefs* before being taught ideals and *commandments,* or vice versa, is, as already mentioned, a controversy within and among diverse religious approaches and traditions.

On the level of cultural initiation, a religious educator might plausibly state that all initiation into the valuative life of a community is, in fact, entrance into the historical framework within which religious ideals and ideas are given concrete and continuous expression. If society is religiously perceived, then the ideals flowing from the principles are, in fact, the "language" of the culture. These ideals stipulate what "loyalty," or "service to God," requires. Likewise, the "literature"—the creative and spontaneous cultural expression of the individual within the community—provides existential links to God and to the sanctified community for people of diverse temperament, circumstance, and endowment. Each will express his or her "service" in a somewhat different way, yet without violating the normative ideals—the "language" that God demands of the community.

As for the "whole person" who has been successfully educated, he or she may be defined by the religious educator as one who adheres to the patterns of religious life, historically unfolding in the community, on the basis of his or her affirmation of religious doctrines that sustain and legitimate these normative patterns. The noble person is loyal to the culture that is the framework for the concrete life of the religious ideals; he or she achieves self-realization through congenial negotiations between his or her disposition and "the teaching" of the religious community. This community, for its part, provides diverse modes of sainthood and heroism, so that adherence to God's will does not require intolerable self-denial.

(In some contemporary writings on theology and religious education it has been suggested that the "whole person," serving God "with all his (or her) heart," is not to be understood in doctrinal terms but in existential categories that are congenial to the deliberative-inductive orientation in education. In this view, religion is understood differently; to be an integrated person *is* to live in faith.[18] Faith, in this conception, is not synonymous with belief in doctrines or adherence to *a priori* truths but constitutes the entire encounter of the person with reality, including the self as it is perceived. To have faith is thus to be a certain kind of person, and not necessarily to believe a certain doctrine. The relationship between this conception and normative ones, between the doctrines "believed" and the faith "expressed" by the entire personality, will be discussed in later chapters.)

## Religious Jewish Ideologies and Normative-Ideational Theory

The more traditional the religious Jewish educator is, the more likely he or she is to "do" normative philosophy of education in ways considerably different from non-Jewish teachers. Moreover, the more traditional Jewish educator can be expected to apply a normative-ideational conception of religious education somewhat differently from a liberal educator.

The traditional instructor is likely to argue (a) that operative ideals precede, in religious life and education, the formulation of ideas or principles; (b) that Jewish religion is as intrinsically concerned with cultural and historical "language" as with *Weltanschauung* and that Jewish civilization cannot be detached from religious faith and norms; and thus (c) that all personal as well as social ideals are inherently religious unless they have been corrupted. Thus, the traditional Jewish religionist will understand the crisis of modern Jewish identity as occasioned by the attempt to be Jewish without religion, or to "make do" with a fragmentary notion of religion. This person will argue that whereas it is possible to be an Englishman without Anglican faith, it is impossible to be Jewish without Judaism, for the cultural heritage of England and the ideal "images of humanity" in Western civilization, although channeled by religion and shaped by Christian vision, were not engendered by these elements, nor are they intrinsically dependent upon them. The traditional-minded normative Jewish educator, more than a liberal colleague, can therefore be expected to insist that all normative-ideational understandings of education are subservient to religious faith and commitment.

If the traditional-liberal continuum is roughly reflected in the ideological spectrum of Orthodox, Conservative, and Reform Judaism, we may conjecture that various stated philosophical positions concerning Jewish religious education correspond to traditional-liberal options in normative-ideational educational thought. For example, we find Reform educational thinkers arguing for explicit instruction in the beliefs of Judaism and its world view and more concerned with the articulation of Jewish faith than are their Conservative and Orthodox counterparts. Likewise, ideal embodiments of principles would appear among Reform educators to be more universal, more clearly dependent on philosophical than on cultural foundations. The Conservative educator, judging from current curricular materials and programmatic statements, would also tend to differ from an Orthodox colleague about the relative importance of basic *aggadah* (principles) and *halakhah* (ideal embodiments); although the Conservative teacher would consider halakhah crucially important, he or she might consider certain aspects of the halakhah to constitute not the *language* (the essence) but the *literature* (acceptable forms of individual expression) of Jewish religious culture. The Orthodox Jew, in contra-distinction to the Reform one, will usually maintain that Jewish theological discourse is more "literature" than "language." The traditionalist will tend to see the "whole person" as emerging from a life of correct belief and comprehensive participation, whereas the liberal-minded religionist can be expected to emphasize the significance of faith as an existential category of religious life.[19]

However, all religious Jewish educators, and many who do not specifically define themselves as religious but who locate educational norms in the cultural heritage of Judaism (such as cultural Zionists), will be able to agree that Jewish religious tradition contains principles and norms, a cultural *language* and models of humanity; in short, that it generates a normative philosophy of education. Therefore, an educator "armed with Judaism," which includes Bible and Talmud, Midrash and philosophy, scholarship and models of piety, may confidently go out "into the world" to examine the elements that must be considered if the theory ("Judaism") is to be effective in producing Jewish persons. Through the normative Jewish philosophy of education, as formulated by our expositors of Judaism, whether traditionalist or liberal, we can confidently say what Judaism teaches, demands, and implies and what, therefore, constitute ideal objectives.[20] If the conception of *a priori* ideal objectives is accepted, the subject for research and deliberation is "merely" practical. The only educational questions, after the norms have been theologically uncovered and clarified, are, How much Judaism can be taught under the prevailing circumstances? To whom? How?

This way of approaching educational discourse is certainly plausible and can be defended even by those who do not agree that "Judaism" is a once-and-for-all eternal verity or Idea. If education toward a world view and toward specific social and individual ideals is legitimate, if initiation into a historical tradition is indispensable for cultural continuity and personal identity, and if society has the right and duty to propose ideal models of being and doing, then Judaism, no less than any consistent and complex world view (whether "Western Civilization," Hinduism, or in perhaps a less comprehensive manner, Marxism or "the American way of life") may also propose such models. Thus, it makes theoretical sense to ask a teacher, How much "Judaism" is known or observed in this school? How "Jewish" is the atmosphere? Are the teachers in this school "religious"?

## The Historical Crisis of Normative-Ideational Religious Education

The problem is that since the Enlightenment and the Emancipation, the previously described method of operation has not held true for increasing numbers of Jews. There are, of course, ultra-traditionalist communities in which a normative-ideational philosophy of Jewish education, based on religion as the only primary source of world view, is naturally and smoothly applied to the home and the school, but these communities pay the price, though they might not consider it so, of living outside the modern spiritual context. In addition, there are communities of modern Orthodox Jews who use the term "Judaism" in connection with their ideal objectives in education with a large degree of self-confidence and increasing theological refinement. Yet social and educational research indicates that, among these Jews, there is existential unease, tension between "open" and sectarian tendencies, and often educational unclarity.[21] Reform and Conservative Judaism, like modern Orthodoxy, have arisen to confront the new circumstances, problems, and insights associated with modernity. However, many adherents of these movements have admitted that the confrontation is incomplete or only partially successful;[22] even when Judaism's ideal objectives are formulated in new and relevant theological terms and testify to a desire that the tradition be enhanced by modernity, Judaism often appears to lose its claim to comprehensiveness or retains the stigma of outlandishness. In other words, non-Orthodox educators, positing their normative educational philosophies on the basis of their conceptions of Judaism, can claim no greater success in bridging the gap between "Judaism" and the practice of the Jewish people than can Orthodox educators. In fact, only the Orthodox may claim large-scale communal and educational successes. However, as Heilman has shown, the Orthodox often pay for their success in the coin of quality and integrity. Although they live in the modern world consciously and even self-consciously, they tend to deal with it superficially or in a compartmentalized fashion.[23]

## Prophets and Priests: Then and Now

In a sense, the contemporary problems of normative-ideational education are not totally new; there is something perennial about them. After all, ideal objectives are termed "ideal" not only because they are highly desirable but also because they do not correspond to reality. There is always a gap between what the ideal person will do, understand, and be and the behavior and the attainments of most people. Ideal theological objectives, as Soloveitchik intimates, are prophetic; the educational aspiration is for each person to be a prophet.[24] But this does not correspond to any sustained historical reality. As Ahad Ha-Am noted,[25] this gap was recognized institutionally in the function and status of the priest, whom we may consider the realistic educator. The priest was bound by the vision and "the Word" of his prophetic mentor but not by his rhetoric of absoluteness nor by his corresponding impatience with realities. We may say that the prophet perennially presents a normative-ideational philosophy of education; the priest must apply it to the data "out there"—in the needs, limitations, tensions, and moods of ordinary people. Ahad Ha-Am's priest, the practical educator, is totally dependent on the prophet for "ideal objectives" but relates realistically and thus effectively to the elements shaping the community and the individual in their historic situations. The prophet, distressed because not all people are prophets, is yet dependent on the priest who moderates and humanizes his teaching, and the priest knows that he must obey the prophet: that if he brings "strange fires" to his altar, he will die.

So, when we say that normative-ideational philosophy of Jewish education as it derives from the sources of Judaism and as mediated by theological interpretations of Jewish tradition is not "working," we do not mean that most Jews fail to conform to prophetic standards, for the gap between pristine theory and practical reality is inevitable. The problem—or rather, the problematic situation—is that Jewish priests who speak in the name of classic prophets are ignored and shifted aside to make room for popularizers of more relevant seers. And many present-day priests do not appear to represent any prophet at all.

Therefore, the gap between theory and practice that every normative philosophy of education acknowledges and that is indigenous to every human situation has changed in kind; imperfection has become incongruence. For the gap can be educationally negotiated only if a community assumes that the stated ideal *is* ideal, that it should be accorded at least nominal reverence and that it will, with luck, fare better in the future than in the present. In such a case, every falling away from the prophetic-theoretical ideal is attributable to human weakness, and ignoring the priest's "translation into reality" of the prophetic imperative is sinful or an admission of ignorance. But when the ideal is not *believed* and it is rumored that the priests themselves, despite their professions, do not really believe it—unless they are benighted or "clerical"—it no longer makes sense to speak of a "normal" gap between the ideal and the realities. The old normative philosophy of education finds itself speaking to, *or next to,* a practical reality that has quite different prophets (philosophers, social scientists, ideologists) and listens attentively to *its* priests (politicians, columnists, tennis instructors) and their ideals/commandments (to pursue hobbies, academic degrees, and so forth).

In such a situation of virtual apostasy, any normative-ideational approach that posits ideal objectives of Judaism becomes virtually impossible. Any sincere and knowledgeable interpretation of Judaism that relates seriously to the data of the tradition becomes automatically suspect. And those who wish to carry on Jewish education on a normative-ideational basis without serious confrontation with deliberative-inductive insights can do this in only one of three ways, all of which are severely limited in appeal, in normative seriousness, or in intellectual comprehensiveness.

1. The normative-ideational approach can address itself exclusively to those who, however shallow their actual commitment, articulate and in some practical way give evidence of their belief in the ideal objectives of normative Judaism. The normative-ideational teachers will seek out, as it were, the righteous remnant and give these individuals "honest" Jewish education. The approach is explicative with regard to Judaism; there is little justification or apologetics. The tradition is declared to be normative. The teacher may, to cite an example, teach that Jewish males are required to pray three times each day and will hope that (male) pupils will do so. The teacher is likely to refer to the talmudic Sages in a normatively present tense and will generally use a formula such as "Our Sages (*Hazal*) say . . . "

2. The normative-ideational approach can be used objectively, to present the Jewish tradition to the community that has an expressed desire to perpetuate Jewish identity and is not averse to using the normative tradition as a historical framework for examining the cultural heritage. "Judaism," in this case, is explicated as a normative corpus, but it is not, *a priori,* normative. The cultural assumption of the educator is that every Jew should know the tradition "on its own terms"; that is, as the educator understands them. The pupil is then entrusted with the decision of what to do with "the tradition." The normative "ideal objective" is knowledge of what historically were Judaism's ideal objectives. (Naturally, this is based on some, often unexamined, theological doctrine of Judaism; ironically, often the very doctrine that the teacher has rejected as normative for himself or herself.) The teacher will therefore point out that "Judaism has taught that Jewish males are required to pray three times each day" but will not expect pupils to draw prayerful conclusions from this datum. The talmudic Sages, too, will be referred to historically: "The Rabbis said (or thought) . . . " The use of this approach is widespread in non-Orthodox Jewish education in Israel.

3. Finally, the normative approach can be used in teaching those who are conscious of an ideal-vacuum, who are "looking for something," and whose nascent Jewish identity makes Judaism a visible option. In this case, "Judaism," with its principles and ideals, its cultural heritage and its models of personality and self-fulfillment, is explicitly presented as competing with other "philosophies of life." The rhetoric of this approach is more apologetic than directly prescriptive, and it shuns historicity. When pupils are taught that Jewish males are required to pray thrice daily, the ramifications drawn are existential ones; for example, the teacher may discuss how important prayer is "in a world where nobody listens to anyone else any more" and may add a rationale for the fact that women need not pray three times a day, such as "women are closer to God all the time." The talmudic Sages will be cast in a theosophic light; the teacher will reflect, "Our Sages knew what we're just finding out . . . "

In the three models of contemporary unexamined normative-ideational approaches, the focus of education is a known and objective substance entitled Judaism. In the first case, it is assumed or hoped that the pupils adhere to that minority which "believes in Judaism," for whom Judaism is entitled to determine normatively what education—ideals, initiation, wholeness—is all about. Judaism is not compromised in the educational process, but most of the Jews do not believe it, staying away from the school or paying lip service to verbalized norms.

In the second case, "Judaism" is, if it is possible, even more of an objective and historically imposed reality. For Judaism is a historical fact; it is hoped that Judaism is relevant as a resource. But the religion is taught to be known *about* and to provide a historical and cultural basis for collective memory and identity.

In the third case, Judaism is, first and foremost, a practical theology that is presented as a perennial mode of existential orientation. Theology is not, therefore, viewed as a mode of making the normative tradition accessible to the present by innovative thinking—and re-thinking—with regard to it, but it is considered synonymous with the normative tradition itself. Judaism *is* a "philosophy of life."

In all three cases in which the normative-ideational approach is used and useable without any conscious recourse to deliberative-inductive thinking, the assumption is made that the problem is known and that the normative philosophy of education, flowing from interpretations of Judaism, contains solutions. In each case, the problem is "not enough Judaism" and the solution is "more Judaism." For a large number of Jews, and probably the majority of them, however, there is no such problem, and consequently the solution is irrelevant.

What there undoubtedly is, even among many Jews who are not particularly concerned with theologically articulated norms of Judaism, is a problematic situation, "a consciousness of conditions that we wish were otherwise," a state of unease. This problematic situation, or symptom, is characterized by a decline of interest in Jewish identity and in those contents, commitments, and modes that have historically characterized it. The unease is felt by those who wish for Jewish identity to be perpetuated and who themselves are alienated, partially or totally, from the traditional commitments and meanings.

Those who suffer from the unease note with alarm that Jewish identity is being depleted: The manifestations include a low birth rate, a high rate of intermarriage, a lack of commitment to Jewish religious tradition, and a declining or purely symbolic concern with the national movement of the Jewish people—with Zionism.

If we examine this unease through the prism of the deliberative-inductive approach, we must recall that symptoms are not themselves the problem. Problems, in this approach, are never obvious, and all of the statistical and social symptoms just mentioned are obvious in the extreme. The problem, as we have noted, is analogous to the diagnosis, the cause of the symptoms. Why are Jews losing interest in Jewish identification? What is causing the symptoms? Clearly, the solution or solutions for this particular situation of distress cannot be located or constructively examined until the problem itself has been disclosed. Problems, the deliberative-inductive educator tells us, are disclosed by experts. And the Jewish world has both secular and religious experts, who urge us to "see" the problem in misguided religious definitions of Judaism or in misguided secular self-understandings, respectively.

## The Problematic Situation in Jewish Education

The symptoms engendering Jewish collective discomfort are precisely exemplified in the area of Jewish education. In recent years, these problems have been diversely documented, and various diagnoses and solutions have been put forward. Ackerman and Himmelfarb,[26] for example, have elaborated on the malfunctioning of what are sometimes called "topics" of Jewish education—that is, the environment, the teachers, the pupils, and the subject matter. As they point out, the overall symptom (namely, the declining interest in Jewish education) is reflected in localized symptoms in each of these "topics" and in the "unhealthy" relationships among them. Thus, the community and the home are usually indifferent to what the religious school does and have no cultural stake in the subjects taught there; children are aware of the apathy of their parents and respond to the Jewish school with boredom and undisciplined behavior; the Jewish teaching profession lacks status and adequate compensation and therefore few young people wish to enter the profession; and religious subject matter, though ostensibly based on a normative philosophy, reflects a nostalgically remembered social reality that is not meaningful to pupils, not mastered by (untrained) teachers, and not functional in the community as it is.

The malfunctioning of the "topics of education" is only the most visible symptom of the hidden disease of contemporary Jewish life, and the educators often find themselves scapegoats for the problematic situation of modern Jewry as such in the post-Emancipation world. For, whatever the problem, it surely is that of the Jews, not simply of Jewish education. Many Jews have ceased to see in Judaism a source of norms and of significance; it is not an option of meaning for them. Judaism, however interpreted, does not integrate their lives, shape them culturally, or provide them with an image of humanity against which they measure themselves. Fein has pointed out that when Judaism has become a choice rather than a condition, and when even the implications of choosing Jewishness have become obscured, Jewish education has ceased to be necessary in any functional sense:

The demise of the organic Jewish community meant that an educator could no longer assume he was teaching children skills they would need to make their way in adult society . . . there is little opportunity to translate Jewish cognitions into Jewish behavior.[27]

Under such conditions, a normative conception of Jewish religious education is applied by teachers who do not know enough about Judaism or do not know what they would consider success in teaching Judaism, to children who know that it is not meant to be taken seriously, for a community that has only a hazy and weakening sense of its identity. This has been starkly illustrated in Schoem's ethnographic study of an American Jewish afternoon school.[28] Teachers in this school spoke of "the Jewish way of life" as though their feelings, beliefs, values, and thoughts were framed by Jewish knowledge and understanding, and they acted as though many of their pupils, too, were committed Jews. Yet, states Schoem, in fact neither the staff nor the parents embodied that "Jewish way of life."

In what was a typical classroom lesson, a seventh grade teacher asked the students to describe in what ways the Sabbath differed from other days of the week. In response to a student's answer that 'on the Sabbath we pray,' the teacher said, 'But you pray every day.' In this case, not only was the teacher's response completely detached from reality, but the student who answered was also speaking in theoretical terms. Many of the students in the class had not been to a prayer service on the Sabbath for up to six months or more. When the teacher, who managed a restaurant on Friday evenings, then began to speak about why we don't work on the Sabbath, students giggled incredulously because of the question's absurdity. Clearly, this lesson, that was being discussed in first person terms, was in the students' minds, about a people that was far removed from their own reality.[29]

One parent in that particular community described "being Jewish" as "what you're not. It's not what you believe in. . . . But being Jewish doesn't entail believing in anything in particular." And a pupil described "the problem" of Hebrew school as follows: "It's too long. You get home from school and then right away you have to go to Hebrew school. And then you eat dinner and sometimes there's no time for homework."[30]

The problematic situation is perhaps not comprehensively or definitely researched in an ethnographic study, but everyone who has taught "normatively" in a non-normative setting will read these conversations with a shock of recognition. And if what Schoem is describing reflects findings of other, more statistical, research, it will give us more than an inkling of what the problematic situation indicates; namely, that normative-ideational approaches to religious education by themselves are usually no longer sufficient.

One does not have to agree with this diagnosis—that is, this formulation of the problem—in order to be conscious of "a situation that we wish were otherwise." Therefore, those who know what the social-educational realities are and who wish Jewish religious education to be neither academically detached nor narrowly sectarian cannot disregard the conceptual framework that takes problematic situations seriously—as an invitation to new discoveries and larger insights.

This deliberative-inductive framework is religiously suspect when it views all norms with antagonism, when its adherents insist that the truths of the deliberative-inductive orientation are exclusive and comprehensive. But its use does not necessarily militate against religious education. Indeed, if brought into confrontation with a normative tradition through an adequate theology, it may invite a broader understanding of religion and education, which will help us to solve problems as well as to locate them.

# 3 Secular Diagnoses of Educational Crisis

## WHICH PROBLEM ARE WE LOOKING FOR?

In viewing the situation of religious education through the prism of the deliberative-inductive orientation, we must keep a crucial fact in mind: Problematic situations, those obvious indications of malfunctioning that initiate deliberation (with a view to locating the problem; that is, diagnosing "the disease" itself), are problematic only to those who find a given situation uncomfortable. Thus, the problematic situation we have described, in which a loss of Jewish identity is indicated through the prism of specifically educational symptoms, is not equally disturbing to everyone. For example, bored pupils in unruly Hebrew schools are most problematic to teachers who have to cope with them and who sense that the wildness testifies to a collective emptiness. Or, an avoidance by teachers of material that they have difficulty in understanding or believing and a subsequent tendency to move into uninformed discussion or games designed to evoke interest—or at least order—in the classroom is especially distressing to scholars and to those committed to the literary tradition of Judaism, who see in such "flight from subject matter"[1] evidence of poor teacher training and recruitment, lack of community interest in "maintaining standards," and a component of assimilation.

Stated more generally, the decline in Jewish identification occasions cultural unease among those who think there is something wrong with the erosion of Jewish life and who worry about Jewish survival. The symptoms of Jewish entropy lead such people to search for "the problem of Judaism" and, ultimately, in terms of their delineation of the problem, to put forward plausible solutions.

The Jews who have no such cultural concerns are differently unsettled. What causes them discomfort—*their* problematic situation—has to do with anti-Semitism, minority status and disability, and persecution. For them, what is problematic is not loss of identity but the historical failures and continued difficulties of assimilation. They may locate the problem in historical relationships between Jews and non-Jews, Christian theology, and, perhaps, economic relationships and abnormalities best explained in socio-psychological categories. They seek to define precisely "the problem of the Jews" and to posit solutions in social revolution, in the progressive rationalization of human relationships, or in a socio-psychological conception of Zionism.[2]

For such Jews, whose cultural concerns are not Jewishly defined, religion and religious education are not generally an issue, unless they can be shown to heighten anti-Semitism or to impinge on the freedom of individuals to manage (or overcome) their condition according to their own circumstances, convictions, and abilities. If the "problem of the Jews" is viewed as amenable to political solution, as in Herzlian Zionism, "religion" may be tolerated and given due (yet apathetic) respect (including budgetary allocations for education) as long as it does not become "coercion" and does not attempt to move beyond its strictly defined and limited institutions. If it is believed to be a negative factor that is intrinsically divisive and causes prejudice, it will be fought and condemned, generally on a broad front that unites all free thinkers (or revolutionaries, progressives, and so forth) who may together denounce all benighted and reactionary believers. Sometimes, those for whom "the Jewish condition" is the problem have expressed themselves in virulent polemics against the undesirable consequences of Judaism. Their self-hatred has been termed pathological; it may simply be considered the tragic awareness of a problem that appears insoluble.[3]

Our concern is not with these, but with those, especially educators, for whom Judaism is their *cultural* problem, who sense that the former ways of maintaining equilibrium and satisfaction no longer seem to work. These former ways are, in the case of education, curricula and frameworks that were based on what was once a satisfactory normative philosophy. When this normative philosophy of Jewish education can speak convincingly only to a small minority and is rescued for some of the others only by the transformation of what was normative into objective historical data, then, in the opinion of these educators, a deliberation process must be undertaken that will seek to determine what the problem is and what possible solutions are. For some, this will lead to a revised but (they believe) historically continuous normative philosophy of

Jewish education; others, more iconoclastic and radical, state that normative philosophy constitutes a misleading and overly metaphysical nomenclature for present understandings of problems, viable approaches, and tentative solutions.[4]

It can be posited that the deliberative literature of modern Jewish history concerning the cultural issues of Jewish life and education (not the political ones!) revolves around the question of whether the "problem" is the loss of religious faith and loyalty that constituted the essence of Jewish civilization, at least in the centuries of exile, or whether the obstinate insistence on religious definitions of Jewishness in a secular age is itself the problem. In other words, is the problem of Judaism its "religious" straitjacket or the "corrosive effects" of secularism? In the first case, solutions are proffered in terms of "return" to or re-discovery of "authentic" religious Judaism, or religious Reform or religious "relevance," a new synthesis between the modern secular culture and religious tradition, or new understandings (theologies) that allegedly leave the essence of religion unchanged but apply it conceptually and practically in perhaps revolutionary ways. In the second case, solutions are concerned with secular re-interpretations or re-discoveries of pre-rabbinic Judaism, cultural nationalism, or an existential humanism that accords the Jew a non-mysterious, non-symbolic and "normal" status in the family of nations.

A study dealing with religious Jewish education cannot ignore the arguments directed against "organized religion" and religious belief by its "worldly" or secular opponents. We may mention three reasons for this:

1. If normative philosophy of education has "broken down" for most Jews, and this breakdown occasions deliberation, the deliberation must take into account what is said by those for whom it has broken down. In fact, a refusal to consider "what is going on in the world" is implausible even within the normative-ideational model, except for the religious educators who agree to absolute conceptual and social isolation and who are concerned only with the insulated observant community.

2. If religious education is to be concerned with truth, the theoretical discussion that guides it must be ready to learn from the experience of modern people's search for truth or, at least, to relate to it. Minimally, this calls for a reasoned argument concerning why modern secular claims are false. It is sectarian to speak of religious verities without seeking to understand what claims of truth are being made "out there" and what methods are being used to discover "the truth."[5]

3. Most Jews, it need hardly be pointed out, are not sectarian. Indeed, most of them live in a modern-secularized world. They have studied at uni-

versities and expect their children, even when they are currently receiving Jewish education, to do likewise. At these universities, as well as in the school systems that prepare young people for college admission and achievement, certain assumptions prevail regarding the nature of communicable knowledge, virtue, and the legitimate means of acquiring knowledge and virtue. For the most part, the number of hours of television pupils have watched before they enter school is greater than the total number of hours of religious education they will receive throughout their lives. Jewish parents, even when they desire religious education, may be hostile to instruction that disparages their own secular convictions. Teachers, even when they claim adequate knowledge of the traditional subject matter of Judaism, may be intellectually uncomfortable with it or, conversely, may suffer from the alienation that is their lot in the larger community.

In short, the fact that most people, most learning, and most virtue in modern society is not religious in any traditional sense constitutes an important datum in deliberation on religious education which, *as* religious education, will be concerned with restoring to use and health some workable conception of religious norms and ideal objectives. It also explains why most religious people ''in the world'' think and act as though the irreligion of their neighbors and friends cannot be ascribed to perversity and wickedness.[6]

In relating seriously to those to whom traditional religious norms do not speak and to the culture that does speak to them, religious educators who continue to take norms seriously are not assured of convincing everyone (or for that matter, anyone). In fact, when educators communicate with these individuals seriously, their conception of the ideal communication may subtly change. But, in listening to those who have been angered, frustrated, or made to feel vaguely guilty or apathetic about religious conceptions of Jewish education, teachers can learn, and they may be rewarded by becoming, if not convincing, at least plausible to those whom they engage in discussion.

To this course of action there are only two alternatives. One, which unfortunately is frequently adopted in the larger community, is for religious educators not to take themselves seriously; to consider themselves autobiographical quirks, relics who should be tolerated for their contribution to Jewish survival even as they are pitied (and pity themselves) for their fixations. The second is for religious educators not to take the larger community (i.e., the Jewish people and the world in which it lives) seriously. In this case, the teachers gain a warm community but lose a people. For security they pay the price of encounter with what most Jews consider knowledge, wisdom, and insights. Conversely, if religious educators have ''worldly'' knowledge but refuse to confront it, they buy certainty in the coin of compartmentalization. In either case, they are likely to lose most parents, pupils, and teachers, who will see in them quaint specimens of nostalgia, parochialism, and stunted vision.

That there is a problematic situation is clear. Let us now survey non-religious formulations of the problem, based on diverse forms of inquiry, and the solutions that flow from secular diagnoses of contemporary Jewish discomfort.

Four major arguments may be advanced against religion and religious education. We shall classify them as (1) the philosophical; (2) the cultural; (3) the anti-theological; and (4) the educational. The first and fourth apply to all religious education; the second and third are addressed specifically to the symbiosis of Jewish existence and religion.

## The Philosophical-Secular Diagnosis

The philosophical location of the problem flows from a scientific-secular world view. It may be succinctly stated as follows: The three-storied universe of pre-scientific Western civilization, in which the inscrutable but unquestionably moral purposes of Providence provide a final cause for all things, no longer appears compelling or reasonable to most educated people. This view has been shown, to the satisfaction of the trans-national community of scholarship, to be an "unnecessary hypothesis" to explain reality and generally useless in solving human problems.[7] Thus, classic religious faith and commitment are seen as eccentric or representing personal (rather than moral) values. Religious convictions and commitments are tolerated in liberal society but must remain private; schools and curricula should not deal with it. And although some modern philosophers, reflecting on scientific culture, equate metaphysics with poetry, the sciences have suggested to many modern thinkers that the traditional notions are pretentious and absurd.[8]

Paton[9] has summarized what the diverse disciplines seem to imply about the validity of the traditional religious world view. Physics intimates a mechanical world destined, by the second law of thermodynamics, to a cold death in which there will be no trace of any consciousness or any value; biology places human beings on the scale of evolution, engendered by chance mutations; psychology replaces the soul with the psyche; and history exposes all perennial truth as historical-cultural developments. The Bible must be placed, therefore, in the perspective of variegated religious texts, put in the same bookshelf with them, and, like them, analyzed with the tools of comparative literature and anthropology, for human beliefs and norms constitute the subject matter of the sociologist, the psychologist, the historian, the anthropologist.

Franz Rosenzweig, though speaking from the perspective of a religious person, was aware of what religious Jewish conviction had to confront:

> Just as a student of William James knows how to put every 'religious experience' into the correct cubby-hole of the psychology of religion, and a Freudian student can analyze the experience into its elements of the old yet ever new story, so a student of Wellhausen will trace every commandment back to its human folkloristic origin, and a student of Max Weber derive it from the special structure of a people. Psychological analysis finds the solution to all enigmas in self-delusion, and historical sociology finds it in mass delusion . . . [10]

The university, that "yeshiva" of modern secular culture, has divided the knowable world into distinct disciplines, which, through their discrete methods of research, unceremoniously categorize the "unique" truths of religion for study; their ontological claims are discounted in advance and then objectively described. God is the subject of human belief, of "religious experience"; the Torah can be traced to its origins, and the uniqueness of Israel is to be found in (not uncommon) mass delusion.

Russell speaks in clear and dispassionately analytical terms when he writes that all religious statements can be understood as psychological or sociological ones. "If A loves B the relation . . . consists of certain states of mind of A. Even an atheist must admit that a man can love God. It follows that love of God is a state of the man who feels it, and not properly a relational fact."[11] The analytical philosopher is doing with words and concepts what science does with things; many modern philosophers bridle at such restrictions yet insist that truth originates in human reason, which shapes research. All beyond that is unknowable or subjective.

Thus, for the secular Jewish educator, the religious definition of Judaism in terms of a past religious world is the problem. So, modern Jewish life and education must undergo a worldly transformation. The secular Jewish educator admits that Jewish culture was traditionally religious but points out that this was true of most cultures. Jews can maintain a collective identity in the modern world and be fully integrated and authentic within it only to the extent that they do what other nations and cultures have done. In this view, the reason for the widespread falling away from Jewish loyalty (the problematic situation) is not that children are not given adequate religious education, but rather that religion is still too "normative" in defining Jewishness (the problem). To build a Jewish future on religious affirmations and obligations is hopeless. In the general human-scientific culture of today, ontological and valuative assumptions are made that are incongruous with the Jewish—or any other—religion. Modern people, nurtured on scientific method and achievement and initiated into humanistic-secular philosophies, believe in the individual's autonomy and in the individual's responsibility for the creation and maintenance of his or her values. They have been taught that it is possible to locate and solve the real problems humanity faces; they believe in the individual's capacity to exploit the environment intelligently and in the capacity for self-understanding so that life can become less tragic and warped than it must inevitably be when people are ignorant.

Although elements of tragedy are intrinsic to human life, modern secular teachers, even and especially in a world without God, wish to inculcate serenity, courage, and dignity in their pupils. And in their view, religion is absolutely at loggerheads with this world view. Religion shackles people to dogmas, limiting the scope of legitimate inquiry; values are imposed on them; dignity is bought at the price of mindless obedience; and the absurdity of human existence is dispelled or obscured by myths.

For the non-religious Jewish educator, therefore, the problem of Jewish identification and loyalty lies in the residual belief of most Jews that Jewishness is, at least in its public-cultural manifestations, a religious affair that assumes specific personal beliefs and that, therefore, one who wishes to enter the mainstream of modern civilization must leave the Jewish people. The alternatives seem to be limited to assimilation or petrification; one can either talk intelligently to Jews *or* pray with them; those one can pray with are loyal, "good" Jews, whereas those one can talk to do not pray and assume that they are not "good Jews."

Secular Jewish education, especially through Zionism and in the State of Israel, has been making the attempt to draw consistent educational theory from modern thought and life. Whether respectfully or critically, religion has been seen "in historical perspective"; Jewish culture has been identified as primarily and essentially national. New existential models of "good Jews" have emerged, such as the *chalutz* (the pioneer), the Jewish scholar, the humane and humanistic Jew. These are men and women who harness contemporary knowledge and intelligence to the solution of human problems in a Jewish social framework. At times they are academics who find their culture neither too holy nor too irrelevant for scholarly commitment; usually they are people who love their own tradition for its (to them) special way of articulating universal values. For some national thinkers and educators, the loss of religious faith was perceived as tragic; others were glad to have discovered that the moral principles underlying their heritage could be severed from what were deemed outworn forms and dogmas. And there was a third group who saw in the national renaissance an opportunity for a radical metamorphosis of Jewishness, a transvaluation, an uninhibited acceptance of science, serving the human will for self-making, resting on Jewish hope for self-understanding and self-improvement.[12]

The latter tendency, so vehemently expressed by writers like Brenner and Berdischevski, finds concrete social-ideological illustration in the written advice to an Israeli youth leader of Hashomer Hatzair who, during the course of routine work among immigrant children, comes across youngsters who are religious. The *madrich* (youth leader) is warned against hasty and unkind condemnation of such children but is reminded of his or her ideological obligation as a positivistic irreligious Jew; for "of course it is our intention to get them to understand that their belief in God lacks logic and justification and that religion is the fruit of reactionary regimes and that it has no right to exist among those who are fighting for a progressive social order." The *madrich* must eventually explain that while "no one will force him [the child] to believe or to reject belief," yet "the materialistic foundation of the world . . . leaves no room for higher supernatural forces in man's consciousness . . . "[13]

This approach is perhaps of greater historical than philosophical interest, for the very radicalism of its intent to make Jewish education conform to secular-modern (in this case *Marxist* to boot!) views of reality may be considered idiosyncratic. Secularism can generally afford to be much less militant. If the patterns of culture are "secular as a matter of course," asks Rotenstreich rhetorically, "why fight for something that is given, something that exists objectively, even automatically?"[14]

### The Cultural Location of the "Religious Problem"

The cultural argument for non-religious Jewish education, though beholden to modern secular thought, bases itself on what are believed to be internal historical-national grounds. Judaism and Jewish civilization, it is maintained, are misrepresented and distorted when they are categorized as "religion." True, in Western Emancipation society, religious self-definition enabled Jews to hold on to a limited Jewish identity while gaining civic equality, but this definition perverted not only historic Jewish culture but also the religious aspects of this culture. It was, as Ahad Ha-Am characterized it, "slavery in the midst of freedom," the loss of national dignity and even of a comprehensive religious life as constituted by the halakhah—in exchange for the freedom of confessional associations and the privilege of writing for theological journals researching the Jewish past.[15]

The secular Jewish exponent of "Yiddishkeit" insists that Judaism was never a religion, and points out that the Hebrew language has no term for "re-

ligion.'' Never did Jews accept a normative creed, and those who attempted
to set down such a creed were soon challenged. Likewise, a Jew does not gain
status as a member of the Jewish people by virtue of his or her religious affirmations; one can be an irreligious Jew in a sense that one cannot be an ''irreligious Catholic.'' Jewishness is a matter of national consciousness. In the
words of Dubnow:

> What is the power that welds us into a compact organism? Religion and
> race do not account for our survival, because the agnostics are in the front ranks
> of all our national movements. The 'something' that holds us together is the
> common historical destiny of all the scattered parts of the Jewish nation.[16]

Moreover, it is claimed that the insistence of certain Jews on defining themselves as Jewish only in religious or theological terms testifies to the degree of
cultural assimilation they have undergone.[17]

The view that ''Judaism'' is the national life of the Jewish people and that
the over-emphasis on or exclusive concern with its religious elements is the
result of the abnormal conditions of the Diaspora was given profuse expression
in the writings of Enlightenment poets and essayists in Eastern Europe. They
argued that in ancient Israel, when the Jewish people still lived a normal life
in its own land, there were outspoken controversies between secular and religious authorities and viewpoints—between kings and prophets, and between
Pharisees and Saducees—just as existed among other peoples. ''Religious''
Jews were then, as now, a party, a point of view, a puritan tendency.[18]

If, nevertheless, traditional Jewish culture was so ''religious,'' this could
be attributed to the exaggeratedly ''spiritual'' forms Jewish life assumed under
abnormal and unterritorial conditions and to the religious nature of pre-modern
culture as well. Even the Talmud, that great religious code of Jewry, gives
evidence of the national character of Judaism; the talmudic halakhah itself
agrees that a Jew is anyone born of a Jewish mother and that a thorough-going
apostate is only the one who disassociates himself from the Jewish people, for
''an Israelite who sins is still an Israelite.''[19]

If thus says the Talmud, all the more national and ''natural'' is the great
treasury of ancient Hebrew life, the Bible. The early Zionist educator Ben-
Zion Mossenson depicted the Bible as central in real Hebrew education because it ''presents the full life of our people in our land''; it pictures Hebrew
life ''at home and in the fields, in times of peace and of war.''[20] For Segal, a
later educational theorist of the non-religious Me'uchad kibbutz movement,
the ''holiness'' unnaturally attached to the great biblical stories deprives young
people of an authentic and attractive national literature.[21] Taught to view the

colorful stories and poems of the Bible, already watered down by the clerical rabbinic editors, as "religious," youngsters have no choice but to turn to non-Jewish tales when in search of "a good story." The religious interpretation of Jewish history and literature has, for people like Segal, profoundly anti-national consequences; it is a cause of cultural assimilation.

The cultural objection to religious education is more mildly articulated by cultural Zionists like Ahad Ha-Am and tradition-oriented educators such as Zuta.[22] Although he was opposed to the radical rejection of Jewish tradition by teachers like Mossenson, Ahad Ha-Am insisted that the moral values of Judaism are not intrinsically tied to religion; Judaism lives not only by a sacred tradition but also by a "law of the heart" that expresses the deepest spiritual insights available for the national spirit in diverse ages in new situations.[23] The exclusively "religious" conception of Jewish civilization served well in the Diaspora; it was used by the nation to assure its survival in adverse conditions. In modern society, however, it invites national apostasy—those who cannot in good conscience be religious feel that they do not belong. Religion as a social cultural requirement closes options of human affiliation and expression that a nation, which constitutes a microcosm of humanity, must make available.

Worst of all, Jews' religious self-understanding creates a dualism in their lives. In religious matters, they are Jewish; in all other spheres, they are "human." This dichotomy, so widespread in Emancipation society, is unnatural and undignified. If we liberate ourselves from the religious self-definition that currently functions in a society in which the secular domain is "where the action is," we can re-integrate the Jew. He will be a Jewish human being, rather than "a Jew in his home and a man on the street." This Jewish individual will have respect and empathy for all Jewish culture but will see in it a specific (Jewish) expression of universal human values and, like all adherents of national culture, will select from the historical treasure house in accordance with his true needs and sensibilities.[24]

Although the Enlightenment world view comes to fullest expression today in Israel and in the theoretical writings connected with the General-State (non-religious) school system, it has been articulated by national thinkers in the Diaspora as well, even by some for whom the religious element was a dominant feature of Jewish culture. These "non-religious" writers often insisted that religion was intrinsic to "Yiddishkeit." As Yudel Mark expressed it:

We cannot say that we are discarding everything religious because then we would discard almost everything. . . . We do not wish to compare the Jewish religion to Christian religions, and we do not wish to imitate alien models. The survival of the Jewish people is our chief goal, and we wish to preserve, as much as possible, Jewish differentness. But we are also faced with the problem of the *impossibility* of persisting in the old ways . . . [in their] inviolability and entirety.[25]

Mordecai Kaplan, in his many writings, beginning with *Judaism as a Civilization,* has argued that Jewish religion, as *all* religion, is the super-structure of a civilization. Like all religions, Judaism is inherently attached to a culture; it establishes norms (commandments) for the achievement of salvation (human happiness and self-realization). Its faith component is limited to a view, an optimistic orientation to the world; namely, that the cosmos is so constituted that a human being's highest aspirations can be realized. The "power" that "makes for salvation" is termed God; but the term "God" is constantly reinterpreted in line with a culture's development, its progress in devising methods of inquiry, and, correspondingly, its changing conceptions of salvation.[26] Many of Kaplan's disciples and associates, especially in the Conservative and Reform branches of American Judaism, have given educational expression to his Reconstructionist view of Jewish religion-nationhood. Thus, Shulweis has attacked the "new Jewish theologians" and their "theoretic debates over salvation." He is concerned with "the more fundamental efforts to preserve the integrity of our civilization. . . . We must resist the social 'advantage' of dichotomizing ourselves into natural and supernatural Jews, secular and religious Jews, just as we have resisted the Christian dualism of law and spirit, ritual and ethics, flesh and soul. The danger of our turning into a nation like all other nations must not be overcome by our becoming a religion like all other religions. Both forms of collective imitation threaten the uniqueness and authenticity of Jewish religious civilization."[27]

Judaism, in the cultural-national view, requires not a religious theory of education, which will apply religious—that is, non-Jewish—theologies to Jewish education, but a humane ideal that can be translated into a curriculum of Yiddishkeit. Such a curriculum will incorporate the religious dimension of Jewish civilization. It will make the child realize, in the words of Goodman, that "my people, my culture, is the channel that leads me to humanity."[28]

### The "Problem" of Theology: A Secular Diagnosis

The philosophical-secular position, as we have seen, views religion and religious Judaism with historical curiosity or with descriptive objectivity, and the cultural position objects, at times militantly, to the consideration of what is *naturally* a part of Jewish culture or heritage as the whole of it. The *anti-theological approach,* however, is never objectively detached or culturally empathetic. It is fervent and highly ideological. Its point of view is not that

Judaism (or other religions) is "no longer needed" to explain reality, but that it is, in this historical situation, exposed as false. Moreover, religious belief is morally suspect for its insistence on heteronomous norms that are often spiritually deficient or are obstacles to dealing rationally with the social, political, and existential situations confronting modern Jews.[29] Consequently, religious Jews, who insist on the supernatural source of the commandments and shy away from intelligent examination of their sources and effects, are the enemies of realism and progress. Those who have been existentially "thrown" into Jewish culture and peoplehood must consciously fight against "Judaism" in order to locate the real challenge facing them and to live by ideals that experience shows to be meaningful.

The historical foci of this anti-religious ideology are the Holocaust and the State of Israel, not only because they are said to constitute "falsifications" of Judaism's truth claims but also because they illustrate what are seen to be congenital flaws in religion and religious consciousness.

In the Holocaust, it is argued, the plausibility of classic Jewish belief in a "God of history" was irrevocably destroyed; in the words of Rubenstein, God died at Auschwitz.[30] And not only did God not save, but also those who believed in Him were paralyzed into inaction by their faith. The Jewish partisans in the war against Hitler were usually Zionists or Communists, for these were the Jews who had relinquished the belief in a supernatural salvation and believed that people alone are responsible for change and salvation.

The basic unreality of religiously grounded principle is seen to be exposed in the catastrophe of the Holocaust. Since religion depends on God, people are freed of responsibility and human passivity is excused and justified. The Midrashic (theological) treatment of the Holocaust reveals that no classic religious "answer" to human suffering is to be found in the Jewish tradition. Moreover, Judaism created the conceptual framework that explained why the Jews were the worst victims of human cruelty. For Jewish religion made the Jewish people a chosen people, hence a symbol; it remained only for Judaism's daughter religion to make a symbolic status of virtue into one of vice. In either case, religious symbolic status dehumanized the Jews; as dehumanized symbols, they died at Auschwitz.

Classic religious Judaism's theologians have called it a religion of history, but, argues Scholem, Messianism (the belief in historic significance and vindication) means not only that history has a consummation and thus an ultimate meaning but also that nothing historical that is pre-Messianic is ultimately serious;[31] thus, paradoxically, Messianism induces believers to withdraw from history or, alternatively, to be unperturbed when they act irresponsibly within it. In either case, the consequence may be destructive. For those who renounce

Messianic belief and religious trust, the history of Jews appears as the tragedy of a theological misreading of reality.

If the Holocaust exposes the Messianic dimension of Jewish religion as misleading and false, the State of Israel reveals how covenant categories of collective existence that do not depend on territory render the building of a normal national life impossible.[32] More concretely, the collective life of the Jews in the State of Israel exposes the deficiencies of halakhah as a corpus of law, grounded in a religious doctrine. Halakhah, codified in the Diaspora, was shaped to deal with communities; it cannot comprehend, much less cope with, the complexities of a modern, liberal, pluralist society. Thus, all reactionary, anti-democratic, and illiberal manifestations and tendencies arise—or find natural allies—among "the religious." They are said to be xenophobic, indifferent to humanistic values, authoritarian.[33]

For the anti-religious secularist, religion looks "comfortable," and the religious person's belief is even "enviable"—for the religious individual "has an answer to all questions." But this grudging admission is tinged with irony and not a little malice. For, in a dynamic society that functions in a world of confusion and rapid change, the "comfort" provided by "religious answers" is said to bespeak ignorance of issues and moral insensitivity. And, indeed, against the broad social canvas of Israel, halakhah is accused of being lacking in the humanistic virtues of intelligence and sensitivity. It discriminates against women, stigmatizes bastards, and insists that what should be private convictions be public norms. Thus, the insult of religious coercion is added to the injury of cultural-moral petrification. And no better demonstration of halakhah's weakness is to be found than its reliance on non-Jews for the maintenance of essential services; in what is declared to be its natural habitat, *Eretz Yisrael*, Jewish religious law can function only with the help of those who are not bound by it.[34]

Religious education, implemented in Israel through the State religious schools and the Independent (Agudat Yisrael) system, exemplifies these flaws. In religious schools, conformity of behavior is demanded of teachers and pupils alike. No serious questioning of sacred texts or notions is permitted, and the ideal envisioned is a "Torah State" in which modern conceptions of freedom of conscience and the moral authority of the individual alone to decide on the articulation of his or her beliefs may be flouted with impunity. Even more than in the Diaspora religious school (which, it is agreed, at least serves a vital function in fostering Jewish identification), the Israeli religious school is charged with incongruence—either irrelevant to the ethos of the national renaissance or distorting it. The religious educational system and its constituency can be accused either of refusing to create a new Jewish culture or of co-opting secular nationalism for an irresponsible Messianism—wedded to archaic halakhah. If the passive religious Jew is to be pitied for being alienated from the most vibrant visions and achievements of modern times, the latter, nationalistic Messianists, represented by the Gush Emunim movement, are to be feared. For this group not only views political issues through a prism of theological fantasy, which is dangerous enough, but also insists on defining Zionism in a stipulatively religious manner, which, whether by design or not, creates a sense of alienation in secular Jews. The latter are made to feel less Jewish than religious Jews, warned that they have no authentic "Jewish culture," and eventually led to wonder in which sense and why Israel is significant to them.[35]

## *The Secular View of the Educational Problematic Situation*

The specifically educational objections of secular Jewish education theorists are, of course, implied and sometimes explicitly stated in arguments that we have called philosophical-secular, cultural, and anti-theological. Nevertheless, the educational objections to religious instruction should be reiterated and spelled out in the terms that characterize educational discourse:

1. It has been argued that religious education leans to authority rather than to freedom, to imitation rather than to development, to tradition rather than to experience. In the words of Adar, it is concerned not with the child but with religion.[36] It is thus necessarily indoctrinatory. Although some religious educators may be more open and flexible in their approach than others and may take the child's stages of development and interests into consideration, even these, like all religious educators, aim to inculcate religious doctrines and practices.

2. Religious education militates against autonomy. It "liberates" individuals—at the price of freedom—from responsible striving for their ideals, offering them the comfort that these ideals already have some supernatural "reality" in another world and therefore are not really dependent upon the individual.[37] Thus, whereas many religious educators insist on a necessary link between moral education and religion, between character building and faith, secular educational theorists maintain that there is no such connection and that adherence to tradition may often have adverse affects on moral character.[38]

3. The claim of religious educators that they alone assure Jewish identification and survival and that secular education cannot transmit Jewish values and loyalty is countered by the argument that such an instrumental understanding of religion is deficient on two counts. First, it is false to religion's own (non-instrumental) conception of itself and constitutes, in fact, a secular ar-

gument—that one should practice religion not because of its allegedly true contents but for its social value. This is, for some educational theorists and psychologists, an invitation to hypocrisy and "verbalization."[39] Religion may in fact be effective in furthering identity, but only when it is believed; values do not become believable simply because they can be shown to be useful. Lies are never educationally justified, not even the lie that religion is true. Moreover, the efficacy of religion in strengthening Jewish loyalties is questionable in the contemporary age, when, as has been pointed out, an exclusive identification of Jewishness with religion is more likely to have the opposite effect—of discouraging Jewish affiliation among secular people.

4. Religious education, even in the Diaspora society that has little choice but to define itself religiously, is not functional. In other words, one does not learn anything in the Jewish school that must be acquired in order to act plausibly or competently, or in order to succeed in life. Thus, the four classic "topics of education" (the teacher, the learner, the subject matter, and the environment) are chronically "out of gear" in the religious school. The pupils, concerned neither with religion nor Jewish identity, are unmotivated and know that nothing that they will need to do well "out there" is related to what they are studying; the teacher, although probably concerned about "Jewish identity," is either troubled or skeptical about religion, or, alternatively, is very "religious" but totally incompatible in thinking with pupils and parents. The subject matter, if it is tradition, is too difficult for sophisticated treatment by meagerly trained teachers and thus appears naive and foolish to pupils in comparison with what they learn in general subjects (and schools). It is thus learned by rote, or evaded by "discussion" or other forms of avoidance. As for the parents, who are secular in their life styles and assumptions and largely ignorant of the religious tradition they in fact reject, they cannot have a clear idea of what they want the "religious" school to achieve. Thus, they cannot be supportive, and they express their confusion and indifference in contradictory ways that are all equally annoying. They look down on the Jewish teacher, give piano lessons priority over Hebrew school, and complain that children are "becoming too religious" or, conversely, that "they don't learn anything in Hebrew school." "Don't make him a rabbi" and "She's not learning anything" are, in fact, two sides of the same coin.

5. To say that religious education is not truly functional has a cultural corollary. If religious teaching is successful, it alienates the child from the cultural world considered significant by parents and children. It either ignores what is important cognitively and valuatively, thus creating an inauthentic religious sentiment of escape, or it imperialistically attempts to incorporate secular wis-

dom, thus making everything religious in a way that systematically blurs the distinction between dogma and universal understandings based on scientific inquiry.

The secular positions that imply the superfluity of religious educational theory have been summarized in this chapter at some length for two reasons. (1) A theory of religious education must demonstrate its value in the world in which these secular positions prevail and are taken for granted. (2) Such a theory cannot blind itself to the problems located by modern thought and research, for psychological, sociological, and historical knowledge are necessary components of all educational theory. What we know in these fields is largely the consequence of modern research made available through disciplines heavily influenced by secular modes of thought.

In other words, Jewish religious educational theory not only must "know how to answer the heretic" but also must attentively listen to the questions being asked. For it may not be decided in advance that certain questions being asked in the contemporary world have no relevance to religious answers or that solutions put forward to secularly conceived problems have no relationship to genuine unease.

# 4　Religious Responses to Secular Solutions

## THE STATUS OF SECULAR DELIBERATION: PROBLEM OR SOLUTION?

In the previous chapter, we surveyed what may be called secular or untraditional hypotheses about the problem of Judaism and Jewish education in the contemporary world. The search for this problem and the subsequently proposed solutions arose from a state of unease experienced as a crisis. This crisis, evidenced by symptoms of "disease"—of malfunctioning—indicated that previous understandings of "Judaism" and consequent "normative philosophies of Jewish education" were no longer to be considered adequate ways of dealing with the new social circumstances and spiritual orientations.

The resulting discomfort, "the problematic situation," induced those who had cultural loyalties to their Jewishness but could no longer believe in the "historical-habitual" norms of the Jewish people to look for a way out of the unease, a solution to the problem of modern Jewish existence. But before they could hope for a solution, they had to define the problem. Before they could hope to cure the disease, they had to arrive at a diagnosis. This, as we have seen, they did in the following ways:

1. They reflected on modern thought and its "liberation" from religion, and they attempted to place Jewish collective experience and aspirations within the framework of general developments that promised greater self-understanding and human fulfillment through science and secularization.

2. They sought to locate the national foci of Jewish identity in the historical tradition of the Jewish people, hoping to give—or restore—to the "non-religious" components of Jewish culture the centrality and dignity these

elements deserved. In this way, they hoped to "correct" religious-Orthodox readings of Jewish history, more accurately depict the Jewish spirit, and provide a solid basis for their own (no longer religious) sense of Jewish cultural continuity.

3. At times, they expressed a determination to change the nature of historic Judaism on the basis of what they experienced as a breakdown of the theological tradition. That tradition was declared to malfunction in present circumstances, and the desire for Jewish survival and happiness was said to require the courage of radical change and metamorphosis.

The secular diagnoses generally negated normative philosophies of education based on tradition or theologically formulated "ideal objectives": They called for deliberation that would locate the "real" problems and offer requisite solutions. These solutions, it was indicated, would be characterized by more freedom from tradition and more emphasis on "real" experience and challenges. The solutions took educational shape in Bundist, ethnic, and (most enduringly) secular Zionist schools, youth movements, and camps. As if in response to the scornful anti-Zionist remark of the famed German-Jewish philosopher Herman Cohen, "Those bums wish to be happy,"[1] the Zionists declared, "Yes, we do." They thought that the disdain for happiness, which Cohen considered a moral imperative in an unredeemed world, was simply an inability to face realities; it was unease masking as nobility. And, as already noted, the problem, according to secular thinkers and educators, was to be found in the narrow and unjustified self-understanding that made Judaism, in principle and in "essence," a religious affair.

But, of course, this secular formulation of the problem was not a self-evident truth. The unwillingness or inability of Jews to believe in "the tradition" and its norms and religious meanings could also be interpreted as sinful or, at least, tragic. Thus, Yechezkel Kaufmann, who admitted that his contemporaries appeared unable to believe in the religious values of the Jewish tradition, nevertheless held that these values alone explained Jewish history and made continued national existence feasible. Taking issue with Ahad Ha-Am, for whom Jewish religion in the Diaspora was an expression of the national "organism's" will to survive, Kaufmann insisted that it was not the case that the Jews had kept to their faith in order to perpetuate the nation. Rather, the nation had survived in order to embody its highest value: religious faith, which alone was the source of the nation's "national will." Thus, he wrote mournfully:

Our situation is indeed tragic, the situation of all those whose faith has been destroyed and who have no hope of returning to it but whose hearts still cling to the national entity that draws its life force from the faith. It is hard to reconcile ourselves to the idea that our nationalism derives from a faith that no longer exists in our hearts. That is why we try to find some other basis for our nationalism and devise a "natural nationalism" or a "spiritual nationalism" or some other explanation.[2]

If Kaufmann's polemic with "spiritual nationalism" is aimed at Ahad Ha-Am and his disciples, his argument with "natural nationalism" is directed at the anti-metaphysical school of Klatzkin and such educators as Mossenson. Klatzkin has posited that Jewish life was maintained throughout the exile because of halakhah and the social and quasi-political institutions built in accordance with the halakhic regimen. Because the faith assumptions behind halakhah are no longer believed by most Jews, halakhah is doomed to continued attrition and ultimate demise. Thus, Jewish life in the Diaspora is destined to disappear, except for a small sectarian and non-modern minority. Klatzkin insisted that the only modern Jews who will survive as Jews are those who decide to reconstitute themselves as a "normal" nation, distinguished from others by language and territory—and whatever culture they choose to create within this language and land.[3] To this line of thought Kaufmann responded that even secular Jews were impelled to come to *Eretz Yisrael* by what remained of their (religious) national value systems: "The nationalist movement itself, even though it arose among secularists and even though some schools of thought within it are opposed to religion and fight it, came into being, directly or indirectly, only by virtue of the religious faith. . . . Anyone who recognizes that religion was not only a means of survival but, as a faith, the source of the nation's will to survive, must necessarily deduce from the decline of religion not only the extinction of the Diaspora but also the extinction of the entire nation."[4]

The foregoing is not cited in order to refute the secular diagnoses of modern Jewish discomfort scholastically but merely to indicate that secular interpretations of the problematic situation did not dispel the unease; Cohen's "fear" that "those bums" would be happy was at least premature. Nor is it meant to disparage their seeking to relate new secular realities to the existential situation of modern Jews. Their deliberation, whether or not it arrived at a sound diagnosis, was certainly legitimate, arising out of genuine unease. After all, it was not they, the "heretics," who created the problematic situation! Their unease, and the failure of normative Jewish education to "achieve its ideal objectives" with them, arose in an environment that was religious—and that they perceived to be oppressive, reactionary, and insensitive to significant and revolutionary events. Yet, the way in which secular Jews located the problem of contemporary Jewish crisis is not obviously correct, nor are its educational solutions necessarily the way to extricate modern Jewry from its problematic situation. In education, as in medicine, there are different schools of thought, differing definitions of health and disease, and varying reasons for "trusting" a teacher or a healer, or questioning his or her judgment.

It has been said that those who are not engaged in solving a problem are themselves part of the problem. The controversy between secular and religious understandings of the contemporary Jewish crisis is a case in point. We have seen that secular Jews consider religious Jews' insistence on normative and theological understandings of Judaism to be the cause of assimilation and a drain on the vitality of Jewish culture; they claim that because of religious definitions and understandings Judaism is kept shackled to medieval moorings, and this prevents its full development and saps its potential in the modern age.

Conversely, for religious thinkers and educators, the weakness of the Jewish people is often ascribed to non-religiosity, which is equated with assimilation or believed to lead inevitably to cultural impoverishment and historical extinction. They argue that if Jews will "return to religion" the symptoms will disappear: Marriages will increase, birth rates will rise, intermarriage will be unthinkable, Jewish education will thrive, and Jewish communities will experience a spiritual renaissance.[5]

An advantage enjoyed by religious respondents to secular deliberation is that they can dialectically incorporate insights made available through the secular discussions; the drawback is that, in using the categories established by the secular-oriented thinkers and educators, the religious arguments may sound like a rebuttal and an apology. Thus, when the secularist claims that modern thought is antithetical to religion, the religious thinker not only responds that religion is perennial but also is likely to buttress this claim with findings (or at least quotations) from modern philosophy and scholarship.

Moreover, when religious thinkers insist that Judaism is fundamentally a religious culture, they may well refer to failures in transmitting Jewish culture in secular form. For them, the crisis of modern history, rather than testifying to religious obsolescence, is an opportunity for new theology, enhanced by contemporary insights. Finally, when they argue that Jewish education that is conceived as non-religious will not be truly Jewish, they may also utilize universal categories prominent in modern discourse and question whether non-religious education is genuinely educational.

This use of contemporary categories is not illegitimate; indeed, it enhances communicability. But it is legitimate to use "general" knowledge only when the religious educational thinker recognizes that the defense of religious education and its rehabilitation involves a serious encounter with the deliberative orientation, despite its usually "secular" contexts. This recognition not only prevents dishonesty in the conduct of controversy with the non-normative "world" of secularism but also may facilitate the discovery, within the religious tradition, of a religiosity that is not *only* normative.

In examining the religious diagnoses, we shall use the same categories that were identified in the preceding chapter's discussion of secular diagnoses. The fact that the same criteria can be used to describe secular and religious approaches to the problem illustrates what we have pointed out earlier. Religious deliberation must admit to the debt of contemporary theology and religious educational theory to modern currents of thought and study, even as it insists upon the relevance of religious sensibility and possibility of, as well as the need for, its adequate theological articulation under all historical circumstances.

## The Philosophical Enlightenment and Crypto-Theologies

It can be argued that in every critique of a world view, particular beliefs and operative ideals are implicitly articulated. The description of the "universe" that is being attacked is generally tailored to the belief that is said to have replaced it for "serious" thinkers. This is as true of the "one-dimensional" world of the scientist (so designated by the traditional religious believer) as it is of "the three-storied universe" of the believer (thus referred to by the positivist). Ideological thinkers, often incisive about the problematics of world views that conflict with theirs, are seldom capable of criticizing the "self-understood" assumptions of their own epoch and culture. In light of this, such Jewish thinkers as Fackenheim have suggested that a central function of philosophy of religion is to bring hidden or unconscious beliefs to consciousness and articulation—so that they may be openly criticized or defended.[6]

This is no less true of objective-scientific beliefs, in all their variety, than of overtly religious ones; there have been many similarly heated philosophical controversies among scientists about objectivity and its relationship to inquiry and values.[7] All beliefs, at given times and in given contexts, appear problematic. One may argue that some beliefs are, on the whole, more plausible, open to more universal forms of verification, or more germane to human self-understanding. But none is served by dogmatic indifference to new challenges; all must deal with new knowledge in order to remain viable.

For traditional religion, the advent of modern science is such a challenge, as is the consciousness occasioned by technology and enhanced human control over environments. Though we must distinguish between science, as a universe of inquiry and control, and scientism, as a world view and a crypto-theology, we cannot ignore the fact that living in a scientific world creates, for sensitive people, feelings of incongruence and "dislocation" in their lives within the religious tradition. We now can switch on an electric bulb as evening approaches and then proceed with our activities; why then, if the *Shema* is to be recited "when you lie down [to sleep]," is the advent of darkness nevertheless the prescribed time for the evening prayer?* Observant individuals may be uncomfortable with certain types of religious authority and may wonder whether "the authority" understands the sociological and psychological context of the particular religious problem being addressed. Those who study the Bible at universities ask—or suppress—reasonable questions about Divine revelation. Our historical consciousness creates difficulties for our convictions about eternal truths, and our scientific habits of thought at times lead us to compartmentalization or confusion with regard to our patterns of reverence and humility. Yet it can be posited that the challenge is not, in principle, to religious world view and *faith,* but to problematic *theologies,* and to antiquated (and polemically celebrated) "models" of three-storied universes.[8]

Indeed, the advent of modern science as a dominant cultural "model of reality" has created neutral tools that can be used ideologically in various ways. There is, for example, the scientific study of religion itself. Some have used scientific modes of inquiry into religion for purposes of debunking; others, of different belief, have deduced from this scholarship that religion is, despite "old-fashioned" opinion to the contrary, a lasting human concern. Relating religion to the existential, as well as to the psychological and social, factors constituting human experience seems to produce insight into the question of why, despite all expectations to the contrary, it has failed to disappear. Although psychologists and social scientists take no position *qua* scientists with regard to the truth of specific religious propositions, they have discussed how religion is not necessarily synonymous with the "superstition" deplored by the rationalist but is intrinsic to the language of the psyche and to the sense of society. Jung has suggested a phenomenology of religion based upon an all-pervasive unconscious;[9] although his thesis is probably unacceptable to most religious believers, it is far removed from Freud's thesis that the basic religious dimension of "depth" is born in the quite-unmysterious experience of early childhood.[10] It is perhaps ironic that the positivistic Freud was soundly rebuked by Popper as pseudo-scientific; it is certainly ironic that Freud, who considered religion as illusion and neurosis, has been credited with spiritual "breakthroughs" that cast new light on religion and complement it.[11]

New social realities, created by a scientific culture, have created new religious problems for theology, have suggested new avenues to channel reli-

---

*The *Shema,* the biblical credo of Jewish faith, is to be said morning and evening (Deut. 6:7) as interpreted by the Talmud (Tractate Berakhot, chap. 1).

gious consciousness, and, for religious people, have enlarged the scope of religious deliberation. The problem of freedom and human dignity in a mechanized world, the issue of humanity's use and misuse of the planet that has been "entrusted" to it, the dilemmas of medical ethics—such questions have become the subjects of religious discussion. And to the extent that religious people have failed to discuss them, they have been accused of compromising religion's claims to relevance and to scope. These questions would not have arisen in their current form and with this degree of intensity in a world without technology and scientific inquiry. What has happened is that science and the demise of "the three-storied universe" have invited new religious deliberation.

Moreover, not only scientific discovery but also secularizing philosophies, once they were seen as making "faith claims" of their own, could be (and were) called upon—and disputed—in principled discourse and controversy about truth and value. These conversations, though sometimes shattering previous convictions, were also opportunities for deeper understandings of religious traditions. The secular existentialism, which sharpened sensitivities *vis-à-vis* the chaotic and the absurd in human existence, also insisted on total human responsibility. It was this that led religious existentialists to emphasize choice, to dwell solemnly on God's transcendence, and to debunk "peace-of-mind" religiosity.[12] Analytical philosophy, which concerned itself with the exploration of meaningful rhetoric and the exposure of non-sense, was invoked by theologians and religious-minded philosophers to clarify "religious language."[13] In fact, in all schools of thought, philosophers have themselves debated the theological implications and significances that may legitimately be attached to diverse metaphysical (and "anti-metaphysical") systems. Thomas[14] has shown how Kant has been variously interpreted by religious and anti-religious thinkers; Fackenheim has examined how Hegel's disciples have drawn diverse conclusions about religion from his philosophy.[15] In a study by Macquarrie,[16] the reader is briefly introduced to the entire spectrum of philosophical orientations in the modern world—many of them explicitly based on the contemporary scientific culture—and to the theological responses *and manifestations* associated with each of them.

Sociologists and historians of contemporary religion have created typologies of response to the secular philosophical challenge to religion. From the perspective of contemporary intellectual sensibility, the non-conformist is now often the one who is willing to take religion seriously. For unabashed "heretics" like Walter Kaufmann, militantly secular world views, no less than scholastic theologies, are deficient in poetic sensitivity.[17]

For Jews, whose religion is intimately related to the particular historical culture of one people, the challenge of the secular Enlightenment to national or cultural "identity" may be considered *sui generis*. Even Orthodox writers, such as Lichtenstein,[18] readily agree that secular Jews are not in the same category as secular Catholics—if, indeed, it makes sense to speak of "secular Catholics" at all. Likewise, secular Jews are not really like secular non-Anglican Englishmen, possessing a clear national identity but disclaiming a religious one. Non-religious Jews, as long as they admit to a Jewish identity, are bound *to* a religious heritage even when, as non-religious individuals, they declare themselves not bound *by* it.

Mordecai Kaplan dealt at length with this perplexing problem. He understood religion to be a serious concern with the salvational potential of human ideals and deeds. For him, the problem of "secular" Jews was not that they could not accept traditional doctrines that ran counter to the modern world view, but that they refused to see their values and salvational achievements as truly serious—that is, *as religious*.[19]

Yet most Jews do not accept this conception of religion, and many self-sacrificing *chalutzim* would have rejected it. Secular Jews understand themselves as unable to relate "religiously," as commanded and significant, to the normative traditions of Judaism. At the same time, they know themselves to be Jews, and they seek foci of Jewishness—of activity and attachment. Moreover, they wish this activity and attachment to be somehow *serious* and to have a vocabulary of symbols that articulate that Judaism *is* a serious concern. However, many Jews have discovered that a secular consciousness cannot easily adhere to a symbolic language needed to sustain a framework of absolutely serious commitment and significance. In this situation we find that Jews tend to give up the symbols and the ultimate seriousness of their Jewishness, or to give up their secularism—and sometimes their Jewish identity.

Those who give up the symbols of serious concern are likely to resign themselves to a Jewishness of nostalgia, surface activity, project-oriented community. Those who give up secularism, who seek "real" symbols and concern, will, in some cases, become ultra-traditional Jews. In other cases, they will opt for gurus or evangelical sects. The ultra-traditionalists will leave "only" the modern world; the sectarians will leave the Jewish people.

As for the ones who remained secular, who live Judaism as non-religious activity and community, they will probably lose their children—who fail to understand why their parents are so parochial as to limit serious concern with the salvational potential of human ideals and deeds to Israel and Soviet Jewry, especially as they are proud citizens of other countries.

Milton Himmelfarb has given literary expression to this diagnosis of the problem.[20] *Inter alia,* he notes that while in pre-revolutionary Russia *gymnasium* students had contempt for official teachers of religion, the contempt is currently reserved for official university lecturers in dialectical materialism. "Now," he wrote in 1967, "all kinds of people are Russian Orthodox or pre–Russian Orthodox."

Of Joseph Brodsky, the young man sentenced to a killing term in the North for daring to write poetry without an official poet's license, one hears that he has a Russian Orthodox cross over his cot. Is that because he, too, is now Russian Orthodox, or is it because a cross is the only religious symbol this Jew can find?

Turning to Israel, Himmelfarb continued:

In Israel the so-called oriental immigrants have taken the dominant Ashkenazim as models for how to be modern and up-to-date. One thing they learn quickly is that modern Israelis aren't religious, that to be religious is the way not to be modern. I heard the following story from a professor at the Hebrew University. . . .
. . . During military service this man's son became a noncommissioned officer and with his new stripes he was assigned one afternoon to a new unit and barracks, where he was both senior and the only Askhenazi. The next morning he put on his tefillin and prayed. The other soldiers stared and a few began to cry. Later he discovered the reason. Here was their noncom, an Ashkenazi of the Ashkenazim, praying—and with tefillin. They had been deceived. All of the sacrifice of habit and feeling and belief they had thought necessary was unnecessary. It was possible both to be *moderni* and to put on tefillin.[21]

According to Himmelfarb, Brodsky left the Jewish people for reasons diametrically opposed to those that made cultural Zionists of people like Ahad Ha-Am. The latter believed that it was the anachronistic religiosity of Jewish culture that was the problem; Himmelfarb found the problem in an ideology of secularism that leads, in the absence of tefillin, to a search for other symbols—and, consequently, estrangement and apostasy.

There are, it appears, at least two ways to locate the philosophical problem of modern Judaism.

## The Nature of Jewish Culture and Religion

The argument concerning whether Jewish culture is or is not essentially religious leads necessarily to an examination of what "essentially" constitutes "religion," how each religious culture is unique, and what they all share to render the general term "religion" meaningful. When Jews declare that Jewish civilization need not be interpreted as a necessarily religious phenomenon, they may be making one of several statements:

1. That Judaism, the national culture of the Jewish people, is too different from what is considered "religion" in the surrounding culture to make that term useful.

2. That Judaism "essentially" anticipates the non-religious scientific and humanistic world view, although it had "religious" manifestations in religious epochs.

3. That Judaism is an abstraction, connoting reflective self-understandings of Jews and the problems they are called upon to solve as a group.

Obviously, a view of Judaism that is abstractly theological and liturgical and does not take the concrete realities of the Jewish people in varying historical circumstances into account is partial and distorting. Such religious and purely theological understandings have indeed led to inconsistencies and presented post-Emancipation Jewries with the apparently insoluble problem of how Judaism, as a universalistic and monotheistic faith, could conceive of a God Who makes specific normative-halakhic demands upon the Jew alone.[22] In less theological terms, the religious abstraction of Judaism from the Jewish history and culture that gave it content and context has, for those whose Judaism meant that they were "of Mosaic persuasion," raised the specter of dual loyalty. When consistent, Jewishness that was only "religious" had to reject much religious material that dealt with the main subject of Jewish religiosity: God's relationship to His people.[23]

However, if it is implausible to comprehend Jewish religion without the historical Jews and their culture, the converse is also true. The attempt to formulate a Jewishness that is confined to a secular culture that can, in principle, be seen and inhabited without religion, created its own anomalies and distortions. The long-standing debate in Israel about education for "Jewish consciousness" well illustrates the dilemma of secular civilization. What gave rise to this debate and discussion was the unease felt by the generation of Zionist founders at what they considered the "un-Jewish" character of the younger generation. Those who were being educated in the general (i.e., non-Orthodox) schools were feared to be deficient in Jewish sensibility and culture. For example, they did not know what the portion of the week was, they were not proud of the age-old heritage, and they were alienated from Jewish communities in the Diaspora and from religious Jews everywhere. The resolution of the Knesset in 1959, which requested that the Ministry of Education rectify educational deficiencies of "Jewishness," stated that "the strengthening of the Jewish consciousness of the youth of Israel (is) . . . one of the important educational means of preserving the unity and integrity of the Jewish people and its historical continuity throughout the generations.''[24] Thereafter, the Ministry set forth guidelines for ''Jewish consciousness'' that included a more sympathetic view of Jewish history in the eras of dispersion, greater attention to the spiritual heritage (including the study of the oral tradition), and concern with contemporary Jewry and Jewish communities.

Such attempts were criticized as nostalgic or chauvinistic by opponents of the program, who stated that the new guidelines were a sinister attempt to smuggle religion into national Jewish education through a back door.[25] These opponents considered *religion* the educational problem that secular Zionism had to solve. But one can discern quite another problem with secular-cultural conceptions of Jewishness in the defense of the program put forward by its secular supporters. For example, a Minister of Education, insisting on the centrality of Jewish values in Israeli-Jewish education, stated that children in the Israeli school must believe that people were created in the image of God; yet, he added, this need not be based ''on the assumption of God's existence.'' Statements such as this one spelled out the inconsistencies in the Ahad Ha-Am position, which thought to secularize Jewish ''culture'' without impinging on its spiritual ''essence.''[26]

Let us continue the non-secular analysis of the ''problematic situation'' of modern Jews with another example of ''obvious unease.'' It has been observed that many Israeli youngsters have principled problems with a ''Jewish state'' that is democratic and has non-Jewish citizens; conversely, they often have difficulty in explaining why the ''Zionism is racism'' argument is libelous. This, we suggest, is largely a result of their misunderstanding of the relationship between the Jewish (religious) tradition and Zionism, even in its secular ''rebellious'' embodiment. For, in fact, Zionism, as a spiritual and cultural movement, notwithstanding its general rebellion against the traditional religious life of the ghetto, was directed toward a solution of the specifically Jewish problems of cultural continuity despite—and even through—modernity. It did not consistently rebel against the historical self-understanding of the Jews as a people whose unity was ideational and normative rather than territorial, if for no other reason than that the faith in a return to *Eretz Yisrael* was part of that idea of Judaism. *Eretz Yisrael* was part of the ''system'' of Jewish belief and practice, as well as a focus of longing and anticipation.

It was this that made the national ideology persuasive and also problematic. Zionists could thrill to the vision of an ''ingathering of the exiles'' even when they no longer expected a divinely sent Messiah, because the religious concept was now being understood in a new national manner. But the religious concept was still *there,* because secular cultural nationalism continued to insist that territorial residence (in *Eretz Yisrael*), in the past and in the present, was irrelevant to Jewish national status. The "traditional" notion that one could be a Jew outside of *Eretz Yisrael* unto the tenth (and twentieth) generation—because Jewish "identity" was conferred by God through Torah—also meant that non-Jews could live in *Eretz Yisrael,* even as citizens of a Jewish state, without thereby gaining a Jewish national identity—for "Jewish identity" was participation, no matter how rebelliously, in the community of the covenant. Zionism, even in its secular-cultural forms, was thus an extremely "Jewish" affair that required some theological knowledge and even sophistication to be fully grasped, even though it was primarily addressed to those who wished no traffic with theology!

Of course, within secular Zionism there have been those who regretted this state of affairs and wished to carry the Zionist rebellion against the tradition to what they considered a consistent and logical conclusion. These writers held the position that "Judaism" is an abstraction and, in terms of building a healthy national life, perhaps even an obstruction. The radical wing of this group were the "Hebrews" or "Canaanites," who proposed ideological and educational alternatives to Jewish-Zionist education. They urged that the State of Israel view itself as a normal national polity rather than as, in some respects, a Jewish community that has not "liberated" itself from religiously grounded cultural assumptions.[27] But proponents of this school of thought, at least in its radical manifestations, agree that accomplishing this would require a clear disengagement from the Jews of the Diaspora. They admit that a radical "liberation" of this kind would mean that Israel could in no sense continue to be viewed as a solution, real or potential, to "the Jewish problem" (though Jews, like others who wished to build a new nation, would be welcome).[28]

The cultural difficulties and debates from within are reinforced by pervasive images and attitudes from without that also occasion unease. The State of Israel, no less than the Jewish people as such in pre-State days, is often portrayed as "abnormal"; that is, it is viewed symbolically. Zionists may have fervently wished to cease playing a role in the symbolic mythic systems of others and to be viewed and treated simply as human beings.[29] (The "wandering Jews" wished to be "at ease in Zion.") However, like their opponents the Diaspora assimilationists, the "normalizing" Zionists found that declarations of new consciousness or new self-understanding did not necessarily affect—or affect benignly—the consciousness or understanding of others. Israel, no matter how prominent the secular face of its Jewish culture, remained the "nation that dwells alone." Indeed, one may posit with Ben-Horin that since Zionism constituted a rebuttal to theological declarations that Judaism is fossilized and archaic, secular and cultural Jewish nationalism made Judaism an even more acute theological problem for non-Jews than it had been.[30]

Yaakov Herzog, the statesman-scholar, once pointed out that the failure to comprehend the religious and theological aspects of Jewish national life in the reborn State of Israel brought with it political naïveté and handicaps. The problem, he intimated, was not that Israel had not yet secularized Jewish existence but that secular Jews did not recognize the miraculous-religious character of Jewish national return to *Eretz Yisrael*. Thus, they could not comprehend how and why this event constituted a scandal (that is, a wrong miracle) among those of other religious persuasions.[31]

With regard to the character of "Jewishness," too, there are diverse ways of locating the problem.

## Religious Crisis and Theological Re-assessment

We have seen that secular Jewish thinkers and educators view both the Holocaust and the rise of Israel as radically "dislocating" previous Messianic and normative (halakhic) concepts and patterns. That these developments—the Holocaust and Israel—are indeed traumatic and world-shaking is virtually undisputed. But the diagnosis of anti-theological secularists that religion is the spiritual problem of modern Jewry and that it prevents a reasoned rejection of halakhah and vital rethinking and innovation in ethics and cultural dispositions is open to question. Those who are deliberating about the cause of Jewish unease in light of these events must determine, if we may use Kuhn's conceptual framework, whether these events and developments are to be viewed within the paradigm of religious tradition or as "counter-instances."[32] In the first case, the new circumstances are viewed as occasions for theological enlargement of the tradition; the assumption is that the traditional faith (the old paradigm) can deal with the new circumstances. In the second case, the new situation is seen as demonstrating the implausibility of the paradigm and the need for new paradigms. Where the Holocaust and the State of Israel are viewed as problems or puzzles, they demand new theology and perhaps halakhic innovations; where these events are considered counter-instances, they call for new *faiths*. In the former case, there is theological expansion; in the latter case, there is religious rejection and conversion to secular convictions.

"Post-religious" thinkers see the events and circumstances of contemporary Jewish history as counter-instances; to religious thinkers, these events are puzzles. In contra-distinction to the anti-theological secularist, who believes that the old model is beyond repair and thus places it in a limited (and now rejected) halakhic perspective, the religious thinker insists that the tradition remains alive and is therefore capable of shedding light on new situations and absorbing their perceived significance. The position of the latter has been given succinct theoretical expression by Strauss:

> Within a living tradition, the new is not the opposite of the old but its deepening; one does not understand the old in its depth unless one understands it in the light of such deepening; the new does not emerge through the rejection or annihilation of the old but through its metamorphosis or reshaping.[33]

In the spirit of Strauss's thesis we find much religious faith and thought being re-examined in the generation after the Holocaust. Schindler[34] has studied the religious responses of those who have lived through this tragedy; although some lost their faith during those years, in many cases the piety of the confrontation puts all "systematic" religious responses to shame. Thus, although the Holocaust is a catastrophe that cannot be ignored by religious or secular Jews, it is not self-evident that one must see it as contradictory to Jewish religiosity. Just as secular Jews may legitimately ask their religious fellows how they maintain faith in God's goodness, so may the latter remind their secular counterparts that the classic faith in humanity has, through the Holocaust, been faced with its most severe test.

Ben-Sasson[35] has surveyed theological responses to the Holocaust and has found that not all theologies related to it concern themselves primarily with the redemptive pole of religious faith, with the problem of God's "saving Presence." Some are predominantly halakhic and ask, not about the meaning of the event, but what the proper normative response to chaos and catastrophe should be. Conversely, not all religious thinking that deals with the new predicaments of Judaism in the age of Israel is concerned with the halakhic problems related to the transformation of the Jewish community into Jewish society. Werblowsky, for example, has drawn attention to the "crises of Messianism" that are elicited by intimations of imminent redemption.[36] In the specific terms of the contemporary situation, one may question whether (and how) the image of the envisioned Messiah is affected by radical change from political powerlessness to social and halakhic responsibility. Rabbi Kook, in the early years of this century, already foresaw this crisis and warned against the over-spiritualization of religious visions.[37] Visions of return and consummation, he cautioned, are always realized only in a concrete and "worldly" context. Thus, the Messianic crisis, which may be called the shock of partial realization of a vision and a consciousness of (at least partial) responsibility for its implementation—and the subsequent fear of failure—is common to both religious and secular Jews in Israel.

Nevertheless, the halakhic-normative issue is undoubtedly *the* central one regarding the viability of religious tradition in Israel. Secular thinkers consider halakhah archaic in the State of Israel, for to them it is the ill-fated attempt to maintain the legal framework of exilic community. Religious thinkers, sharing a consciousness of unease, ask probing questions while searching for the problem: Have the development and interpretation of halakhah been slowed down by conservative reactions to modern antinomianism? Are those who interpret halakhah not willing or competent to do so in terms of the bodies of knowledge available and valued in a secularized society? How can its future interpreters be educated not to consider rigidity, on the one hand, and "cognitive surrender" to secular conceptions of humanity and society, on the other hand, as the only available options? Moreover, how should one explain the passive willingness of secular Jews to "put up with" an official Jewish religion (and religious establishment) that they declare to be intellectually and spiritually unacceptable to them? Is this because they make a conscious sacrifice of principle for national unity and harmony? Is it because they are secretly in agreement with religious principles but "lazy"? What would a genuine Jewish consensus in a Jewish state really look like?

These and related questions are crucial to religious deliberation on the problem raised by Zionism and Israel for traditional Judaism. Through such questions, the issue of Jewish law may be seen in the context of a general philosophical and sociological problem of modern people in present-day society as well as in explicitly theological terms. No one will claim that even a liberal Jewish society should live without norms, and no culturally sensitive Jew maintains that the Jewish religious tradition is not a significant resource for norms in a Jewish polity. Nor will knowledgeable Jews declare that the religious teachers of Jewry, as the tradition transmits their teachings, did not deal with such problems as autonomy and heteronomy, morality and commandment, mundane public realities and ideal embodiments.

Yet religious teachers are aware that not all traditional declarations or decisions can be incorporated into a new situation. Indeed, it can be shown that the ultra-Orthodox community in Israel and in the Diaspora ignores specific halakhic rulings of previous epochs because they are seen to be inappropriate.[38] On the other hand, the conservative and even reactionary tendencies in much religious teaching and decision making may be understood as a form of "guarding the fort" against a secular public. As many religious leaders see it, the secular public anticipates the solution of problems only from within social-scientific frames of reference; thus, this public is insensitive to the internal religious dilemma—how to negotiate the tension between holiness and its accessibility, how to be both reverent and relevant.

Educators concerned with religious education in Israel, both Orthodox and non-Orthodox, have pointed out that the cluster of problems concerned with the relationship between society and the individual—that is, the problems of authority and freedom, of "heritage" and "experience," are perennial and inherent in human life.[39] There is discussion and debate, and there are shifting lines of affirmation and affiliation. "Religion" and "Judaism" do not set self-contained or consistently clear *a priori* guidelines for every conceivable situation or temperament. The practical questions of religion, like those of morality, are in principle never definitively answered, for every situation makes demands and reveals new problems and possibilities.[40]

Seen in this perspective, the problem of religion is aroused and sharpened for Jews by the Holocaust and the State of Israel, but the problem need hardly be conceived as a counter-instance. The concerns of Jewish religion are not changed by these events, though the specific issues may be traumatically novel. These concerns include the relationship between morality and power (and powerlessness!); the nature of people and their ability (or inability) to be responsible; the promise of religion to supply humanity with intimations of meaning in a highly ambiguous world. Indeed, the existential importance of the questions themselves will be ascribed by the religious person to what he or she considers their religious source.

### The Nature of Education

Obviously, all the issues raised in this chapter are, in their operative ramifications, also educational ones. Nevertheless, we have mentioned certain objections to religious education voiced by secular writers, which are more directly concerned with schools, instruction, and human development—that is, with explicit features of "educational theory." These objections, however, while plausible and fruitful in educational diagnosis, are themselves based on philosophical commitments, cultural understandings and perceptions, and specific interpretations of historical development. They may thus be considered crypto-theological and should be carefully scrutinized for their philosophical underpinnings.[41] Here we shall limit ourselves to several illustrations.

1. The claim that all religious education is indoctrination deserves a respectful hearing. Yet it must be borne in mind that the boundary line between education and indoctrination is determined by philosophical judgments with regard to the nature of learning, the child, authority, and value. And educators in democratic societies, despite their different viewpoints, do attempt to arrive at some consensus to ward off the totalitarianism that is abhorrent to all of them. Thus, Perry has pointed out that one cannot make the distinction be-

tween education and indoctrination without referring to the valuative context. For we do speak of Nazi indoctrination but shun the term "democratic indoctrination."

Why does the critic [of indoctrination] find the Nazi method, the communist method, the strict parental or scholastic method objectionable? Because it is narrow, rigid, and authoritarian. But if he is against these things he must be *for* their opposites; namely, breadth, flexibility and freedom.[42]

Phenix has even presented the thesis that education is fundamentally a religious activity.[43] Is this statement at loggerheads with Perry's? We maintain that it is not, but clearly, Phenix's view and similar ones prevalent among religious educators require discussion and analysis of the term "religion." We shall deal with this issue in subsequent chapters. Yet from what has already been said, it can be seen that what constitutes education and what is justly labeled indoctrination is largely dependent on convictions about truth, knowledge, and "the good."[44]

2. The relationship between autonomy and authority, between creative individuality and doctrinal loyalty, is perhaps the focal issue engaging religious educators in their debate with non-religious colleagues. However, the assumption that religion speaks for authority at the expense of autonomy is not universally acknowledged by religious educators and is a subject of much theological debate. Buber, for example, would not have agreed to a conception of religion that suppressed the individual's innovative self-realization, nor would existentialist thinkers like Becker grant that freedom and individuality are served by secularism.[45] Even such Jewish traditionalists as Berkovits and Falk insist that religion and tradition present accessible models for autonomy, reason, and personal decision making.[46]

Likewise, the statement that religious education is in principle concerned with religion and not with the child invites exploration of what various theorists understand by "religion" and how (psychologically, sociologically, theologically) they view "the child"—in his or her society and in his or her solitude.[47]

3. The secular educator argues against the "religious" distinction—first expressed in modern educational Jewish writings by Weisel—between *Torat Elohim* and *Torat Ha-adam,* "religious" versus "worldly" knowledge.[48] However, religious thinkers who have addressed themselves to educational questions, such as Soloveitchik, have suggested that comprehensive human existence is marked by a duality of "confrontation" and orientation. Indeed, a survey of contemporary thought would indicate that the world of the enlightened and scientific person is itself often compartmentalized and suffers the dis-

tinction between knowledge of the world and self-knowledge, between objective inquiry and conviction. This is not invariably the case, of course, and many thinkers are uncomfortable with this principled distinction.[49] But the dispute seems to divide not so much scientists and religious believers as people of diverse temperament, philosophical orientation, and experience.

It is true that certain post-Emancipation "religious" ideologies of accommodation in Western Europe did distinguish between Jewish (i.e., religious) and "general" culture and education, but this distinction is not indigenous to the historical normative philosophy of education or to much of modern Jewish educational thought in principle. In fact, national Jewish ideologies of the last century have been normative in their educational blueprints of culture and peoplehood; yet, (or therefore!) they were polemically insistent on blending the "Jewish" and the "human" in education while stressing the worth of Jewish particularity and its unquestionable legitimacy. As for theologically based conceptions, no less Western a "theological" thinker than Franz Rosenzweig insisted that religious education makes a whole "Jewish person," and the neo-Hasidic Rabbi Avraham Chein extolled Abraham, the paradigm of an integrated person.[50]

4. The malfunctioning of—and the poor relationships among—the elements of religious education (the teacher, the pupil, the environment, and the subject matter) have been much discussed, and not only by secular writers. It is the secular educators who speak of this crisis with the most pathos, for this malfunctioning was their first encounter with the problematic situation of modern Judaism.

But this does not necessarily point to the inherent deficiencies of religious education. Rather, the malfunctioning of religious education may be traced to the problems faced by religious—and for that matter, non-religious—educators, whose practice is not guided by theory or who, conversely, do not permit the realities "out there" in the world to inform them about workable applications of their principles.

To "have a theory," for the religious educator, requires a careful examination of religion, of the specific tradition that is taught and, consequently, of feasible conceptions of subject matter and their use in the cultivation of ideal personalities. To "have principles" but not to examine their application is quite simply, as already noted, not to be an educator. An educational situation in which principles are unclear and in which subject matter is arbitrarily selected is likely to be unsuccessful. This has been amply demonstrated in religious Jewish education.

Because secular Jewish education is younger and has been in the service of revolutionary and vibrant ideals, this dilemma was less obviously present in non-religious Jewish schooling until recent years. Today, non-religious educators are also asking "what went wrong." It may be that they, too, have insufficiently examined the values and principles that guide them. However paradoxical it sounds, there may be an element "out there in the world," in the child, that they have ignored or discounted: the element of the human being's religiosity.

# 5 The Scholar, the Believer, and the Educator

Our previous discussion on the secular climate of the modern world and the status of religious thought, life, and education in modern society was not designed to refute secular views or to demonstrate the truth of religion. If theoretical examinations of religion (psychological, sociological, historical, or even philosophical) cannot prove the veracity of religious beliefs, polemics are certainly not qualified to do so. What both theory and polemics can do is to point to functions and intentions in religious life and, possibly, to indicate how education might reflect religious orientations, theology, and culture.

The purpose of the preceding chapters was mainly to lay the groundwork for a discussion of religious education. Such a discussion clearly is substantively dependent on the ways in which people understand religious experience, the way they talk about it, and the manner in which they initiate young people into the fellowship shaped by it. In the introductory chapters to this book we noted first that diverse secular world views, in Western society and in secular Jewish ideologies, are themselves convictions, which, like religious ones, deserve both respectful attention (for the experience they reflect) and critical analysis (in terms of universal experience and stores of wisdom). Second, we attempted to show that cultural definitions of Jewishness that relegate the religious aspects of Jewish civilization and history to a secondary or insignificant position are themselves secular "translations" and interpretations of the religious tradition (however justified such re-interpretation may be). Third, we noted that problems arising within the (Jewish) religious tradition as a result of historical events (e.g., the Holocaust) are as likely to engender new religious affirmations as rejections, to lead to new theological formulations no less than to a renunciation of all meaning in history. Finally, we pointed out that clear-cut educational statements on the nature of secular and religious education are inevitably based on specific philosophical and theological understandings of such initially formal terms as "freedom," "self-realization," and "the educated person," as well as ontological conceptions concerning "the child," "the world," and "knowledge."

We may now go on to note that neither "secularism" nor "religion" is, in itself, as clear-cut or as monolithic as it appears from within particular "religious" or "secular" ideologies. Both these terms are difficult to define. It is not accidental that modern non-religious education has itself been unclear as to the sources of its humanism. (Is it Jewish? Greek? Judeo-Christian?) We have already pointed out that in secular Jewish education there is often a serious grappling with the problem of the Bible's "sanctity" and with the question of how to translate theological concepts into religiously "neutral" (or cautious) but existentially "serious" ones.[1]

Our discussion thus far on "secular" versus "religious" world views and religious education may therefore almost be described as *stipulative*. The term "religion" has been used in the sense of "the claims or thoughts of those who think positively or negatively about religion and who call themselves 'religious' or 'secular.' " Among Jews, religion is often an institutionally prominent yet existentially marginal expression of "identity" in non-Jewish society. More pointedly, Diaspora religiosity, except in the case of the observant Orthodox, is often viewed in synagogue or Hebrew school or summer camp terms; it is a highly stylized group experience. In Israel, the inclination of Orthodoxy to use the term "religious" as referring only to itself is institutionalized and taken for granted in political and social discourse. Not only do the Orthodox consider all others "non-religious," but also the non-Orthodox, no matter what their beliefs, generally accept the appellation of themselves as "non-believers." (When Mordecai Bar-On, a well-known "non-religious" personality, became interested in the transcendental aspects of his Jewishness some years ago, he described his feelings, convictions, and commitments in an essay entitled "The Faith of a Non-Believer."[2])

Consequently, if we were to limit ourselves to the commonplace usage of the term "religion," both in the Diaspora and in Israel, our entire discussion of religious issues in Jewish education would be confined to schools and other frameworks that define themselves as "religious," and would have to accept as axiomatic that Israeli "non-religious" education has nothing to do with religion. We would thus be forced to deem a lesson in an Israeli general school on the book of Job irrelevant to religion and a current events class in an American Sunday school "religious."

## THEOLOGY, RELIGIOUS DEFINITIONS, AND EDUCATION

Jews are traditionally reluctant to occupy themselves with religious definitions. There are several reasons for this:

1. The Jewish tradition emphasizes practical-normative religiosity rather than doctrinal or intellectual formulations, and thus "theology" is suspect.

2. Those most consciously and intensively committed to Jewish religious life tend to view their religious obligations and meanings as too unique for communicable discourse.

3. Secular Jews fear the "hidden ideology" of a religious discussion (i.e., the view that Judaism is a religion), whereas religious Jews suspect academic attempts to reduce religion to culture (i.e., the view that it is not "really" a religion).

It is indeed nigh impossible to escape a hidden declaration of one's own beliefs in defining or examining religion, and this fact must at least be stated. This is as true of definitions that are narrow or even opinionated (i.e., "this is what I believe" or, conversely, "what I think primitive or pathological persons believe") as it is of definitions that are so broad as to be (for believers in specific faiths) bland, making every possible conviction somehow "religious." Likewise, students of religion are often so scientific in their convictions that their descriptions of religion betray relativistic or reductionistic biases. The former (relativism) is perhaps related to their wide knowledge, which is not related to any specific religious commitment; the latter (reductionism) bespeaks an inability to accept any degree of religiosity as cognitively serious.

Conscious or hidden convictions are also expressed in the often apologetic (and tendentious) distinction drawn in religious studies between "good" or "healthy" religion and "bad" or "neurotic" religion.[3] This distinction may be legitimate when it is theological; that is, when it is made from within a religious tradition and reflects a specific religious faith and orientation. However, it is often presented as an "objective" distinction, drawing upon criteria that are external to religious faith and community. Although Jews are prominent exponents of this tendentious distinction when it is made within the scholarly community, they have also been among its principal victims—especially when "objective, evolutionary" concepts of religion actually articulate a bias among non-Jewish believers *vis-à-vis* the "archaic" mother religion.

From all that has been said, it might seem best to leave "religion" undefined and to allow each group to appropriate the term as it wishes. This course of action is, however, not feasible for those who deal with religious educational theory. Fundamental questions of policy and practice depend on conceptual clarity with regard to the nature of religion and the character of a given religious tradition; these policy-practice questions must be addressed to teachers as well as to subject matter, to children as learners and to schools as frameworks of socialization.

We shall illustrate with random questions that cannot be answered without conceptual clarifications about "Jewish religion." We shall formulate these questions in terms of the four elements, or "topics," of education (teachers, environments, subject matter, and pupils), to which we have already alluded.

I. *With regard to teachers:*
   A. When may a person be considered qualified for religious teaching?
   B. Is a specific conviction or life-style a pre-requisite for teaching in a religious school? If so, will this be a requirement for instructors in all subjects or only for teachers of subjects stipulated as "religious"? Or does it suffice for the teacher to have a firm intellectual grasp of the tradition, its texts, and its recommended experiences?
   C. If a teacher is committed to religious practice and has religious conviction, is doctrinal conformity required or merely commitment to using the community's theological language? Does commitment to a religious life-style (as, for example, embodied in a certain standard of halakhic observance) require that the teacher be loyal to its *details* or "only" to its principles?

II. *With regard to schools and their environment:*
   A. What is the point of view of the environment? (Is it secular? Pagan? Judeo-Christian?)
   B. Is the school to represent the environment, or to oppose or educate it?
   C. Should there be separate schools for religious instruction, or should there be integration of all learning in a single environment?
   D. Should the school attempt to "evaluate" religious learning in ways drawn from "secular" studies, or is religious knowledge "absorbed" from the texts and teachers, who create a specifically "religious" atmosphere in the school?
   E. Who is to decide religious matters? The rabbi (or religious authority)? The educators? Parents? Social scientists?
   F. What is an appropriate policy with regard to persons or institutions of different religious conviction, within Judaism or without?
   G. Can non-observant parents be involved in policy making? What if they define themselves as religious but are not what the school considers observant or "really" religious?

III. *With regard to subject matter:*
   A. What *is* "religious subject matter"? (The Bible? Nature? Talmud? Moral and human relations deliberation?)
   B. Which texts and experiences are *most crucial* in conveying religiously valuable knowledge?
   C. Is there a specifically religious way of teaching this subject matter? If so, is this specifically religious way necessarily congruent with the teaching of "non-religious" subjects, or should it be seen as totally different?
   D. How should "non-religious" subjects be taught? *Are* there non-religious subjects?
   E. If there are, should they perhaps not be taught?
   F. Is religious subject matter intended to give knowledge or conviction?

IV. *With regard to pupils:*
   A. Are children naturally religious, or must they be socialized into religious culture against natural (and untamed) inclinations? Or both?
   B. Do children have stages of religious development that must be considered in curriculum planning? Do theories of psychological or moral development reflect philosophical biases, or are they neutral?
   C. Should children be encouraged to raise religious and other principled questions about Judaism, even if the teacher has no clear-cut answers?
   D. Is the aim of religious education to bestow meaning on children's lives or to familiarize them with obligation, or both? How do texts and experiences do this? How will children perceive teachers who teach on the basis of convictions that are problematic to them?

All these questions and others—for the possible combinations are numerous—necessarily arise in the deliberation of principled religious educators. They can be answered "by ear" (i.e., by listening to the community) or by "insight" (i.e., by looking within for what one "knows" to be true.) In traditional communities the ear and insight often suffice because the individual members *listen* to one another as members of the community and together *look* to a truth that is not only within but also "above" them. The decline of religious community and the rise of historical consciousness and psychological introspection has changed that for the majority of communities. Religion must therefore be critically examined. Then, perhaps, it will itself be discovered to be a framework for criticizing unexamined social and scientific convictions that in our education easily become dogmatic, stifling "growth" and inhibiting "the examined and worthwhile life." In any case, not to examine religion analytically and empirically in an age when everything else is examined in this way may well lead to social and educational practices that are more arbitrary, divisive, and incomprehensible than they need be.


## UNDERSTANDING RELIGION: PARTICULAR FAITHS AND UNIVERSAL RELIGIOSITY

If, then, we seek to understand religion systematically for the sake of educational theory, what kind of examination is legitimate? Wach, citing Scheler, states that religion should be explored phenomenologically; that is, one should "let manifestations of the religious experience speak for themselves rather than force them into any pre-conceived scheme [of history, psychology, or sociology]."[4] Yet Wach also points out that there are two discrete ways of discovering the nature of religious experience:

> One way is to appropriate the historical formulation of one religion, denomination, or school of religious thought. The other is to start from "where I am"; that is, the potential range of personal experience. The "I" can be either an individual or a plural—a collective or corporate "I." William James uses the personal approach; the collective approach seems to be the intention of Alan Richardson in his claim that it is "the actual faith and worship and experience of the living Church which must provide the data of theology." This (distinction) agrees with the so-called existential emphasis upon what is my own as opposed to that which is common, general, organized, or institutionalized.[5]

> Which of the two ways will be undertaken, or how the two may be combined, will depend largely on the conviction of the researcher and on his or her own religious experience (or lack of it). Thus, if one believes that "religious experience" is an illusion and specific religions are deceptions and self-deceptions, one will dismiss both of these methods and turn to social and behavioral science for comprehensive understanding of religion. If one believes that there is religious experience but that it cannot be isolated because it is identical with general experience, one need not turn to either mystical experience or "the living Church" to discover the truth about religion; one must deal simply with the ideal imagination and its ongoing enterprise of transforming the merely envisioned into concrete reality. For those who identify all "real" religious experience solely with their own historical religion, obviously only the first way mentioned by Wach will seem justified. Conversely, those who hold that there is genuine religious experience and that it can be identified by means of definite criteria, which can be applied to any of its expressions, will be drawn to "the personal approach" of William James.[6]

Usually, modern discussion concerning religion and religious education that is not outspokenly secular or humanistic (i.e., the first and second of the aforementioned views) tends to adopt *either* the "one religion" *or* "the potential range of personal experience" approach. Indeed, much debate is engendered by this insistence on exclusive alternatives, and, as we shall see, much educational controversy. The universalists appear to believe that reliance on a specific religious tradition makes arbitrary and subjectivistic assumptions on the basis of some exclusive revelation allegedly bestowed upon its adherents. Conversely, the particularists suspect that universalists claiming to take all religions seriously actually believe in none; that "dealing in all religions" is a tactic of academics designed to make religion a part of "the humanities."

In later chapters, the educational and specifically curricular difficulties that arise from this polarity will be discussed, and we shall argue for a view of religious educational theory that encompasses both *explicit* (particular, historical) religion and *implicit* (universal, existential) religiosity. Here it should merely be mentioned that an insistence on treating Judaism as totally unrelated to "religion in general" is difficult to defend; conversely, religion seen only through the prism of "the potential range of human experience" also can be shown to yield an inaccurate view of Judaism.

It is true of Judaism, and, I believe, of any religious faith, that "religion" becomes meaningful within the experience of a particular group and that it is mediated by a specific culture. Wach[7] points out that religion inevitably takes in the realm of thought, action, and fellowship. *Fellowships* are different. So are the myths and doctrines that are the *thought* components of religion, and the cults, which are crucial—though not comprehensive—features of religious *action.*

The Jewish tradition, of course, is insistent on its uniqueness, on seeing *its* "actual faith and worship and experience as a living *people* [as providing] the data of theology," to paraphrase Richardson. The Bible and rabbinic literature are hardly comprehensible outside the theological framework of the singular covenant between God and Israel—through the Torah. The unabashedly particularistic medieval thinker and poet Yehuda Ha-Levi has described the historic Jewish community as the exclusive framework of true religious experience. And even the prince of rationalistic Jewish philosophy, Maimonides, declared that it is God's Torah—revealed through Moses—that established *the* fellowship in which human beings may reach moral perfection and rise in thought to the love and knowledge of God.[8]

But "the potential range of human experience" with religion takes in more than Israel, also in the faith of Israel. It is not apologetic to reiterate that the Jewish tradition does not accept the dictum of "no salvation outside the

Church'' (although this has sometimes been stated in an apologetic context). In rabbinic thought, the Noachide commandments are assumed to have been revealed to all mankind, and although Gentiles have at times been seen through negative moral stereotypes, they are sometimes lauded for their spirituality.[9]

Furthermore, the view that only one historical religion is a proper basis for understanding ''real'' religious experience because it expresses a unique and revealed truth is grounded on the dual assumption that (1) religion is always a good thing and it is bad not to possess religious truth, and (2) the adherents of one's own religion are the only ones who possess such truth. The Jewish tradition, in both its ancient sources and its historical development, although it articulates diverse opinions and reflects varying social situations, does not unambiguously teach either of these. Religion, the service of deities, is not in itself ''a good thing''; indeed, all nations have gods (idols), and they are a *bad* thing (although the view is also expressed that some of these deities are, for the Gentiles, an acceptable way of worshipping God).[10] The Bible seems to be concerned with right belief (religion) but declares that to have no religion is merely ''foolish''—not wicked.[11] Wicked and false beliefs are religious ones (e.g., worshipping a false god). Conversely, it should be noted, seminal discussions regarding Christians and Moslems and desirable relations with these groups were concerned with the truth to be found in their religions. Noteworthy is the halakhic decision of Rabbi Menachem Ha-Meiri that those nations ''bound by the bonds of religion'' are to be considered non-idolatrous—i.e., these religions adhere to the criteria of Judaism *vis-à-vis* man's moral obligations.[12] No less a particularist than Rabbi Moses Sofer, a radical exponent of modern ultra-Orthodoxy, argued against the ''enlightened Jews'' for their denial of all religion *as such*.[13]

Jewish sources and Jewish thought recognize in religion a universal and potentially communicable phenomenon. A religion is positively evaluated if it rests on the moral criteria of what rabbinic Judaism calls the seven Noachide (*revealed*) commandments. Nevertheless, Judaism, like all religions, may properly see itself in a certain sense as comprehensible only from within; not all ''general'' categories are necessarily or precisely translatable into the specific terms of Jewish tradition and experience, and not everything that Jews perceive as ''Judaism'' is accurately portrayed in ''universal'' religious categories. Thus, such general treatment must in principle be circumscribed: It describes aspects, it analyzes, it offers food for thought. But it is not exhaustive.

The consequences of this imperfect congruence between general religious theory and particular religions (and the experience of individuals within religious fellowships) are two-fold: First, a particular faith experience (in our case, the Jewish one) may not be reduced to ''religion in general,'' and a theory of religious education may not simply judge or evaluate a religious educational conception by its "general religiosity." Second, a theory of religion and religious education must be recognized *to be a theory*— that is, a universal construct that describes and (in education) establishes general norms, with the understanding that the description and the norms are not absolutely precise or adequate with regard to any particular situation. Each particular religion is practical, distinctive, and not completely contained within any universal statement of the essence or the "nature" of religion. And every believer in a specific religious tradition is committed to the position that what is *heard* within is more than what can be said or understood outside the faithful community.

## DEFINING RELIGION IN ITS ESSENCE: THE SCHOLARS SPEAK

Defining the characteristics of religion or locating its "essence" is notoriously difficult. The general definition of religion, among diverse thinkers and scholars, has varied from "belief in an ever-living God . . . holding moral relations with mankind" to "an attempt to express the complete reality of goodness through every aspect of our being." For Whitehead, it is "what man does with his solitude"; for Schleiermacher, how he lives with his feeling of "absolute dependence." MacMurray considers religion to deal with "realization of ideal states of relationship," whereas Allport speaks of man's "intention-orientation" as corresponding to the classic theological conception of "love of God."[14] These descriptions, as Alston points out,[15] may be seen as features of religion, as definitions, or as essences constituting the "heart of religion." But, he argues, it is problematic to see any of them as both sufficient and necessary. For there are religions that are not concerned with ethics, many that do not believe in monotheism, and even several that seem to manage without a clear conception of deity. Alston proposes dealing with what he terms "religion-making characteristics." These include (1) belief in supernatural beings; (2) a distinction between sacred and profane objects; (3) ritual acts focused on sacred objects; (4) a moral code believed to be sanctioned by the gods; (5) characteristically religious feelings, such as awe and mystery, which are aroused on religious occasions and are connected with divinity; (6) prayer and other forms of communication with gods; (7) a world view encompassing a general picture of the world and the place of the individual within it—somehow connected to an "over-all purpose or point of the world" and an indication of how the individual fits into it; (8) a more or less total organization of one's life based on the world view; and (9) a social group bound together by the above.

Alston claims that the degree to which a phenomenon may be called religious depends on the number (and intensity) of such characteristics.

When enough of these characteristics are present to a sufficient degree, we have a religion. It seems that . . . this is as precise as we can be.
. . . There are cultural phenomena that embody all of these characteristics to a marked degree. They are the ideally clear paradigm classes of religion, such as Roman Catholicism, Orthodox Judaism, and Orphism. These are the cases to which the term "religion" applies most certainly and unmistakably. However, there can be a variety of cases that differ from the paradigm in different ways and to different degrees, by one or another of the religion-making characteristics dropping out more or less . . . [16]

The religious characteristics mentioned by Alston all deal in some way with "ultimate concern" (to use Tillich's celebrated term)[17] and the expression of this concern in thought, practice, and fellowship. Ultimate concern has an object generally held to be transcendent, since the concern is "ultimate"; the non-ultimate is identified with the non-sacred. Since it is related to responsibility, religion tends to posit a moral code authorized by the Divine. It initiates moments in which "what it's really all about" comes into sharp focus, and it requires communion with the object of ultimate concern. Religion demands seeing the world in terms of what is mysterious and humanity's relationship to the mystery, and it requires a social element to assure stability and collective expression.

Yet Alston notes that not every characteristic must be present in every religion. Along similar lines, Yinger[18] has pointed out that not everyone will agree that religion always has to do with conscience or with the "ultimate" or the supernatural. A diagram of his clarifies some possible views and distinctions.

|  | *Supernatural world view necessary* | *Supernatural world view not necessary* |
|---|---|---|
| *Religion deals only with ultimate concerns* | A  y | C |
| *Religion deals also with immediate and utilitarian concerns* | ———  x  ——— | |
|  | B | D |

(Reprinted with permission of Macmillan Publishing Company from *The Scientific Study of Religion* by J. Milton Yinger. Copyright © 1970 by J. Milton Yinger.)

One matter to be pondered on the basis of this representation is that some people who consider themselves religious feel that they can dispense with a supernaturalistic world view. Another is that much religion seems to deal with immediate and utilitarian (not "ultimate") matters within the context of a supernatural world view. In a certain sense, one might even speak of people relating "religiously" to mundane concerns that lack all objects of transcendence.

Furthermore, while everyone would agree that A is religious, yet, despite what some people might do or feel, few would seriously argue that D by itself can be defined as "religiosity." As Yinger points out:

> A group of sportsmen may *know* that the Green Bay Packers are the best football team in the world. They may celebrate that fact with calendrical rites every Sunday afternoon throughout the autumn. But only so far as these beliefs and practices become connected with their deepest concerns—that is, move toward C—do they take on a religious quality.[19]

It is common to find B identified with "magic" (as distinguished from true religion or "advanced" religion); those who disagree erase line x. The identification of C with religion may be considered reductionistic, since it implies that a person's existential philosophy is synonymous with his or her religion; line y represents the problematic boundary between supernaturalistic and naturalistic (perhaps philosophical) faith.

In any case, the status of B and C is controversial. With regard to B, it may be asserted that immediate and utilitarian concerns relate to the functioning of the whole person and that, consequently, people legitimately link ultimate concerns to social stability, even to physical protection against natural disaster. As for C, ultimate concern without an object that is as ultimate as the concern itself is problematic. For, as Tillich points out, ultimate concern not only demands ultimate commitment but also promises ultimate meaning.[20] Thus, even those who feel uncomfortable with the term supernatural may agree to refer religious sentiment to the "transcendental." The status of B and C will therefore largely depend on the language of communities (e.g., Catholics and Unitarians), on the biases of the disciplines within which thinkers and scientists are anchored, and on the cultural and social context in which the theologian or educator is speaking.

Yet, no matter how ambiguous B and C may be, it would be implausible to say that A is *not* religious phenomenologically (i.e., regardless of whether there really *are* ultimate concerns, as religious people understand them, related to a transcendent source that "draws" people and nourishes them in an ultimate way), for that would be tantamount to saying that the term "religion" has no meaning. Thus, we would seem to be on solid ground in stating that religion that is understood to be such by everyone would be characterized by (a) some kind of ultimate concern or attitude and (b) some belief in and relationship to the supernatural or transcendental that is somehow above and "beyond" the world, yet accessible to people. "Ultimate concern" and "transcendence" may be called root terms of religion.

These are formal terms; they do not signify a particular content until they are related to a particular tradition or insight-pattern. Thus, the ultimate may be the most existentially true, which people must encounter whether they wish to or not, such as death or solitude, and the "above and beyond" may be identified with the challenge, as well as the source of strength to deal with it.[21] Such an understanding would be closely related to Whitehead's idea of religion, "what man does with his solitariness."

In more recognizable and classic religious understandings, the ultimate may be "the inexpressible" who names Himself in human experience (in some process or event of revelation); in these cases, ultimate concern is to be "close to" Him and to "serve" Him.

Yet this general and formal definition, which allows for a variety of religious phenomena and sentiments, does not mean that everyone or everything is religious. Scientific theories may be based on secular convictions that *are* secular because they "explain away" one or both of the aforementioned root terms.[22] Freud, for example, looked upon religious beliefs as illusions, projections of infantile dependency wishes and (thus) neurotic.[23] This secular denial of religion must itself be seen as anchored in an orientation, a conception of ideal selfhood and of ultimate concern, but it denies a "beyond" dimension, a transcendent object of the ideal; indeed, it often argues against the usefulness (and, of course, the existence) of such an object. A different form of irreligion is that associated with "the God of the philosophers": In this case, there is an object of ultimate concern, but He demands nothing and cannot promise human self-realization; He is "there" to be contemplated, but He has no relationship to man and to his concerns.[24]

Denials of religion from secular perspectives (i.e., the elimination of one of the two root terms) must be clearly distinguished from controversies with regard to their content. Different believers may take issue with the ultimate concerns of others and with their perceptions of the object "beyond" these concerns—that is, they may declare that others have false or heretical beliefs. In other words, certain religious people may claim that others are idolatrous, i.e., that their concerns are not really ultimate and that they are worshipping or serving an object that is unworthy of absolute devotion. Here, unlike the case of the secularist, the argument is not about the worth of religion as such but about the truth or untruth of a specific religion.

## RELIGIOUS ULTIMACY AND DIMENSIONS OF COMMITMENT: EDUCATIONAL DELINEATIONS

Phenix has described "ultimate concern" for the educational enterprise.[25] He notes five major aspects of ultimacy:

First of all, the ultimate is *most important.* "Ultimate concern is belief or conduct in relation to whatever is considered of greatest importance." It thus occasions "complete seriousness" and gives rise to awe and reverence.

Second, it has supreme worth. That is, in addition to being most important, it is also *most valuable;* its importance is "personally perceived and appropriated." Whereas the "most important" can be general and neutral, the most valuable makes a judgment with regard to good and evil. "Hence the religious outlook is concerned with grading matters of supreme importance in scales of reverence to persons of good and evil."

Third, ultimacy seeks *depth;* it searches out the deeper significance of things. "The religious person does not take his life experiences at face value but tries to discern the more profound meanings and purposes to which they point." Depth implies a sense of the realm in which "the most searching questions" will lead all inquiry to the boundary "where knowledge shades off into mystery." It thus is an awareness of the boundaries of human existence and of the final limitations that condition the human quest and the human understanding.

Fourth, ultimacy involves *totality* or *comprehensiveness.* Unlike mundane matters, which are partial, one-sided, or fragmentary, having to do with specific goods or limited goals, religion "is one's comprehensive life orientation. It is what one makes of his life as a whole." Consequently, most religious ultimate concerns include questions about origins and the source of the world and inquire into the genesis of individual personality ("Where does it come from?"). This question, of course, is related to depth as well as to comprehensiveness. In like manner, the question of destinies and the consummation of things is raised ("Where are things going?"), as well as the connection between origins and destinies. (Thus, for example, redemption is seen as the consummation of Creation.)

Fifth, ultimacy raises the valuative question about right conduct and orientation that flows from the ontological, epistemological, and axiological aspects noted earlier. What is the good way of life? What is the will of God?[26]

Those who are in principle irreligious will not agree that certain things are in themselves most important or most valuable, that there is a depth and "mystery" behind things, that origins have significance beyond the curiosity that can be satisfied by inquiry into relevant scientific disciplines, and that purpose or significance is "built into" reality. They may agree that some of these elements are useful to human culture and correspond to human experience, but they will deny their link to a transcendent object of ultimacy; for them religion is not a good or true or deep way to expand knowledge and enhance human life. They do not believe in religious education, although they may well agree that religion should be taught in schools to enable pupils to understand culture and its expressions in art, literature, and philosophy.[27]

But what is the specific content of ultimacy? What is important, valuable, comprehensive, right? Here each religious tradition, through its sacred literature and its oral teachings, its social structures, and the symbols it possesses for "pointing toward" the ultimate, can be expected to make material statements (in the form of doctrines) about each aspect of ultimacy. Thus Judaism, as a historical and literary religious tradition, posits that the world is neither illusion nor triviality but an arena of man's activity and God's creation. In this tradition, social life has ultimate *value*. God's goodness and Providence are believed to be beyond human comprehension, although people may—and perhaps should—question God to the limits of their understanding and fervor (the examples of Abraham and Job come to mind) and are bidden to know God "in all His ways" and to be "whole with the Lord." The Bible, Talmud, and Midrash speak of origins, of purposes, and of a "way," in the context of a particular story and a particular language. Thus, for example, God "created the world only for the Torah" and in the knowledge that Israel would accept the Torah.[28] The Jewish tradition gives concrete expression, in its own cultural contexts, to each element of "ultimacy." This is particular, but it is also related to a general theory. Let us examine why this is so.

## A GENERAL THEORY OF PARTICULARITY

We have already mentioned Wach's thesis that religion is universally expressed through three fundamental modes: thought, practice, and fellowship. Since religion deals with the inexpressible, namely, "the ultimate" in its relationship to the individual and human concern with the ultimate, the expression is necessarily symbolic to a large degree. One cannot express the relationship in a mundane way without limiting it, making it ludicrous.[29] There are symbolically expressed concepts, doctrines, and world views; there are symbolic rites and practices that, *inter alia,* bind persons in the religious community and create a fellowship in which partly symbolic beliefs and actions set the parameters of association. (However, we must note with Leibman[30] that the academic discussion of religion often has a Protestant bias, which underestimates the importance of religious practice that is *not* symbolic. For, in fact, much religious practice incumbent on members of the religious fellowship constitutes concrete moral action—normative prescriptions of behavior "between man and man.")

Since specific religions are expressed through specific fellowships, we may speak of religious commitment as taking on specific content within communities. Glock and Stark,[31] in their analysis of what they consider "the core dimensions of religiosity," speak of a "considerable consensus" among the world's religions "as to the more general areas in which religiosity ought to be manifested." They describe five such dimensions that shape religious communities: *belief, knowledge, practice,* (religious) *experience,* and *consequence.* The life in a religious community inculcates certain beliefs, requires the acquisition of certain sacred knowledge, demands certain practice, and anticipates certain (individual) religious experience. And it is geared to create a certain "type" who is the result of such beliefs, knowledge, practice, and experience. Glock and Stark's assumption is that community defines the context within which people believe, know, practice, and experience religion and become certain types of (religious) persons.

Let us spell out the "dimensions of religious commitment" as described by Glock and Stark, with elaborations and clarifications based on the conceptions of other scholars we have cited.

1. *The belief dimension.* Religion, in symbol or fellowship, inculcates and expresses normative clusters of ideas concerning origins, ends, and desirable actions. A religious person is expected to hold these beliefs, although not all beliefs are necessarily dogmas that must be affirmed in one uniform manner. That is, diverse theologies may offer discrete understandings of the basic principles. The principles are axiomatic in the "language" of the religious "believing" community; the understandings may vary.

2. *The knowledge dimension.* There is a corpus of religious knowledge that is shared by believers; it is considered most valuable because of its connection to the belief framework. This knowledge may be considered the source of true belief or a reflection of it. The religious person's knowledge concerns origins and purposes; it suggests ways to come closer to the ultimate; thus it will enhance sensitivity to value and depth. This knowledge is sacred; it is "God's word" or a testimony to His presence.

3. *The practice dimension.* Religion has to do with practice and action that includes, but is not necessarily limited to, cult or worship. All actions performed with a religious intention, whether they are symbolic or concretely moral, may be included. The religious intention in action constitutes an individual's practical endeavors to achieve perfection, to be close to God, to do good.

4. *The experience dimension.* Religious fellowships are media of religious experience that may be viewed as an anticipated outcome of "proper" belief, knowledge, and practice or as immediate and revelatory. This experience, though made possible by the community, must be personal. A man or woman who has never had an unmediated experience of the truth of his or her relationship to the divine, despite his or her belief, knowledge, and diligent practice of religion, may be defined *as not yet* fully religious. In such a case, the community will seek to persuade such an individual that his or her knowledge, practice, or belief is deficient or that he or she is not yet mature religiously. But, of course, it is possible that the lack of religious experience arises not from an irrelevant understanding of the beliefs but from a formulation of them that is not conducive to religious understanding. It may be that the knowledge is inadequately delineated, interpreted, or transmitted. It may be that traditional rites have lost their power to engender religious experience, at least in their traditional contexts, and have become "empty."[32]

In such a case, the religious thinker, scholar, or prophetic personality is called upon to revitalize belief, knowledge, and practice. Reformation, declares Wach, is "a universal phenomenon required by the dialectics of religious life."[33]

5. Finally, religion has a *consequence dimension,* which may be broadly formulated as identifying "the kind of person one may expect to result from being a member of a particular religious community." In the language of Jewish tradition, one may say that religion expresses itself "consequentially" through model personalities who embody virtue and righteousness and who constitute, in their being and behavior, also as publicly perceived, a *kiddush ha-Shem,* a "sanctification of God's name."

We must add that *all* of these dimensions are, in principle, individual as well as communal, for ultimate concern is, in one sense, a personal achievement. Belief is not only a shared language but also a way of making sense of things, an individual's "closing the gap" between what is known (by everybody) and what might be considered "a full picture" by an individual. A conception of sacred knowledge is a community's understanding of what constitutes the most important subject matter for education, but it is also a personal habit and an avenue of religious experience. Practice, especially in its non-symbolic aspects, is related to moral self-esteem and a sense of "walking with God" as well as a form of communal "signaling."

But the converse—that "experience" is communal as well as individual and that it arises out of fellowship as well as solitude—must not be forgotten. Turner has referred to the threshold experience, or "the liminoid experience," which is "a transformative experience that goes to the root of each person's being and finds in that root something profoundly communal and shared."[34] In this experience, the absence of equality, the lack of sincerity, the hierarchy of status in society are "undone"—kinship and unity are restored, and the community is perceived as truly holy and godly.

## CATEGORIES, COMMONPLACES, AND THE SPECIFICITY OF JUDAISM

The fundamental categories discussed previously can be applied to—and located within—Judaism as a religious tradition and culture. With Judaism as a historic religious phenomenon one finds the root concepts of "ultimate concern" and its "object," as well as the relationship between immediate concerns and God (Yinger's B—see earlier). The various modes of religiosity can be readily located as well. One can speak, without distorting the tradition, of Jewish beliefs, sacred knowledge and texts, practice, and community and the consequential "ideal religious personality." Judaism has diverse theologies and stable symbols; it has contexts that cultivate specific kinds of religious experience. Judaism is thus "general" in formal terms of ultimacy and dimensions of religious commitment. But it is also different, and this difference is no less relevant to Jewish educational deliberation than its conformity to general conceptions of religion.

The difference is not only that Judaism is a specific religion but also that it has idiosyncratic national features. Its religious specificity is generic: Judaism, like every religion, supplies its own cultural-religious contents and concepts to the formal commonplaces. Its beliefs, practices, and patterns of fellowship are its own.

Its idiosyncrasy is in its seemingly supra-religious historical character. One can plausibly claim to be a secular Jew in a way that one could not claim to be say, a secular Catholic. There are those who will seriously claim that "Jewishness" concerns itself exclusively with fellowship and requires no beliefs and rites. This may be historically inaccurate and tendentious, and it may be normatively questionable, but in fact there are Jews who do insist on this, and their status as Jews is not thereby called into question.

Furthermore, many dimensions of communal and personal life, such as the intellectual, the ethical, and the affiliative, may be viewed as not "exactly" or necessarily religious, as falling into Yinger's C and D categories. In other words, they may deal with ultimate concerns but not with God; they may not be ultimate for a given person but merely aspects of a Jewish sub-identity that is ethnic. Thus, certain people may consider it important to read—and, indeed, do read—Jewish books and to have Jewish libraries without attaching religious significance to this; they may believe in "Jewish ethics" as incumbent upon them without using the theological term *mitzvah* with regard to these norms, and they may affirm Jewish fellowship simply by supporting Israel or living in Israel.

That such "secular" Judaism appears to be possible for many people, and that those who are "religious" do not exclude from the community those who are "secular Jews," is possible because Judaism is idiosyncratically a religious teaching that is intertwined with a national consciousness. In fact, the specific content of religion—of God's word, Torah—is not simply ideas and norms concerning origins, purposes, and means that delineate the proper understanding and desirable relationships between the individual and the object of ultimate concern. Torah is also a story of events, and not just of (religious) experiences; it is "Jewish culture" as well as God's demands upon history and culture.

*Torah,* therefore, is a key concept of Jewishness; it is a specific instance of the root terms of religion, spelling out the fundamental modes of its Jewish expression. But it is also national, cultural. This is not because Torah is less than religion, but because Jewish religion does not leave nationality out of its scope. God is seen as acting in history as well as in the soul. But even someone who rejects "religion" can appropriate Torah as a comprehensive cultural concept.

So too, the key concept of *Messianism.* Messianism is a specific Jewish-religious content of purpose, but some of its ramifications are national enough to have been adopted by secular Zionism. A third key concept, *Am Yisrael* (the people of Israel), is even more clearly idiosyncratic; one cannot be Jewish in a religious sense without membership in the "ethnic" Jewish people. And yet, *Am Yisrael* is a religious conception, with remembered origins in divine revelation, with its anticipated "end" in the universal Kingdom of Heaven.

The term *God of Israel* is a specific Jewish expression denoting "the object of ultimate concern." But the general monotheistic content is, from the Jewish point of view, enlarged by a cultural-historical one: the God of Israel is God as He was experienced by the people of Israel. "Religious experience," in a non-propositional sense,[35] is also national.

A fifth key term, *Eretz Yisrael,* appears almost completely idiosyncratic (although it corresponds in large degree to the general religious concern with "God's world" and the individual's "place" in the "space" in which he or she does "God's will"). However, to many, *Eretz Yisrael* seems to be so strictly national that some modern liberal thinkers spoke of it as a stage now outgrown, or as a symbol (e.g., "Zion") no longer requiring a concrete territory. And yet, the conceptions of holiness and covenant, which relate these five key terms to one another and integrate them, cannot be understood in the Jewish tradition without *Eretz Yisrael.* It is the land in which commandment and norm are applicable in the most comprehensive manner and in which *Am Yisrael* will experience God's kingdom in historical redemption.

Thus, the five key terms of the Jewish religious tradition; i.e., the terms through which the notion of "covenant" may be seen to take on meaning, are both within the theoretical-formal structure of religion and yet, in varying degrees, idiosyncratic enough to be translated into secular-historical terms.[36] (That is, it is plausible to see them as specific Jewish and collective instances of Yinger's D.) Even the least idiosyncratic of the key terms has puzzled students of Judaism who, sometimes maliciously, have asked how a monotheistic nation could insist on having a God of its own, on being "chosen." The *most* idiosyncratic term, *Eretz Yisrael,* is often detached from religion, notably in secular Zionism. But one need only read the Bible to see how *Eretz Yisrael* is portrayed as a covenantal datum.

An insistence on maintaining and using these key terms in any theory of Judaism that professes clarity of definition and normative explication exposes to view the problem of interpretation. What cannot be "dropped" must be interpreted whenever, to paraphrase Rawidowicz, loyalty is challenged by alienation.[37] New situations and new knowledge—indeed, everything we believe to be true—must be related to Judaism. The key terms are thus the building blocks of new theologies and ideologies of Judaism. In a sense, therefore, they are also formal terms, like "ultimate concern," which must be brought into relationships and examined in diverse contexts. The entire sacred tradition of Judaism is, on ideational, halakhic, and existential grounds, such an examination; as "sacred tradition," it is paradigmatic for any normative Judaism.

The key concepts of Judaism may therefore be called, following Schwab, *commonplaces.* Schwab defines commonplaces as "foci of attention within an area of interest which fulfill two conditions: (a) they demand the attention of serious investigators; (b) their scrutiny generates diverse investigations and consequent diversities of definitions, doctrines and emphases."[38] In a certain sense, the specific (and religiously idiosyncratic) commonplaces of Judaism are thus also open in terms of content. They are, however, less open ("formal'') than the root terms of religion (''ultimacy and its object'') because they draw on and are accountable to specific experiences reported and reflected upon in a corpus of sacred writings. They deal with a specific culture and history that nourishes them and which must be interpreted.

We may sum up our discussion of the key terms, or commonplaces, of Judaism as follows:

1. Each of these terms is religious in a universally communicable way, for each is connected to the root term of religion and to the modes in which religion is articulated (action) and by which it is framed (fellowship). Yet, each is to some extent idiosyncratic (as well as specific to the given religion called Judaism) insofar as it points toward ''national'' or ''cultural'' memories, events, and aspirations as well as to universal religious experiences.

2. Each term is a ''commonplace'' because (a) the tradition cannot function without these terms and they are therefore the language of the tradition's transmission; and (b) the specific content of each commonplace is ambiguous until it is related to a specific historical, theological-ideological, or normative-halakhic context. Each traditional teaching, law, or story is the description of such a context and mandates precise contents of the commonplace within it. Each such teaching inevitably suggests other contexts, meanings, and relationships among the commonplaces. The Midrashic enterprise may be viewed as constructed on this ideational and cultural foundation.

3. Each commonplace, when it must be defined or explained outside a specific legal, historical context (i.e., in abstract theological terms), can only be explained or defined relationally. Thus, for example, the God of Israel is He Who chose the people of Israel by giving them the Torah, which is to be fully implemented in *Eretz Yisrael* and which, if fully carried out, will lead to the perfection of society and the Messianic age. Or, the Torah is the way in which *Am Yisrael* has related to the God of Israel in seeking to make the world what it was designed to be in that society for which *Am Yisrael* is specifically responsible. (From the differences between these two relational definitions, it appears that no way of linking commonplaces is theologically neutral.)

4. Despite the organic relationship among these commonplaces, it appears that in the ongoing discussion of Jewish obligation and significance they will generally be graded hierarchically. The modern ''secular'' Zionist will place either *Eretz Yisrael* or *Am Yisrael* at the top and will understand the God of Israel, Torah, and Messianism in the terms of the two higher concepts. Neo-Orthodoxy will, at least experientially, make all the other commonplaces dependent on Torah, whereas classical Reform will consider the God of Israel as preceding the other commonplaces.

5. All commonplaces have their own derivative value concepts, which, as we learn from Kadushin,[39] function independently and enter into delineating and clarifying relationships with one another and with the commonplaces themselves. Thus, a derivative value concept (sub-commonplace) of the God of Israel is *Shekhinah,* which, for example, "dwells with Israel in its exile" (the latter, a derivative of *Eretz Yisrael*). Torah engenders both halakhah and aggadah—and one who studies halakhot each day is assured of a place in the world to come, which is a derivative of Messiah. But halakhah and aggadah also represent norms and spontaneity, two different expressions of Jewish religion and culture.[40]

6. Each of the commonplaces is related to the root terms of religion and to the modes, or "dimensions," of religious expression and life. To take the least likely example: *Eretz Yisrael* is, in the Jewish tradition, a special land, enjoying particular providence; and living in it is a prerequisite for the observance of certain commandments of the Torah. Moreover, "there is no prophecy outside of *Eretz Yisrael*" and, at the end of days, all nations will ascend to Jerusalem to serve God, though it is the land "assigned" especially to the people of Israel by the Creator.[41]

7. Theologically, all commonplaces are indispensable for an understanding of Judaism, even though they may be variously graded in different ideological understandings. Educationally, however, the commonplace of Torah is generally considered the primary one. The reason for this is that the more Torah one learns, the more one is initiated into and becomes competent to deal with the "language" of Judaism and the discourse through which the commonplaces are located, distinguished, and integrated. "Learning Torah" is, therefore, learning the language of Judaism. Educationally speaking, God is a prior commonplace only for the prophetic aspect of the evolving religious personality. Yet, under certain circumstances and for specific individuals, any one of the commonplaces may be the best (or only) way "into" Judaism. Thus, many contemporary Jews re-entered Judaism through *Eretz Yisrael;* others, through the experience of being "thrown" into Jewish destiny (i.e., *Am Yisrael*) in the Hitler epoch.

8. The terminology of relationship among the commonplaces is generally (and classically) theological; for example, Israel was "chosen" by God. However, because of the cultural dimension of Judaism, the terms may be related in historical-existential ways; for example, being a Jew is sometimes experienced as a unique destiny that involves certain obligations. In our era, Rosenzweig has suggested that the fundamental words of relationship are creation, revelation, and redemption, and Buber has shown how these terms may be

understood phenomenologically without recourse to conventional religious pre-suppositions.[42]

In light of the foregoing, we may now suggest that religious educational thinking must show how learners are helped to cultivate the experience of ultimate concern as they are introduced into a fellowship. The fellowship is "holy" in its devotion to ultimate questions as a more-than-individual challenge; it speaks a language of specific contents that address the object of ultimate concern through the various dimensions of religious commitment.

In each such community, the actual life of the fellowship, even in its aspects that are not explicitly ultimate, may be expected to take on religious significance, lest the term "ultimate" be spiritualized out of responsible existence and become synonymous with sublime but possibly trivial symbolic enactments. The actuality and comprehensiveness of spiritual concern are evidenced in Judaism by the fact that its commonplaces assume an inherent and organic relationship between culture and faith, history and covenant, nationhood and religion.

Religious Jewish education is an initiation into the commonplaces of Judaism and into the literature that connects them, enlarges their application, and challenges previous understandings. In this process of initiation, Judaism will be related to "general religious" categories if it is to establish its relevance for the "uncommitted" and maintain its normative significance beyond childhood.

Although Jewish education is religious, it is not "religious education in general," and it cannot make do with a "general" religious theory of education. For to educate religiously is always to inculcate allegiance to a certain fellowship, to some specific cluster of experiences of God. It is always to teach a particular language of religious expression and a commitment to its perpetuation. To the extent that there is a religious education "in general," it is based on a theology of a religious community or a religion that presumes to be universal and thus to be the dialectical heir of all "particularistic" ones. When its practitioners are not aware of this crypto-theology, general education is often abstractly philosophical and moralistic, supporting unacknowledged ends that express in symbolic forms the assumptions of secular culture. For Jews, therefore, "general" religious education is vacuous or assimilatory. Conversely, Jewishness without an anchor in ultimate concern is apt to lead to sterile nostalgia or provincial particularism.

## A SECONDARY RELATIONSHIP TO RELIGION

We have gotten ahead of ourselves. On the basis of a description of the way in which religion functions, how Jewish religion may be understood—existentially, culturally, philosophically—we have already begun to sketch a normative philosophy of Jewish education to replace the one that broke down at the wake of modernity.

Actually, what we have tried to do is to legitimate religion in terms that may allow it to compete, respectably if not always successfully, with the dominant secular world view. Jewish tradition, we have intimated, can be seen as complex and positive. Religion, philosophically viewed, is quite different from what the iconoclasts portray and what certain picaresque sectarians represent. Our argument has been that, philosophically, education partakes of a religious dimension, and that those who relinquished it because of their unease with traditional norms in the modern world may have misunderstood it. Our analysis suggested the possibility of a positive evaluation, based on an appreciation of the functions played by religion in the life of society and the individual, as these functions are described by scholars and thinkers.

But, of course, a description of the function and "worth" of a religious tradition means only that, other things being equal, a normative philosophy of religious education is philosophically defensible, and that one who experiences religion in his or her life is justified in educating in light of a religious conviction. But a second-order description of how religion functions cannot create more than a second-order relationship to tradition, to use Schweid's pithy phrase.[43] All the programs of "Jewish consciousness" in Israeli general schools, and the diverse study units in the Diaspora designed to make Judaism more relevant, are, at best, instruction about Judaism, clarification of existential issues through a Jewish cultural medium. It is hoped that these programs make religious education interesting; they do not make religious belief, practice, or fellowship normative.

Now we must recall that the deliberation-inquiry model that we discussed in previous chapters arose for Jewish educators out of a situation of unease, out of a desire to change an uncomfortable set of circumstances—a "problematic situation." We should recall, too, that this model negates the assumption of any *a priori* truth in problem solving.

The problematic situation that expressed itself in a gradual moving away from a religious normative conception of Jewish education was that many Jews could no longer sustain a first-order relationship to religious tradition. They no longer experienced it as true, or they found its truth as they experienced it marginal in terms of other comprehensive truth claims and experiences in the secular scientific world.

The problematic situation of most Jews, to paraphrase Heschel, was that religion was not a problem. It was not a problem because the scientific culture was, by conviction, indifferent to problems that could not be solved in principle. The modern society did not believe in questions to which there were no objective empirical answers. It did not make Marcel's distinction between a problem and a mystery, between a solvable puzzle and an existential predicament.[44]

Schweid points out that those who developed feasible "secondary relationships to tradition," remaining attached to "tradition" but in fact neither concerned with its specific contents nor bound by it, had all received an education in which the tradition conveyed specific contents and demanded commitment.[45] They found that one can *instruct* about a tradition in a secondary relationship, but one cannot *teach* it; one cannot educate toward commitment to it.

Furthermore, a secondary relationship to tradition invites second-order instruction. A second-order teaching of a tradition makes no demands; it is objective. "The Rabbis taught" is substantially the same as "Einstein (or Freud) taught"; the only difference is that the pupil and the teacher are more likely to consider Einstein and Freud reliable. Likewise, when second-order philosophy justifies a tradition, it shows why it is in principle still defensible; actually, it serves to save those who still believe in it from the stigma of eccentricity. Second-order justification makes my friend or colleague of a different faith appear more reasonable to me; his philosophical reflections and rhetoric are "interesting," and I am happy to learn that his tradition deals with issues that are indicated in mine as well. I am not "converted" to another faith by second-order justification but reconciled to its existence. On the other hand, first-order teaching and thinking is concerned primarily not with what Jews have said in defense of Judaism and how they have explained its beneficent functioning but how, under new circumstances or in conditions of changed consciousness, it has been seen as *still true*. It is a normative-Midrashic enterprise, making religious truth accessible to those who are commanded.[46]

Religious education must be shown to be defensible, even in a second-order way, because otherwise its legitimacy will be denied by the larger community to which we all belong; without this legitimation it will fail to enlist "serious" teachers and curriculum workers. But religious education, as a normative enterprise, begins with a first-order commitment to its truth. Normative philosophy of religious education is not embraced because of its legitimacy but because of what has been experienced through the symbols that are being transmitted and what the holy community means to its members.

## THEOLOGY OF EDUCATION

Religious truth and meaning are usually articulated in theological conceptions that reflect basic religious orientations. Even in modern times, in which religion is experienced as problematic, theology fulfills the function of explicating and justifying religious experience. It does this both in a first-order manner, articulating obligation and continued relevance, and in a second-order one, expressing for the outsider religion's structure and philosophical plausibility. If definitions of religion and descriptions of the functions of religion give us a syllabus for religion courses or "civilization" studies about religion, religious theologies, in their first-order dimension of normative explication and ("Midrashic") interpretation, propose religious curricula. They argue for concepts of education that are at least potentially restorative of normative philosophy of education.

In these orientations, as they theologically confront modernity, we thus find open or hidden curricula recommendations. An examination of religious thought will therefore expose to view theologies of education; that is, what "religious theorists" would consider religiously acceptable educationally. For the *educational* theorist who deals with religious education, theologies of education are normative data for the construction of an educational theory. Without a theology of education, religious education lacks substantive principles and guidelines. Even as a theology of education alone will yield an education that mainly exhorts, a theory of religious education that ignores theology will be reductionistic—confusing fellowship and social interaction, identifying ultimate concern with psychological needs.

In the following chapters we shall examine characteristic religious orientations in their modern theological forms. In searching for the religious curricula suggested or intimated by them, we shall be able to formulate alternative theologies of education and suggest patterns of integration among them.

To this task—of discovering and formulating a "theology of education"—we shall now address ourselves.

# 6    Explicit and Implicit Religious Life and Teaching

There are, says Fowler,[1] "master stories" that "we tell ourselves and by which we interpret and respond to the events which impinge on our lives. Our master stories are the characterizations of the patterns of power-in-action that disclose the ultimate meanings of our lives." Master stories are basic faith understandings of reality and value by which we work. For example, one person's master story may be "The universal vocation of persons is the humanization of humankind." Another's may be "It won't make any difference a hundred years from now." These two individual master stories shape basic approaches to the world; in the first case, reaching out constantly for human self-realization, responsibility, and involvement, and in the second, stoic perspective and a degree of existential remoteness.

The experience of people may be considered recognizably religious when their master stories are shaped and affirmed by the "stories" that constitute the traditions of a faith. They hear these traditional stories and believe them, and the stories become a paradigm of action for them. That is, the traditional stories are deemed worthy of being absorbed into one's master story, of exemplifying it. For the person whose master story is "People are good when they do God's will," a dramatic religious Jewish story is the Binding of Isaac. If the person's master story is "God helps those who help themselves," the story of Hanukkah and Hasmonean heroism will be especially meaningful.

Stories that evoke or affirm a religious experience of truth thus reflect different master stories; they are often elaborate and intricate. Let us look at six such stories.

A. And thou shalt love the Lord thy God with all thy heart, and with all thy soul . . . (Deut. 6:5). Rabbi Akiva says: With all thy soul—even if He takes thy soul from thee. . . .

When Rabbi Akiva was taken out to be killed by the Romans, it was the time for the reading of the *Shema,* and they kept flaying his flesh with iron combs, yet he accepted upon himself the yoke of the kingdom of Heaven [i.e., he recited the *Shema*].

His disciples said to him: Even now, master? He said to them: All my days I was troubled by this exposition: "With all thy soul"—even if He take thy soul from thee. I said, if only it were in my power to fulfill this. And now that it is in my power, shall I not fulfill it?

He kept prolonging [the word] One, until his spirit left him while [still] saying One. A voiced issued from Heaven and said: Happy are you, Rabbi Akiva, that your spirit has left you at One.[2]

In a sense, this is a terrifying story. It was Rabbi Akiva who had made the halakhic ruling that the scriptural command to love God "with all thy soul" meant "even when He takes your soul." And it is he whom the Romans torture to death, and when they do so, it happens to be the time for the recitation of the *Shema*. Rabbi Akiva's "story" is that one recites the *Shema* at the proper time regardless of the circumstances; this is what he apparently meant in his ruling "even when He takes thy soul from thee," and he himself exemplifies this teaching. The disciples have difficulty with this "story." Can one "receive the yoke of the kingdom of Heaven"[3] when the kingdom is so blatantly absent? Can he "believe" it while being tortured? Akiva repeats, through his halakhic explication, his master story. What the Romans are doing is existentially irrelevant. Life is defined by accepting God's kingdom through the halakhah, and Akiva himself had the privilege to expound part of it. It is, at that moment, not primarily the time of his death, but the time for the recitation of the *Shema*. That the *Shema* takes precedence over other things, such as confession of sins, meditation, or other preparations for death Akiva "knows" from the words "with all thy soul."

Berkovits[4] has shown how this story both shaped and affirmed the "story" of Jews during the Holocaust. It is reflected in responsa of the Holocaust period and in the attitude of some Jews during that terrible time that the Nazis could "go to hell," that they were, in a sense, a "mere" natural catastrophe.

B. A story that is not unrelated, although its context is incomparably milder, has been told by Heschel. He relates how, in his first months as a student in Berlin, he went through "moments of profound bitterness."

I felt very much alone with my own problems and anxieties. I walked alone in the evenings through the magnificent streets of Berlin. I admired the solidarity of its architecture, the overwhelming drive and power of a dynamic civilization. There were concerts, theatres, and lectures by famous scholars about the latest theories and inventions, and I was pondering whether to go to the new Max Reinhardt play or to a lecture about the theory of relativity.

Suddenly I noticed the sun had gone down, evening had arrived.

*From what time may one recite the* Shema *in the evening?*

I had forgotten God—I had forgotten Sinai—I had forgotten that sunset is my business—that my task is "to restore the world to the kingship of God the Lord."

So I began to utter the words of the evening prayer:

"Blessed are Thou, Lord our God, King of the Universe, Who by His word brings on the evenings . . . "

Heschel, contemplating the story he had undergone, reflectively ties it together with part of his master story. "It is such happiness to belong to an order of the divine will."[5]

C. The following narrative expresses the same master story, albeit in very different circumstances. It is June 1967, the Friday of the Six Day War. An Orthodox kibbutz member relates:

We are riding in the desert. Zalman reminds me that it's Friday. Almost candle-lighting time. We take all the *mukze** out of our pockets and put it into knapsacks. We say *Shabbat Shalom* and continue riding.

The convoy stops. We get off. Gather together a *minyan*. From the second jeep, the driver gets out, takes off his military cap and puts on a *kipah*. . . . We begin *L'chu neranenu,*† and other men join in. . . . We finish our prayers. . . . The Commanding Officer declares: "Zalman will make *kiddush!*‡ Zalman stands in the middle of the highway. In the desert echo the words: " . . . and in love and favor He has given us His Holy Sabbath as an inheritance, a memorial of the creation of the world."[6]

D. A very different kind of story is the following: The Mishnah, in a warning to witnesses against testifying too readily against persons accused of capital crimes, declares:

Therefore was man created single to teach you that whoever destroys a single soul is considered by Scripture to have destroyed an entire world, and

---

*Objects that Jewish law forbids handling on the Sabbath.

†The opening psalm of the Sabbath eve prayers.

‡Sanctification of the Sabbath over a cup of wine.

whoever sustains one soul, Scripture regards him as having sustained a complete world, and he was created single to keep peace among the human creatures, that no man may say to his fellow, My father was greater than your father.

And to tell you the greatness of the King Who is king over all kings, the Holy One, blessed be He; for a man stamps many coins in one mold and they are all alike. But the King Who is king over all kings, the Holy One, blessed be He, stamped every man in the mold of the first man, yet not one of them resembles his fellow. Hence it is said: How great are Thy works, O Lord. (Ps. 92:6)[7]

The "master story" is that the imprint of God's work is on every man and on historical events. God's hand can be seen in all, though there are different perspectives. In the uniqueness of individuals and of moments, God is present.

E. Consider the following, written by an Israeli soldier after the Six Day War. Describing his excitement at the conquest of Jerusalem, he states:

In the air hung a sense of great and holy hours. When I asked a fellow soldier, a member of Kibbutz Sha'ar Ha-Amakim, at the Rockefeller Museum, before the conquest of the Temple Mount, "What have you got to say?" he answered me with a verse from the Bible: "I was glad when they said to me, let us go to the house of the Lord. Our feet were standing in thy gates, Jerusalem, Jerusalem that is built as a city that is tied together." The fellow smiled as he cited this verse. Maybe because it isn't fitting for a member of Hashomer Hatzair to speak thus. But I saw his eyes and I knew that that was what he felt. [Later at the Western Wall] . . . I looked at soldiers and officers: I saw their tears and their wordless prayers, and I knew that they sensed what I did. . . . I understood that not only my religious [i.e., Orthodox] friends and I felt grandeur and sanctity, but that they too felt it, with no less power and depth. . . . [8]

F. A related master story is indicated in Buber's description of an argument he had with an old Gentile German thinker. The colleague was dismayed at Buber's seemingly facile use of the word "God." As Buber tells it, the man cried out:

How can you bring yourself to say "God" time after time? How can you expect that your readers will take the word in the sense in which you wish it to be taken? What you mean by the name of God is something above all human grasp and comprehension, but in speaking about it you have lowered it to human conceptualization. What word of human speech is so misused, so defiled, so desecrated as this . . . ?

Buber, in response, admitted that "it is the most heavy-laden of all human words. None has become so soiled, so mutilated."

Just for this reason I may not abandon it. Generations of men have laid the burden of their anxious lives upon this word and weighed it to the ground; it lies in the dust and bears their whole burden. [Yet] where might I find a word like it to describe the highest! If I took the purest, most sparkling concept from the inner treasure-chamber of the philosophers, I could only capture thereby an unbinding product of thought. I could not capture the presence of Him whom the generations of men have honoured with their awesome living and dying. . . . We must esteem those who interdict it [the name, God] because they rebel against the injustice and wrong which are so readily referred to "God" for authorization. But we must not give it up . . . we can raise it up from the ground and set it over an hour of great care.

Following this exchange, Buber relates his "story":

It had become very light in the room. . . . The old man stood up, came over to me, laid his hand on my shoulder, and spoke: "Let us be friends." The conversation was completed. For where two or three are truly together, they are together in the name of God.[9]

These six stories point to two inherent components in the way people understand religion; all are meant to communicate something paradigmatic about religious experiences. The first three stories are explicitly nourished by a normative tradition; the last three are more rooted in the personal encounter of individuals with transcendence, with a perception of "depth" that is related and points to "faith."

The two differing religious understandings illustrated in these stories are invariably the subject of theological and phenomenological typologies and, often, of polemics. For instance, Tillich speaks of the "cosmological" versus the "ontological" type of faith. From a kindred philosophical perspective, Buber speaks of "religion" versus "religiosity," arguing for the priority of the latter. James speaks of "institutional" as opposed to "personal" religion. Berger has written of the differentiation between deductive and inductive religion, and Smith makes a distinction between a "cumulative tradition" and "faith."[10]

We shall term the former religious understanding, highlighted and perhaps exemplified by our first three stories, *explicit religion* and the latter understanding, which is characteristic of our second group of stories, *implicit religion*. Explicit religion concerns itself with what we believe and practice as loyal adherents of a specific faith, as members of a believing community; it sets down norms that prevail in our fellowship, norms that are incumbent upon those whom "we" will recognize as "religious." Implicit religion deals with existential encounters, occasioned by looking within and up in an attitude of faith; it connotes reverence, openness, and search for meaning. Implicit religion begins not with God's demand but with human hopes and fears, with perception rather than tradition, with the depth of questions rather than with the authority of answers. In explicit religion we come into contact with God when we do His will; in implicit religion, it is when we become conscious of a unique significance that is in us, in moments, and in events and that is perceived in the relations between persons.

Both dimensions[11] convey certainty and bespeak truth to religious believers; they both "surround" the believing person. But the relationship between these orientations is unstable, and they co-exist in varying proportions within different people. This instability and diversity make possible religious life and community that can be shared by men and women of diverse temperaments and talents, and it generates much religious creativity, but it also invites theological and educational corruptions—for either of these dimensions may overpower or suppress the other. As we shall see, the danger of such corruption is particularly acute in the modern age, in which religion and religious education have made various systematic, often dogmatic, attempts to deal with the challenge of modernity.

The instability of the relationship between explicit and implicit religion in the life of faith is inherent and constant. It stems to a large degree from the fact that each of these dimensions conveys distinct and seemingly incongruous messages and guidelines to the believer and the educator. The (explicitly religious) story of Rabbi Akiva seems to be "saying" that God is to be approached only through halakhah; that the blackness of historical reality is mitigated only by human love-through-obedience; conversely, in the (implicitly religious) story of the Israeli soldier praying and weeping at the Western Wall, God is "seen" in the unique moment, and those who are "religious" realize that even the seemingly "irreligious" are in His presence. Similarly, Buber and his non-Jewish colleague were "together in the name of God," although they did not share a normative faith community. On the other hand, Zalman, taking the *muzke* out of his pockets in a military jeep and making *kiddush* in the desert, is spiritually peculiar, perhaps incomprehensible, to a non-Jew. So, too, is Heschel, who distanced himself from his "cultural" surroundings when he began to *daven Maariv*—to recite the evening prayer.

In specifically educational terms, *explicit* and *implicit* religion appear to have contradictory orientations with regard to five discrete issues: (1) What is truth and how is it transmitted? (2) What do we mean by norms and obligations? (3) What is the proper relationship between religious truth as experienced and other realms of knowledge and meaning? (4) How shall one relate to religious traditions other than one's own? (5) What are the parameters of the educated religious personality?

Let us briefly comment on the "messages," the "master stories" conveyed by explicit and implicit religion, respectively, in these five areas:

1. In its pure form, and in its more "consistent" manifestations, explicit religious sentiment considers truth "at its highest" to be knowable only from within the community of the covenant. For this is the truth of revelation, comprehended through historical experience or existential grace. One is born into the community that was "chosen" for God's message and that sought and found God in a particular experience, which dictated a normative mode of "standing before" Him. The norms of the community provide the avenue to ultimate understanding. Thus, explicit religion may be superficially explained to outsiders, but its essence is not communicable to them. For example, no matter how well non-Jews understand "religion," they will not have thereby grasped what "Torah" really is; the truth of Torah can be understood only by those who are commanded. The talmudic Sage Shammai was justifiably impatient with the three Gentiles who wished to become proselytes. They set "ignorant" conditions for conversion and therefore had to be rejected. Not knowing the right answers, they asked the wrong questions. They did not know the truth about Judaism and so, in Shammai's opinion, were incapable of finding it. He therefore had no compunction about driving them out.[12]

In the implicit religious approach, truth is first and foremost individual and thus, in principle, universal. That which makes a person human, rather than what makes him or her a member of a particular faith community, is of primary importance. While shying away from the term "absolute truth" in any propositional or dogmatic sense,[13] the implicitly religious personality views the individual as a fundamentally religious being who will be able to achieve self-discovery only by entering the religious dimension of existence. The specific goals of religious life may be highly individual, but the way is at least partially communicable because the teacher can refer authentically to his or her own search and can draw upon the models provided by seminal personalities in diverse religious traditions. This implies, of course, that discrete religions are illustrative of universal insights ("truths") and may—indeed, must—be justified before the bar of universal experience, including the child's. Truth is discovered by delving into experience; by eliciting the child's questions, and not the *a priori* "right" ones. When Hillel confronted the aforementioned proselytes, he considered what their questions meant to *them* and accepted this meaning as worthy even before leading them to a search for answers—through *their* study of Torah.[14]

2. The religious sense of norm and obligation, as distinct from "general" moral purposes and the behavior dictated by such norms, derives from the explicit aspect of religion. Explicit religious rules may be said to be "ends in themselves," not means leading to extrinsic ends. Laws and doctrines of explicit religion have been compared with the rules of chess or, for that matter, those of any formal system: The laws define "the game." In Judaism, for example, the explicit orientation encourages the identification of the religious life with a comprehensive sacramental-halakhic discipline (or, in its more "liberal" manifestations, with explicit and clear theological truths). The individual, when in doubt as to the correct religious response to a situation, is expected to ask an expert—or, to "look it up." Not to have recourse to the norms as objectively located within a corpus bearing God's will is not religion, as that term is defined by the explicit thinker or educator. Thus, Rackman, writing about the Sabbath and the relationship between its law and its significance, says:

The Torah, to the devotee of Halachah, is God's revealed will, not only with respect to what man shall do but also with respect to what man shall fulfill. To apprehend these ends, however, requires more than philosophical analysis of some general ideas set forth in the Bible. It is not enough to say that the Sabbath is a day of rest. One must also study the detailed prescriptions with respect to rest so that one may better understand the goals of the Sabbath in the light of the prescriptions, for if one considers the end alone, without regard to the detailed prescriptions, one will always be reading into the Bible what one wants to find there. It is God's ends we are to seek, not our own.[15]

Although Rackman is concerned with human creativity in interpretation, he insists that the law is God's, and people attain dignity and holiness through their responsibility for maintaining the norms that are the essence of religion.

Conversely, implicit religion neither desires nor is able to impose normative patterns of dogma, behavior, or experience, although it does connect an individual's moral striving with religious sensitivity and responsibility. God's will is never finally congealed through/in a particular religious tradition, and no historical community may presume to speak authoritatively for God.

Implicit religion insists that no text or tradition is *a priori* normative; individuals must decide (and bear responsibility for deciding) what is required of them, and this flows from what is truly significant to them. They may, of course, be encouraged to make a particular tradition their framework, and it behooves the teacher to point out that all religious men and women have some cultural framework, but it signifies no failure on the part of the teacher if the pupil decides otherwise. What the religious teacher must do is to cultivate in the pupil the moral strength, power, maturity—in short, faith—to make decisions that express his or her self, in a way that society can live with. Anything more than that is, religiously speaking, "taking God's name in vain" and closing the gates of faith in order to salvage lifeless dogma.

Thus, Buber discusses the charge that religious education is unwarranted because it is opposed to "the total openness" of youth, which "gives itself to life's boundlessness." Youth "has not yet sworn allegiance to any one truth for whose sake it would close its eyes to all other perspectives," Buber comments:

> This admonition would be justified if religion were really, by nature, the dispenser of fixed orientations and norms, or a sum of dogmas and rules. By nature, however, it is neither. Dogmas and rules are merely the result, subject to change, of the human mind's endeavour to make comprehensible, by a symbolic order of the knowable and doable, the working of the unconditional it experiences within itself. Primary reality is constituted by the unconditional's effect upon the human mind, which, sustained by the force of its own vision, unflinchingly faces the Supreme Power.[16]

Therefore, implicitly religious educators consider teaching that measures success by religious observance to be a form of indoctrination. The teacher may expose children to a tradition, set an example of how one can live religiously within that tradition, and even teach competence within it. The decision—to accept or reject—must be the pupil's.

3. From the explicitly religious perspective it is clear that truth is "internal" to the holy community. From this perspective it appears illogical, and even perverse, to justify religious beliefs and practices in terms of other realms of knowledge—be they philosophical, moral, or scientific. The external justification of explicit religion, except as a temporary or didactic device, must be seen as a betrayal of the highest truth. One may appeal to some external criteria when this is done for apologetic purposes (in the sense of "know what to answer to the heretic"); in such a case one must not be overly scrupulous about intellectual standards but simply must deal with the problem of the non-believer as best one can. However, a serious recourse to a non-religious realm for legitimation, is, in effect, an admission of its higher truth. The justifying principle has become, as it were, more unquestionable than the word of God. Thus consistent explicit religionists, seeking to explain their beliefs, basically limit themselves to spelling them out, describing them, drawing conclusions from them. The truth to which they testify is *given;* its meaning is *experienced;* it can be only partially "translated" into terms intelligible to "outsiders," and what can be explained is easily distorted. Thus, Joseph B. Soloveitchik, describing the dilemma of "the lonely man of faith," notes that "the act of faith

is unique and cannot be fully translated into cultural categories''; modern ''majestic man'' is ''searching not for a faith in all its singularity and otherness, but for religious culture.''[17] His method of ''explaining himself'' is therefore often that of drawing analogies between Torah and other realms of knowledge, or bodies of data that are ''also'' self-evident and invite explication. (For example, the Torah may be compared with nature, or halakhah with scientific law.)[18] Thus, too, when seriously grappling with other realms of knowledge, the explicit religionist tends to hold a compartmentalized position: Religious truth is so different from other kinds that it cannot benefit from the methods and tools used to investigate the latter. The ''other'' truths deal with qualitatively different data, which have religious relevance only because God created them and gave to human beings the intelligence to expose them to view. The world of ''general'' knowledge tends to be ''neutralized'' religiously; one may use it, enjoy it, and appreciate it. It cannot, however, really inform or direct the personality of the religious individual.

Aaron Soloveitchik,[19] for instance, makes the interesting distinction between ''theoretical'' and ''practical'' studies. ''Practical'' studies are those that are legitimately *educative*; that build character; ''theoretical'' studies merely convey information. They are justifiable as long as they do not attempt to be ''practical.'' Thus, all Torah studies are ''practical,'' even when they deal with seemingly irrelevant material; driving lessons, physics, and literature are ''theoretical.'' They convey facts and competences.

Conversely, implicit believers have no compunctions about appealing to general philosophical or existential categories in justifying their religious views and commitments, since they maintain that their faith flows from universal aspects of human experience that may and, ultimately, must be thought about reflectively and systematically. For them, there is no problem in explaining a religious point of view in terms extrinsic to it, for nothing is in principle outside human (potentially religious) experience. One may say that religious answers are legitimate and justified only as they can be seen to be answers to questions arising out of experience, out of all perceived relationships between a person and the environment. Thus, it makes sense, in implicit religious education, to begin a Child's Introduction to the Bible with an opening paragraph such as the one we find in Newman's textbook:

How can a fly walk on the ceiling without falling off?
What are clouds made of?
When does a seed grow into a tree?
Have *you* ever wondered about such things?
Have *you* ever asked such questions?[20]

The child's curiosity is thus awakened; he or she is made to wonder, to formulate a question to which the story of Creation is an answer. The same questions that lead to inquiry in all fields are those that arouse religious inquiry: A person's search is the beginning of all wisdom to the extent that it is motivated by his or her ultimate concern for most comprehensive and profound understanding. The implicit "man of faith" feels comfortable with inductive methods of religious inquiry and is not disturbed by the question, "Where will it lead?"—for it cannot lead to aught but more comprehensive understanding, perhaps "touched by the divine." There really are no "other realms"—the very notion testifies, in the eyes of the implicitly religious person, to a lack of religious "wholeness."

4. For the explicitly religious person, religion as such is neither a blessing nor a source of value. It is *this person's* religion, not religiosity, that is true. Other religions, to the extent that they incorporate "the true" religion's moral norms of universal obligation, are acceptable—although, from an explicit perspective, they seem largely superfluous. (For example, a "pure" explicitly Jewish person would argue that people could, in principle, accept the seven Noachide commandments without being Christians and Moslems.) To the extent, however, that other religions base themselves upon revelations that are not in substantial agreement with the revealed moral code, they are injurious and perverse; one is duty-bound to pray for their demise, for they are embodiments of idolatry. J. B. Soloveitchik, for example, in speaking of Judaism's "confrontation" with the non-Jewish (Christian) world, declares that both faiths await the eschatological moment when one of them will be vindicated.

. . . each faith community is unyielding in its eschatological expectations. . . . it expects man [then] to embrace the faith that this community has been preaching throughout the millenia.[21]

The implicit religious attitude toward other religions proceeds from the assumption that religion is answering a universal need, arising in its various historical forms in response to a universal quest for an accessible spiritual reality. Whereas the explicit orientation is antagonistic to "untrue" religions but quite comfortable with secular humanism, the disdain of the implicit person is reserved for the shallowness and cultural poverty of the secular person who cannot appreciate all religion because he or she takes specific literary traditions too literally.[22] From the implicit standpoint, all religions have truth in them, especially as they highlight the implicit dimension of faith; since no religion has a monopoly on truth, each religious person and community has much to learn from others. As for the claim to an exclusive and comprehensive truth, it betrays the explicit (thus parochial and narrow-minded) nature of the community or person and exposes the individual as captive to untruth, for he or she is incapable of spiritual growth.

5. The "pure" explicit religious educator wishes to cultivate the pious and observant person; the "pure" implicit religious educator hopes to foster a spiritual personality. The former's pupil will be a loyal servant of God, as that ideal is understood within a particular religious community, and will be a reliable member of that community. One can, therefore, "do" religion "with" him or her. A significant proportion of religious experience is in the encounter with fellow believers, and communication takes place in the language that only they understand and live by.

When Zalman reminds his fellow soldiers that "it's almost candle-lighting time," everyone who is an insider knows what that means and what must be done: to take the *mukze* out of one's pockets. Those outside the community, even if in the same jeep or tank, do not know exactly what "candle-lighting time" is or what one has to do about it. From the inside, religion is inexplicable without such communication; from the outside, the forms of communication appear arbitrary and quaint.

If the outsider is an implicitly religious person, he or she will argue that one's religious obligation is not to "do ritual acts" but to be "true to oneself" and honest with God (however the individual understands God). With the implicit sensibility, the religious demand is for authenticity, not for conformity. Viewed from without, the exemplary implicit pupil appears to be "wild" and self-centered, never more concerned with his or her own ego than when he or she claims to be dwelling on the Divine. Yet the implicitly religious person is likely to consider Zalman, the "explicit Jew," a formalist, socialized into "meaningless" conventions.

It will be recalled that what we are here dealing with, in a typological manner, is the forms of religious experience as they look from the inside. Our concern is with the "essence" or "functions" of religion not as seen from social scientific or humanistic perspectives, as was the case in the previous chapters, but as seen from within (though it will be noted that the implicit dimension of religion is more "open" to such scientific or humanistic findings and more ready to incorporate them into religious sensibility and self-understanding). For we are positing that normative educational conceptions, which are the viable foundation of religious curricula, are based on what people really believe and experience religiously, and not on what they can say in defense of a religious orientation. A defense of religious life, we have argued, merely clears the ground; it makes religious faith and education plausible. But such "second-order" articulation of "what a religion believes" or philosophical justification of such beliefs, does not make religion normative for anyone. Religions "from within" are not primary arguments but stories and contexts, which are enacted—and inhabited—before they are analyzed and explained.

Nevertheless, it should be obvious that what people are ready to commit themselves to as true, which experiences of theirs they trust and how they will live within the stories they tell, cannot be divorced from a cultural and historical set of circumstances. Nor can their "systematic theologies," in which they explain themselves, ignore the spiritual context in which they are meant to be plausible. And if modern religious education is partially dependent on modern theology—which reflects and explains an "acceptable" and authentically experienced religious life—then one must ask how religious experience and thought in the contemporary age are affected by the context in which they find themselves. This, we need hardly remind ourselves, is a context of secularism, of a philosophical commitment to the autonomy of reason and of a scientific world view. The social context of the modern world is one of professed pluralism in "an open society"; the historical consciousness of the age is one that locates religion among dynamic cultural phenomena; the privatization of religion in what Katz has called "the neutral society" is axiomatic.[23]

We have already discussed the secular world view and diverse religious responses. Nevertheless, it will be appropriate to note several points that are germane to the interaction between modern scientific culture and religion. This interaction, no less than it influences the way religion is studied, shapes the life of religion itself.

1. On the sociological plane, it should be borne in mind that the traditional religious communities were socially multi-functional and constituted a holistic "world" for their members. When a rabbi taught the laws of Passover to *"ha-olam"* (literally, "the world"), he was speaking to a universe comprising all significant persons. In the pluralistic "open" society, this "world" has disintegrated or has become compartmentalized from large and significant segments of life (and "worlds") for most of its members. In certain cases and in small groups, the communities have become sectarian, zealous bastions of defensive and threatened "cognitive minorities," groups who know that they are "different" and develop strategies for maintaining their commitments and concepts of knowledge.[24]

2. On the philosophical-theological plane, one observes that objective-rationalistic ("positive") theologies, which are based on philosophical arguments for particular revealed traditions, have been severely undermined. Religion that is "imposed from above" is largely unbelievable to modern people,

who tend to accept (whether in sophisticated or popularized forms) the post-Kantian conviction that metaphysics conveys no real knowledge. They thus naturally incline to Spinoza's insistence that prophecy deals with goodness rather than with truth. Most people in the contemporary world have either studied or absorbed—profoundly or superficially—the various functional approaches to religion that originate in the university and impose universal needs, hopes, and perceptions upon religious life and belief.[25]

3. On the educational plane, given the basic assumptions of scientific-minded people, it makes more sense to study *about* religions than to be initiated *into* them.[26] However, to the extent that scientific inquiry is perceived as unqualified to deal with an individual's search for meaning and commitment, room can be made, with a boost from existential psychology and philosophy, for a subjective sphere in which religion is a requisite "dimension" of life. In this way, religion can be viewed as a cultural option and, for some, an existential one. Moreover, cumulative religious traditions may be studied to enrich contemporary experience; the variously explicit-historical communities of faith embody, albeit in characteristically mythic form, psychological wisdom and quasi-philosophical insight. Since these insights document and store aspects of a person's inner life, it would be culturally wasteful to ignore the traditions that incorporate them.

Thus, Maddon distinguishes between "religion as a quality of experience" (i.e., what we are calling implicit religion) and "religion as a structure of special doctrine" (i.e., explicit religion). He wishes, like Dewey, "to strip away the trappings of structured religion and to find the religious spirit which actually pervades the affairs of everyday life." Yet he insists that we should not disregard the old "supernatural" religions.

It is conceivable that our supernaturally minded ancestors struggled for insights that they grasped only vaguely and could express only symbolically. To ignore their spadework, even though much further work remains to be done, would be a waste of resources.[27]

Maddon's statement is a faithful reflection of the dominant philosophical approach to religious education: Religion can be experienced by the modern person only as an existential orientation. Most modern thinkers and educators understand defensible and, thus, authentically meaningful religious experience as an artifact of a partially redeemable heritage, if radically reworked by contemporary philosophy of religion. This extreme implicitness and privatization are well illustrated by Becker's theological assertion that only God is the source of freedom, since man's relationship to society is always one of bondage—either the bondage of acceptance (or norms) or the bondage of rejection.[28] God, it is posited, makes possible the integrity of the individual.

In brief: For the modern "implicit" consciousness, explicit "ritual" forms may be preserved because of their congeniality to what "makes sense" symbolically, to maintain a modicum of historical continuity, or to foster fellowship. But explicit religion, it is argued, is not imposed by God, and in the larger universe of cultural discourse, "the neutral society," it is not even clear what "imposed by God" is supposed to mean. Thus, explicit religion should be given more dignified treatment than positivists are wont to give it, for it is a vehicle of significant experience in the past and, for some, in the present. But it may as readily be researched as respected, for it is human in origin and development; it is a product of human culture. Therefore, religious education, if it is to deal with what people may truly believe, must be education for openness and integration. Only this is defensible in light of everything else we know. And for the person who has experienced uniqueness in the midst of the everyday, and significance-calling-to-commitment, it is perhaps synonymous with education itself. For the ultimate object is finally unified with the subject who has ultimate concerns, and the ultimate—that is, religious—understanding and obligation are, as Buber puts it, "not in Heaven," but in the human heart.[29]

We should consider also, in the case of Jewish religious education in the post-Emancipation era, the desire of Jews to be amalgamated into the national (non-Jewish) community, which, after all, was supposed to be "neutral" religiously. In this context we readily understand the basis of a religious education that is supplementary and highly "ideational" and which, even when it builds on publicly articulated respect of ethnic and religious differences, yet operates in the midst of a pervasive civilization that tolerates but hardly respects the explicit norms of others.[30]

But even sociologists, who within their disciplines are careful to bracket their own religious experience, note that there has not been a universal throng to implicit faith that holds to a bemused respect for archaic explicit religion. Most people, in entering the secular world, have not thereby become more spiritual and existential in their religious orientation; they have simply become secular. At the same time, for many sophisticated and not-so-sophisticated people in today's society religion has been "returned to," in blatantly explicit forms. Berger has called this "the deductive possibility," the neo-Orthodox phenomenon in which, in ways echoed in Heschel's experience in Berlin, "the authority of the tradition is regained. It becomes subjectively real to the individual and can then be perceived again as objective reality."[31]

This "re-conversion" experience does not come out of the blue; it is related to the partiality of implicit religion as it is experienced and, consequently, analyzed. Thus, writers such as Kurzweil and Fackenheim[32] (the one close to neo-Orthodoxy, the other with roots in religious liberalism) have posed almost identical questions about implicit religion and its dependence on general justification; namely, Once you have psychologized, sociologized, and philosophized religion so that the remaining experience may maintain authenticity, what do you *really* believe? Are the ensuing (or perhaps *a priori*) historicism and relativism of this enterprise the real belief of the implicit culture? And if so, what is the implicitly religious personality but a highly personal achievement of morally and spiritually gifted individuals? Stating this differently: If one leaves the field of "real" knowledge to science and its "objective" avenues of inquiry and has made religion a merely subjective affair, what are the religious contents and claims that are to be educationally transmitted? Moreover, granting that philosophical reflection and even social scientific research with regard to religious life are legitimate and even a requisite for spiritual equilibrium in the present-day world, must they not have something to reflect upon? Can philosophy create faith? Can science recommend it cogently? And, if not, how will anyone be educated toward religion through philosophy or social science that can explain and even regulate religion but that cannot be expected to engender it? If all meaningful religion is going to be implicit, then all people must be prophets! But that is impossible, and, in any case, leaves no task for education as a social and socializing enterprise.[33]

Such questions, asked by people who are imbued with modern consciousness and competent in using its methods, testify to a response to modernity that is the opposite of the purely implicit one: the "re-discovery" of pristine "objective" religious truth by those who have "been through" modernity. The same contemporary situation that has suggested the identification of religion with its implicit aspects has also engendered, as a counter-response, the return to communities in which the revealed Word is the highest truth, which judges all reason and culture by revealed criteria. Moreover, the sharp distinction that the re-discoverer can make between his or her truth and "religion" allows the analytical study of "religion" to proceed apace. The choice to these returners (*"baalai tshuvah"*) appears to be between Torah and valuative anarchy and atheism. Torah, as explicit Word, is both eternally true and yet, at least for a believing elite, structured by modern consciousness. Neo-

Orthodoxy, the modern pristine explicit religion, is both objective and existential; a-historical, yet a genuine witness to historical continuity.

It cannot be denied that seminal religious teachers and thinkers, in our time as in previous epochs, have characteristically written and lived in profound awareness of the dialectic between explicit and implicit religion in Judaism. In our century, such religious personalities as Abraham Isaac Kook, Joseph B. Soloveitchik, Abraham Joshua Heschel, and Franz Rosenzweig, to mention several, have articulated theologies that struggle with the question of how inner illumination is consistent with law, how openness and innovation may be nourished by loyalty and reverence.

However, these thinkers, although often addressing themselves to educational questions, have not been primarily concerned with the "translation" of their theologies into religious educational theory. Moreover, they did not systematically write theologies of education; that is, comprehensive and consistent guidelines for the cultivation of the religious personality. The main reason for this is that they focused their attention, in most cases, on only one of the four elements that must be dealt with descriptively and prescriptively in a normative philosophy of religious education. Their main interest, as religious thinkers, was with the subject matter; they dealt with "Judaism," its significance and its norms, its world view and its message. They did not usually state what they, as theologians, would have liked teachers to do, in terms of what teachers believe and can communicate or what pupils will understand and appreciate. They were not specific about curricula problems in specific environments. Therefore, what they had to say about education often appeared ambiguous, or preachy.[34]

As a result, the modern religious Jewish educator, after having read profound and enriching theological exegeses and essays written by such men of vision and learning, still looks for more programmatic writing on the subject of religious education. And, as the educational writing becomes more programmatic, it seems to become more polemical. Some theoreticians, proceeding from an explicit orientation, seem to be arguing that education should (or can) do no more than socialize the young person into the religious fellowship of common belief and observance. Others, positing an implicitly religious position, maintain that religious education is no more than cultivating the individuality of the spiritual person.

These theological conceptions of religious education are generally one-sided, either "explicit" or "implicit," not because the writers are indifferent to the dialectic between the two, nor because they deny the value of either. Rather, the one-sidedness of the authors is occasioned by their *educational* concern, by their conviction that, given the nature of Judaism, children, and the modern world, *this* or *that* is what the school should do—and that this pre-scription is Jewishly (i.e., theologically) legitimate or even mandated by the tradition and its principles.

The educator, having been impressed with the axiom that "education can't do everything," finds that a similar notion seems to guide the theological-educational thinkers. These thinkers appear to be forcing the educator to choose between alternatives, to teach either "explicitly" or "implicitly."

Thus, Isaac Breuer, a neo-Orthodox and a very explicit thinker, defines a religious Jew as one who lives under the yoke of the commandments. He de-cries "the terrible solitude of individualism" and insists that the individual is obedient to the law not "because he is convinced of the divinity of the national law but because the nation's will ranks higher than his own and binds him."[35] On the other hand, an implicit thinker such as Martin Buber will insist that religion is concerned with encounter—the religious life of the young person concerns itself with "awakening" rather than an imposition—for "nothing is incapable of becoming a receptacle of revelation."[36]

The teacher will find these theological guidelines articulated in conceptions of curriculum more specific than the foregoing. Leibovitz informs the educator that Jewish religion is to be conceived as training in the observance of the com-mandments.[37] Marvin Fox declares that "The Hebrew Day School is obligated to stand openly against the exaggerated notion of freedom from authority which endangers our young people." He declares that the Jewish school must supply "moral knowledge" and moral sensitivity. "In learning and practicing such *mitzvoth* (commandments, religious actions) as *Tzedakah* (charity), *hach-nasat orchim* (hospitality), *bikkur cholim* (visiting the sick), and many others, the student discovers important moral principles and follows important prac-tical precepts."[38]

Conversely, Kushner tells the teacher that when children ask about God, they are asking for help in understanding their own experiences and are striving for self-realization. It is helping children with this, argues Kushner, that con-stitutes the religious teacher's primary challenge.[39] Similarly, albeit from a more communal perspective, Cohen insists that the educated Jew "will view operationally the various interpretations of Judaism now current in Jewish life." He suggests, therefore, that American Jewry has to frame its own life, regardless of what any previous generation of Jews did.[40] The approach, as noted, is more communal than is Kushner's, but the emphasis here too is on man's quest, the centrality of questions and problems, the shift of focus from authority to authenticity.

Both approaches, the explicit and the implicit, are modern. They posit dif-fering interpretations of the implications of modern thought. They seek an essence and a core of Jewish tradition to be transmitted, be it in law or in spirit, in acceptance or struggle, that will enable the educator to present a consistent and perhaps untroubled approach to tradition on the one hand and to modern science and philosophy on the other. But each approach points in a direction that may easily become one-sided, substituting dogma for dialectic. It may become overly and unrealistically normative or excessively deliberative, emptying the religious tradition of substance. For the dialectic that is maintained in the mind, and even in the system, of the explicit or implicit theologian tends to become blurred as his or her theology becomes an educational guideline. As the guidelines are translated into materials and practice, all aspirations to comprehensive religiosity that has both "awe" and "love" in its fabric may be totally lost or denied.

In order to define, to describe and, in effect, to re-discover a philosophy of religious Jewish education, we must, at this stage, deal with three questions:

1. What do explicit and implicit theologians of education say about Judaism and Jewish education, and what are their prescriptions for "good" religious education?

2. How do the explicit and implicit orientations, once they have left or before they have reached the theological plane of system and dialectic, "translate" into texts and teaching? What do explicit and implicit Jewish education actually "do" with tradition, and with the child?

3. How can explicit and implicit theologies of education, with their very distinct curricula guidelines, be brought into a fruitful confrontation?

In dealing with the questions pertaining to a theology of Jewish education, especially the third, we shall discover that religious education requires not merely a theology but also an educational theory that partially translates explicit and implicit religious conceptions into sociological and psychological ones. Only on the basis of such a theory, which incorporates social scientific elements into the theory of teaching, shall we find ourselves equipped to more clearly define and describe a philosophy of religious Jewish education.

The theology of Jewish education is the subject of our examination in Part 2. In Part 3, we shall see where theology of Jewish education has taken us and what requires description and analysis beyond the realm of theology. In this way, the religious ideas of the theologian can be rendered educationally meaningful and feasible; one can "get a handle on" the explicit and implicit religious experiences that underlie the ideas, thus ensuring that the ideas will not be perceived as educationally irrelevant or ethereally "spiritual."

# Part Two

---

# THEOLOGY OF JEWISH EDUCATION

# 7  Norms Despite Modernity:
## Explicit Educational Theology

## EDUCATORS DISCUSS THE TALMUD

At the time this chapter was being written, a group of curriculum writers at the Hebrew University's Melton Centre for Jewish Education in the Diaspora, including this author, met frequently to discuss ways of teaching the oral tradition in the Jewish school. Diverse approaches were presented to the group and were analyzed and evaluated by the participants, who represented differing outlooks and variegated educational experience.

One evening, a member of our curriculum group, herself an experienced Talmud teacher and educational theoretician, illustrated her orientation by teaching us a *sugyah* (talmudic issue) that drew on discussions in two tractates of the Babylonian Talmud. The issue was the mandatory recitation of the Hallel (an order of psalms of praise) on joyous festivals and possible reasons why it is not recited on Purim, although it is read on every other holiday that commemorates God's saving acts. Here are some of the points made concerning the passages we studied:

▪ One would expect the recitation of the Hallel to be mandatory on Purim. If its reading is required on Passover, when Israel was delivered "only" from slavery, it should obviously (*a fortiori*) also be recited on Purim, when Israel was saved from certain death.

▪ One need not recite the Hallel on Purim, since the prophets prescribed the reading of *Megillat Esther* (the Book of Esther) for that day. The reading of that scroll, being a form of praise to God analogous to the Hallel, makes the recitation of the latter superfluous.

▪ One does not read the Hallel on Purim, since these psalms mark only salvational events that occurred in the Land of Israel but not those, like Purim, that occurred outside the Land. (In this connection the Talmud raises the question of why, then, the salvation in Egypt deserves to be celebrated by the chanting of the Hallel. One possible answer proposed in the Talmud: that before Israel entered the Land, salvation in other countries could be marked in this way, but not afterward.)

▪ One is obliged to recite the Hallel on Passover but not on Purim because, in the former case the subjugation to Pharaoh ended on the day of Exodus, whereas in the latter case the rule of King Ahasuerus endured.[1]

The educators who participated in this lesson and the ensuing discussion had several interlocked concerns:

1. They wished to understand the text, to comprehend the *subject matter*. This meant, first of all, that they wished to understand the line of argument (a desire many readers may share). Moreover, if they were less than conversant in talmudic rhetoric, they wished to catch the *form* of the argument, in which religious norms were deduced from set patterns of exegesis—in which one "learned out" (arrived at) norms from (unaccustomed) modes of legal discussion.

2. They had to find themselves *as teachers* in this context. They were obliged to measure the degree of relevance, for themselves, of procedures whereby one deduces how and when to recite psalms of praise and of a system of "rules" concerning the equivalence of a narrative (the Book of Esther) to such psalms on a specified occasion.

3. They had to think of the sensibilities of *pupils* with regard to this text. It was necessary for them to evaluate how such a "language," if it were conceded to be intrinsic to Jewish religious tradition and existence, could be conveyed to learners who were not "inside" the language, to whom it appeared incomprehensible and quaint.

4. They had to take *the environment* into consideration, to decide whether teaching this "language" was worthwhile given the situation of contemporary Jews, what the chances of success might be, and what other contents would have to be sacrificed to give the investment in such Talmud teaching a chance of success.

Not surprisingly, therefore, the interchange during the lesson and in the subsequent discussion touched on these discrete issues. For example:

1. When the Talmud insists that the reading of the Book of Esther is equivalent to the recitation of the Hallel, does this mean that, in a situation in which

no "proper" (parchment) scroll is available, one should therefore recite the Hallel on Purim? This was obviously a *subject-matter* question, and it led "naturally" to "looking up" the answer in the *Mishnah Brura,* an authoritative code of Jewish legal practice. (The answer found therein was that in such a case one should indeed recite the Hallel on Purim.[2])

2. Instead of spending time comparing the status of Passover and Purim with regard to the recitation of the Hallel, shouldn't we, *the teachers,* invite the pupils to think through the meaning inherent in reciting psalms of praise? Would it not be more meaningful to discuss the significance of public readings of salvational epics (like the Book of Esther) and to compare them with the communal chanting of psalms as a form of public thanksgiving than to introduce pupils into legal discussions? What "happens" to a person saying the Hallel? How should one celebrate Purim? How much of the text under discussion should one know and teach in order to conduct that discussion within the framework of the Jewish tradition?

3. How can the talmudic text be simplified or clarified for teaching purposes so that *the uninitiated pupil* will understand and come to appreciate it? How can the "language" of rabbinic discourse be made clear to one who lives within a different "tradition of logic"?

4. What exactly is the pupil's benefit from such a study unit, however simplified? Doesn't the legal formalism of the material relate to *a world, a community,* that is aeons removed from that of the Jewish child? Can the material, however presented, lead to questions of concern to him or her? For not only is the "language" incomprehensible to the child but also, in most cases, neither the child nor his or her parents *ever* recite the Hallel, even on Passover, which, in the talmudic discussion, is *assumed.*

With regard to each of the issues raised, there were, of course, different points of view, which appeared to be anchored in two discrete sensibilities and orientations.

For some in our group, the subject matter—the text—was seen as constituting the spiritual reality being encountered. They indicated, by intonation and idiom as well as by argument, that Judaism should be seen as a language, a method, a "sea" that requires competent navigation. Their approach was largely deontological, that is, geared to internal "ground rules" by which the system "functions"; the teacher, it was implied, could be evaluated largely in light of his or her ability to teach Judaism, i.e., *this* language as exemplified in *this* text. These members of our group accepted as *Jewishly self-understood* that the recitation or non-recitation of the Hallel on Purim was deduced from a legal context and that theological significance was intrinsically located in that context. Their sensibility was one of loyalty, of taking the tradition as a measure of their understanding, of appreciation for the perennial and a satisfaction at knowing how to participate in it.

On the other hand, there were those in our group who raised questions that indicated their concern with the pupil and the environment as valuative issues for the teacher. They asked about the relevance and significance of the Talmud; they tended to see the talmudic text and its mode of reasoning as a historical datum. They maintained that although the Talmud admittedly was a central expression of Judaism in its historical development, and thus of the Jews' dialogue with God through practice and faith, it must be evaluated anew in new situations. These group members gave expression to their orientation by intonations of perplexity. They countered the (self-conscious) competence of their text-oriented colleagues with (overly) patient reasonableness. They intimated that competence may be mis-channeled and that scholarship may be religiously flawed when it becomes a substitute for religious sensitivity.

To a participant observer, it seems clear that the two viewpoints disclosed in the discussion were what we have called explicit and implicit orientations. And each is characterized by a predilection for certain emphases in the educational situation (subject matter and teacher competence versus environments and significance-perceived-by-pupils) and by characteristic strengths and weaknesses.

The implicitly religious members of our curriculum group seemed to take more seriously the society in which they wished to educate; they appeared more adequately to speak its language and to reflect its spiritual concerns. Although they were more traditionally "religious" than most in their society, even their religious sensibility could be said to be negotiated by methods and disciplines that explain and seek to deal non-judgmentally with diverse outlooks. On the other hand, they tended to speak the "language of tradition" less competently than their explicit-minded colleagues and to value classic competence less. They had not learned the "language" to such a great degree, perhaps because they assigned less importance to it; they gave priority to communicability and relevance.

Conversely, the explicitly religious members of the group appeared to be more "inside" the tradition, to be more comfortable with it and, thus, more alive to its inherent and specific spiritual import and potentialities. But their position was no less paradoxical than that of the implicit-minded colleagues who accepted their (secularized) society and belonged to it, yet were "more religious" than the majority of its members. For the explicit religionists in the group also were modern and shared with their implicit colleagues the knowledge and consciousness of modernity. Thus, their relationship to the normative corpus was clearly more self-conscious than that of simple "religious" Jews; they were *traditionalists* rather than *traditional*. Therefore, they were not identical with most of the normative thinkers with whom they (perhaps even enthusiastically) agreed. Indeed, they often defended normative thinkers for what might be called "the wrong reasons." This is a strength, for they understood the nature of the society that their community would have liked to reshape in the image of its normative tradition. But it is also a weakness, for "their" community did not seem to really need them, and, indeed, may have misunderstood or even distrusted them.

In any case, the crisis of modernity for the religious tradition is diversely reflected in the two orientations. The implicit group is close enough to the larger (secular) public to be comprehensible but is unclear or ambivalent about its specifically Jewish religious message. The explicit group has an unambiguous Word to convey and bears a distinctive tradition but faces severe difficulties in communicating the contents it wishes to transmit. Moreover, this group is more likely to describe and defend the normative community than actually to embody its sensibilities unreflectively.

As a result, the theological function of each of the two orientations is likely to be different as well. The implicit theologian represents what the religious-minded person may possibly experience "religiously" within the modern world and gives this experience a language; the explicit theologian describes the normative community of believers phenomenologically and defends its way of life as an existential option *even* in the modern world.

Because of this, the "movement" from the thinker to the textbook can be expected to differ in the two cases. The implicit theologian, turning to education, suggests a path for those who have lost, if not their way, at least their signposts; the explicit theological educational thinker etches a landscape, sometimes a new one, around those walking an old and trodden path that seems—to most modernists—not to lead anywhere.

In this chapter, we shall attempt to illustrate how explicit theologians suggest guidelines for religious education. They examine, through a "normative" text, their relationship to the educational community that is their existential "hinterland."

## EXPLICIT THEOLOGIANS OF EDUCATION

Isaiah Leibowitz is a prominent Israeli religious thinker whose theology exemplifies a radically explicit tendency and who has expressed himself on religious education.

In his essay "Education for [the Observance of] Mitzvot," Leibowitz applies to education the view of Jewish religion that he has developed in numerous writings, namely, the differentiation between religion "as a means to fulfill some spiritual or social or educational need" and religion "as an end in itself . . . not as an instrument for attaining or imparting values, but rather [as] a supreme and ultimate goal."[3] The first view Leibowitz rejects; in his opinion, it is based on a fundamentally non-normative approach to religion. Such instrumental religiosity will always, and quite naturally, be adapted to one's needs, desires, and goals—in other words, to one's real (non-religious) values.

The opposite view constitutes what is, in his opinion, "Torah for its own sake"—and not for the sake of values extrinsic to it. The *end* of religion in this view is *to be religious* or, stated more theologically, "to serve God." The end of "real" religion is not even morality. Morality as such is a general human aspiration and social need; it can be deduced from reason and it is not a specifically Jewish religious concern. Moreover, it can be achieved without any specific religious commandment or commitment.[4]

Religion, states Leibowitz, presents itself first and foremost as an institutional framework that encompasses and imposes a life-style and public norms. These norms and social institutions, in Judaism, define the community of Israel. One of the central social institutions is the educational one. The task of education, in fact, is to initiate children into the institutional life of society.

Leibowitz admits that Jewish religion also has "a subjective side." Judaism is not exhausted by the institutional aspect; it is also "an emotional and existential experience." But historic Judaism, he maintains, is in essence "an institutionalized religion which includes religiosity and emotion." What is crucial in the relationship between the two is that "the latter [what we call 'implicit'] characteristics flow from the institutions; the institutions are not based on emotional experiences."

The question of religious life and education thus is presented as offering two alternative responses: Either one attempts to inculcate a certain religious attitude "by spiritual means and influence" or one educates toward a specific life-style and to specific institutions that enhance the ability of the individual to achieve spiritual growth. Leibowitz's answer is unambiguous. Since the individual's spirituality must be kept "free" (that is, the responsibility for choosing religious life "for its own sake" is the individual's), and since observing Judaism for the sake of values not derived from the *mitzvot* is not a genuine service of God but of human (secular) ideals, the educational program must be to teach the observance of the commandments. Religious education is required, therefore, to cultivate the religious Jew who is, first of all, one who observes the commandments.

If we are speaking [here] not of ambiguous "religiosity," but of the Jewish religion, we cannot evade the fact that the meaning of the original historical Hebrew concept of religiousness is observance of *mitzvot*. . . . There is no significance in religion in isolation from the traditional-historical reality of the Jewish people, and any religion which does not flow from this reality but rather is superimposed on it for the satisfaction of its members' needs—is not a Jewish religious phenomenon but is rather a general human psychological phenomenon.[5]

True, the goal of education is not to be equated with the existential goal of human religious life. This ultimate goal is personal and subjective and is expressed in the term "love of God." But education as a societal institution does not legitimately concern itself with this pinnacle of human self-realization. Only the normative commandments and their inculcation are entrusted to society. Only through the normative commandments may one reach the goal of religion, for the "love of God," which is a personal and "subjective" achievement, is possible only for the person who has been properly educated—to observance.

Religious education is only the imposition of the yoke of the *mitzvot,* even though it is obvious that study and observance of the *mitzvot* do not exhaust the [ends of] the Torah. In the Torah itself, though it is in its entirety an end in itself—there are elements which are means and others which are ends. . . . The essence of religion is located in the commandment: "Thou shalt love the Lord thy God." Nevertheless it is not possible for religious education to convey more than the tools . . . of religion—the practical commandments—and no education in the world has the power to give man more than the training to achieve the end [of religion]. Everything beyond that—or above that—is not within the realm of educational influence but is given over to the personal and inner decision and determination of the individual—after he has received his educational preparation for the task. The religious values cannot be taught, they can only be acquired. Education is no more than a method, and no more can be bestowed [through education] than the methodological tools.[6]

Leibowitz thus proposes a consistent deontological approach to religion and religious education.[7] Jewish religion as a public phenomenon is defined and given its substance by halakhah; anything else is not properly termed Judaism. Halakhah is normative because those who "play the game" of Judaism by its rules accept the authority of the talmudic Sages who established its historic normative patterns. A religious Jew is one who commits himself or herself to serve God through the pattern of this Judaism and within the historic community that is loyal to it. The commandments are not merely one way to be moral; they are *the* way (at least for Jews) to be *religious*. Religion aims to bring people to "the love of God"; this is the only end, to which the commandments are the exclusive means.

Religious education must therefore be thoroughly (what we have termed) explicit. Children must be initiated into the commandments (i.e., the religious life of the community), and these commandments should not be legitimated on non-religious grounds. Furthermore, teachers should speak of values only within the context of a religious intention; in other words, they should inculcate the value of dutiful and competent observance. Indeed, educating for faith outside this specific religious intention might even be considered indoctrination, for it stifles the "free spirit" of the pupil. It is the Torah, through its norms, that "teaches values" rather than teachers. Educators have the task of transmitting that part of the Torah that will allow individuals to develop themselves in the personal enterprise that is religious self-realization, "love of God." What the Torah teaches, according to Leibowitz, is that people must be free of needs and impulses in defining themselves; the acceptance of the yoke of the *mitzvot* is an expression of freedom, making possible the development of inner religiosity in the sense of the full humanity of the person who is distinct from the beasts in that he or she "stands before God," and *only* in that sense.[8]

A similar orientation is found in the writings of Isaac Breuer, who is also a consistent explicit religious thinker:

Every religion desires to educate. But the oneness, the integrity with God, which causes the free, moral deed to bubble up out of the source of inner conviction is not the *beginning* but the *goal* of education.[9]

Religion, states Breuer, requires "the unconstrained conviction of the personality"; yet this conviction is only "the crowning conclusion" of the educational process. If "religion" is taught by appealing to the pupils' subjectivity and by soliciting their conviction, it "becomes the support of the weak" and "burdens the strong, who might like to adhere to it, with the grave torture of conscience which makes them . . . hypocrites or constrains them to break with religion and prematurely stand on their own feet."

For Breuer, religion requires absolute conviction, but this cannot be taught, only acquired. With what, then, does religious education deal? If Judaism cannot be taught, what is taught in the Jewish school? Breuer resolves the problem by defining Judaism not as religion, but as law. Education teaches allegiance to the law of the nation. For, "It [Judaism] is the law which the Jewish nation . . . received from God's hands at Mount Sinai and ordains to its members.

The primary addressee of the revelation is not the individual but the nation. . . . ''

The revelation binds individuals because they are loyal members of the nation, *not* because each individual has had a religious experience. ''If it were delivered to individuals, how could it bind successive generations? Could not these . . . be justified in demanding revelation for themselves also?'' Therefore, one who is a loyal son or daughter of the nation observes the law as a national duty. The nation does not demand religious conviction. Yet the law of the nation is the way for the individual to achieve religiosity: ''While for the nation an end in itself, the divine law is for the Jewish individual *means to his education.*''

One observes the law because one has been taught that the commandments are the substance of the national life of Israel. However,

On the path of obedience of deed towards the Jewish national will, the Jew wrests for himself his religion, his God. The nation is mediator between him and God. The heteronomy of the Jewish national will leads to the autonomy of the free Jewish personality through the law to freedom in the law.

One obeys the law because that is what ''being a Jew'' demands and means. But the national requirement (of observance) is known to educate the individual toward personal conviction, which can be achieved only within the nation.

A comprehensive theological approach that is based on explicitly religious assumptions is that of Rabbi Joseph B. Soloveitchik. Soloveitchik, in his essays, has developed typologies that culminate in ideal figures, most prominently ''halakhic man'' and ''the lonely man of faith.''[10] In each case, the ideal is a creative and spiritual person who embodies ''knowledge'' and ''majesty'' on the one hand and ''religion'' and ''covenantal commitment'' on the other. The individual in question therefore understands his world and ''orders'' it but also seeks self-understanding, significance, and salvation. The whole person, the model of spiritual integration, is halakhic and faithful; he is one for whom such ''implicit'' characteristics as cognitive curiosity, philosophical understanding, and ethical striving and system building are subjugated to the demands of the divinely ordained covenant. These demands, represented by halakhah, seek to shape all reality; the halakhic norm that distinguishes the self-understanding of the covenantal community imposes itself on the ''majestic'' community, thereby to integrate the human world and to place the secular (knowledge) and the sacred (normative commitment) into a proper, divinely designed relationship.

The Halakhah sees in the ethico-moral norm (the revealed law) a uniting force. The norm which originates in the covenantal community addresses itself almost exclusively to the majestic community where its realization takes place. . . . The norm, in the opinion of the Halakhah, is the tentacle by which the covenant, like the ivy, attaches itself to and spreads over the world of majesty.[11]

But the imposed law does not merely demand commitment and "surrender"; at a higher stage, after people have accepted its norms and made their home within the Torah, it invites them to creativity. Those who have accepted the "holiness of place"; that is, those who have located themselves within the confines of the Torah and submitted to it as the "situation" demanding absolute commitment, are enabled—or invited—to transform halakhah from competence-commitment to self-knowledge–creativity. Through such self-knowledge, covenantal man too discovers that he is created not only from dust but also in the image of God, and that he may understand majestically not only nature but also the instrument of covenant, the Torah itself. He may become a prophetic personality whose halakhic vision and implementation are themselves God's Torah.[12]

Such self-making through the Torah is vouchsafed only to those who have previously surrendered completely to the Torah and its norms, who have sat at the feet of scholars and have reverently sought to understand their teachings. Thus, the knowledge of what is required by the covenant that demands control over human creativity ("majesty") is a requisite for self-knowledge. Halakhah and the norms that it imposes must be accepted before individuals can be whole and achieve their spiritual potential. As for the world of majesty, of the individual's own achievement as a cultural and creative being, it is spiritually neutral in isolation from the (revealed) norm; it is *good* when subjugated to the norm, and it becomes *demonic* when it insists upon shaping religion according to its own needs, standards, and understanding.[13]

In terms of Lamm's models of instruction, referred to in a previous chapter—*imitation, molding,* and *development*[14]—we seem to have, in explicit theologies of education, an unambiguous *imitation model:* Educated Jews are those who observe the *mitzvot;* that is, they do what their elders do. As for the teacher, he or she is an agent of society, charged with the task of inculcating patterns of normative behavior. Likewise, goals of instruction are uniform (for everyone must learn to observe the *mitzvot*) and extrinsic to the interests of the individual child.

Leibowitz, Breuer, and Soloveitchik might argue that the pattern of explicit Jewish education they propose is imitative only because Judaism considers the norms that must be learned requisite for individual development. Although

Lamm defines the development model as one that aims for freedom not only from specific acts but also from dictated principles, it could be argued that explicit religious education combines *imitation* and *development*. For, in its rigorously systematic form, explicit religious theology also tends to see principles as individual—that is, as a reflective mode that expresses the individual's love of God. This theology is predicated on the law because it is viewed as the only way to achieve individual development (knowledge and love of God) as "seen" by those who attained the highest such knowledge and love, the prophetic personalities, for whom Moses is "model" and mentor.

In other words, we may say that an explicit educational approach is designed to teach pupils to trust in the religiously structured and disciplined society. For this society, as a covenant community, furnishes the instruments with which the individual can achieve self-development. Moreover, these instruments (norms) will be maintained by the person who has reached the heights of self-development because he or she has experienced this way as true. And from the heights of "knowledge of God" the developed (self-)educated person will bear responsibility not only for maintaining but also for interpreting the norms, to ensure that they remain accessible and speak adequately to a given social and historical situation. The developed personality will be both "bearer of tradition" and qualified to offer, on the basis of the tradition itself, new understandings of it. This person will be qualified not only because he or she has achieved individual knowledge of God but also because this knowledge derives from obedience. The individual indeed respects his or her own insights but also has reverence for the covenantal community and its sages that made these insights possible. The historical and societal framework within which he or she achieved this spirituality is never forgotten. Indeed, the developed personality trusts the framework, even in the educational enterprise, more than his or her appropriation of it.[15]

We may now summarize the salient features of systematic explicit theology as it seeks to prescribe guidelines for religious Jewish education:

1. Judaism connotes a specific institutional entity that imposes norms on those who may legitimately be considered members of a historically continuous Jewish people.

2. The norms and normative frameworks of Judaism are transmitted from generation to generation by Jewish society, but they originate with God, Who communicated them to prophetic personalities. Judaism is the way that God has provided for serving Him, for being close to Him, for achieving salvation. The Jewish tradition articulates that belief and transmits its content. (What constitutes such closeness and salvation for non-Jews appears to be adherence to the moral norms of the Torah.[16])

3. The achievement of (religious) salvation is the reward for keeping faith with the historical religion of Judaism. It is possible for people (Jews and non-Jews) to reach great heights of aesthetic, philosophical, and even moral achievement without subservience to the Torah, but they cannot attain self-realization.[17] Religious self-realization that worships less than the transcendent God Who is known primarily through His commandments is idolatry.

4. Knowledge of God, which is the religious goal of obedience to His commandments, is an individual matter and is achieved in varying degrees. Not all persons are prophets or sages. Consequently, it is not the task of religious educators to teach subjective-existential faith (i.e., love of God), which is, perhaps, possible only for prophets. However, it is proper to teach trust in God when "trust" is within the context of the Torah and instills confidence in the way of the Torah. Teaching more than that is presumptuous; moreover, teachers who attempt it will invariably fail. Pupils with strong personalities will reject the "religious knowledge" of others, wishing to shape their own; those with weak personalities will not comprehend "religious knowledge" and will corrupt what they accept.

Thus, what is to be taught is merely the service of God and trust that this service is of supreme significance. This teaching is to be seen as the indispensable instrument through which the individual achieves religious self-realization. For it is assumed that where there is no imposed "service" there can be no committed knowledge and love.

5. The religious experience that is to be transmitted and "caught" in religious education is, therefore, faith in the Torah and in those who "explain it" and the trusting experience of being part of a faithful people. This faith-trust appears as a formal and social pattern of activities; specifically, studying the Torah and carrying out the *mitzvot*—and doing this competently—together with other Jews who are similarly commanded. Explicit religious education is, therefore, socialization into the holy community.

6. Since there is no higher value in society than "the service of God," Jewish religious education must explicate the Torah on its own terms. When children ask for rationales for observance and for trust in Torah, they should be given answers from within the Torah itself. If this is not satisfactory, they may be given examples of other "data" (in addition to the commandments) that are also difficult to fathom, that "we don't understand." This, the fundamental religious sentiment cultivated in the explicitly religious school, is loyalty to the commandments and to the community of covenant; theologically, the dominant motif is the element of depth and mystery in the divine will and in the individual's relationship to it. Existentially, the central experience

is one of being anchored in eternal truths within which people "dwell" and develop.

Explicit Jewish religiosity, as expounded by such thinkers as Leibowitz, Breuer, and Soloveitchik, is a theological confrontation with modernity. It is one highly consistent and sophisticated interpretation of Judaism that uses, in footnotes even if not always in texts, the categories and conceptions of modern thought and modern scholarship. In this theology, scientific inquiry is not denounced or rejected, but it is normatively neutralized and placed in subservience to revealed religious truth. Explicit religious doctrine also appears to accept the modern doctrine of autonomy, but this is referred to individual conviction rather than to practice. Theology is posited to be a variegated matter and, in principle, each person may choose how to reflect on the essentials of social imperative.[18] But the responsibility (of choice) is not crushing, for the loneliness of modern man is redeemed through the community of covenant. Explicit religious thought does not, ostensibly, fetter the mind, yet it demands the service of God as institutionally presented to the individual as a measure of covenantal belonging. It conveys legitimacy on the university, sanctions scientific research and technological development, and even supports an attitude of guarded openness toward the general (non-Jewish) society, when it has a moral philosophy compatible with revelation and even derived by it.

## AN EXPLICIT RELIGIOUS TEXT

How does "pure" explicit religion look in the classroom? Or, rather, what type of classroom do explicit theologians have in mind when they speak of education in the covenantal community?

Before we look briefly at a text that reflects an explicitly religious ideal, we must bear in mind two qualifying considerations: first, that the explicit theologians sympathetically describe and defend an existing community that is not dependent on their thought for its life; second, that all theological theory, by the time it is "translated" into religious curriculum, has inevitably undergone many transformations.

With regard to the first consideration, let us remember that, unlike implicit theologians, who wish to "coax" individuals into community and who thus are a type of prophet or sage for their disciples, explicit theologians speak, often to "outsiders," on behalf of existing prophets and sages *and teachers* who themselves have an ambivalent attitude toward the theologians' "philosophical translation" of their internal and existential truth.[19] So, we need not expect an "explicit" text or teacher to subscribe to all the theologian's philosophy as essential to proper education or intrinsic to the life-style and belief of the community—although it is usually considered good as far as it goes, i.e., as far as explicit religiosity can be explicated in modern conceptual terms.

With regard to the second point, we should note Fox's reminder that theological conceptions and guidelines will have been variously negotiated by the time they reach the classroom.[20] Curriculum writers will have made them understandable to teachers, teachers will have brought their biases to the material they have been charged to transmit, communities will have generously or meagerly funded the educational materials and teachers to make such transmission feasible. Moreover, the materials prepared on the alleged basis of religious educational thought have been graded by psychologists for emotional healthfulness and have been checked by rabbis for communal acceptability.

We now turn to an explicit textbook, *Torah as Our Guide* by Walter Orenstein and Hertz Frankel.[21] A perusal of the text yields the conclusion that the authors view the religious tradition as a normative one that is to be imposed on the learners. To them, such an imposition constitutes authentic education, allowing Jews to achieve the heights of significant life.

The book is primarily concerned with "customs and ceremonies, or traditions and observance," described as "one of the most vital subjects taught in Hebrew schools." (p. ix. All excerpts from *Torah as Our Guide* are reprinted by permission of the publisher, Hebrew Publishing Company, copyright © 1960. All rights reserved.) Yet the authors are well aware of the difficulties that face them: The environment created by society and parents is a problem, as are the children who are the products of such homes and such a society. And it is admitted that successful education means facing these problems and dealing with them. Thus, the observances that are assumed to constitute a "vital subject" are admittedly most difficult to teach because they are often "an object of controversy." There is controversy because many children "come from non-practicing homes, or from homes in which Jewish observances are practiced in varying degrees. Parents may often disagree with a school or teacher for having made their youngster aware that they are negligent in some of their religious duties" (*ibid.*).

Moreover, the authors realize that creating loyalty to the subject matter is going to create conflict between educated young Jews and their parents and that this is an educational problem. The solution they seek is accommodation on the part of the parents.

It is the duty of the parents to study and try to understand the important practices that the child has been taught in the school. They should encourage the child to observe these practices and try to make gradual changes in their own observances. Such an approach is necessary so as to minimize conflict in the child, and so that neither parent nor Hebrew school falls in the esteem of that child (*ibid.*).

However, this appeal, to assure its plausibility, is addressed only to those who define themselves as traditional:

> The handling of this delicate matter [Jewish observance] should prove to be acceptable to all schools of religious instruction, whether they be Orthodox, modern Orthodox, conservative or moderately conservative, as the treatise is developed along traditional lines, in the historic continuity to which all segments of the Jewish faith adhere (p. x).

This obviously does not include *all* schools of religious instruction.

The explicitness of the religious approach underlying *Torah as Our Guide* is exemplified by the section dealing with *chukim,* those laws in the Torah for which no explanation is given. Introducing brief discussions on such *chukim* as the laws of *shaatnez* (the prohibition of wearing a garment made of both wool and linen), tattooing, and shaving the corners of the beard, the text tells us:

> As you know from reading the chapter on the dietary laws, there are certain laws in the Torah that were not explained and, therefore, we do not know the reasons for them. We were told by G-D through Moses that such laws are to be obeyed even though we do not know why we must obey them. These laws go under the general classification of "Chukim" (pp. 41–42).

Here, the talmudic-rabbinic explanation of *chukim,* as cited by Rashi on Num. 19:2, is introduced. Obviously, however, some pupils may be expected to ask, "Why? Why did God tell us to observe laws that appear to have no reason, that don't seem to make sense?" Let us examine how the text "fields" this eventuality.

> "But, why should we obey laws when we don't know the reason for them?"
> How often does this question come up in class? Although it may be asked by only one member of the class, it is probably in the minds of most, just as surely as it is in the minds of most of you reading this chapter. . . .
> Have you ever asked yourself why we need reasons? Well, let us tell you. When Columbus said that the world was round nobody believed him. His theory had to be investigated and proved correct before it was accepted. After all, Columbus was only a human being; he could have been wrong.

It took a long time before the world accepted the theory that the world was round. But why do we look for reasons in the Torah? Is it to find out whether the laws in the Torah are right? To find out whether G-D's laws are justifiable? Surely we know that G-D is right in everything that He wills. Can we question the ways of G-D? Can we question any law He has given us in His Holy Torah? Surely we do not need reasons for that purpose (pp. 42–43).

Thus, the question has been placed in what the authors consider the proper context and perspective. Rather than being told that he or she is asking a *wrong* question, the child is being commended for asking a good question, which, however, does not apply to the Torah. The child is told that justification is proper only in science, since people are fallible. In science, explications of theory require justification so that we can judge whether the theory is correct and deserving of explication. This is not so in the case of Torah; therefore, all justification questions ("Why should this elicit our consent and commitment?") should be reformulated as explication questions ("Why did God command it? What can we fathom of the mystery?") Thus:

There is another purpose, however, in looking for reasons, which is applicable to our Torah. We look for reasons so that we can understand things.

It will be noted that this applies both to science and to the Torah, albeit in somewhat different ways, since both nature and Judaism come from God.

In classrooms all over the world, subjects like science, mathematics, geography, psychology and astronomy are studied to learn the laws of G-D in nature. We are always trying to learn more and more about the world we live in by understanding the reasons for things. When our rabbis studied the Torah, they found many deep meanings to the laws given by G-D. They taught these meanings to their students and studied them among themselves. Logical reasons were even given for some of the "Chukim." To this day, rabbis are finding new ideas in the Torah. This is the beauty of Torah. We never know everything about it. The more we study it, the more we learn about it (pp. 42–43).

Here, the self-understood truth of the Torah is explained by an analogy to nature, which is also a self-understood datum. Scientific inquiry into nature is then made analogous to rabbinical study of the Torah. The "ideas" about the Torah are thus similar to scientific theories. However, the Torah is different because of its unconditional truth, because of its absolute value and depth.

So you see, we don't have to know the reason for a certain law in order to obey it. We obey these laws because they are given to us by G-D. Since He gave them to us, we know that they are right. Who knows, perhaps the "Chukim" were purposely given without reasons, just to test our faith in G-D (p. 43).

The inherent philosophy is that Jews obey God through the Torah. *Taamai hamitzvot,* rationales for the commandments, are seen not as justifications for their observance but as a feature of the commandments themselves, as their intellectual component. Thus, we are told, a part of the intellectual aspect of religious life may be a consciousness of the fact that one cannot understand everything. In this sense, the *chukim* are a cornerstone of explicit religious sensibility.

An analysis of this textbook yields the following principles and ideals:

1. A good Jew is a religious one who knows the laws of the Torah and observes them, even though the non-religious world does not always appreciate them. One must therefore learn these laws and remain faithful to them under all circumstances.

2. The commandments of the Torah are the way in which God teaches the truths that good people live by. The relationship between the specific commandment and a moral idea is not always clear to those who are not observant, but if the reason for the commandment is explained to the non-religious Jew, he or she will often "see the light." For example, those who do not say blessings before eating can be seen to be no different from people who eat at a restaurant and then refuse to pay their bill (p. 6). A particular *taam* (reason) is viewed as "what the Torah wishes to teach us," i.e., it is intrinsic to the commandment.

3. The religious life prescribed by the Torah is the key to appreciation of the mystery and depth of our experience: with God (in prayer), with our fellow human beings, with nature. The world is truly in God's hands, in ways we cannot fathom (though as we grow in wisdom, we can hope to understand more!) but that are intimately related to the observance of the *mitzvot.* Thus, a Polish statesman stops a pogrom, realizing that the accusation that Jews drink blood must be false—since he once saw a pious Jewish woman throw away precious eggs rather than cook eggs with blood spots in them (pp. 32–33). The person who stubbornly observes the Sabbath despite the demand of a Gentile governor that he sell him goods discovers that the governor was just trying to prove the Jew's piety to some skeptical guests (pp. 215–218). And miraculous deeds are done for those who deserve them, to reward their trust in God and

to strengthen it. (Thus, for example [pp. 89–91], Abraham "joins" a minyan on Yom Kippur in Hebron when "the tenth man" has suddenly died.)

4. For explicit theologians, history may be neutralized to give eternal religious truths their meta-historical due. In explicit education, historical inquiry and consciousness are suspected of undermining Judaism's normative character. There is therefore no attempt to place any feature of Judaism within a significant historical context. Judaism in its entirety is eternal; it is simply given expression in diverse texts (e.g., Bible, Midrash, Talmud) and reflected through the prism of various saintly personalities.

Thus, when a historical development must be alluded to, it is rendered almost parenthetical. For example, in the lesson on the synagogue, the child is instructed that "when the Temple in Jerusalem was destroyed and the Jews were exiled to Babylonia, the new type of house of worship, the synagogue, increased in importance" (p. 83). Moses, in surveying the camp of Israel before the revelation at Mount Sinai, convinces the merchants to rejoice together with the scholars at the coming event. To their complaint that they will have no time to study and thus are deprived of a share in the Torah, Moses replies that they do have a share in it.

> It will be up to you to support the Yeshivoth and Talmud Torahs where the Torah will be studied. . . . Moreover, after you finish your day's work or business, you are going to join some Torah circle in the evening, you are going to attend the services at the "Shul" daily and Sabbath and "Yom Tov," you are going to follow the teachings . . . just the same as the others (p. 180).

5. It is assumed that older people, especially teachers, know what is good for children. Though they teach the tradition in a kindly manner, they will resort even to physical punishment in order to save the noble character of a child who might otherwise come to spiritual harm (pp. 45–48).

6. It is clear to the writers that the world of the pupil does not necessarily reflect normative Judaism. This normative Judaism is discussed in terms of what "we do" but it is admitted that this is not always what "you" are doing. Thus, in the discussion on the commandment of tefillin as it appears in the Torah, we are told that "it is found in a paragraph that we recite three times a day; a paragraph you have recited many times in Hebrew School" (p. 11). Then, in the next paragraph, the writer continues: "Surely, you have recited this paragraph [of the *Shema*] more than once, perhaps even in its English version" (p. 12). The norms are presented pleasantly, with understanding for the circumstances of the child and with patience. But they are not altered. The normative reference group, "we," the writers, teachers, and our community, represent Judaism.

7. The attitude of the text toward non-Jews is tolerant, sometimes appreciative, yet somehow remote. The non-Jewish world is the "frame" in which Jews carry out their religion. Non-Jewish religion is not alluded to, and the morality of non-Jews is what they have learned from the Bible, the Jewish "contribution to mankind" (p. 187). For the explicitly religious demands made on Gentiles by the Torah is a moral one; this is what the Bible "teaches" mankind.

On the other hand, non-religious Jews are delinquent, though they are not necessarily to blame. The religious Jew must make them understand the truth. (It is not accidental that the State of Israel is mentioned only once, and in a philanthropic context.) The pluralism that is legitimate *vis-à-vis* non-Jews does not encompass non-religious Jews. (Explicitly religious Jews who wish to sanction Zionism must proceed from other theological premises than those of the writers of this textbook; for example, the dialectical one of Gush Emunim.)

8. General culture is congenial with Jewish religious life, but it is valuatively neutral; the character of the Jewish boy or girl is legitimately shaped by the Torah alone. For example, although Joe, one of the children in the book, is a yeshiva student, he plays football with all the boys. Yet he never plays on the Sabbath (Shabbos), and he always keeps his head covered (pp. 4–7). The Gentile environment sometimes invites children to faulty values, but the Torah "way" is obviously the only source of true values. For example, a Jewish girl who feels that the Torah discriminates against women ("Many girls feel that all the Jewish laws are for the men . . . ") should simply attempt to understand Judaism more profoundly.

In Judaism everyone has his or her job. Would you say that a woman is inferior because she doesn't go out and earn a living? Of course not! Her job is taking care of the house and raising the family. It is certainly as important as earning the money, perhaps even more so (p. 95).

Here, even an aspect of general culture that has been adopted by most traditional women is presented as dubious in terms of Torah norms.

The textbook we have reviewed is an interesting and thoughtful one, which bears testimony to a very pristine explicit religiosity and to a lucid normative philosophy of education. It transmits an unambiguous "master story," but it is also sensitive to the surroundings. It makes a serious effort to translate explicit norms into education in a less-than-congenial environment without surrendering or diluting them in the process. However, the extremely normative and explicit approach it represents is clearly fraught with great difficulties, not merely in social and educational senses but also in religious ones.

## SEVERAL PROBLEMS WITH EXPLICIT THEOLOGY OF EDUCATION IN EDUCATIONAL PRACTICE

In our brief discussion we have noted how several explicit Jewish theologians "make room" for implicit features of religiosity. But the venture of educational translation of even sophisticated explicit theology exposes theoretical and practical problems that are not apparent or visible in the normative theology itself. We shall mention several examples, suggested by our discussion of the textbook *Torah as Our Guide*.

1. The assumption that children must be taught loyalty and trust before they can understand, that they must be socialized completely before they can express their individuality in the only area that is really important (religion) seems to imply that children must be indoctrinated before they can be educated (by themselves). In practice, when children express their individuality by asking "justifying questions" about Judaism ("Why is it worthy of my allegiance?"), these questions are to be "fielded" as explicatory ones ("What did God mean when he commanded us that . . . ?"). This can be legitimated by the claim that the fact of human psychological and spiritual development is that "habit precedes reason" and that what would be considered indoctrination at a more advanced age is really, for young children, the education suitable for them.[22] And yet, if individuality cannot be taught but only the norms of the religious community, must the educator do nothing to assure that individuals will eventually achieve individuality? On the other hand, if children are to be allowed to ask justifying questions in school, to prepare them for ultimately realizing their individuality, how can their continued loyalty and religiosity be assured, especially in their secular surroundings that constantly tempt them with "false" beliefs?

2. Although it may be philosophically true that respect for children in explicit education means not "forcing values on them," how can the commandments and Judaism be taught without a demonstration that they are valuable? One solution is to teach the "philosophy" of the *mitzvot* as intrinsic to them, but isn't this "teaching values"? In that case, isn't the "freedom of the mind" recommended by explicit theology of education merely a sanction for extraordinary individuals to develop their own theological nuances whereas most people are expected to merely learn the requisite dogmas of Judaism, attractively called "philosophy of Judaism"?

3. Teaching "what the Torah tells us" about the meaning of the *mitzvot* through rabbinic interpretation is clearly predicated upon the assumption of the fundamental a-historicity of Judaism. How should this be "integrated" with what the child learns in general studies? After all, if these subjects are consid-

ered legitmate (though distinct from the world of values) and graduates of the explicitly religious school may without compunction study at universities, must general subjects not be studied in accordance with their own methodologies? And, certainly in the social sciences, are these methodologies not imbued with historical consciousness? Or should social sciences and humanities in fact be discouraged to the advantage of such studies as computer science, mathematics, and natural science, which can be presented in their technological (i.e., a-historical) aspects?

If, however, the legitimacy of all "secular subjects" is taken seriously, can one expect most teachers to develop the theological sophistication that permits them competently and comfortably to distinguish between the world of Torah and the world of general culture? What would be required, in terms of teacher training and curriculum construction, to make even the sophisticated teacher succeed with this approach? Paradoxically, it appears that a serious approach to general studies in the explicitly religious school requires teacher training that has a philosophical orientation!

4. If "autonomy" means that the mind is left free but the will must be educated to full participation in what is religiously normative (i.e., the Torah), does this mean that all impulses that endanger exclusive loyalty to the normative community are incompatible with religious values? If so, doesn't this imply not only compartmentalization *vis-à-vis* secular subjects but also the inability to deal with the issues raised by them in an appropriately valuative manner? (Such valuative questions would include: How does a computer culture threaten privacy in a free society? Are some forms of nuclear physics morally suspect?)

Likewise, is any pluralistic attitude and empathy for differing views among Jews ruled out if these do not belong to the normative community? Is it possible, within explicit religious educational frameworks, to foster religious sympathy with Zionism?

5. In short, does the explicitly religious approach require that, in the practical educational enterprise, one choose between autonomy and loyalty, between Judaism and culture, and between community and individuality, leaving the dialectical tensions and conceptual integrations to the philosophers?

These questions necessarily arise when explicit theology is moved into the classroom. The explicit educator finds that the normative philosophy is difficult to apply; it is not "practical." Not all children are equally talented; not all teachers can be expected to understand the philosophy and carry it out; the explicit community is uncomfortable with the sophisticated philosophy that "explains" its life in the contemporary marketplace of ideas and distrusts it.

Thus, in the explicitly religious classroom, texts such as *Torah as Our Guide* are likely to appear more congenial to educational practitioners than anything written or proposed by an explicit-minded theologian such as Soloveitchik.

The resulting perplexity is one that the theologian of implicit religious education is pleased to address. Indeed, the implicit theologian believes that his or her approach resolves the problem of modern religious education. To an implicit thinker, the perplexity betrays a conception of religion that is all text and no context, all tradition and no relevance.

We shall now examine such implicit theology of education and look at a representative unit of religious study.

# 8  Encounter and Deliberation: Implicit Educational Theology

## CONTEMPORARY JEWISH THOUGHT: THE IMPLICIT MOOD

Explicit religious educators have a normative philosophy of religious education (although, in the contemporary world, this philosophy is admittedly not simple to apply, and it will not speak to the non-committed). Nevertheless, explicit religious educators know what Judaism is and what it demands; if they find it impossible to convey the experience and the substance of real Judaism adequately to the community-at-large, they are comforted in the fact that a saving remnant of "real Jews" stand behind them and give Judaism a concrete presence. The crisis of religious education is one of Jews who have "moved away" from religion, who do not say the *Shema* three times a day as "we do." The recommended strategy is entrenchment, religious segregation, and normative visibility; what is required is strengthening the "dimensions of religious commitment." There must be more knowledge, devoted practice, firm belief, and normatively guided religious experience.

Martin Buber, who has already been cited as the most far-reaching implicit Jewish thinker of this century, paraphrases the explicit approach succinctly, but he does so only in order to demolish it:

You want true community—but where else can you hear its law if not in the word God spoke to His people? And how can you distinguish between what in God's word seems to you still fresh and applicable and what antiquated and spent? There is no other way: if you want to be Jews and to realize Judaism, you must return to pious submission to God and His law. [Reprinted by permission of Schocken Books Inc. from *On Judaism* by Martin Buber. Copyright © 1967 by Schocken Books Inc.][1]

Buber reacts to this explicitly religious approach with passion and scorn:

> . . . we would not want to exchange our giddy insecurity and our untrammeled poverty for your confidence and your riches. For to you God is the one who created once, and then no more; but to us He is the One of whom people profess that He 'renews the work of creation every day. . . . ' To you God is Being who revealed Himself once and never again. But to us, he speaks out of the burning bush of the present, and out of the Urim and Tummim of our innermost hearts.
>
> We honor the law, the armor of our peoplehood that was forged by venerable forces. . . . But we shall resist those who, invoking the already existing law, want to keep us from receiving new weapons from the hands of the living God. But we can tolerate nothing that comes between us and the realization of God. [Reprinted by permission of Schocken Books Inc. from *On Judaism* by Martin Buber. Copyright © 1967 by Schocken Books Inc.][2]

Buber insists on an unequivocable distinction between (implicit) "religiosity" and (explicit) "religion." "Religiosity starts anew with every young person, shaken to his very core by the mystery; religion wants to force him into a system stabilized for all time."[3] Religion is identified with passivity, preservation, the "organizing principle"; religiosity is active, bespeaking renewal, creativity.

Buber's conception of religiosity and religious education is predicated on his belief that people find God wherever they encounter reality as "Thou," as the "place" wherein they are challenged—and confirmed—by the Absolute, Who meets them as Person. When people are "open" to such an encounter they will find God: He is present whenever and wherever "man lets Him in." Religious faith is not assent to doctrines but an orientation to life and to the presence of God in and "behind" all things and events. Religious education is not a form of taming and training young people who would, without it, remain wild and primitive. Rather, it is making them sensitive to the presence of the "unconditional" in the life of each person, indicating how it has been present in the life and memory of the historical community, thus enabling the young people to encounter their own selves within this community. Not all parts of the life and memory of this historical community are "close" to this "unconditional" or to the pupils, but the entire story and tradition relate a religious truth of struggle and dialogue.

That God is merciful is an abstract statement; to penetrate the religious truth that lies beyond it, we must not shrink from opening the Bible to one of its most awful passages, the one where God rejects Saul, His anointed . . . because he spared the life of Agag, the conquered king of the Amalekites. Let us not resist the shudder that seizes us, but let us follow where it leads as the soul of the people struggled for an understanding of God. We shall then come to that wonderous passage in the Talmud where . . . God rejoices in Goliath's soul and answers the angels who remind Him of David: 'It is incumbent upon Me to turn them into friends.' Here we see a religious truth. [Reprinted by permission of Schocken Books Inc. from *On Judaism* by Martin Buber. Copyright © 1967 by Schocken Books Inc.][4]

The widespread secular assumption that youth cannot be expected to be concerned with religion is, in Buber's opinion, based on mistaken, explicit conceptions of religion. Since youth ''is the time of total openness'' characterized by a ''quest for knowledge that knows no limits other than those set by its own experience,'' it is, in fact, the time of life when real (i.e., implicit) religion is inherent in spiritual experience. ''At some time or other, be it ever so fleeting or dim, every man is affected by the power of the unconditional. The time of life when this happens to all we call youth . . . what the total openness of youth signifies is that its mind is open not merely to all, but to the All.''[5]

Education begins with relationship; the educator selects from and ''gathers in the constructive forces in the world. He distinguishes, rejects and confirms in himself, in his self which is filled with the world.''[6] The educator is the representative of a community that is open to the world and turned to God. The Jewish religious educator will ''gather in'' the world through the prism of the historical community of Israel, but the beginning of wisdom is not loyalty to the community. First comes youthful spontaneity; ''reverence for the form'' is acquired only after ''the pupil . . . has ventured far out on the way to his achievement.''[7] Any other way leads to resignation or rebellion.

Samuel Hugo Bergman, a contemporary of Buber and like him a Zionist humanist, also insists that true religiosity cannot rely on ''the law.''

In a clash between written law and conscience, the highest authority is the man with a conscience. . . . It is for this reason that history admires those passionately moral heroes who rebelled against the law for the sake of the inner ethical demand.

Thus, the well-known Psalms verse (119:126) invoked in the Talmud to legitimate innovation is cited by Bergman in a manifestly ''implicit'' fashion: ''It is time for thee, Lord, to work; for they have made void your law.''[8]

For Bergman, the moral decision that is at the core of religious life ''is always a decision between a higher value and a lower value.'' The individual cannot be relieved of this responsibility. ''Whenever we are told that God commanded something which we consider immoral, we ought to answer: it is inconceivable that God commanded it.''[9] The danger in explicit faith, what

Bergman calls the "way . . . of obedience," lies in the fact that "it releases a person from personal responsibility." However, Bergman is also aware that "the second way of faith," the implicit one, may lead to an excessive confidence in people and their understanding. He demands, therefore, a synthesis, "an inner truth that is loyal to both oneself and to a higher revelation, and at the same time, is conscious of the limitations of man."[10] But this inner religious truth may not contradict the believer's moral or logical reason.

Bergman insists, therefore, on an "expansion" of Jewish ethics. He takes issue with the view that only the law (the halakhah) creates ethics and applauds Leon Roth for his essay in which "he showed all the difficulties of this one-sided position, by pointing out that the Halakhah itself is dependent on the moral development of a Jew—for 'That which is moral to one generation seems immoral to another.' "[11]

Here, as in Buber's writings, we have the consciousness of a tradition that is appropriated through struggle and reshaped by it. Implicitly religious individuals of Bergman's persuasion see the tradition as the product of an encounter with God, but they nevertheless start with their present situation and their contemporary insights. At the same time, they are anchored in the community to which they reach out. But the bridge between the two is not easily built or traversed.

Life is surely not easy. It is a difficult burden. And it is hard to know why God couldn't overcome Amalek without the help of Moses' lifted hands. And why did God need to try Abraham? These are the most disconcerting and arduous of questions for us, the generation of the Holocaust. Of course, the easiest systematic answer is that of heresy: there is no God and that's all there is to it. But if there were no God, there is no place for Israel in the world, because we are His 'witnesses,' as Isaiah said (43:10). Another answer, which is perhaps more suited to a modern Jew, is that man *grows* by the crises that he goes through, and our fathers may have been right when they said that a man should bless God for the evil that befalls him as well as the good. I don't know.

. . . Once, at a time of great personal trouble and desperation, I took up the *siddur* and opened it. I was alone in the room and I read aloud the thirtieth Psalm, and when I came to the last part, 'Thou hast turned for me my mourning into dancing; thou hast put off my sackcloth and girded me with gladness, . . . ' I was filled with the blessedness of the passage. It was not a 'religious mystic experience,' it was simply the emanation of power from the prayer of a great poet who had been in similar trouble and had been delivered from it.[12]

This is reminiscent of the two soldiers on their way to the Western Wall during the Six Day War cited previously (Chapter 6). In both cases the master story is that God is present and "girds with strength" those who meet Him in life, those who have the "faith" needed to recognize His always astonishing presence.

Implicitly oriented theology should not be viewed as inherently antagonistic to the patterns of explicit religion. Implicit theologians generally are cognizant of the community and wish to make their home within it, just as explicit religious thinkers, who insist on the primacy of norms and authority, hope that collectively binding commandments will lead toward individual saintliness. But implicitly oriented people think and feel from within a different universe of discourse from explicitly oriented thinkers. Yet, just as explicit educators are not necessarily Orthodox, so implicit ones are not always anti-nomian.

For example, the thought of Rabbi Abraham Isaac Kook, the first Chief Rabbi of modern *Eretz Yisrael,* was largely nourished by implicitly religious assumptions and experiences; yet he was a completely halakhic, Orthodox Jew. Kook insisted on the falsehood of all partial perceptions of reality; there is truth, he claimed, in all religious insight. Sinfulness is synonymous with lack of harmony and falsehood, with lack of comprehensiveness. Holiness, on the other hand, corresponds to a state of harmony between spirituality and concrete manifestations of life. In a startling comment, Kook decried "the concentration on a diet of study alone" in religious education, which "weakens the power of the nation." [13] Though the false fantasies and messiahs of Jewish history "confused the world and caused great harm,"

. . . amidst all the evil they caused, there was not lost the tiny element of good hidden in them. They exemplified a psychic renewal as opposed to the sole dependence on the one foundation, the study of texts, and indoctrination in the disciplined, practical performance of commandments. This served to remind the people of the healthy basis of the nation's earlier life, when the divine light had shone in her midst, and her prophets had seen divine visions. [14]

The contemporary national renewal, despite its regrettable manifestations of irreligion, constitutes a revitalization. Religious leadership cannot content itself with "the surface study of the Torah which is concerned directly with the practical aspects of life." What is needed are "mighty men of God [who] will embrace in their being all the general and particular forces needed for the nation's revival." Through the integration achieved by these "mighty men of God" between "all the forces of feeling and thought," the boundaries separating human souls will be broken down, and the resulting renaissance of the Jewish people will inspire the world. "Through the divine spirit pulsating in its being, [Israel] . . . will stir to life the spirit of all nations that have grown weary with the burden of life in its grossness that has become unbearably oppressive." The problem of Israel is its narrow spiritualization, centered in texts: that of the nations, material "grossness," the inability to perceive the divine in the prosaic world. Holiness will be restored to humanity when the former returns to material concreteness and the latter is "stirred to life by the spirit of Jewish life."[15]

Abraham Joshua Heschel, who has been cited in a previous chapter in an explicit religious context, has emphasized in both his theological and his educational writings the importance and primacy of the implicit element. He decries the tendency of (explicit) religion "to become an end in itself, to seclude the holy . . . as if the task were not to enoble human nature." Thus, religion "has often done more to canonize prejudices than to wrestle for truth; to petrify the sacred than to sanctify the secular." Heschel insists that

> . . . we must recover the situations which both precede and correspond to the theological formulations; we must recall the questions which religious doctrines are trying to answer, *the antecedents of religious commitment*, the presupposition of faith.[16]

The reason for religious crisis is that religion is taught and expressed as a series of answers to the ultimate questions without proper concern for the questions themselves. The answers are given by rote, but the questions have been forgotten.

In line with this differentiation between *answers* and *questions*, Heschel distinguishes between *theology* and *depth theology*. "The theme of theology is the content of believing; the theme of depth theology is the act of believing, its purpose being to explore the depth of faith, the substratum out of which belief arises." All religious issues, therefore, have two dimensions and can be looked at from the two perspectives, which we are calling explicit and implicit. In Heschel's words: Theology declares, depth theology evokes; theology demands believing and obedience, depth theology hopes for responding and appreciation.

> Theology deals with permanent facts; depth theology deals with moments.
> Dogma and ritual are permanent possessions of religion; moments come and go. Theology abstracts and generalizes. It subsists apart from all that goes on in the world. It preserves the legacy; it perpetuates tradition. Yet without the spontaneity of the person, response and inner identification, without the sympathy of understanding, the body of tradition crumbles between the fingers.
> Theology speaks for the people; depth theology speaks for the individual. . . .

. . . Theology is in the books; depth theology is in the hearts. The former is doctrine, the latter an event. Theologies divide us; depth theology unites us.[17]

The careful reader will note that Heschel believes theology without depth theology to be useless. Indeed, though "theology speaks for the people" it, rather than the depth theology of the individual, divides us. In other words, the basic questions are common to all people; specific religions constitute diverse answers. The "substratum out of which belief arises" is not only individual but also universal. Therefore, Jewish religious education must show the meaningfulness of Judaism's answers to the questions that arise in the soul, at great moments, in the lives of human beings. Judaism must be shown to evoke inner spirituality. Thus, halakhah is a response to the problem of the soul: "how to live nobly in an animal environment, how to persuade and train the tongue and senses to behave in agreement with the insights of the ages." Unfortunately, we often do not teach Judaism "as an answer to the questions of inner life," and this misrepresents and distorts it. "Judaism is *not* legalism; this is precisely what the opponents of Judaism claim. It is an answer to the ultimate problems of the individual and of society."[18]

Jewish education must not only teach children how to recite blessings but also evoke in them the wonder at creation that spurs a tradition to formulate blessings and prescribe their recitation. In a plea reminiscent of Buber, Heschel declares: "What we need more than anything else is not *textbooks* but *textpeople*."[19] What is required are people who have "gathered in" the tradition and know how to relate its answers to the questions that lie behind them. The teacher must evoke the question so that the answers of the Jewish tradition will fall into a spiritually meaningful context.

We may now summarize the significant features of implicit religious Jewish thought as articulated by theologians who represent its mood.

1. Judaism, as a framework for religious experience, embodies and connotes the historical encounter(s) between Jews and God. The experience of the Jewish people becomes "present" to the individual who turns to Jewish tradition, for it evokes ever-new encounters. Through struggle with the tradition one learns to respond to the religious requirement of the present moment: openness to the demands of the spirit in the midst of specific and concrete realities.

2. The norms of the Jewish tradition are generally not seen as binding *a priori*, although certain thinkers, especially in Hasidically oriented forms of Orthodoxy, may take norms for granted. More commonly, however, these norms are not primary in religious life but merely invite appropriation if they

are understood "still" to answer fundamental questions that Jews—as "human beings in sacred community"—ask. These questions, however, are particular instances of universal concerns. They deal with proper and profound relationships and understandings, with the realms of responsibility, love, appreciation, and wisdom. Thus, the foundations of religion are common to all sensitive persons; different religions give distinct, yet not unrelated, responses to the human quest. In a sense, a superior religion is one that is most demanding of total confrontation, most comprehensive and rich in cultural articulation of existential truths.

3. Since primary feeling and experience give rise to norms and dogma (rather than the other way around), one need not fear that young people have a natural aversion to religion. With regard to "true" (implicit) religion, the opposite is the case. Children "still" ask questions and are not embarrassed by their amazement. Their spontaneity and fearless questioning are the hallmarks of true religiosity.

4. It is the task of the teacher to assist the young person in discovering the world and God's presence in it. The teacher can do this only as a genuine religious personality, a "textperson" who "gathers in" the world through the prism of his or her experience and who bestows, through dialogue, the message that wonder and love are not *childish* but *faithful*.

5. The educated person does not automatically trust tradition, wise people, or texts. He or she is responsible for his or her religious life. Just as religious people of our past made decisions, so must each one of us. Thus, whereas the religious school should teach respect for the tradition, since it constitutes a record of the Jewish people's decision making, the adherence of the pupil to the tradition is never self-understood; it is dependent on the pupil's agreement that the tradition conveys significant answers to important questions.

6. The religious person "reaches out" to God in moments of solitude; his or her membership in the community is not only a source of enrichment but also at times appears to be a concession. This largely explains the personal and inner or subjective emphases of implicit religious education.

7. Finally, the assumptions of implicit religiosity are that the present situation must be taken seriously as the "place" of the individual's existential reality and that tradition must be brought before the bar of "this hour's" judgment. This implies that secular culture must be treated with the respect due to one's "real" environment. The implicit religious thinker is seldom indifferent to scientific study and analysis of religion that reflect experience as challenge and response and thus are germane to religious wisdom. Yet, although the culture of the world and the age must be addressed as part of a general openness, their specific message may be severely criticized. They may be judged to be

asking the wrong questions, explaining away amazement, or "drowning out" the presence of the Thou. Paradoxically, the implicit religious thinker, open to the secular world, may be a more severe critic of it than an explicit religious colleague. The latter, having "put that world in its place," is often content to meet it on a technological, seemingly non-valuative plane.

## AN IMPLICITLY ORIENTED TEACHING UNIT

An important and ambitious example of implicitly grounded religious Jewish education is *Genesis: The Teacher's Guide* (1966) and the revised edition, *Genesis: A New Teacher's Guide* (1979), produced by the Melton Center, Jewish Theological Seminary of America.[20] Although the didactic differences between the first and second editions are substantial, it appears that the more frontal and "down-to-earth" methodology of the revised *Guide* is not the result of philosophical change of heart but rather of pedagogical difficulties occasioned by the original "open-ended" deliberation approach. For this reason, we shall, in our present theological-philosophical discussion, refer to the two texts as a single unit. In fact, we shall more frequently refer to the original *Guide* for its more uninhibited articulation of the philosophical principles that underlie this curriculum project.

The writers of the *Guide* assume not only that the larger world in which pupils live is a valuative one for them—this is also grudgingly admitted by the explicitly religious writers of *Torah is Our Guide*—but also that it is, in many ways, valuable. The general world is seen and appreciated as one in which reasoning is fostered in learning and is intrinsic to it. It is recognized—and not dismissed out of hand—that in the general school the evolutionary nature of religious culture is assumed and that *there* one quite naturally engages in comparative study of "ancient myths." The self-image of that general culture is one of criticism and clarification; norms are arrived at through deliberation on alternative understandings and courses of action, not by dogmatic proclamation and automatic endorsement. The writers share this modern self-image, though, because they are religious Jews, not without criticism or qualification. They wish children to become religious, but they agree that if religion is to be considered "serious" by children (and adults) it must be shown to deal with "serious" questions, examined through sources deserving serious study and deliberation. Indeed, a valued religious tradition, including a Jewish one, may best be presented as an ongoing inquiry into moral and existential issues. In this way the Jewish tradition can be "discovered" as not only the culture of a historical community but also a cogent system of responses to human questions about the ultimate. For the Jewish child, it is hoped, this historical deliberation will be perceived as a worthy focus of profound study and of reasoned identification.

In introducing the first edition of the *Guide,* the editor states:

> . . . underlying the questions suggested for the teacher's use is a great respect for the students' capacity to think. It was often the case in the past that students felt that "learning Torah" involved a suppression of their reasoning power. This would happen at a time in their lives when their intellectual strengths and acquired skills were growing rapidly. In our day, it is also true that . . . an even greater demand is made on the students' critical ability than before. Religious studies which preclude inquiry or critical analysis suffer as a consequence. It is the premise of this book that our students must be challenged to apply themselves fully, with reason and feeling, to comprehending the text.[21]

Because religious studies should be conducted with awareness of what happens in general studies and in relationship to the valid truth claims being made in the general world, religious teaching must never transgress against accepted general canons of truth. Thus, the revised *Guide* urges the teacher "not to teach anything to your students that they will have to *unlearn* later, e.g., false information which will have to be discarded at a later date."[22]

In principle, this does not militate against teaching any religious truth, for conflicts between religion and science are based on mistaken views of religion (and science). Religion deals with the meaning of data as they are discovered in experience; it is a different way of looking at things from the scientific method. Therefore, scientific facts should not be either pushed aside as irrelevant or concealed as dangerous; they should, rather, provide the context within which meanings are sought and located. Thus, students as well as teachers are told that the unit uses the historical approach, which sets "the text back into its original cultural environment or milieu, by comparing it to the cultures which may have existed at the same time." An example of this approach: Pupils learn that Sarah's giving of her maid Hagar to Abraham as a concubine was within the tradition of the ancient Near East.[23] Similarly, the biblical Creation story is compared with the Babylonian narrative Enuma Elish and the Noah story with the epic of Gilgamesh. All stories, the biblical as well as the Babylonian, are described as myths; a myth is defined as an "extended metaphor." (The teacher has already been introduced to the concept of biblical and religious language as metaphorical language.[24])

The historical approach, which makes the learner sensitive to the diverse context in which religious insight arises, is also evident in the description of the Bible. The exposition strives for objectivity and holds norms and belief statements at a distance, though the writers gladly admit that their aim is to cultivate religious Jews who believe *in* certain religious ideas and ideals. Thus, we are told that the Bible is a collection of many books "which are considered holy by the people of Israel." The Jews took great pains to keep and preserve these books, for "they fervently believed that these books were the inspired words of God, a sacred literature."[25]

Since the Jewish tradition must be correlated with other serious realms of knowledge with which the pupils are assumed to be acquainted, the question of the Bible's "truth" is negotiated through (a) treating the Bible as great literature, which can be read and appreciated even if the characters depicted are not "real," and (b) considering the biblical truth to be a metaphorical one. The Bible expresses, in its own way, true ideas about God, people, and the world. Thus, we are told, "Whether or not creation as depicted in Genesis 1–2:4 is rooted in reality is not important. What is important are the ideas the Bible attempts to teach us by means of this story."[26]

How does the *Guide* suggest teaching a narrative that seems to be unambiguously explicit, one that teaches obedience and "unreasoning" commitment? Such a narrative is the Binding of Isaac. (It is not surprising that an explicit thinker such as Leibowitz considers this story to be the central symbol of Jewish faith.[27])

In approaching the Binding of Isaac, the revised *Guide* discusses the issue of "total faith."

Bascially you want to teach that probably *one should have blind faith only in God*. Now, this does not mean that one should have no commitments, but that whatever *other* commitments one has, the commitment to God has to take priority.[28]

However, total faith as exemplified in the Binding of Isaac is, as noted, an extremely explicit notion and thus presents an acute problem for the implicit religious educational orientation. Indeed, the writers themselves define "total faith" as it is portrayed in this story as "doing exactly what is demanded of one, disregarding one's own sense of morality and feelings of conscience." But this is immediately placed in a more implicit context by the comment that "Abraham had total faith in God because of his previous experience with Him." Then, in the course of the lesson, total faith is transformed into total commitment to one's conscience and moral judgment. Obedience to God is "translated" (and not without justification *vis-à-vis* the sources of Judaism) into moral behavior. And a further qualification is made:

Total commitment to any man or ideal may come into conflict with one's commitment to God. (Some people will substitute conscience or moral judgment for the word "God.")[29]

   As an example of how one's total commitment to God may come into conflict with other commitments, the class is presented with the dilemma of a medical doctor in Nazi Germany who is commanded to experiment upon Jews. The doctor has to decide whether his belief in God takes priority over his belief in Nazism. In the former case, he would know that "life had to be preserved [God's Law]," that "the Hippocratic Oath had to be followed," that "one's conscience had to be followed," and so forth.[30] Abraham's (explicitly) blind faith has been identified with (implicit) commitment to one's highest values. To "have blind faith only in God" means, in line with Bergman's teachings, to identify one's highest moral understanding with His will.

   In line with this approach, the *Guide* (1966) initiates pupils into sophisticated moral deliberation on issues that arise in the text of Genesis. The text is seen as posing questions about what is morally right—more specifically, what alternative course of action has moral priority in given perennial situations. The Bible is approached as a model that suggests how to assign such priorities. Thus, students learn to become sensitive to the questions underlying human existence; in Heschel's terms, they become religious through depth theology. They are aided in locating the questions "behind" the answers of the Bible; in this way, they are invited to adhere to Jewish theology, to accept the Jewish tradition's way of being religious. To illustrate: The story of Creation is understood as arousing and answering such questions as, "What is a human being's position in the world? To what extent may one exploit nature for one's own needs?" The *Guide* presents an ethical dilemma: On the one hand, human beings were created in God's image, and they are the pinnacle of Creation; on the other hand, as God's handiwork, all creatures possess sanctity. We are thus in a situation in which we may—indeed, must—exploit the world in order to survive; yet, at the same time, we may never lose our reverence for it. Pupils are asked to decide which moral alternative seems just to them on the basis of the biblical model and the tension expressed within it between "God's image" (control) and "God's creatures" (reverence). For example, the use of bird feathers for the decoration of hats is presumably indefensible because it violates most blatantly the sanctity of Creation, whereas the killing of seals by Eskimos to make clothing appears to be acceptable, since "if we were to regard everything in creation as sacred and inviolable, man would be unable to survive."[31]

The *Guide* sees in the tradition not only an ongoing inquiry into fundamental religious Jewish *ideas* (i.e., basic sacred answers of Jews to ultimate
questions) but also the translation of these ideas into social patterns of religious
life. In discussing the Sabbath, one of the few commandments that can be con-
textually dealt with in a study of Genesis, the Student's *Guide* tells us that
people are commanded to rest on the seventh day because, in the words of the
commandment, God rested on that day. However, this is problematic. "Surely
the commandment does not mean to teach that God became physically tired
from the work of Creation and therefore rested, as man does. Why then, does
the commandment use the word [He rested]? The Rabbis of long ago struggled
with this question and offered the following answer. . . . " This is followed
by a midrash that expresses the idea that, although God never tires, He wishes
people to rest and "to use the seven days of the Creation week as a model for
their own behavior. . . . "[32]
After explaining some of the ideas that can be deduced from this model,
the writers continue:

Jewish tradition developed many laws and rules of behavior for the Sabbath. The purpose of these laws was to remind the people of the meaning of
the Sabbath and to help them live according to its spirit. Their aim was to encourage the people to create a personal world of "holiness" for one day each
week.

These laws made the Sabbath a day of relaxation and pleasure. But the model
of Creation indicates that it should be not only that but also "a day in which
people could find satisfaction in that which already exists and not try to make
something new" and a day of study "especially of those things which might
help us to understand better how we should behave towards God and man."[33]
The *Guide* then elaborates on some of the laws and notes that "these laws
continue in our own day to guide the behavior of large numbers of Jews who
try to obey Jewish law and tradition." After the explanation of major Sabbath
laws, the *Guide* describes, with great warmth yet without preaching, a Jewish
home in which the laws and customs of Jewish tradition are observed.[34]

The *Guide*'s pattern of religious inquiry may be stated as follows:
1. The text of the Torah is analyzed to determine which religious ideas it
is expressing.
2. These ideas are seen as answers to fundamental questions; the analysis
helps us to understand these questions and to see the biblical ideas as a basic

way to respond to them. These answers, the Jewish religious tradition, have developed through a collective tradition of asking questions and experiencing a response that was believed to be God's will.

3. The Jewish tradition thus develops through a confrontation with past responses, in an awareness of the "presence" of the perennial questions and of the tradition of past answers.

4. The Rabbis believed themselves to be clarifying the basic ideas of the Bible; they also developed patterns of behavior that would guide people toward an appreciation and understanding of these ideas. The laws illustrate how the ideas can become "operative" in the lives of people. But the ideas are primary: They justify the laws, and they (the ideas) themselves are justified by the spiritual experience of the learners in grappling with basic issues.

Like the authors of *Torah as Our Guide,* the explicit religious text discussed in the previous chapter, the writers of the Genesis Teacher and Student *Guides* are aware of the secular environment in which Jewish religious education is conducted. *Torah as Our Guide,* it will be recalled, suggests that the pupil *may* have said the *Shema,* "even in English," which "we say" three times a day; similarly, *Genesis: The Student's Guide* tells pupils that "large numbers of Jews . . . try to obey Jewish law and tradition."

But the differences are clear. For the former, the observance of the law is loyalty to God's will, and *we* observe it. For the latter, the law is the result of a human struggle to understand God's will as it is intimated by existential encounters leading to a historical formulation of ideas that testify to and bear traces of divinity. This law illustrates how to live these ideas, how Jews have lived them; *Genesis: The Student's Guide* cannot bring itself to say that *we* observe them. The secular world in which the children live is, for the teacher using *Genesis: The Teacher's Guide,* existentially present and significant, in ways that would be suspect to the explicitly religious teacher using *Torah as Our Guide.*

Our analysis of *Genesis: The Teacher's [and Student's] Guide* yields the following implicit religious orientation and "message":

1. A good Jew is, to the greatest possible extent, a religious one. This means that Jews should ideally appropriate the experience of the Jewish people with God by struggling with what that experience means to them. This grappling with the experience of the Jewish people requires knowledge of tradition, the kind of spiritual awareness that makes the tradition potentially meaningful, and the modern sensibility and knowledge that provide a relevant context for Jewish (and non-Jewish) quests for meaning.

2. Religious sensitivity and commitment are not primarily a matter of doctrines or practical norms, although the religiously sensitive person may find a given doctrinal formulation congenial to his or her understanding of the Ultimate and may be expected to find beauty and significance in traditional patterns of religious practice. Furthermore, religious Jewish education will aid and encourage young Jews to link traditional conceptions and practices to their cultural-religious identity. These orientations and patterns, which are the heritage of the young Jew, are shown to be ways of giving his or her innate religiosity comprehensive expression. But these patterns are shown to be options of religious response rather than binding norms.

3. The central *problem* behind the *problematic situation* of irreligion and alienation from Jewish religious culture is in the failure of most "religious" and "irreligious" people to concern themselves with the questions behind the specific (doctrinal and practical) answers of tradition. If the questions will be brought back into consciousness, the answers will regain their appropriate context. Then, too, it will be apparent that there is no conflict, in principle, between scientific inquiry and religion. Religion will be understood as dealing with relationships and significance, not with the processes that are the subject of scientific research.

4. Non-Jewish religions, too, offer distinctive answers to the perennial human questions. These answers are not always in agreement with the Jewish ones, but they and the Jewish answers arise out of a common situational "ground" of human experience, variously and richly interpreted. Thus, Enuma Elish, like the biblical story, is "a Semitic myth of beginnings."[35] The description is not overtly judgmental, yet it is intimated that the ideas of that story are less sublime, less deserving of assent than the biblical one.

5. Teachers themselves struggle with tradition and are charged with the responsibility to help children do likewise. However, the choice of how to relate to the tradition is ultimately the student's, and the teacher should not seek to impose norms beyond those of spiritual awareness (of Ultimacy), knowledge (of tradition and its ties to other realms of wisdom), and morally responsible choice. If the teacher can evoke these values in the learners through the prism of Jewish tradition, he or she is succeeding.

6. In the context of the modern situation and in the framework of the school, the method of inquiry—of rational deliberation—is most useful in educating toward existential choice and religious individuality. Deliberation does not assume *a priori* norms; it harnesses the reasoning powers of children, helps them locate problems, and generates or exposes to view alternative responses. Given the complexity of most problematic situations, decision making may be

assumed to be largely dependent on individualized "subjective" considerations.

*Just as explicit religious teaching is attuned to the normative-ideational orientation in education, so is implicit religious teaching congenial to the deliberative-inductive one.*[36]

## THE IMPLICIT THEOLOGIAN AND THE EDUCATIONAL COMMUNITY

In the previous chapter, we saw that when explicit educational theology is translated into educational prescriptions and practice, it often loses the tensions inherent in the theology itself. The theologians who have emphasized the explicit features of the tradition for the sake of philosophical plausibility and consistency find their ideas "translated" into textbooks and classroom situations in narrow, and even sectarian, ways. Lacking the sophistication of the theologians in the realm of abstract ideas and more realistic about the world "out there," many teachers consider the dialectics of religious thought to be frills—and educationally useless or confusing. Thus, explicit religious education tends to be rigid and to lack breadth.

Let us also bear in mind that, with regard to their community, explicit theologians play a primarily *reflective* role: The norms that they laud can be "objectively" described as exemplifying a real community. These theologians are dependent on the community for the objective reality they depict; the community and its educators, to the extent that they respect and need these thinkers, value their thought for representing the institutions (to the "outside world") and enriching the intellectual dimension of their faith. But the theologians' function is intrinsically secondary, and their thought is usually too complex to be translated into education without distortion or simplification. More specifically, the educational *goal* of the explicit educator—to foster the development of loyal, observant Jews—is not often seen in a (theologically reflective) context of the long-range *intention* to create uniquely spiritual individuals through the unique way of the normative tradition.[37]

However, the theologian standing behind the implicit religious educator discovers that his or her teachings are also liable to be distorted in educational "translation." This situation is different from the distortions to which explicit theology is vulnerable, but it is no less acute.

First, as we have seen, the implicit theologian deems the secular world existentially serious. The critical accommodation that the theologian makes to it *in principle* tends, in the classroom, to corrode the tradition and its foundations. Berger terms this "inductive religion"; that is, a surrender to secular commitments that retain a religious terminology.[38] In other words, the educational ideology that is open to and "at home in" the secular world too readily becomes an *expression* of that world rather than a *confrontation* or *conversation* with it. The (non-admitted) norms of modernity, which religious education wishes to expose as principles-ideals deserving of serious religious critique, become "self-understood." Religious norms, accordingly, tend to become historical-descriptive ("The Rabbis struggled . . . ").

Second, the categories of "ultimate relationship" that the implicit Jewish theologian finds in Judaism through such key terms as "Creation," "Revelation," and "Redemption" are not as accessible to teachers and pupils as they are to theologians, and they often appear superfluous to the non-theologian. Why speak of Creation, Revelation, and Redemption when, to the non-theologian, the meaning of these terms is exhausted by the ideas of *origins, existential "presentness,"* and *ends*—concepts that are, for many, vaguely religious but do not seem to require specifically Jewish ways of articulation or enrichment?

Theologians find special significance in the "Jewish language" because they know the tradition well, and they are insiders. They are nourished by Judaism's spiritual syntax and can use it associatively and creatively. Their search for meaning within this tradition is based on an admission, rarely overtly stated, that it has a call on their loyalty; the meanings they perceive within it are linked to their normative commitments. But they are urging a perception of significance on people whose commitments and loyalties are not so clear or so specifically Jewish. We may say that the teacher who follows the implicit theologian suggests to children that they be faithful to the Jewish tradition on the grounds that it evokes individual religiosity. But the children, in the contemporary "open" society, may find more evocation elsewhere.

Therefore, the implicit religious teacher must appeal to the child Jewishly on national grounds. ("This is *our* religious culture.") But that national culture is not really "present" to the child. A child's "we-ness" is generally not Jewish; Jewishness connotes a "religion." Thus, learning *his* or *her* tradition is, in fact, more like learning *a* tradition. Religious education as a deliberation on implicit religion tends to become an exercise in comparative religion. The implicit theologians, unlike the explicit ones, are more Jewishly commited than the community they serve. They cannot help the educator solve his or her problem, for the problem (why be Jewish?) is absent from their experience.

For they, unlike the community that reveres them (however vaguely), are deeply rooted in a tradition that is *also* explicit, or they are national Jews in some meaningful sense.

We may now re-state the dilemma. Explicit religious education has a normative philosophy of education, but it is not convincing to most Jews in the modern age. Implicit religious education can be shown to be philosophically plausible, relevant to the modern person, and linked to scientific inquiry or reflection upon religion. But it has no normative philosophy of education beyond what amounts to a commitment to existential virtues that should be embodied in teachers and "caught" by pupils. Jewishly speaking, this commitment lacks specificity or religious depth; it is either culturally "universal" or simply national.

Explicit religious education thus seems appropriate either for the very wise or the very simple: those who associate themselves with the dialectical tensions of explicit theology, on the one hand, and those who are so unreflectively "normative" that they actually require no theology and cannot understand one, on the other hand. As for implicit religious education, it seems appropriate for the very sensitive and philosophically astute—who, however, are not sure that they need it—and the indifferent and secular-minded—who always threaten to declare it innocuous.

Our thesis is that theology and educational theory that are only explicit or implicit are religiously and educationally distorted. Religiously, the distortion is contained in the assumption that faithfulness is concerned with *either* God *or* Torah, with transcendence *or* immanence. And the educational deficiency is located in the assumption that education exclusively "does" either socialization (into norms) or individualization (for self-realization).

We believe that the religious and educational tendency toward overly explicit or implicit religious teaching is largely an outcome of a desire to deal consistently with modern thought and culture. Jewish thinkers and educators have wished to "solve the problem" of religion in the contemporary world with an explicit vengeance or with implicit reasonableness.

We suggest that the problem is not one that can or should be totally solved. Perhaps there is a danger in too much integration between culture and religious faith. Perhaps, paradoxically, integration that is too complete may be purchased at the price of religious *wholeness*. Our assumption is that religious "wholeness" must incorporate both explicit and implicit dimensions, that it is religiously distorted to view any religious tradition, the Jewish included, as "in essence" only one or the other.

But is this necessarily true, or is it only one educator's hope, artificially imposed on the tradition to meet his ideal for education that incorporates both norms and deliberation? A contemporary sage, Rabbi Abraham Y. Karelitz (the "Hazon Ish"), understood *Trust* as synonymous with passivity and obedience and stated that only complete submission to the law of the Torah can assure high ethical standards (which cannot be achieved "in accordance with natural tendencies").[39] Was he not, perhaps, expressing the genuine teaching of Judaism? On what basis did Rabbi Karelitz's contemporary, Rabbi Abraham I. Kook, believe that "the fear of Heaven must not suppress man's natural morality, for then the fear of Heaven is no longer pure . . . [and that] every word of the Torah must be preceded by worldliness"?[40] Was *he* speaking for the authentic tradition?

We have seen that religious believers and thinkers express and defend one orientation or the other. But is the Jewish tradition itself, in its primary sources and methods, really both implicit and explicit? If so, in which sense? And how can this be determined? In addressing ourselves to these questions, we cannot rely only on theologians: They are important, but they too have an agenda, and they speak within a particular context. They too cite Scripture selectively.

Yet these questions must be addressed by the philosophy of religious education. For the "wholeness" demanded of the teacher in the Jewish classroom must be based, *inter alia,* on a conception of Judaism that makes such a demand. If this cannot be done—and shown—Jewish religious education that tries to take norms and deliberation seriously will be compelled to ignore (at least partially) its "subject matter."

Indeed, such a state of affairs is quite prevalent in Jewish education. It is usually ascribed to ignorance of the religious tradition. But shouldn't the theorist of Jewish education substantiate that charge by indicating what a "whole" theology of Jewish education, drawing upon the biblical and rabbinic tradition, would look like?

# 9 Standards and Spontaneity: A Theology of Jewish Education

In our discussion of the individual's relationship to ultimacy and to the "dimensions of religious commitment" that delineate fellowship we set the stage for our description of religious traditions as both "explicit" and "implicit." Religions, we noted, speak to a variety of human beings in different and changing situations and invite all of them to membership in community and to the expression of "ultimate concern" within it. Ultimate concern cannot be the same for everyone, and not everyone can "see" God in the same way, because people are different from one another and undergo life experiences in specific ways. Yet, at the same time, dimensions of religious commitment delineate the ways to express ultimate concern through fellowship in which God is "heard" in community. These dimensions must be shared with others: One cannot live in fellowship only with oneself.

Sometimes those of a "liberal temperament" will be annoyed at the constricting beliefs, practices, and anticipations of a particular religious tradition at their specific time and place and in their individual circumstances. Such (implicit) persons, if they are anchored in the community, are likely to be its innovative spirits or even, at times, its prophetic personalities. Conversely, there are those for whom God's majesty and transcendence are dominant motives in religious life. Their joy is in revelation; they distrust human perceptions of the divine that are more than footnotes to sacred texts. Such people stand guard over the tradition, assuring that change will be minimal and "within the tradition," congruent with its "innate" religious sentiment.[1]

In Jewish religious terms, certain people are most attracted to Job and his questions; others to Deuteronomy and its answers. For those religiously constituted by imagination, hope is more precious than stability, and they will risk some order for larger vistas of the possible. Others, religiously shaped by cumulative tradition, find order most true and beautiful and fear for the stability of forms that ''contain'' the holy and make it accessible.

How does the Jewish religious tradition negotiate explicit and implicit religious factors? How does it teach normativeness and choice? Or is it, perhaps, not a ''religion'' in the general sense discussed earlier but rather an (explicit) Law or an (implicit) orientation?

## HALAKHAH AND AGGADAH

It is often posited that the distinction between what we are calling the explicit and the implicit aspects of Judaism is synonymous with the difference between *halakhah*—the normative law—and *aggadah*—the non-legal feature of the tradition. The former is binding, communal, ''objective''; the latter is spontaneous, individual, reflective. Heschel has compared halakhah with prose and aggadah with poetry. Whereas everyone has to speak prose, not everyone writes (or needs to understand) poetry. Yet, both are needed:

The inter-relationship of halakhah and aggadah is the very heart of Judaism. Halakhah without aggadah is dead, aggadah without halakhah is wild.[2]

Bialik has also given literary expression to the need for both (explicit) halakhah and (implicit) aggadah.

The shafts of the aggadah dart hither and thither, wavering as though shot into the air from a slackened bow-string; those of the halakhah fly straight and true, strongly and unswervingly, as if sped from a taut bow. Aggadah gives you air in which to breathe; halakhah, a place to stand on, solid bedrock. . . . A people that has not learned to combine halakhah with aggadah delivers itself to eternal confusion and runs the danger of forgetting the one direct way from the will to the deed, from the effort to the realization.[3]

Bialik was questioning the ideology of his generation, one that had rebelled against all authority and that wished to create a national renaissance on implicit-aggadic bases alone. Implied in his polemic is that the search for a Judaism that is all aggadah and no halakhah, based on a rejection of religious coercion, may undermine the venture of the Jewish national movement.

However, viewing the halakhic pole of Judaism as its explicit one and the aggadic pole as its implicit one has been questioned. Sometimes the aggadah is stringent and even grim, spelling out coercive aspects of human existence. Sometimes halakhah is flexible and mindful of individual differences.[4] Furthermore, there are certain basic beliefs and "values" of Judaism that are often identified with "the essence" of Jewish faith. These concepts or action-values are found in biblical, talmudic, and Midrashic statements or stories no less than in laws. Is the story of Creation halakhic? No, but it is certainly explicit, establishing God's sovereignty. Is God's choice of Abraham an implicit-religion narrative? No, but it is not halakhic.

All people (including saints and theologians) quote Scripture for their own purposes, and one can assemble an impressive number of implicit or explicit sources with the claim that "they are what Judaism really is." This "real Judaism" will not necessarily be halakhic. Indeed, a Reform theologian is likely to find the "essence" of Judaism in aggadic material understood explicitly ("Jews believe that . . . ") and may point to the historical development of halakhah as evidence of Judaism's implicit view of law, resulting from the human "struggle" to translate ideals into norms.[5]

In fact, not only are there different verses and Midrashic passages that can be cited in support of one viewpoint or another but also the same passages can be variously interpreted. We have seen how the Binding of Isaac, which Leibowitz terms the "symbol of Judaism" for its portrayal of Abraham's blind obedience to God's will, undergoes an "implicit" metamorphosis in the Melton Center's *Genesis: The Teacher's Guide* and becomes associated with morality.[6] From the other direction, when Joseph B. Soloveitchik writes that "The halakhah has always insisted that . . . " followed by a doctrinal statement about what "Judaism teaches," he is, as Novak points out, positing a concept of "ideal Torah" or "*a priori* halakhah" that makes Halakhah-Law synonymous with Theology-Aggadah.[7] Novak, taking issue with this, states that Judaism has a history, and that in this history both halakhah and aggadah undergo a process. There is, in Jewish history, "the development of legal precepts—that is, statements of what Jews are to do—and of theological concepts . . . describing these experiences which define what Jews are."[8] These are two poles, both of which "involve a Jew's relationship with his own people, the external world and the transcendent God" but in no period have the "precepts and concepts been emphasized at the expense of the other."

Halakhah and aggadah are the content of Judaism. . . . Since Judaism is inconceivable without either halakhah or aggadah, they comprise its indispensible prerequisites, the inter-relationships of which it is the task of Jewish philosophy to understand.[9]

In his view, "halakhah is the data (of Judaism) and . . . aggadah is the model which widens the perspective found in the data." Novak insists that aggadah (as "model") is no less Judaism than the law, for aggadah is the explication of "the grounding of the commandment" and emphasizes "the transcendent ground of the commandment in a realm beyond man's comprehension."[10] In other words, the categories of the aggadah are imposed, or "given," as well. We should add that, conversely, if the aggadah (theology) assumes that people must be free to be meaningfully commanded, then there must be an implicit element in the halakhah as well. We must be active partners in understanding and interpreting what we are "bound to do."

Wurzburger, from a more strictly Orthodox perspective, also questions whether the normative-explicit can be facilely identified with the legal-halakhic aspects of Judaism, for certain key terms and assumptions that are non-halakhic are "essential" in Judaism. Wurzburger speaks of "meta-halakhic propositions" that, "unlike general aggadic concepts, form an integral part of the halakhic system," which would make no sense without them. (For example, the halakhic requirement to serve God is dependent on such non-halakhic assertions as He exists, He took Israel as His people, and so forth.) Moreover, Wurzburger insists that "the halakhic datum . . . is never a pure *given*."

Just as scientific data are not mere sensations but become scientifically relevant (i.e., *data*) only through activities (selection, interpretation, construction, etc.) of the human mind, so does the halakhic datum presuppose an act of interpretation on the part of the individual thinker.[11]

Yet all decisions arrived at by *bona fide* halakhic procedures on the part of individuals have the status of halakhic data. Therefore, the specific content of halakhah is not synonymous with the given, just as aggadah is not always synonymous with spontaneity and freedom (certainly not if it is "meta ha lakhic"—i.e., basic—belief).

Rosenzweig has also pondered the distinction between the imposed-Divine and the chosen-human in Judaism. Significantly, for this twentieth-century man of history and science, the "aggadah" of God's choosing Israel is, on the face of it, more "imposed" than the commandments of the Torah. And yet:

I was startled by Nahum Glatzer's words that only the election of the people of Israel has divine origin, but all the details of the Law come from man alone. I should have formulated this—and have actually done so to myself—in much the same way, but when one hears one's own ideas uttered by someone else, they suddenly become problematic. Can we really draw so rigid a boundary between what is divine and what is human? We must keep in mind the obvious fact that a Law, as a whole, is the prerequisite for being chosen, the law whereby divine election is turned into human electing, and the passive state of a people being chosen and set apart is changed into the activity on the people's side of doing the deed which sets it apart.[12]

Where then, if not in halakhah and aggadah, may the explicit and implicit poles of the Jewish religious tradition be located?

## MODELS AND THEORIES

A possible approach to the problem is suggested by Ferre's thesis regarding the differences between models and theories and the distinctive ways in which models and theories are used in science and religion.[13]

Ferre posits that models, in science as well as in religion, are distinct, simplified ways of understanding complex realities. However, there are two important distinctions between scientific and religious models.

First, the theological model is metaphysical and comprehensive. It presents a total picture of "what is to count" as reality. The theological model is like the scientific one in that it proposes ways to "see" realities, but it differs in that it claims to have a vision of all reality. (When, therefore, a scientific model is represented as absolutely comprehensive, as a "vision of all reality," it must be seen as a theological or metaphysical one.)

The theological model is, in a certain sense, unfalsifiable, since it takes in—or has a language for dealing with—all possible situations. However, when people who take their own experience seriously find that aspects of this experience do not correspond with what the model seems to be saying, they then create theories through which they attempt to solve the problems that have arisen between the tradition (actually, the model as previously understood) and new experience. The function of these theories is to *protect the model,* by interpreting and relating the key terms that constitute the model to everything else that is experienced, known, and believed.

This leads to another distinction between the scientific and the theological model. Scientific models may, in principle, be tested for their adequacy. For example, although we currently have a scientific model that suggests we "see" molecules as billiard balls, "perhaps more powerful electron microscopes will one day permit a point-for-point comparison of billiard balls and simple molecules."[14] Consequently, in science, models are changed or exchanged with relative ease, in line with new and accumulating knowledge and ways of "seeing things"—resulting in new theoretical assertions. But theological models are, in principle, not given to such testing, for the model itself represents the ultimate in human understanding with regard to the ineffable truth that it *points to*. The theological model says, as it were: "This is the way you may see what is unknowable"; moreover, as a comprehensive system of metaphors that is normative and valuative, the model declares: "This is the way you are to see it." All (internal theological) theories about the model are built on the assumption that the model remains comprehensively true; when this is not believed or no longer held true, the making of new theories becomes superfluous.

Therefore, the relationship between theory and model in the case of theological models is the opposite of the relationship in the case of scientific ones. In the scientific enterprise, models are readily changed. In theology, by contrast, theories are changed in light of new insights, situations, and knowledge, but the model itself is sacred. To change the model, i.e., to change its key terms or metaphors and their inter-relationship, is to change *the religion;* whereas to change the (religious) theory is merely to change *the theology.* Thus, the basic model-terms or metaphors, " . . . those at key positions within the overarching model of reality are defended at all costs . . . a change in model signals a religious revolution that may sweep away that which has received the devotion of multitudes over the ages."[15]

Berkovits's attempt to define Jewish philosophy in relationship to certain "facts" and "events" is germane to Ferre's categories and our discussion here. For Berkovits, Jewish religious thought "is determined by one element that is variable and another that is constant." The variable element is the intellectual and scholarly equipment used in building a specific philosophy. The constant elements are "facts and events."

 . . . [P]hilosophies are the thoughts of men: they are Jewish because they attempt to render Judaism intellectually meaningful. Implied in such a position is, of course, the insight that Judaism is not identical with a philosophy or a theology. If it were we would be moving around in a circle. The philosophy, the theology, the metaphysics, are the variables. Judaism contains the element of constancy because it is founded not on ideas but on certain facts and events. These facts and events do have their philosophical, theological and metaphysical relevance. But such relevance is always a matter of change and as such subject to change.[16]

The "events" include not only such occurrences as the Exodus but also the *mitzvah,* whose "essential quality lies in the fact that it was actually addressed as a command of God to the Jewish people." And it includes God

Himself, "Who revealed Himself to Israel, who acts in history and is known to men by the events of His manifestations."[17] In Ferre's terms, these facts and events are the model itself, whereas "the philosophy, the theology" and, we may add, halakhic rulings making the *mitzvah* accessible in new circumstances are the theories that, in relating it to new situations, defend it and expand it. Thus, when Saadya Gaon in the tenth century stated that he undertook his philosophical work "so that what we have learned from the prophets of God may be clarified for us in actuality,"[18] we may understand this statement as a *theoretical* defense of the *model* ("learned from the prophets of God") for his time.

The "constants," the "objective Judaism"—that is, the model itself with its imposed metaphors of ineffable reality— is not only the substance of *mitzvah* but also those meta-halakhic propositions that may be considered root theories, such as "God charged Israel to observe His commandments." Such statements, which Judaism historically has considered facts, are theological components of the model itself, "to be defended at all costs." Thus, when the talmudic Sage Hillel discovered that the law of the Torah commanding the canceling of debts at the Jubilee created social injustice (for no one wished to lend money to the poor when the Jubilee release was at hand) and that consequently one of the highest-level models "within the overarching model of reality"— that God commanded the *mitzvot* and that they were good—was endangered, he instituted the prosbul, which allowed debts to be transferred to the courts rather than canceled.[19] Thus, he protected by halakhic innovation the model that has as one of its key metaphors God's giving Israel the commandments. And, as scholars such as Rackman have argued, the cultural-philosophical conditions of modernity require new halakhic thought and decision making in order (in terms of the conception we have used) to protect the model. Defending it is mandatory, because it is believed to be given by God; this defense, however, involves its expansion.

*The model itself, therefore, corresponds to explicit religion.* The model is "imposed," and to reject or change it is apostasy. It is transmitted by a community that "protects" the model, is loyal to it, embodies it. The individuals within the community attempt to understand it and apply it, thus testifying to its claim on them and to its truth. And in order to be defended, the model itself must have, among its principles, the one of openness; the "Oral Torah" was also "given" at Mount Sinai.[20]

How, in the contemporary situation of crisis, may the model and its protective theories be viewed? There appear to be three possibilities.

1. The individuals—and the community—can shut out all threats to the model by denying the significance of any experience that is not adequately

"covered" by previous theories (theologies and halakhic decisions) that once defended the model. Past theories are thus deemed to be features of the model itself. In this view, theology and perennial faith are identical; all past halakhic rulings are indistinguishable from the *mitzvah* itself, and any qualification or re-examination of a previous theory is seen as an attack on the model itself. Therefore, the need for new theories (which defend and expand the model) must be vitiated by denial of the legitimacy of new challenges. In this religious approach, everything of religious value is explicit. Religious people must live in a segregated community, and education is to be equated with successful initiation into the community.

2. Conversely, the authority of the model can be totally denied or its relevance called into question. The individual can look upon religion with "scientific eyes." In this case the assumption is that religious models are really (faulty) scientific hypotheses and that they should be exchanged for better ones as human experience and knowledge grow. New theories to defend old models are deemed evasive and dishonest. One should not ask, "How can we understand this faith (new aggadah) and apply it (halakhic innovation)?" One merely explains why one does not believe the model and why only the benighted remain loyal to it. As in the previous paragraph, religion is denied its implicitness. But here, education about religion is historical-descriptive alone.

3. For the model to be preserved and protected, a third way is indicated. The individual and his or her (interpreting) community look upon the model as sacred, revealed knowledge and religious obligation. In examining historical theories (Midrashic, halakhic, philosophical), they learn how these theories made the model accessible, and they may view the acceptance by Jews of these theoretical expansions of the model as integral to what Torah means. For the model always became accessible through theories, and each theory not only contains a response to the situation but also is an analysis of and "teaching" about the meaning of the model itself. The key terms and demands of the model are authoritative, for they set the rule and value framework for what "believing in" and "practicing" Judaism means. Because of their very normativeness, they require frequent interpretation, but former interpretations—which have constituted the meaning of the model itself—are normative as transmitted unless they can be shown to threaten the viability of the model.[21] Moreover, the data of the model (*mitzvot*, meta-halakhic propositions) dis-allow certain theories, metaphors, and practices and insist on the use of others. Rothschild makes it clear that, whereas metaphor must be used "where literal descriptions fail us," the question of which metaphor is used remains crucial.[22] "God the Creator" is a "kosher" metaphor authorized by the model; "God the Beget-

ter'' is not. For certain metaphors belong to the model and others are ''lifted'' from other models (religious faiths).

This option embodies the application of implicit religion to the model (explicit religion). But the application arises out of (a) a secure knowledge of the model as it has been understood through past theories; (b) a familiarity with the methods authorized by the model for dealing with it; and (c) learning how to ''do'' theoretical work on a corpus of transmitted heritage, which is, to the learner, ''objective,'' existing independently of the learner and introducing him or her to a language of understanding and commitment.[23]

We may now summarize. For religion to be only explicit means that everything ''handed down'' is the model itself. The model may be very broad, but it was given that way (by God, by tradition, by holier people than those alive today), and it cannot expand. The alternative to acceptance is rejection. Conversely, for religion to be only implicit means that the theories by which reality is interpreted are not related to any normative model. Thus, the theories are not communicative or meaningful (outside of some private prophetical insight), or they are crypto-theological—that is, they relate to and defend unacknowledged or unadmitted models that are not articulated—for the sake of defending the norm of ''objective and detached inquiry.''

Judaism, like all comprehensive models of value and knowledge, must therefore be viewed as both explicit and implicit, not only because it includes both revelation and commentary but also because each (revelation-model and commentary-theory) requires the other to remain accessible, to have a cultural-historical context.[24]

In discussing the method of determining what ''the essence'' of Judaism is, examining the claims of those who declare that it is ''basically'' explicit or implicit, we mentioned that either view can be readily documented. The Jewish tradition has an abundance of proof-texts and, in our generation, the Jewish school is amply provided with a choice of anthologies.

In an earlier chapter, we too, like the theologians, quoted Scripture and Talmud. We did so to indicate that there are diverse narratives that elaborate on ''master stories'' within Judaism reflecting explicit and implicit religious experience. For instance, we cited the story of Rabbi Akiva's reciting of the *Shema* at the moment of his death to illustrate the following explicit ''master story'': ''People are good when they do God's will (no matter what the circumstances).'' This master story is indeed a constituent element of the model. That is: One who says that people should not do God's will as expressed in His commandments is a non-believer (in the ''model'' of Judaism); such a person will never ask, ''How is His will to be carried out in this situation?'' Conversely, we cited the Mishnah, which ''warns'' witnesses in cases of capital crime to recall that "man was created single to teach you that whoever destroys a single soul is considered by Scripture to have destroyed an entire world," as an example of the implicit religious idea that each individual is unique and significant. This harks back to the model-story of God's Creation and each person as created "in the image of God."[25]

In light of our previous discussion about "key metaphors" within the model and theories (theology, Midrash, halakhic innovation) that maintain the model's "relevance," our question must be expanded: We must ask not only which texts and experiences "represent" explicit and implicit religion but also how the tension is sustained between the key metaphor of the model lying at the base of the story and the theory that suggests expanding meanings, thus evoking different key metaphors. (This question will engage us as an educational issue later on, but at the moment we are concerned with the phenomenological-theological aspect of the problem.)

Let us return to the story of Rabbi Akiva's martyrdom. Why is this so easily characterized as an "explicit religious" story? Rabbi Akiva, so it seems, ignored the unique and shattering personal circumstance of being tortured to death in order to fulfill God's commandment—to "love Him . . . with all thy soul," which, halakhically, means to say the *Shema* at the time prescribed for its recitation "even when He takes thy soul from thee." This obedience, this view of the relationship between God and the individual in terms of a routine, "by the clock" as it were, was startling to Akiva's disciples. The questions they asked their master were apparently implicitly religious: "Why are you ignoring the truth of this moment? Can your relationship to God be one of blind obedience when He is afflicting you? Is this what "serving Him" means in this situation. Isn't there a more significant, a more honest way to respond?" (After all, observance and obedience do not exhaust the model. Abraham, a prime model-figure, not only did God's will but also argued with Him!) Or perhaps they were wondering whether there is any theory that can make sense of the model that demands love of God when He seems to be unworthy of human love.[26]

However, a close reading of the story suggests a greater complexity. We are told that the halakhah of "with all thy soul—even when He takes thy soul from thee" is, in fact, the ruling of Rabbi Akiva himself, who held that every phrase, word, and letter of the Torah has a distinct meaning.[27] It was he himself who had pointed out that the ultimate test of faith in God is in proclaiming love for Him in the most dire circumstances. One may say that these circumstances reveal the truth about an individual "standing before" God. The circumstances were, for Rabbi Akiva, not straits that superseded the halakhah—they put it "in his power" to fulfill it; this power vindicates the existence of the person who has it. One might say that Rabbi Akiva found it providential that the time of his inhuman execution was "the time for the reading of the *Shema*." It was *his* halakhic ruling, and it was *he* who explained—or, rather, located—the "subjective" significance of that hour. In Buber's very implicit words, we may say that the natural event (in this case, "the time . . . ," despite the circumstances) is not only "experienced . . . as revelation" by the witness, but also "he who witnesses the event and sustains it experiences the revelation it contains. This means that he listens to that which the voice, sounding forth from this event, wishes to communicate to him, its witness, to his constitution, to his life, to his sense of duty."[28]

Later generations of Jews made the testimony both more explicit and more implicit. They considered martyrdom a *mitzvah* and recited a formal blessing before death. And they recited the *Shema* at the hour of martyrdom. "The time," in the talmudic-halakhic sense, underwent a revision. *Any* hour was "the time for the reading of the *Shema*" if it was the hour of death. "With all thy soul" became an existential testimony of faith, of recognizing the uniqueness of the hour, evoked by the example of Rabbi Akiva. The model, which demands absolute love of God, is expressed (indeed, becomes articulate) through the (model) *mitzvah* of reciting the *Shema*. It is buttressed and expanded by, in this case, halakhic "theory," corresponding to the individual's autonomy to make rulings, confront situations—and skeptics—with integrity, and, finally, to innovate by seeing the halakhic category of "time" as pertaining not only to the clock (an imposed universal "situation") but also to the perceived situational challenge facing (uniquely) every individual, at his or her moment of truth.

And this too became "explicit," a halakhah "handed down" from one generation to another. It seemed to be part of the model itself, because it expressed and exposed one of the key metaphors of the model, the commandment to "love God with all thy soul." And yet, a time came when it could plausibly be asked whether martyrdom, in the circumstances of national renaissance and of Holocaust, was still a *mitzvah*. Now theoreticians of Judaism, such as Fackenheim, asked whether mass dying was indeed the best way to love God when Israel's enemies wished to destroy it totally.[29]

Agnon expressed this new theory aggadically, yet his description was "explicitly" grounded in key doctrine and metaphor:

When a king of flesh and blood goes forth to war against his enemies, he leads out his soldiers to slay and to be slain. It is hard to say, does he love his soldiers . . . do they matter to him, don't they matter to him. . . . When the soldier is hit . . . and slain, they put another man in his place and the king hardly knows that someone is missing . . . the king has many others to make up for him.

But our king, the King of kings of kings, the Holy One, blessed be He, is a king who delights in life, who loves peace and pursues and loves His people Israel and He chose us from among all the nations. . . . But because of the love He loves us with and we are so few, each and every one of us matters as much before Him as a whole legion, for He hasn't many to put in our place. . . . [30]

And a soldier from Kibbutz Ein Ha-Choresh expressed something like this, without any reference to God, yet with intimations of halakhah in the days of mobilization before the Six Day War, when there were fears of another Holocaust:

> We spoke among ourselves about this [in the days of mobilization]. And we said that this is impossible [i.e., that we will be defeated]. . . . The Jewish people won't forgive a thing like that, that we will let them come in here and wipe us out again. . . . [31]

Soloveitchik has expressed the new demands of the model, that Israel defend itself against destruction, in clear theological-halakhic terms: The establishment of the State of Israel and its defense is "a positive commandment occasioned by a particular time (*mitzvat asai sh'hazman g'rama*)."[32] And while the Hasidic teacher during the Holocaust who preached to his doomed community that "to die for *kiddush ha-Shem* is a great privilege"[33] appears closer to Rabbi Akiva, Agnon and Soloveitchik are also addressing the same key metaphors. And who can say with certainty that the kibbutznik from Ein Ha-Choresh, who, as a secularist, "distrusts" the model, is not?

Our second example of a master story concerned the "warning" administered to witnesses who might testify against the suspect in a capital case. Let us turn to this more implicit story.

It will be recalled that the original warning stresses the value of the individual; it is aggadic in style and content. But the Mishnah wishes to impress the witnesses with the dignity of the human being by appealing to the individual's experience of his own worth ("for me was the world created") and, at the same time, to have this understood "within the model," which is represented here by scriptural commandment:

. . . . And lest you say [after hearing all these exhortations]: Why do we
need this whole trouble [of testifying, seeing that each individual is priceless].
But it has already been said: (Leviticus 5:5) ''And if he was a witness, or saw
or knew of a person's sin; if he does not report it, he shall bear his iniquity.''
And lest you say: Why should we bear the burden of this man's [i.e., the crim-
inal's] blood? It has already been said: (Proverbs 11:10) 'The destruction of
the wicked brings joy.'[34]

It is a *mitzvah* to testify; this may be traced to the meta-halakhic ''model metaphor'' that ''man was created in God's image,'' but it is most directly founded
upon the model metaphor that establishes the Torah as God's Word. The Torah
commands giving testimony; the commandment is imposed on witnesses no
matter how sensitive they are to the uniqueness of every human life. The explicit authority of the Torah, seemingly, may not be questioned.

But, in fact, the Mishnah does not end with the Levitical commandment.
The authority of explicit religion (here, God's commandment) is comple-
mented by an appeal to reason, to moral sense and experience as it is expressed
in a non-normative scriptural passage: Remember that the death of the wicked
brings joy to the world—for the wicked deny, by their deeds, the dignity and
uniqueness of the human being.

An absolutely explicit orientation would have insisted that the law be stated
and obeyed—and would have considered the citation from Proverbs 11:10 an
irrelevancy. (Does God have to explain why he wants us to obey His laws?)
Conversely, a consistently implicit approach would have pointed out merely
that ''man was created single'' and then would have suggested that the individual witness decide what he considered his duty. The Mishnah, however,
presents the valuative opposites within the model itself and determines the halakhah for the case at hand. There is truth in both the explicit and the implicit;
indeed, a good implicit reason can be given for the (explicit) law of the Torah.

And yet, of course, a particular halakhah does not constitute closure for
the issue at hand. The implicit dimension remains and invites further deliberation. Thus the Talmud reports a dispute among the Sages concerning capital
punishment:

A Sanhedrin that puts to death one person in a week of years is called cruel
[''destructive'']. Rabbi Elazar ben Azaryah says: One (person) in seventy
years.
Rabbi Tarfon and Rabbi Akiva say: If we were sitting in the Sanhedrin, no
one would ever have been put to death. Rabbi Shimon ben Gamliel says: They
[R. Tarfon and R. Akiva] would have increased shedders of blood in Israel.[35]

The model is authoritative. But it must be understood and interpreted so
that it will continue to be ''perfect,'' to function comprehensively and justly,

and this requires theoretical and practical deliberation. This deliberation arises out of unease at possibly cruel applications of the Torah or even the fear that *any* application of certain laws of the Torah may be less than perfect, that, therefore, a mechanism must be discovered in the Torah itself to restrict certain of its laws to theory. Thus the interpretations of Rabbi Akiva and Rabbi Tarfon. But the same deliberation evokes a defense of capital punishment. Rabbi Shimon ben Gamliel finds the law morally sensible and warns against having greater concern for the guilty than for the innocent. But this is never a deliberation with no *a priori* principles. The model does set down principles; it is explicit, the eternal "Word of God."

In short, not only are there "explicit" and "implicit" texts and experiences, but also what usually makes the text theologically and pedagogically interesting is the tension between these aspects of religious experience—as they appear in a single story, situation, dialogue. It is noteworthy that in a case in which a text or tradition is blatantly explicit or implicit, it evokes, in exegesis and religious discourse, the "opposite" dimension of religiosity. Thus, as Carlebach points out, the well-known statement of Rabbi Chanina that "He who fulfills a commandment because he is commanded to do so is greater than he who fulfills it although he is not commanded to do so" (a radically explicit opinion) is modified in the ensuing talmudic discourse. The statement is altered to refer to the reward to be expected and not to the intrinsic religious value of the act.[36] Conversely, aspects of the model that appear to be implicit, such as the seven Noachide commandments, which constitute (biblically ordained) universal morality and that are assumed to be known to—and to obligate— Gentiles, are made an aspect of explicit religion by the ruling that only those who observe the Noachide laws because they are revealed are to be considered righteous. Gentiles who observe the commandments because they make sense, rules Maimonides, are merely "wise" but not "pious."[37]

Judaism can be seen, therefore, to have both a theological model that "is defended at all costs" (for the alternative is apostasy, non-belonging) *and* theories that indeed defend and expand the model to assure that its comprehensiveness and its truth will be maintained in light of the human experience of truth and goodness in all human contexts. The model is "from Heaven"; it is imposed, and young people encounter it through the community that constitutes their primary existential situation. But the principle of implicit religion is intrinsic to the model itself, for the model is doomed without it. The Bible, the book that presents the model and the principles of theory making, speaks of the individual's search for God and, concomitantly, God's address to the individual. The revealed (model-giving) literature presents ideal types such as

Abraham: They obey "blindly" and yet engage God in moral dispute; they "rise early" to do His will and yet "walk *before* Him." [38]

The talmudic "religious teaching" preserves and celebrates this tension. For example, in assigning scriptural passages for public reading, the Sages often paired severely explicit texts with very implicit ones. (The readings from the Torah and the Prophets for the morning and afternoon of Yom Kippur are good examples of this. [39]) They "righted" texts that were too exclusively explicit by implicit Midrash and commentary—and vice versa. [40]

Moreover, the Jewish tradition is rich in systematic theological formulations of both explicit-social and implicit-individual perfectability—and consistently points to their inter-relationship. Maimonides, to cite a prominent example, spelled out the explicitly oriented assumption that the two are sequential and interdependent. He declares that the particular revelation (of the Torah and its commandments) is completely fulfilled only when the social order it ordains makes possible the highest individual "perfection of the soul." [41]

The theory that interprets the model of Judaism has produced diverse types of virtue and heroism. Moreover, whereas the model demands fidelity to God's commandments, the theory interprets the model and "protects" it by decrying the immoral person who is despicable despite formal adherence to every letter of the law. [42] Indeed, one will find narratives that "theorize" about the folly of "too much law" or "only" law when God's will would have been better heeded by common sense or moral deliberation. [43] And it would be difficult, on the basis of the data constituent to the model itself, to sustain the (implicit) argument that all commandments between man and God are merely instrumental and that parameters of absolute religious obligation are set by the moral law alone. Such a radically implicit view of Jewish law ignores such data as the (capital) punishment imposable upon the willful Sabbath desecrator and the ritual purification connected with the ashes of the red heifer. [44] How such explicit-theocentric decrees of the model are to be understood is, of course, also an implicit question, because understanding the model is also justifying it. But the explicit dimension remains, and in addition to the justifying aspect there is also the explicative one: How is God's will, which is imposed on us, to be carried out?

To the extent that we have succeeded in clarifying the intrinsically dialectical character of religion and Judaism, the issues of theology of education become more sharply focused and are placed into a different context.

1. Religious education that never gets beyond the explicit dimension is guided (consciously or intuitively) by the wish to maintain a coherent nor-

mative philosophy of religious education in a harsh and antagonistic environment. But the philosophy is unbelievable to most and thus necessarily sectarian—because every theoretical "key" to the model that it wishes to protect at all costs is considered as invaluable and as sacred as the model itself, and every theory must be protected and justified as well as the model. Thus, past implicitness in religion ("theories" that made the model more profoundly understood as well as acceptable) is presented as explicit in order to deny the legitimacy of any potential religious openness and confrontation. The corruptions that ensue, such as dogmatism and compartmentalization, should not, however, be considered intrinsic to religious education as such but the result of a partial theory of religious education that deprives religious instruction of its free "existential" element.

2. Conversely, proponents of religious education who see its only substance in a deliberative spiritual quest do so because they wish, at all costs, for such education to remain communicative in a modern secular society. But its curriculum is likely to become irrelevant because its proponents see Judaism simply as "struggle with tradition," i.e., theory dealing with past theory.[45] The model, i.e., the super-structure of principle-norm, is located, consciously or unconsiously, not within Judaism but within liberal-humanistic culture. Like overly explicit religion, it lacks the tension between revelation and reason, between text and conscience. Thus, it is ultimately not interesting; incapable of evoking "blind" loyalty, it makes a true struggle with tradition existentially idiosyncratic or a playful or academic exercise. The corruptions of purely implicit religious education, however, are also not inherent in religious education but stem from the decision, based on faulty educational theory, to deprive the educational context of its "situationally coercive" element.

## SITUATION, RESPONSIBILITY, FREEDOM

If religion, for those who experience it, is the confrontation with ultimacy through the prism of "dimensions" that, being cultural, are "given" before they are "responded to," then religion must articulate and illuminate all that is true about one's human situation. Inherent in that situation is that the individual must be initiated into community and normative expectations *and* that he or she must choose.

Morris speaks of the moment at which "the individual first discovers himself as existing," the "Existential Moment" at which he realizes that he cannot simply be coerced. This moment, paradoxically, marks the beginning of the sense of responsibility, and it is a startling experience.

It is typified in the insolent remark of the youngster who, after cowering under a severe tongue-lashing from his parents for some allegedly monstrous misdemeanor, blurts out, in sullen defiance, "Well, I didn't *ask* to be born, ya know!"

This remark, states Morris, "is one of the most profound utterances; it is the child's first complete existential thought." However,

. . . the irony is that its shattering importance is to be found not in its truth (it *is* so overpoweringly true that there is no answer to it) but in the fact that it means absolutely nothing! We unhesitatingly consider such a remark idiotic and ridiculous. Why? Because it has the fatal flaw of total irrelevance. "So you did not ask to be born; what a remarkable insight! But you have spoken a vacuous verity. For whether you asked to come or not, *here you are!* Here you are in the world, responsible for yourself."[46]

Morris's example pinpoints an important paradox. Before the "existential moment" children behave; they are socialized, but they are not responsible. After they realize that they are free, the condition of "being here," of being "answerable," becomes inescapable. "Explicitness" corresponds to being presented with "given" factors and finding oneself in the given situation. "Implicitness" connotes *finding oneself,* genuinely choosing within the limits of that situation. Implicitness is the freedom to choose and yet, paradoxically, it appears only in the context of being held responsible for one's choice. Religiously speaking, "being answerable" is explicit, as are many of the unavoidable questions faced by a person born into an "imposed" history or family or specific "imposed" historical circumstances. But the specific answer, given by the person in the situation of a unique individuality, is his or her responsibility. And this, in the modern world especially, is true also of the acceptance of the Torah's explicit authority, of the religious "Teaching."

Here we have a process that begins with recognition of being (held) responsible, moves to the consciousness that a choice must be made, and then leads to an acceptance of what has been chosen as binding—but always within the parameters of "freedom within situation." To be only explicit is not to have come of age, to not yet ask the questions or to have wearied of the ambiguity of true answers. To be only implicit is not to understand that when one grows up, one must decide—and that one will be held responsible, because truth is more than personal preference.

Thus, no matter how ultimacy is conceived and how dimensions of religious commitment are constructed, coercion and freedom are always there— together. Or, as the talmudic sages intimated, thy children (*banayich*), who "didn't ask to be born," should be *bonayich*—thy builders—who may make their mark and exercise their creative powers. And, where the prophet says, "All thy children shall be instructed of the Lord," Rabbi Elazar said in the name of Rabbi Chanina, "Read here not *banayich,* thy children, but *bonayich,* thy builders."[47] The latter, who "do their own thing," not limited to the coercive fact of their biological "situation" but never oblivious to it, are the ones who are "instructed of the Lord" to choose the good.

"To choose the good," if understood as only explicit or implicit, can hardly be said to mean anything. Yet, if religion is often considered repugnant or redundant, it is because those are the ways it so frequently *is* understood.

## Part Three

# A THEORY OF RELIGIOUS JEWISH EDUCATION

# 10 From Theology to Theory of Religious Education

In the first part of this study, we dwelt upon the problems besetting religious Jewish education in our era and described how normative-religious conceptions that had shaped the consciousness and culture of pre-modern generations had been undermined by secular philosophies and socio-political transformations. We surveyed the controversies concerning religious understandings of Judaism and Jewish culture that were brought on by this "breakdown of tradition" and suggested that much of modern Jewish thought constitutes a kind of educational deliberation, an examination of a "problematic situation"—a perceived unease at the apparent "malfunctioning" of Jewishness and its erosion. We discussed the goal of this deliberation: to locate the problem (i.e., what is actually wrong) in present-day Jewish life. This led us to a survey of reasoned objections to Jewish religion in the modern world and to an overview of new religious affirmations and theologies. The latter, we saw, were based to a considerable degree on modern thought and even modern analyses of the religious phenomenon.

In the second section, we focused on the experience of those for whom "Jewish religion" has meaning and presupposes an obligation. We categorized the types of experience that may reasonably be termed "religiously Jewish," suggesting that "master stories," textual elaborations and discourse on them, as well as the experiences they represent and the thought that reflects upon them, may be classified as primarily "explicit" or "implicit." We endeavored to show what a theology of education might look like through the prism of these orientations, considered as parts of a whole. To achieve this bond between explicit and implicit religion conceptually within Judaism, it was proposed that the explicit pole of Jewish religious experience be seen in terms of what can be called "the model of Judaism" and the implicit aspect be viewed in terms of "protective theory." Our thesis was that the model of Judaism corresponds to the tradition's claim of objective truth, as intimated by key metaphors, and that the protective theory constitutes deliberation and development, both theological and halakhic, which assure the continued viability of the model in new "practical" situations. The theory thus expands the model so that it can encompass new perceptions, expanding bodies of knowledge, and diverse "situational" requirements.

We endeavored to demonstrate how Jewish religiosity, despite the crisis engendered by modernity, could cope with the tension and challenges arising out of the encounter—or clash—between perennial wisdom and new understanding, if supplied with adequate theological tools. In more specifically educational terms, we suggested that the balance between explicit and implicit religiosity was germane to the relationship between socialization and initiation on the one hand and individuation and personal growth on the other and that a comprehensive theology of education could furnish religious foundations and rationales for a philosophy of religious education.

Thus, the theology of education proposed in the preceding chapter was based on two fundamental considerations: one theological and the other educational.

1. *Theologically,* we hoped to locate, from within the tradition, a conception of Judaism that could make demands for religious "wholeness" on the educator. This conception would relate seriously both to "the (explicit) religious dimensions of community"—in which received religious principles were translated into norms of world view, practice, and patterns of fellowship—*and* to the (implicit) root term of "ultimate concern" and devotion to its object, God. In Jewish terms, we wished to show how Judaism invites the individual to the particular *dvaikut* (cleaving to God) of which he or she is capable—within the community of Israel.

2. *Educationally,* we sought to avoid the corruptions or distortions occasioned by one-sided explicitness or implicitness. The former, we saw, tended to shelter classic norms against given social and existential realities, whereas the latter appeared to "get along" without recourse to norms. The theology of education we proposed was designed to rehabilitate norms without obscurantism and to vitiate the charges against overly explicit or implicit religious education—of benightedness and superfluity, respectively.

## THE LIMITS OF EDUCATIONAL THEOLOGY

And yet, the educator may still wish to register an objection, saying, on the basis of his or her experience, that *no* theology of education, even an impeccably respectable and balanced one, is directly applicable to the classroom. Even if it be granted that theology does establish guidelines for religious teachers and posit "ideal ends" for religious education, it is nevertheless, except for the few who "theorize" intuitively, pedagogically frustrating. For it does not speak to the main practical issue facing the religious teacher: how to bridge the gap between religious-theological doctrine and the reality "out there" that educational philosophies should be taking into account and that educators must confront; the world that teachers wish to shape.

The thoughtful educator will insist that the whole problem of Jewish religious education began (as did this book) with the widening gap between what a normative (religiously anchored) philosophy of Jewish education assumed—and expected to actualize—and new situations involving communities and individuals who were indifferent to these norms. He or she will assert that education of any normative persuasion, unlike systematic theology, is first and foremost an ongoing negotiation between theoretical aims and ideals and specific never-quite-contained human realities. To this observation of the practitioner, the educational theorist will add that faulty negotiation between ideals and realities inevitably leads to unprincipled or unrealistic selection of subject matter; to bored, resentful, and uncomprehending pupils; to badly prepared or unmotivated teachers; and to a nonsupportive, though confused and vaguely guilt-ridden, community. The educational researcher will be able to demonstrate, on the basis of empirical findings, that a distaste for negotiation between religious principles (as formulated by theologians) and the "elements" of education "out there" often leads schools, teachers, and pupils either to absolute withdrawal from the "realities" into sectarian ghettos or to absolute surrender to "the situation," which "can't be changed anyway."[1]

In short, teachers, theoreticians, and empirical scholars all have good reasons to insist that a *theology* of education is not, by itself, a viable *theory* of education. Theology can enlighten teachers and evaluate the propriety of "aims," but it will always sound more suitable for ivory towers than for classrooms, more preachy than pedagogical. And the religious principles articulated by theologians, which deserve a better fate, will usually receive no more than lip service or scorn from those who "have to get through the school day" (or hour). In a situation in which there is no full-blown *theory* of religious education, neither the educator nor the religious thinker can distinguish negotiation between principles and realities, on the one hand, from surrender to or withdrawal from "the realities," on the other.

Those familiar with the field of Jewish religious education know well the animosity that often results from conversations between thinkers, who may be accused of not knowing the classroom, and teachers, who are routinely blamed for "not doing better." The scholars and philosophers of Judaism, invited to address themselves to the "spirit" or "foundations" of Jewish education, speak to teachers about covenant, reverence, Torah, and holiness, but they fail to state, in educational terms, how these foundations are to be built. Meanwhile, the teachers, frustrated by their inability to "do anything" with these phrases, and feeling both religiously guilty and professionally superior in putting these lofty prescriptions "in their place," become increasingly "practical."[2] Thus, they learn to look down on all Jewish "ideal aims" as useless and to dismiss systematic deliberation on Judaism as "theoretical" and therefore irrelevant. Consequently, such theory as *is* incorporated is only haphazardly congenial to religious Jewish education; the theories that are used have a "no-nonsense" aura about them; they present themselves as more "practical." Also, of course, they are usually located in secular "models of reality," and they are as likely to undermine religious education as to enhance it. Elsewhere, I have summarized the ensuing situation:

> The theologians, far from the milieu of the classroom and the community, can only preach; the practitioners, wearied by preachers and angry at their nebulous guilt, can only set their sights close to the ground, theorizing about their experience through the prism of education or such general fields as sociology of religion or applied psychology. And because of their frustrations with theologians, they seldom ask which of these borrowed theories are compatible with the Jewish religious tradition, however interpreted.[3]


## EDUCATIONAL THEOLOGY IN EDUCATIONAL THEORY

What, exactly, characterizes an educational theory? And how does it differ from a normative philosophy of the kind we can expect in a theology of education?

Moore[4] has aptly described educational theory as a statement, on the basis of a normative philosophy, of what constitutes desirable ends of teaching and learning; as a prescription of what, in given circumstances, are the best means of bringing about this desirable end; and as specific recommendations with regard to achieving the ends by the means decided upon. He summarizes the structure of an educational theory as follows:

(1)  P is desirable as an end.

(2)  In the circumstances, Q is the most effective way of achieving P.

(3)  Therefore, do what Q involves.[5]

The statement that "P is desirable as an end" is, for religious education, within the domain of theology. For the theologian not only articulates a systematic view of what (religious) "P" is but also seeks to demonstrate how and why it is desirable. We have dealt with this terrain of theology in previous chapters, discussing how religion is understood by believing people, how it is viewed as a comprehensive way of understanding reality and translating understanding into responsibility and meaning. As noted earlier, the theology of education that we located on the basis of explicit and implicit concepts of religion was designed to show how religious thought can provide a foundation for a normative philosophy of education. Thus, an adequate theology of religious education may be viewed as that part of educational theory that states normative ideals, clarifies them, and argues for their capacity to create ideal personalities.

But the educational theorist must deal with the second and third questions as well: namely, why is "Q" the best way of achieving "P," and how is "P" to be achieved? Answering these questions will necessarily involve four issues, which have been delineated by Hardie: (a) the original nature of humanity; (b) the production of changes in behavior, as, for example, the formation of habits; (c) the environment; and (d) the idea of value.[6]

Of course, even in terms of these issues, educational theology is crucial for religious education, but it does not deal comprehensively with them, nor can it supply detailed prescriptions. (That is why theology is so frustrating to teachers when it poses as a full-blown theory of education.) Whereas theology *does* posit conceptions of human nature, and it *does* state its "idea of value," it *does not* concern itself directly with the way human nature invites or impedes learning experiences, with the ways the environment "acts" upon people and with how changes of behavior are produced. These educational questions, although they are to be found within the religious tradition, are more generally located and addressed via sociological and psychological inquiry. These disciplines concern themselves with the environment and the personality. They give us theoretical understanding with which to cope with the issues practically germane to teaching.[7]

But the theologian, although not professionally "competent" in these areas, cannot be expected to remain silent or to be indifferent when they are discussed. The theologian's field, religious tradition and faith, is perceived and presented as comprehensive, taking in the "whole person" facing all of reality. (This is true of the explicit thinker as well as the implicit one. Though the former tends to compartmentalize religious and non-religious areas of life, he or she claims to be an authority in distinguishing between the sacred and the profane.[8]) Theologians will insist that their field, religion, has a position about the relationships ideally obtaining between the individual and society, between people and their world and that it has a view about human personality. And, of course, since "P" and the best ways of achieving it ("Q") are intimately related, at least if one insists that means are never neutral with regard to ends, the theologian will insist on contributing to the discussion of means as well.[9]

Yet, theologians are not educators and cannot by themselves answer the question, "Under *these* circumstances—with children at *this* stage of development, in *this* society—what is the best way of transmitting 'P'?" Therefore, if theology is to be true to its religious mandate to be comprehensive and, at the same time, to remain within the bounds of its competence in education, it must be connected to sociological and psychological theories; otherwise, the educator will not really be given guidelines for evoking, cultivating, and strengthening the religious personality. Religious educational thought without bodies of theory that illuminate what we may practically mean by "realizing a certain type of person or society" in view of the "nature" of the child, the "nature" of transmittable knowledge, and the "nature" of the environment in which children and their teachers live will always sound preachy, vacuous, frustrating.

Yet, the fact remains: If the religious thinker is not involved in educational decision making, education will not be anchored in religious principle. At the same time, if teachers and curriculum writers are not provided with adequate theoretical guidelines with which to achieve normative ends, religious norms will be only haphazardly educative. Therefore, in order to ensure that education will neither lose its religious moorings nor be deprived of its pedagogic potential, theology must be partially translated into sociological and psychological theory.

*Translation* connotes locating useful social-scientific conceptions and theories that appear congenial to the theological ideal yet address themselves to the topics of concern in normative educational theology in a religiously neutral manner. The theory sought out is useful because it provides tools with which to explain social and psychological processes, to determine what is educationally feasible, to enable educators to set policy, and to predict likely consequences of policies and practices. For example, one may bring explicit theological thought to bear on education in pedagogically helpful ways by comparing it with social-scientific conceptions of commitment and explanations of processes that establish loyalty. Conversely, implicit theological thinkers, concerned with the individual's religious and spiritual search, will find psychological theories of development and actualization helpful in spelling out the educational ramifications of their theology. These theories, more than theological statements about ultimate concern and *kavannah* (religious intention), will inform educators how development is reflected in cognitive and affective change, how understanding may be fostered, and under which conditions a consciousness characterized by self-esteem and authenticity is most likely to emerge.

A *partial* translation of theology into theory is one that does not deny religious thinkers the opportunity to establish the norm and to participate in the discussion and choice of proximate goals and means.

This demand for the partiality of the translation signifies two things.

First, it means that the theologian will not allow the social-scientific theories to present themselves as simply another and better way of expressing the philosophy—which would make religious insight and thought redundant. Therefore, the theologian will insist that not everything known and believed religiously can be stated in non-religious theoretical terms, even though the "language" of theory is more communicative and seems to make more sense in a secular world than does religious rhetoric. (For example, the idea of "commandments between man and God," an important category in Judaism and Jewish religious thought, can be *somewhat* explained in religiously neutral theoretical terms as commandments between a person and his or her ideal self. The individual being "enlightened" about *mitzvot ben adam la-Makom* is likely to "make sense" of this translation, to "see" what the religious person means by *ben adam la-Makom* by virtue of this explanation. Yet, it is precisely at that moment, when the learner "sees" the theological concept as "really just a religious way of alluding to one's higher self" that the religious thinker and teacher must regretfully but firmly declare this social-scientific understanding to be reductionistic: "That was the closest I could come to explaining it to you. But in the life of religious people it doesn't really mean that.")

Second, the partiality of theological translation into scientific theory means that the religious thinker carefully examines the underlying belief ("model") assumptions of particular theories and disallows competing models (that is, other faiths) that present themselves as "mere" scientific or empirical findings or verities. (For example, a view of human autonomy that presents secular alternatives to a religious view will be disqualified by the religious thinker, who will point out that it seeks to guide educational policy toward "self-realization" by the lights of a competing "religion.")

The question of why religious education requires outside theories may be raised, and often is, in ultra-traditional circles. The claim is made that Judaism possesses, in its own literature, all the theory necessary for educational policy making and practice. Not only does it have a view of human nature, but also the determination of worthy and legitimate goals *and* means are to be found throughout its halakhic and homiletic sources. Moreover, it is asserted, recourse to "non-Jewish theories" is dangerous, for these theories introduce the underlying belief system of a pagan or secular world into Jewish education. The readiness on the part of Jewish religious educators to use them testifies to naïveté or budding apostasy. The reason that modern religious educators think they need psychology and sociology to teach Judaism is either because they do not really understand these disciplines or because these sciences and their cultural assumptions are what they *really* believe in.

This traditionalist argument makes historic sense. After all, generations of Jews gave and received religious education that "understood what it was doing," had policies, and predicted results—without social science. If it is no longer feasible to ignore general theory, it is because Jews live in a situation of modernity; and modern Jewish thought not only *deals* with modernity but also *belongs* to the contemporary world.

Under these circumstances, we maintain, a translation of theology into the language of general theory is educationally necessary, even though the translation must be partial in order to protect the integrity of religious educational philosophy. To substantiate this theory, we shall look again at the crisis and justification of religious education in today's world, as these are reflected in the overt or covert ways that theologians "negotiate" between religion and modernity.

## EXPLICIT AND IMPLICIT THEOLOGIANS AND MODERNITY

Explicit interpreters of Jewish religion, as we have seen, "guard the model" of Judaism. They tend to view previous theoretical expansions of the model as intrinsic to the model itself. They condense out of the information at its core the "philosophy," or world view, of Judaism; they spell out this world view and seek to demonstrate its superiority *vis-à-vis* other metaphysical models. The superiority (i.e., the truth) of the model is generally not argued philosophically, for that would be a re-location of the truth (in the justifying apparatus and *its* model), but existentially and morally. Judaism is known to be good and "right" from within the holy community; it makes people good and potentially "rights" the world.

Implicit orientations legitimate the model by introducing new theories that maintain its accessibility. These theories are justifying theologies. Since this approach is favorably disposed toward innovation (conceptual and halakhic), it requires criteria for differentiating between the "fundamentals" of Judaism (the model) and the historical accretions (former theories that legitimated the model in previous circumstances). The criteria are often philosophical; what is no longer believable is presented as former theory, not the model itself. Explicit thinkers distrust this approach: It appears to "peel away" Judaism, leaving nothing substantive to hold the model together. But the implicit thinker asserts that the alternatives to this approach are apostasy or petrification. (And implicit thinkers are more afraid of rocks than of onions.)

The problem reflected in this controversy—namely, the unstable relationship between traditional transmitted wisdom and new individual and societal experiences organized in bodies of "general" knowledge—was readily contained, or even overlooked, in previous "religious" eras. Then, the social dimensions of religion, the desire for self-realization, and the store of "general truth" were perceived as part of a religiously organic reality, in which there was commandment, salvation, and "natural theology." When religion itself became dubious as a model of reality inherently justified by general knowledge and authorized to guide the individual's quest, the problem came into the open. And this engendered the deliberation we have discussed in previous chapters.

This deliberation provided new and useful reflections—national as well as theological—about the nature and the value of Judaism, but it could not, by and in itself, solve the problem of religious Jewish education; it could not "restore norms." The reason for this, as Aron reminded us,[10] was that there are always various alternative solutions; the location and articulation of the problem itself are highly individual matters and decisions. For deliberation, it will be recalled, looks askance at *a priori* assumptions and commitments, and it is guided by very numerous (conscious and unconscious) strands of personality, experience, and habit. Thus, although deliberation exposes alternatives and permits rational analysis of diverse possibilities (thereby providing plausibility and feasibility for diverse decisions), it does not create norms. Norms arise out of a self-understood model and its *Weltanschauung,* which guides investigation. Deliberation can "only" supply theories that buttress and defend felt norms or explain why previously accepted models have been abandoned. Deliberation, in other words, can generate new theologies but not renewed faith.

As we noted earlier, deliberation as a style of religious thought appears to be most congenial to implicitly religious-minded people, whose view is both more rationalistic-liberal and more individualistic-affective than that of their explicitly religious colleagues. Implicit thinkers rely on theology, i.e., new theory, not only to give systematic expression to their religiosity but also to locate it. (After all, the deliberation began because of a discomfort with the model and what it seemed to say and demand!) Explicit thinkers, on the other hand, being conservative and active-communal by temperament, fear that new theories will ultimately replace the model that protects the timeless character of faith and authorizes the life patterns of the community. They suspect that the new theories are anchored in competing metaphysical models; the axiom that deliberation has no *a priori* principles alarms them. They understand this to mean that the only *a priori* commitment of the deliberators is to a scientific model-conception of reality and its key metaphor of "restoring equilibrium" to the social or individual organism that is threatened by some psychic or cultural imbalance. In opposition to this they declare that the model requires no such adjustment, that "everything is in it,"[11] and that only serious commitment to the fellowship that embodies it can justify it. Religious experience itself, loyally transmitted and anticipated, is the test of religious norms.

But implicitly religious people, too, despite their modern consciousness and their readiness to engage in (theory-producing) deliberation, are ultimately thrown back upon religious experience and commitment. This is because there is no universal agreement that the problem itself is "the religious dimension of life" or that (therefore) the solution should be sought in more implicit religiosity (and theology). For, in fact, as we have seen, many of those engaged in this deliberation, such as the secular Bundists and the Zionists, located the problem not in inadequate theology but in "sentimental" attachments to the (defunct) religious model. For them, the problem was not the lure of secularism but the neurotic or benighted insistence on religion in Jewish culture. Thus, in defending their *location of the problem,* implicitly religious people had to examine their religious conviction and experience in order to justify their religious standpoint and understand their inner "organizing principle." Like explicit religionists, they carried with them a religiosity that had to be articulated and defended. True, explicit religionists considered the religious experience of order, sanity, and rootedness in concrete sacred deeds central, and implicit religionists spoke for the religious meaning experienced in many occurrences and actions that intimated a sacred potential for all events and deeds. But both these groups understood the relationship of the self, the other, and the world in basically religious terms.

Of course, the religious experience of both implicit and explicit religionists remains influenced by modernity. In the case of implicit individuals this is more obvious, since they declare their desire to refurbish their religious model with theories and, thus, meanings drawn from the secular world. But explicit individuals too are possessed of a modern consciousness. They know—and accept—that they must protect the Jewish model against other models and that this defense and confrontation necessitates some theoretical "negotiation." In other words, explicit religionists realize it does not suffice to say that Judaism is (morally, existentially) true; one must (at least) show how the (more true) model works. Unless one is ready to withdraw completely from the secular world, one has to argue that at least some of the cultural assumptions and philosophical convictions of this "world" are compatible with Judaism. That is, the explicit person must be prepared to claim that some features of modern society are not necessarily inherent in competing models—faiths—but are actually "at home" in the model of Judaism itself. One of the tasks of the explicit theologians is to demonstrate this, to make people "realize" how rich the Jewish model is and why, therefore, it does not require enrichment from insights learned through science. The modernity of explicit thinkers is reflected in their tendency to point out that "Judaism has always known that. . . . "

Thus, both explicit *and* implicit religiosity have an ambiguous relationship to the modern world, and an ambivalent one. The implicit approach welcomed modernity, for it appeared to supply new ways of expanding the religious model—and then had to temper its enthusiasm to remain true to its religious experience. Explicit religion distrusted norm-corroding modernity but developed a conscious modern orientation when it learned to express itself in modern theoretical terms that could be somewhat detached from competing (secular) models. This was done by partial appropriation and valuative neutralizing of available theories that were useful in explaining aspects of Judaism and its compatibility with modern society.

The fundamental educational problem of both orientations is that they are marginal in the secular world in which they wish to transmit beliefs, norms, and insights, and they are constantly called upon to explain themselves and justify themselves *vis-à-vis* secular society. In sociological terms, religion represents the "plausibility structure" of a "cognitive minority"; in developmental-psychological terms, it is a stage to be outgrown. The secular society readily admits that implicit religiosity is philosophically communicative and plausible, for "ultimate concern" is assuredly a worthy feature of human existence, but it is seen as devoid of specific cultural content. Explicit tradition is admitted by secular society to have clear norms and contents, but these are readily dismissed, however politely, as philosophically idiosyncratic and culturally foreign. Thus, implicit orientation "speaks its piece" clearly but is charged with having nothing to say; the explicit one has a comprehensive and distinctive message, but only the already convinced will believe and understand it. And to stay convinced, their detractors assert, they must sacrifice the blessings of modern culture and inquiry, or misrepresent and misuse them.

## THEOLOGIANS AND THEIR PUBLICS

Now, what do theologians do with this ambivalence, these loyalties, this hostility, when they address educators?

If they are explicit, they explain what is done in the religious-normative community to which they belong and why the life patterns of that community are desirable and worthy. But since they are not simply "traditional" but possessed of a religious sensibility that is ambivalently engaged with modernity, they cannot merely suggest that educators teach children to do "what Jews have always done." This is the way teachers tend to understand explicit theologians, but it is not really what they are saying. For the problem of secular and sacred studies in the school really concerns them; they are aware of the theological implications of a halakhic or a doctrinally traditional life that is not antagonistic to scientific inquiry. If teachers do not understand their "dialectics," it is because they cannot tell them very much about teacher training, selection from available subject matter, dealing with secular parents, or teaching "situatedness" in a landscape of tradition without an undue narrowing of horizons. Thus, explicit theologians are really relating their convictions, rooted in experience of community yet enlarged by a talent for abstraction, system, and synthesis. They have experienced the tradition as all-embracing; they have learned from this insight and they wish others to learn from it. But what they have learned they did not learn directly from formal education! (Leibowitz admits as much when he states that religious education does not educate but only supplies the tools for self-education.[12]) And the teachers know that the explicit theology was not produced in school and that the theologians are not saying everything they know. Perhaps it cannot all be said! In any case, *they* don't know how to produce absolute loyalty and scientific sophistication by loving both Torah and general culture. They are, in this, practically much wiser than the theologians.

If the theologians are implicitly oriented, they cannot even point to a community that embodies "the model." They may merely articulate their existential certainties and insights and suggest that others share them. They are urging educators to produce disciples or colleagues for them, but they cannot tell them how to do this. What the teachers understand from these theologians is that children must be aided to "awareness" and that the teachers should make decisions with the Jewish tradition "present" as a significant resource. But although the teachers understand this to mean that children must be taken into account prior to subject matter—and, indeed, this is often intimated—they are not given any guidelines concerning the selection of this subject matter except that it must be interesting and relevant. But how will the curriculum writer or teacher ensure that what is interesting is also representative of the tradition that is meant to be "a significant resource"?

One can expect cultural sophistication and the motivation to confront the tradition and immerse oneself in it (without losing sight of the priority of individuals and their "right to choose") in implicit-minded elites (usually having some explicitly religious background). But what about those who simply have no interest in the subject matter, assuming with the secular society to which they belong that it is redundant or idiosyncratic? Should the subject matter then be dispensed with, or made entertaining, or taught "despite" the children, "for their own good"? Which choices will the religiously committed implicit theologian consider genuinely "open," and which are simply tactics? What are the teachers really to believe, and what must they teach?

We see, therefore, that the relationship of theologians to modern culture makes them both indispensable for educational theory and, at the same time, incapable of "explaining themselves" to educators, who, of course, also live in the modern society yet are charged with the task of "teaching Judaism." Theologians, whether explicit or implicit, have made a commitment to modernity, but this commitment is religiously qualified. Modern society understands their religious commitments but views them, from within competing models of reality and truth, with "objective detachment." Because of the theologians' commitment to modernity and the concomitant admission that the disciplines have standards of competence that must be taken seriously, *and in which they are not expert,* their religious categories must be translated into sociological and psychological ones. Otherwise, they are not practically usable in education. And yet, because of the religious ambivalence of the theologian and the ambiguity in the relationship between secular-scientific culture and religion, the translation must be partial.

We may now summarize theoretical and practical reasons for the need to translate religious-theological language into social scientific categories:

- *theoretically,* because theology deals directly only with the normative or with pristinely personal aspects of education. It is a reasoned reflection upon a religious culture through the prism of one educated person's experience of "holy community" or "being." It does not spell out the complex inter-action between tradition and modernity in the thinker's mind and heart (though it tends to state conclusions about these inter-actions in a perplexingly off-handed fashion!), and it does not present, in "objective" terms, what is to be transmitted.

▪ *practically,* because the educational negotiation between the theory ("ideal religious aims") and the realities "out there" (i.e., the practical issues) is side-stepped by theologians, who cannot propose working standards for negotiation. Their listeners perceive them as demanding either *withdrawal* into sectarian community or *surrender* to the secular society. Because theologians are not educational theorists, they do not know what is actually done in the educational situation and how to "move" existing variables into more (normative) desirable constellations. In Moore's terms, although they know all about "P," they know about "Q" only "in general," and they lack expertise in "doing what 'Q' involves."

We thus see why social-scientific categories that characterize general education theory must also be used as building blocks for theory of religious Jewish education, although this was not the case when the normative philosophy of Jewish education could be taken for granted and the (often unarticulated) assumption of "the Torah" about personality, society, learning, and virtue were axiomatic. Then, the gap between the ideal and reality was narrow enough to be categorized as sin or moral frailty. But since this is no longer the case, an educator who wishes to "move" from a theology to a theory of religious education must deal with two questions:

1. How does the philosophy of Judaism that I am adopting as my theology of education hold together in terms of everything else I know and believe, so that I can feasibly defend it and expand it through knowledge and insights gained in my general reading, training, and thinking? How will this comprehensive philosophy be "put across" in teaching, and how will it *come across* as religiously Jewish?

2. Given my commitment to the religious tradition that I hold to be valuable, which has a content I wish to transmit, how can I relate this content to some general theory that is capable of explaining to partial outsiders what the tradition is saying? How can one state theoretically, in a communicable manner, the ways to convey this tradition and its content to *these* particular children, with *these* teachers, in *this* particular situation and society, characterized by its given social and philosophical assumptions?

The first question has an implicitly religious thrust. It is concerned with justification; it is designed to legitimate the tradition for teachers as well as pupils, in terms of a harmonious and integrated world view. The teachers are encouraged to understand what general disciplines can contribute to religious understanding; although they *have* a philosophy of Judaism, it is never finished. The second question leans in an explicitly religious direction. Here, the general (social scientific) theory is not being invited to enlarge the tradition but simply to make it more lucid and to suggest ways of locating educational-didactic problems and solving them. That is, the theory is conceived as a method of more clearly articulating the tradition and teaching it more successfully in concrete (practical) situations. In the first question, there is philosophical "involvement" with the general theory, which is an expression and an embodiment of a situation that is problematic; it is also part of the resolution of what is viewed as an actual and new problem. In the second question, the theory merely illuminates what is already known and "enlightens" those who do not (yet) know it.

Since explicit religious thought is oriented toward the "dimensions of religious commitment," it will find a congenial "general" field for the construction of educational theory in sociological understandings of norms and sociological theories concerning transmission of normative structures. However, the explicit-minded educator will be very sensitive to the danger inherent in the useful sociological theory: that it will carry along with it the competing (metaphysical) model in which it is anchored, which threatens to undermine the model of Judaism. And, as one who guards the model, the explicit educator will wish, together with the religious thinker, to expose that (non-religious) model and point out its inadequacy or falsehood. Nevertheless, this is the theory he or she will wish to use, for the dimensions of religious commitment are social and concern themselves with the social self and its cultivation.

Implicit religious thinking is oriented to the root term of ultimacy. Since, as will be recalled, ultimate commitment and discernment are both individual and dynamic, growing with the individual's widening horizons and capacities, implicit religious education finds psychological theories of cognitive and moral development congenial in that they supply concepts and data for educational theory.

This distinction should, of course, be treated with caution and qualified. As we shall see in the following chapters, relevant sociological theory deals not only with initiation but also with individuality. Some developmental theories are more epigenetic (and deterministic), whereas others may be viewed as frameworks of opportunity and potential. To the extent that sociological theories of education incorporate individual innovation and creativity, they will warn the explicit-minded educator to steer away from a distorted one-sidedness in religious educational theory. Conversely, the *imposed* characteristics of development will remind the implicit-minded educator that the limits set to freedom by the brute facts of the human situation are not to be denied their (explicit) religious expression. Yet, broadly speaking, sociology of knowledge and culture can supply operative understandings of normative (explicit) education; they deal with "what society is actually doing" when children are introduced to norms and what to bear in mind while doing it.

Development theories, on the other hand, are enlightening with regard to who the child is, how "ready" he or she is for a given understanding of a religious insight, and how the conception of *faith* may be understood in terms of personality and its growth and integration.

Theologians of education have made two demands on religious educators: They have asked for a commitment to religion *within* the situation of modernity and a commitment to religion *despite* the secular ideologies of modernity. If the first commitment requires translation of theology into social scientific theory, the second one requires, as we have seen, that this translation always be partial and qualified. Even (or especially) for the implicitly religious teacher, "faith" that is only a religious term for "the integrated personality," rather than a word connoting the trust and truth of a religious life, is redundant. As for explicit-minded educators, they surely cannot agree that society, rather than God, is to be worshipped. The religious corruption that threatens implicit educational theory is the adoption of the general theory that threatens to pre-empt faith and to view it as the faith (theological) model itself. The potential corruption of explicitly oriented religious educational theory is the reverse; the educators' fear of the theory as intimating a competing model may lead to a refusal to relate seriously and with integrity to the theory itself. This may take the form of "lifting" part of it out of its methodological or cultural context, or otherwise misrepresenting it.

The relationship between theology of education and social-scientific theory will always be precarious. Education may be religiously corrupted by theories, and theories may be blatantly and willfully misunderstood "in the name of" religion. But there must be a relationship, for, as we have seen, religious education in the contemporary world requires both the religious thinker and the theoretician of social science. How the latter may best function and how the normative philosopher may fruitfully participate in the educational discussion engendered by their conceptions is the subject of the following chapters.

# 11 Educating the Loyal Jew: Theory of Explicit Teaching

## THE PROCESS OF LEARNING: FROM PHILOSOPHY TO SOCIOLOGY

The non-normative aspects of educational theory, as we have seen, are concerned with the possibilities and limits of change within the human being as a result of purposeful action on the part of educational agents, on the one hand, and the interaction between the person and his or her environment on the other. These aspects of educational theory are based on the assumption that persons are not "completed" at birth and must still develop to "become themselves" and that development can be channeled in ways that society considers desirable.

The question of *how* this change is affected, how people learn, has always preoccupied philosophers and sages (in addition, of course, to their concern with the normative question of *what* should be learned). When Plato, for example, assumed that teaching is merely an act of midwifery—drawing out of the pupil what they already know and must be helped to *recall*—and when the Midrashic Sages spoke of the instruction given the soul before birth and the pre-natal "erasure" of the soul's prior knowledge of the Torah, they solved the problem, as it were, by asserting that the learner "already knew" what he or she learns.[1] The medieval sage and exegete Rashi found that the Torah distinguishes among wisdom, understanding, and knowledge: The first, he explained, refers to what one hears from others and learns, the second is the result of deduction from previously acquired knowledge, and the third is the result of divine inspiration.[2] One could cite many other discussions on the conditions and processes of learning from the rabbinic tradition.

Scheffler[3] has shown how the question of learning is logically dependent on philosophical models of the human mind. He has described three fundamental models of instruction. The first is based on Locke's conception of the child's mind as a *tabula rasa,* receptive to external impressions and waiting to be shaped by the "input of sensory units." The second model, based on Augustine's view of knowledge, refers learning to insight and vision—which teachers need merely "coax" into consciousness. The third flows from Kant's thesis that rational principles are embedded in the structure of the human mind. According to this model, to teach is to cultivate the ability of pupils to use principles by which they can learn and apply rules of cognition and conduct.

The similarity between the models of instruction suggested by Scheffler and Rashi's types of knowledge (as promised by God to Bezalel, the builder of the biblical Tabernacle) indicates that the basic issues of how we learn and how children are changed through purposeful action are rooted in philosophical and theological problems and have perennially been answered on the basis of convictions and assumptions in these realms. Yet, in modern theories of education, the question of how a child is initiated into a culture and how the personality of the child interacts with his or her environment is never detached from sociological and psychological theories. These theories create the ground for empirical research and are enriched or modified by it. And the researcher, unlike many philosophers, can be expected to be conversant with the educational situation.

The juncture at which normative philosophies meet sociology and psychology has been well described by Peters, who has studied the problem of educational initiation into the "language" of rationality, culture, and morality. Peters states that the code of reason by which we live is, in the final analysis, a corpus of intelligent decisions about how to conduct life, decisions made and maintained by those who are "on the inside" of a culture. But how does one get "inside"?

How . . . can this process get started? Obviously the child has to learn to use concepts such as "right," "wrong," and "ought." How else can he do this apart from being initiated into the code of a community, into a tradition?[4]

This necessity, Peters notes, was already elucidated by Aristotle: "the things we have to learn before we can do them, we learn by doing them, e.g., men become builders by building . . . we become just by doing just acts, temperate by doing temperate acts, brave by doing brave acts."[5] "This learning by initiation and doing is a necessity also in the normative domain," states Peters, because of "the paradox of moral education," namely:

. . . given that it is desirable to develop people who conduct themselves rationally, intelligently, and with a fair degree of spontaneity, the brute facts of child development reveal that at the most formative years of a child's development he is incapable of this form of life and impervious to the proper manner of passing it on.[6]

The necessity of cultivating habits, of bringing children into a culture before they have made up their minds, may not seem self-understood and may actually appear authoritarian or indoctrinatory, but only to those who believe, for their own philosophical reasons, that children do not require such initiation and should be given no superfluous "values." However, such a view must also be based on a conception of how much individuality society "can bear," what individuals are likely to succeed at by themselves, and what will constitute "positive" experience.[7] These conceptions, it is obvious, are based on the cumulative wisdom, the thought, and the experience of the adult community.

In short, cultural groups do seek to get those who are being educated "on the inside" of a social pattern of (what constitutes) reality and value, and they must take into account "the brute facts" of child development. This is true of all education, no matter what are the particular values a society wishes to instill in the young. Émile Durkheim expressed himself succinctly on this matter when he said, "In order that there be education, there must be a generation of adults and one of youth, in interaction, and an influence exercised by the first on the second."[8]

Believing that education is "only the means by which society prepares, within the children, the essential conditions of its very existence" (and that the child has an interest in submitting to these requirements), Durkheim could state that education "consists of a methodical socialization of the young generation."[9] Indeed, education appears to be only socialization, exclusively concerned with "the social being."

In each of us . . . there exist two beings which, while inseparable except by abstraction, remain distinct. One is made up of all the mental states that apply only to ourselves and to the events of our personal lives: this is what might be called the individual being. The other is a system of ideas, sentiments and practices which express in us, not our personality, but the group or different groups of which we are a part: these are religious beliefs, moral beliefs and practice, national and professional traditions, collective opinions of every kind. Their totality forms the social being. To constitute this being in each of us is the end of education.[10]

Durkheim's statement appears dualistic and authoritarian. Indeed, Durkheim spoke of society as that "higher being" that may "command" on the basis of "the authority with which it is invested." Yet the appearance is somewhat deceiving, for Durkheim was insistent on the role of the individual human being in maintaining society through creative identification with it. Thus, he stated that morality may "not be internalized in such a way as to be beyond criticism or reflection, the agents *par excellence* of all change."[11] Piaget has reminded us that although Durkheim endowed society with seemingly absolute moral authority, he also asserted that "the society which morality tells us to desire is not society as it appears to itself but society as it really is or tends to be." Here, the reference apparently is to society as perceived by great individuals who were in the right when they came into conflict with public opinion. Thus, "Socrates expressed more faithfully than his judges the morality that suited the society of his time."[12]

## INITIATION AND PLAUSIBILITY STRUCTURE

How society instills in its members its "language" and social reality, or "plausibility structure," has been exhaustively considered by Peter Berger.[13] Like Durkheim, Berger wishes to describe the world of norms and the process of initiation into norms without recourse to God (Whose actions are outside the scope of empirical scientific inquiry), although he is not intent on replacing Him with society.[14]

For Berger, society has an inherently dialectical character: It is the product of humanity, and humanity is the product of society. The dialectical process in which culture is made, legitimated, and maintained has three "moments," or steps: *externalization,* "the ongoing outpouring of human being into the world, both in the physical and mental activity of men," *objectivation,* wherein the products of this activity attain "a reality which confronts its original producers as a facticity external to and other than themselves," and *internalization,* wherein this (seemingly "objective" and "external") reality is reappropriated by people "transforming it once again from structures of the objective world into structures of the subjective consciousness."[15]

The process of externalization, of human "outpouring" or expressing, states Berger, is rooted in the very "constitution" of man; it is inherent in his nature. Unlike the other higher mammals, "who are born with an essentially completed organism, man is curiously 'unfinished' at birth." One *becomes man* through interaction with a physical and human environment. The development of personality and the appropriation of culture "are not somehow superimposed as alien mutations upon the biological development of man, but they are grounded in it." Man's world is an "open" one, fashioned by his own activity. In speaking, acting, responding, man makes a world for himself, though he is also and always "in a world that antedates his appearance. But unlike other mammals, this world is not simply given, prefabricated for him."[16]

Because of this double relationship to the world (i.e., it is "there" and it must be "made" for people to "become" themselves), human existence is an ongoing "balancing act" between people (and their bodies) and their world. People are constantly in the process of "catching up with themselves." It is through this "catching up" process whereby people produce a world in which they can locate themselves and realize themselves. And in the same process whereby they produce a world (which, in a sense, is already there to be responded to), they produce themselves. They produce themselves in a world, and this "human world" is culture.[17]

The world of culture is readily apprehended as "second nature," but, being humanly produced, it is emphatically *not* nature. Constantly made and remade by people, its structures are "inherently precarious and predestined to change." People must build worlds to become human, but it is difficult to keep these worlds "going." And one of the main difficulties, if not the main one, lies in the fact that "the world" produced by culture must be transmitted to others and is maintained only through re-enforcement by others who live in the same world. For "the world-building activity of man is always and invariably a collective enterprise."[18]

The "world" that must be transmitted to be "kept going" appears orderly and normative because of a "plausibility structure" that makes a specific ordering of reality seem "right," that establishes certain criteria for what will constitute knowledge, and that has its own ways of legitimating its order. In the very process of externalization, in which persons "catch up with" and "make" their world, they yet see "the world" as an objective fact. "The humanly produced world becomes something 'out there.' " It attains the character of objective reality in a double sense: (a) culture "confronts" a person as "an assemblage of objects" in the world existing outside his or her own consciousness, and (b) culture—unlike any constructions of the subjective consciousness of the solitary individual—may be experienced and apprehended "in company." Thus, to be in culture means to share in a particular world of objectivities with others. Society, indeed, imposes itself on the individual, controlling and coercing, bringing those who do not take it seriously back into line, compelling individuals to relate to it as objective, as real. Thus, society provides individuals with an "objective" identity and imposes its predefined patterns upon them—even as this objective identity must be produced and for which the individual, like everyone else, is responsible.

But although this *objectification* assigns roles to the individuals, it does not give the "sub-identity" that makes one see oneself in terms of these roles.[19] In other words, the *apprehension* of "the world" created by people as external "facticity" is not to be confused with *internalization*. In internalization, the meanings of society become, for given individuals, *their* meanings; they do not merely possess these meanings or express them: they represent them. (E.g., a man not only *is*, "objectively," a father; he *feels like* a father and identifies with the role.) And just as externalization must take place in community, so too must the internalization. The individual "appropriates the world in conversation with others . . . both identity and world remain real to him only as long as he can continue the conversation."[20]

The dialectic of externalization, objectification, and identification always takes in all of its three "moments." Even as the individual is "formed" by conversation, he or she participates and thus co-produces the (seemingly) objective world. It may be said, states Berger, "that the individual keeps 'talking back' to the world that formed him and thereby continues to maintain the latter as reality." The socially constructed world is an ongoing "nomizing" activity. Language itself is the primary nomizing activity, for it declares a given item or phenomenon to be *this* and not *that;* language provides the foundation and the means whereby the cognitive and valuative edifice of "knowledge" is built. "In what it 'knows' every society imposes a common order of interpretation upon experience that becomes objective knowledge. . . . "[21]

When this "objective knowledge" is internalized, when individuals appropriate the cognitive and normative "reality" that enables them to "make sense" of their experience (in terms of everything they know "objectively"), they live "an ordered and meaningful life in a social world. Society is the guardian of order and meaning not only objectively, in its institutional structures, but also subjectively, in its structuring of individual consciousness." Thus, both "society" and its individual participants seek to "hold on" to each other, for separation entails the danger of meaninglessness, of "a world of disorder, senselessness, and madness." To be in society is "sane" precisely in the sense of being shielded from the ultimate insanity of such anomic terror. Since, in marginal situations, the order that regulates everyday life becomes problematic, revealing "the innate precariousness of all social worlds," every society develops procedures helping such situations to remain within the reality as "officially" defined. One important way in which the social reality protects itself and its participants is to have itself taken for granted. An internalization of this "second-nature" quality of society (i.e., of the objectivation of society) means that, in denying it, one denies oneself. Sociology is endowed with an ontological dimension; nomos and cosmos become co-extensive and, at this point, the power(s) that rule and protect this cosmos become the focus of society's most powerful instrument of self-protection. For they (the divine powers) endow the nomos with a stability that human beings cannot provide.[22] Here, then, are two essential traits and tasks of religion. "Religion legitimates social institutions by bestowing upon them an ultimately valid ontological status," and it integrates into the "sane" and meaningful world the marginal experiences that threaten "reality."[23]

The usefulness of Durkheim and Berger's theses concerning cultural initiation and cultural "becoming" for religious educational theory is obvious. Also obvious is the discrepancy between these theses and the religious model. Lindenthal,[24] writing about the influence of traditional Judaism on Durkheim, alludes to both of these features. He notes that for the sociological theorist, religious ritual is an expression of the unity of society and cites the *minyan* as a textual example of Durkheim's philosophy. Yet, although Durkheim's ideas seem much influenced by Judaism, Judaism is opposed to Durkheim's central idea, to what we may call his model-idea.

According to Durkheim, God is society "apothesized"; society is the real God. This is the absolute negation of Jewish precepts which strictly forbid the worship of any entity physical or social outside of a true living God. Religion is not, to the observant Jew, a system of ideas by which the individuals represent to themselves the society of which they are members. . . . [25]

## THE CONTRIBUTION OF SOCIALIZATION THEORIES TO EXPLICIT RELIGIOUS EDUCATION

Yet, perhaps paradoxically, sociological theories of initiation are especially important to the explicit dimensions of religious education. The theorists we have mentioned agree with explicit theological thinkers that (a) there is an outside reality that is "there" for the human being, which appears as an objective reality and which imposes itself, cognitively and normatively, upon him or her; and (b) human scientific and cultural endeavors reveal man's wishes to gain dignity through his own efforts, although the (resulting) human nomos requires the religious anchor of cosmic meaning to gain ontological validity. Thus, the explicitly directed religious thinker J.B. Soloveitchik, describes "majestic man," or "Adam the first," as one who uses his intelligence to shape a rational and dignified existence: "Adam [the first] distinguishes himself and not only in the realm of scientific theory but in that of the ethico-moral and aesthetic gestures as well. He legislates norms which he invests with validity and great worth."[26]

However:

> . . . thinkers throughout the centuries . . . knew very well that the human, creative cultural gesture is incomplete if it does not relate itself to a higher *modus existentiae*. . . . They tried to endow the whole creative gesture with intrinsic worth and with ultimate and unconditioned validity.[27]

Here we have the movement from social "rightness" to religion; it is noteworthy that the sophisticated explicit thinker is ready, on one level, to understand "religion" as the buttress of the majestic world, objectivating it by projecting the human nomos onto the transcendent cosmos.

The sociologically oriented theses of Durkheim and Berger state that human beings are born incomplete; they are not truly human until they are cultured, and they do not "know" reality until they are introduced into a certain language through which it may be perceived. We live in "plausibility structures" through which society controls and coerces. Yet, this is done through externalization as well as internalization; children must learn to respond and to articulate even as they become part of a social "reality" that both makes demands and protects.

The social dimensions of religion—religion in its visible explicit aspects—are indeed such a world. Children are initiated into habits (externalizations) of the social world, and only as they slowly become human (in terms of that social world) do they learn meaning and responsibility: *meaning,* in terms of what the social world "says" to the child and how he or she will internalize it; *responsibility,* for continuing and maintaining it. The religious quest, as Allport has remarked, begins with conformity to culture.

> At first the religious practices prescribed for the young child have no meaning for him, at least none of the meaning that they will later come to have. He regards the ritual as something that his group . . . engages in, and learns that to perform the required act is to cement his identification with those who provide him security, affection, approval.[28]

Habit, therefore, (to paraphrase Peters) precedes reason. Habit as perceived by the child is the behavior, and even the assumptions, of the educating person, who externalizes on behalf of the community and represents its (as it were) objective knowledge.

As we will recall from Glock and Stark,[29] the community is concerned about diverse dimensions of "social knowledge." Religious individuals, liv-

ing in a community, are expected to hold certain beliefs (or principled understandings of reality and value) in common with others; they are expected to
agree that certain bodies of knowledge are sacred and thus most important and
worthy of study; they are required to have a commitment to and competence
in specific prescribed practices, and they are initiated into the anticipation that
they will undergo certain kinds of desirable religious experiences.

The previously described "dimensions of religious commitment" constitute the plausibility structure, the social world of religious community—thus,
the framework for the explicit aspects of religious educational theory. First,
the initiating community teaches—usually by indirection—certain beliefs. The
"indirect" teaching of beliefs is achieved by habit; that is, by stimulation of
a desire to be like those who represent the social reality. The individual being
socialized imitates these people and learns to "speak their language."[30] Second, the initiating community places before the child a corpus of sacred literature and the methods considered most appropriate for studying and
comprehending it. Third, it inculcates certain practices and habits as normative
("do as we do") and places the child within situations (such as collective celebration, prayer, and study) that evoke glimpses of the deeper reality, as the
community understands this reality (i.e., religious "experience"). The commitments are expected to be affirmed and "acted out" before they can be fully
understood or maturely reflected upon, for it is assumed that only the maturing
person can shape with reason the raw material of habit. That is, *only in the
maturing person is objectivation recognized as a collective responsibility, externalization as affecting social knowledge, and internalization as intimating
existential choices.*

With regard to those normative beliefs and practices, the community demands loyalty. But it conveys to the child that, in exchange, it will furnish
reliability, psychic security, and meaningful social intercourse—in short *a
world.* The Jewish child learns what *"baruch ha-Shem"* ("thank God")
means and when this utterance is appropriate; that white shirts or one's best
dress is "part of Shabbat"; and that the "time for candle-lighting" is a generally understood situation and obligation.

Of course, individual self-esteem and the capacity for spontaneity must be
respected at every age, and the ability of young people to "catch up with themselves in the world" can be warped by an over-emphasis on exclusively explicit religion, at any age. Because of the differences among human beings,
externalizations always express the particular person and his or her tendencies
as well as the society being "caught up with"; as Elkind states, children have
a "cognitive conceit" that makes the absolute wisdom of the teaching community never completely credible to them.[31] Yet, the child needs the "world"

in which there is routine and "expectability," in which there is symbol and sanity. The sense of belonging *to* a world is required by every human being living *in* the world. If properly fostered, it will enable the individual to search, with increasing competence and confidence, for meaning and understanding throughout life.[32]

The cognitive framework for the assumptions and norms of the community is constituted by the texts of the tradition, by Torah. The child is taught *Chumash,* Talmud, Midrash, and fixed prayer because they are sacred literature; that is, the authorized literature for learning the "language," the as-it-were objective reality, "the world" transmitted through the tradition. This corpus of literature is different from the non-sacred because the latter does not "impose itself" and makes no claims on members of the religious community. For religious community members, it is not what constitutes the *religious* world and that must be maintained at all costs. One may study Shakespeare with friends and colleagues of diverse faiths (communities) because this text is not *Torah:* It is not normative and neither defines the community nor conveys the dimensions of obligation that delineate it. But the sacred text is sacred not only because it indicates the contours of the faith model but also because its study leads to controversy among those who wish to understand what the faith model means and requires (i.e., it engenders innovative theory about the norms of the community and the significance of its life).

The child is made a participant in events that have a fixed format, from a Passover Seder to the recitation of a blessing upon seeing a rainbow. The tradition becomes the child's. He or she learns competence in handling it and acquires the commitment that derives from the experience of competent, shared doing. The Torah that the child learns is, at first, the Torah and the commandments of the adult community: The adults carry out the commandments not because "it is good for children" to see grownups engaged in such activity but because the adults live in a "reality" in which sanity, reasonableness, and virtue are defined in terms of *mitzvot.* The community, through parents and teachers, informs the child that the Torah is "God's will"; the child believes this not as a precocious theologian or a mature believer, but because he or she has experienced the parent and teacher as speaking for a trustworthy community. That is, parents and teachers have been helping the child to become part of a reality, to "catch up with" himself or herself, to become himself or herself.

The sociological theory enables us to translate the explicit aspects of religious education partially into educational theory. Such sociological categories as we have discussed serve the explicitly religious educational requirements that religious life and instruction be partially liberated from external justifications, that its inner coherence be explained, and that its way of "seeing" a world of reality and value be communicably described.

From sociological translation of explicit theology of education, the prescriptive educational theorist may learn that explicit religiosity cannot exist without social functioning; that, therefore, it makes no sense to speak of the explicitly religious manner in which we believe or act if there is no "we"—an "objective," seemingly solid group reality—that indeed carries out and expects certain forms and expressions of religiosity.

Nisbet[33] has shown how the sociological concepts of Durkheim and the sociologies influenced by him are basically conservative. Like the conservative thinkers of his time, Durkheim argued for the absolute primacy of society and viewed persons as morally and psychologically dependent on society. Without tradition and community, argued the conservatives, humanity was led, not to freedom, but to "intolerable isolation and anguish." In this conservative-sociological tradition, religion, family, and community are binding forms of authority. Religion is especially important because all values are originally sacred ones, and a complete separation between the sacred and the binding is impossible.

Those with explicit religious orientations, in both innocent and sophisticated forms and theories, will certainly find this conservative-sociological thrust congenial and useful in explaining themselves in educational discourse. Explicit religion is "imposed from without or above"; it establishes norms of what "counts" as knowledge, value, "true being," and self-realization. It insists on authority to save the individual from the death of meaninglessness; it sees the divine command behind ethical standards as well as ritual commandments. The sociological theory helps the educator see the explicit orientation as the conservative tendency within religion. Explicit educational theory is concerned with socialization into tradition and community. It stresses, in religious life, the importance of reverence for and loyalty to the forms of shared significance.

## THE EXPLICIT-IMPLICIT DIALECTIC—AND THE CONCEPT OF ALIENATION

At the same time, although sociological theory indicates why education is properly preoccupied with initiation and how initiation "works," it is clearly no *carte blanche* for an overly explicit theology of education. Like explicit religiosity itself, the sociologist must deal with the tension between a coercive and secure social order versus the individuality of its members, who must "keep it going" and whose individuality is as requisite for creative and intelligent "externalization" as it is for authentic "internalization." Before we move to the problematics of sociology for religious educational theory, we shall briefly examine sociology's contribution to understanding this tension, which paradoxically also points to its limitations for religious educational thought.

In our previous discussion, we mentioned Durkheim's distinction between the "social vision" of Socrates and that of his society. Piaget has stated that, according to Durkheim, "the consciences of great individuals . . . were in the right when they came into conflict with public opinion."[34] We will not address the question of what Durkheim's criteria were for belonging to the august assembly of "great individuals." It is clear, however, that he considers it essential, at least in contemporary society, for everyone to have more than loyalty and discipline. Morality requires more than respect for authority and commitment to a group. Beyond these, he tells us:

we must have knowledge, as clear and complete an awareness as possible of the reasons for our conduct. This consciousness confers on our behavior the autonomy that the public conscience from now on requires of every genuinely and completely moral being.[35]

While the demand for discipline and attachment remains, contemporary individuals can know what they are doing through reasoning and thus achieve an intellectual (though not social) autonomy that primitive peoples did not have.[36] Individualism and free thought, says Durkheim, are phenomena "that develop without cessation all through history." True, the individuals get from society the best part of themselves, especially their intellectual and moral culture, and thus, without society, humans would be animals. Yet, "intelligence has become and is becoming increasingly an element of morality. For a long time now, we have imputed social value only to an act that was intentional. That is to say, when the actor pictured ahead of time what the act involved and what bearing it had on the rule."[37]

The concept of society is therefore no refuge for believers in a vacuous traditionalism or a blind conformism. Although individuality is grounded in tradition and community, it must be articulated by individuals: in everyone, through an understanding of his or her loyalties and commitments; in great individuals, in a new (more true) vision than that prevailing in society. The balance between society and the individual is, of course, precarious. On the one hand, society is "normative" and is ignored at the price of human existence; on the other hand, the consciousness and activity of individuals maintain it, and those individuals are thus bidden to think *and* to be committed. The question will naturally arise: What about thought that leads not only to a greater understanding of the norms, but also to dissatisfaction with them? Is this legitimate—and when? Are we to assume that everyone who draws this conclusion and insists on innovation is one of the Socratic thinkers who "sees" society more justly? And can a sociologist answer this question?

The question that arises from a reading of Durkheim may be clarified by an analysis of Berger's concept of *alienation* and its relationship to *objectivation* as an aspect of reality-making. The social world, we recall, is apprehended by the child as "second nature," as an objective "fact" that, in the process of socialization, becomes something "out there." Society compels the individual to see its patterns and cognitive data as "real." And yet, says Berger, since the "objective" social world is both constructed and established by the ongoing "conversation" among people, people do bear responsibility for upholding "the world." At the same time, they are protected by the "nature of the world" in which they live (and survive the intrusion of alien forces of "chaos").

To be protected by the world and yet to be aware that the existence of that world depends on the individual (i.e., you!) creates a tension between socialization and individuation. Socialization makes the "objective" world "out there" accessible, but as soon as externalization is seen not as imitation but as a purposeful "maintaining" of that world, the social world becomes less objective. Furthermore, socialization is never complete because no plausibility structure is so self-understood that people will not ask "why," seeking legitimations of what is socially imposed as the "real world."

Therefore, the internalization of the social world, accepting oneself as part of the "outside" reality, may be considered the "moment" at which socialization and individuation meet. The child is socialized to the extent possible to accept and identify with the "factual" nature of the world, but the child is also the person who must maintain—through "conversation"—the plausibility structure and, when necessary, must modify it and seek new legitimations for it, so that he or she can "live with it." (After all, it is not "simply factual!") Alienation is understood by Berger to be the refusal of an individual to see himself or herself as "co-producer" of the social world. The world becomes completely "objective," thus releasing the person from responsibility.[38] "Stop the world, I'm getting off" is an expression of alienation if the speaker does not realize that this declaration too is an externalization, entering into the social conversation and a part of it. The non-alienated person does not allow the objectification to monopolize the plausibility structure; he or she maintains the tension between being within a reality and being responsible for it.

Now, the way in which people generally try to evade responsibility for the social reality is, as we have seen, to adopt the belief that the gods endow the nomos with a stability that human beings cannot provide; "religion legitimates social institutions by bestowing upon them an ultimately valid ontological status." This is another way of saying that explicit religion, which is *only* handed down and which is an objective reality that makes demands and has static content "from the outside," represents, in Berger's conceptual scheme, an alienated consciousness.[39] The Jew, who speaks of an objective reality or historical datum called Judaism, whether from a religious or a secular vantage point, and who explains why he or she is or is not "religious" (conforming to that stable self-understood facticity) is "alienated." Neither the religious explicit Jew nor the non-religious explicit one (who also "knows" what Judaism is, and that it does not in any sense depend on him or her) bears any responsibility for culture-making. They have forgotten not only that "Judaism" is imposed upon them because of their particular historical and human situation as heirs to and recipients of culture, but also that it depends on their consciousness and maintenance to be what it is. The text requires commentary, just as commentary requires text.

Not to be alienated, therefore, requires internalization (a willingness to embody the social world) *and* externalization (a capacity to act responsibly in maintaining and co-producing it) *and* objectivation (seeing the social world as a value-fact that expresses an existential reality and makes social-moral demands for maintenance). The explicit religious person may insist that the text precedes the commentary, but the sociologists do not "liberate" him or her from speaking out on and establishing the conditions for internalizing the text.[40]

## A RELIGIOUS POLEMIC:
## THE LIMITS OF SOCIOLOGICAL THEORY

Yet it is precisely here that we come upon the limitations of sociology in religious education. For any religious person is, in some sense, an explicitly religious one. This means that he or she considers at least *something* in religion as imposed, as objective. The individual considers some prophecy, or at least aspects of it, as binding.

Religious believers will say of sociology what they also assert about philosophy: that it can ask questions it cannot answer and that, like science, it can provide answers that are not germane to the philosophical questions. Sociology can ask how prophecy functions and why people think that a certain personality is or is not a true prophet, but, in the opinion of the religious person, it cannot state whether a given prophet is a true one and whether the conception of prophecy corresponds to a transcendental truth.

But the sociological theory is not only indifferent to religious convictions and truth claims. There is, behind it, a model staking out a claim that is antithetical to the conviction of the religious person. The sociological "faith" is that a belief in an explicit religious "imposed" truth testifies to alienation. If I accept on sociological "faith" that it is my society that "makes norms" (or the more radical formulation: that a relationship to the divine is "actually" a relationship to society), in which sense will my norms be divine and my relationship religious? Therefore, religious education, although it may use sociology for educational theory, must categorically reject it theologically. Otherwise, the explicit feature of religious education will suffer a reduction to "reverence for tradition" shorn of its ontological claim and specific (theological) content. This reduction, arising out of an unexamined and uncritical use of sociology in (explicit) religious education, will make religious teaching sentimental and classicist, yet without true feeling or continuity. And it is likely to be received by learners as nostalgic and hypocritical.

Undue reliance upon sociological theory creates another, more practical problem. The religious educator, in many contexts and situations of modern life, is called upon to educate religiously where the "organic" community— with its discipline, authority, and self-understood capacity for socialization— is conspicuous in its absence. The child actually lives, in most cases, in a different "objective" community with its own explicit rules (however they may have been hidden or blurred in the secular society, which preaches an individualistic ethos). Sociological theory has shown the educator that everything explicit about religious education is anchored in community, but what should be done when there is no community? Should the religious educator accept the situation and privatize religion, or build ghetto walls around those willing to rehabilitate authoritative religious community, or try something else? Sociologists cannot answer the question; they can only tell those who have made one decision or the other how to act on their decisions, and why.[41]

We have posited that sociological theory is misunderstood and misused in religious education when it is expected to provide religious legitimation. At the same time, we have warned against "lifting" sociological theories out of their contexts and not taking them seriously. The potential misuse is based on the theoretical incongruence between the religious model and the sociological one; the potential for lifting theories out of context suggests that their meaning is fully disclosed only when the sociological model is apprehended and confronted. Let us briefly discuss how explicitly adequate religious education may deal, even polemically, with the competing model and how it may yet be "taken seriously"—as required (at least) by the implicit aspect of religious education.

In Berger's social theory and, specifically, in his concept of alienation it is intimated that explicit religious belief constitutes a "forgetting" of the human "culture-making" character and role; explicit religion is a kind of alienation, a "cop-out," for God is used to enhance the "objectivity" of social reality. Consequently, we may expect "good" (i.e., sociologically approved) religion to be recognized as a human creation, even as people must be understood as shaped by the "normative" society into which fate has "thrown" them.

It is here that the sociological-scientific model must be disputed by theologians who defend the explicit characteristics of their faith. For they believe that their religion is imposed and that their commitment to commandment is not a form of alienation.

We have mentioned Soloveitchik's description of "majestic man," who wishes to endow his creativity "with intrinsic worth and with ultimate and unconditional validity." This description of the secular world seeks to objectify itself by projecting nomos onto cosmos and corresponds closely to Berger's account of alienation. However, Soloveitchik, the explicit thinker, sees this world view as exposing "majestic man's" self-centeredness-leading-to-idolatry, not his forgetting-leading-to-irresponsibility. The moment of excessive objectification of *what should be known as only human* is precisely what the explicit-minded religious person will consider flawed in the scientific model.

Soloveitchik, the religious thinker, will agree with Berger, the sociological one, that the human reality is always "not really objective," but he will point out that, as a result, secular man is always tormented by the question of his ontological worth, even at moments of great achievement. The torment of "majestic man," who cannot forget that the social world is a human construction, tempts him to invest his own creation with ultimate validity. And then he commits the *idolatrous act* of alienation, projecting the majesty that he demands for himself onto the gods he has made. Abraham, in the Midrashic tale, smashes his father Terach's idols,[42] explaining to him that the idols he himself constructs are powerless to help him or his clients, *a fact Terach actually acknowledges*. Therefore, to prevent an alienated consciousness, the explicit theologian insists that cultural authenticity, knowing what is and what is not objective, is predicated on revelation. Religious people accept revelation even though it partially deprives them of the "social construction" of culture and reality, because social construction of absolutely binding nomos is idolatry.

The religious critique of the sociological metaphysic, as that critique is articulated by Soloveitchik, may be summarized as follows: The world of "Adam the first," the cultural creator, is one of externalization and internalization. But when it seeks to objectivize itself by anchoring itself in ultimate reality, it fails; the religion of the creative human world is a mere cultural gesture, and not one of faith. It is an attempt to gain meaning and redemption without any sacrifice of "majesty" and control. It is the scientific model of sociology, which knows of no higher reality than society, that actually invites alienation: either through complete surrender to the "objective" tradition (i.e., worship of society as an idol) or by "walking away" from the religious reality that is so "objective" that it can manage nicely without any specific individual and his or her responsible conversation.[43]

The explicit thinker will insist that only through the religious model, with its explicit pole of objective religious truths demanding externalization and inviting to internalization, can the person who has a grasp of social "reality building" understand the experience of being commanded. Paraphrasing Ecclesiastes, the explicit thinker will agree that all is (ultimate) vanity under the (social) sun. But, echoing the talmudic sages, the explicit thinker will insist that above the sun, there is (objective, transcendental) Torah. Therefore, religious education cannot be based simply on a social-scientific understanding of how tradition "works" in education, because this understanding, albeit important for educational theory, misunderstands religious truth claims. And only these claims can legitimate non-alienated conviction and commitment in young people beyond the age of socialization and, later, enable them to initiate their own children into a tradition that is to be *believed* as well as expressed.

## INTEGRITY, KNOWLEDGE, AND FAITH

And yet, after sociological frames of reference have been considered, something in the plausibility structure of the religious educator *will* be affected, unless the educator did not really take the sociology of knowledge seriously. In other words, can one forget that sincerely arguing religious "truth claims" against sociology seems outlandish in the sociological context we have been using? For the educator, the problem is: Given that a feasible theory for religious education that incorpoates an explicit religious dimension requires sociological "translation" of theological norms, how can the theory be used with integrity without being *believed* as a competitive model of reality? More specifically, will one who teaches Judaism's doctrines and commandments still be able to believe in Judaism, knowing that he or she is socializing children into the community's social reality and evaluating the class's educational achievements in terms of the societal authority and conservative ethos he or she represents? And if sociological knowledge can be shown to corrupt religious teachers by transforming their former truths into teachable "useful fictions," isn't the only alternative not to know the theories? Wouldn't one therefore rather remain in communities that do not confront modernity and that, through isolation, maintain their educational agencies intact and "in their place"—i.e., theoretically innocent, except for authorized theologies of education?

The broad issue of convictions "tainted" by sociological reflection has been systematically addressed by Karl Mannheim.[44] Mannheim has asked whether we can believe in the sphere of "truth as such" if we know what kind of situations create given social realities and if we are aware that social relationships influence our thinking. If every epoch, because of its unique historical situation, has its characteristic consciousness and sees things through its perspective, so that even basic categories of thought change under changed circumstances, isn't the only truth that of sociology—which "really" explains why people act and think as they do?[45]

Mannheim pinpointed the problem by noting that the detachment enabling people to describe data objectively is made from a certain perspective and shapes one's viewpoint. His example:

For the son of a peasant who has grown up in the narrow confines of his village and spends his whole life in the place of his birth, the mode of thinking and speaking characteristic of that village is something that he takes entirely for granted. But for the country lad who goes to the city and adapts himself gradually to city life, the rural mode of living and thinking ceases to be something to be taken for granted. He has won a certain detachment from it, and he distinguishes now, perhaps quite consciously, between "rural" and "urban" modes of thought and ideas. In this distinction lie the first beginnings of that approach which the sociology of knowledge seeks to develop in full detail. That which within a given group is accepted as absolute appears to the outsider conditioned by the group situation and recognized as partial (in this case, as "rural"). [From *Ideology and Utopia* by Karl Mannheim. Reprinted by permission of Harcourt Brace Jovanovich, Inc.][46]

If you learn to see "what used to be absolute" through the prism of a social situation or process, you tend to see not only the partiality of a given view but also the "former" truth in a reductionist manner. Once Marx, for example, "explained" bourgeois philosophy, religion, law, and education in terms of the dialectic of materialism, participant accounts of that bourgeois culture were rendered fundamentally irrelevant to the truth or falsity of actually held beliefs. For in Marx's view the bourgeois ideology "is constituted by those beliefs the primary function of which is either to support or justify class privilege and capitalist forms of social organization, or to force the acceptance of such forms upon otherwise unwilling victims of the system."[47]

In terms of our problem, explicitly oriented religious education, viewed through the prism of sociology of knowledge, *really* is socialization into a "socially constructed reality," and the reasons given by pious people to explain their teaching (and observance) of *mitzvot* can be dismissed as "false consciousness," i.e., ideologically induced rationalizations. Ahad Ha-Am's slogan, "religion preserved our people in the Exile,"[48] which is educationally translated by many secular Israeli educators as "religious education is necessary in the Diaspora," is a species of reductionist sociological thinking about religion and religious education. The paradoxical situation with which we are faced is that the explicit dimension of religious education, if it is to be translated into comprehensive educational theory, requires sociological categories; yet it is precisely from the vantage point of explicit religion guarding the *religious model* that sociological theory, which justifies religious educational practice from an external "ground," appears dangerous. It threatens to transform consciousness, to corrode belief in religious truth, which, as a result of sociological sophistication, is likely to be seen as a historical "group situation" and as a "partial view."

Yet, Mannheim has argued cogently that attaining a detached (sociological) perspective, as in the case of the peasant boy who now speaks of his background as "rural," does not necessarily invalidate the assertions that have been "placed" in their historical or social context by sociology. With regard to the truth of assertions made by participants in a certain culture, three approaches are possible within the context of the sociology of knowledge:

The first is to say that "the absolute validity of an assertion is denied when its structural relationship to a given social situation has been shown." In this way of thinking, the way to annihilate one's opponents is to "expose" the social context of their thought; understanding it is tantamount to disqualifying its claim to truth.[49]

The second possibility is to assert that there is no relationship between a statement's structural relationship to a given social situation and its validity. Proponents of this approach maintain that "the manner in which a statement originates does not affect its validity."[50]

The third approach is to believe "that the mere factual demonstration and identification of the social position of the assertor as yet tells us nothing about the truth value of his assertion," although it does imply "the suspicion that this assertion might represent only a partial view."[51] Unlike the second approach and in response to it, advocates of this way of thinking consider it incorrect to regard the sociology of knowledge as giving no more than a description of the actual conditions under which an assertion arises. "Every complete and thorough sociological analysis of knowledge delimits, in content as well as structure, the view to be analyzed."

What the sociology of knowledge intends to do by its analysis was . . . brought out in the example we cited of the peasant boy. The discovery and identification of his earlier mode of thought as "rural," as contrasted with "urban," already involves the insight that the different perspectives are not merely particular in that they suppose different ranges of vision and different sectors of the total reality, but also in that the interests and the powers of perception of the different perspectives are conditioned by the social situations in which they arose and to which they are relevant. [From *Ideology and Utopia* by Karl Mannheim. Reprinted by permission of Harcourt Brace Jovanovich, Inc.][52]

Hence, according to this third approach, one may still speak of *knowledge* and even of some *objectivity,* but one must reject the "false ideal" of a detached, impersonal point of view. This must be replaced by a vision shaped by people with diverse perspectives, in constant conversation with one another, so that knowledge may be enlarged. True, one can see only from the particular perspective in which one finds oneself, but one can try to see more. One may talk, observe, and develop instruments of comparison.

Of the approaches proposed by Mannheim, two may, in principle, be acceptable to the religious educator who fears that the use of sociological theory may lead to a "sociologizing" of his or her faith commitments: the second and the third. The second approach appears most congenial, for it denies the "structural relationship" between a given situation and the validity of a given statement. In this view, the reasons given by participants for their beliefs will be taken into account more than will casual explanations offered by observers. Thus, Dixon, out of consideration for this approach, argues that serious attention should be paid to participant accounts of belief, to exploring belief systems from an internal point of view, to treating the reasons professed by believers as "conceivably true."[53] From this "internal point of view," the specific situations in which "Providence," "Revelation," "covenant," and "commandment" arise are occasions for the appearance of the truth, occasions chosen by God as suitable for His pedagogical purposes. From this vantage point, Israel was enslaved in order to learn love of the stranger, was made to wander in the desert to acquire faith and love of *Eretz Yisrael,* and was not given to understand some of the commandments in order to teach trust of God, Who "knows the soul of man." Clearly, this approach is most congenial to outspokenly explicit religious educators, who tend, as we have seen, to convert reasons for religion proffered as external justifications into internal explications.[54]

The third approach may also be congruent with a religious education that is not reduced to sociological categories. Moreover, it exposes to view a particular implicit religious contribution to the understanding of sociology's role in educational theory. For although the idea of perspective—of the partiality of human understanding that is always related to a particular social context—may be in principle problematic in relation to "world religions," this need not be the case for Judaism. Judaism is the religious life of the Jewish people and the terms of its covenant with God. This is admitted even by the most thoroughly explicit educators, who, while deeply suspicious of the sociology of knowledge, do agree that God may speak in different ways to diverse people and peoples. After all, they accept the prophecy of Amos, who declared that, as He took Israel out of Egypt, He took the Ethiopians out of the land of Cush.[55] Each nation experienced His saving hand in the context of events and experiences that were unique to it. That Judaism, both as halakhah and as historical events-of-significance, is not binding in practice and in memory upon the (other) nations means *at least* that *this* history (and *this* perspective) is not requisite for a human relationship to *the* truth, though it may be a condition for seeing the truth Jewishly. Therefore, to say that the truth seen from any particular human perspective is partial and that new dimensions of the truth may be discovered in new situations is not necessarily to deny the revealed character of the Torah. In fact, it may simply be a religious insight into the possibilities and obligations inherent in the Oral Torah.

The explicit-minded teacher is likely to prefer the second approach; the implicitly oriented teacher, the third approach. In either case, unless the theology of education is explicitly or implicitly distorted, the educator will "take seriously the reasons for belief" of Jewish tradition—that is, he or she will maintain the integrity of the model. And in both cases, the situation and perspective will be constituent elements of instruction, teaching either divine Providence—"Who knows man's soul"—or human humility, or both, for even prophets see God through the veils of human perspectives and situations. The sociologist, while not a prophet, enables educators to understand more clearly that all teaching takes place in concrete human situations and is built upon a particular culture and a particular fund of perspectives.

# 12 Cultivating the Authentic Jewish Individual: Theory of Implicit Teaching

## PSYCHOLOGICAL SCHOOLS AND EDUCATIONAL MODELS

Implicit religious orientations cast a spotlight on the relationship of the individual to his or her "ultimate concerns" and posit that the vision of ultimacy of which a person is capable is a function of personal development. In order to guide the young person toward faith, therefore, the educator must be able to grasp such concepts as "readiness," "development," and others that denote the individuation that (according to the implicit religionist) characterize the mature, "integrated" religious personality. The young person must become himself or herself and the educator must help to facilitate the "encounter" viewed by implicit religion as the crux of "becoming." Psychology, therefore, can be expected to be of crucial importance for the theory of religious education, especially with regard to its implicit dimensions.

Yet, seemingly, psychologists should be less interested in or hopeful about education than sociologists. For one thing, the psychologist looks upon the educating agent as an "outsider" *vis-à-vis* the developing child and may consider the teacher more apt to sabotage than to foster the child's natural growth. Also, the psychologist, more than the sociologist, is likely to see the child as somehow "programmed by laws of his inner nature" and less amenable to change through education. Nevertheless, the fact is that modern educational theory leans so heavily on psychology that scholars such as Schwab and Hofstadter have called attention to the danger of "the corruption of education by psychology."[1]

Because psychology is so widely regarded as the primary scientific basis of educational theory, and because it is considered authoritative in so many areas of educational practice, it is worthwhile to differentiate, however briefly and superficially, among several prominent schools of psychology and their (diverse) approaches to educational philosophy. For different psychological schools do have different philosophical assumptions, and certain philosophical orientations with regard to teaching and learning are more congenial to some psychological approaches than to others.

Behavioral psychology, for example, which is predicated on the malleability of people through environmental stimuli that condition them, is highly compatible with what, in Scheffler's educational typology, is termed the Impression Model.[2] This approach, with its view of the child as a *tabula rasa* waiting to be "written upon" and shaped by the teacher, seems even more "optimistic" about the degree of socialization that is possible than does that of the sociologists we reviewed in the previous chapter.

The concern with socialization is also focal in classic psychoanalytic theory, with its heavy emphasis on identification ("introjection") in educational activity, but here the starting point is radically different from the Skinnerian-Behavioral one. Freudian thinkers are preoccupied not with the child's conditioning-toward-contentment but with his or her need to live with—and in—civilization despite the *discontent* it engenders in the human organism. The Freudian conception, with its stress on developing an ego that can cope with reality without superfluous deprivations of the id, is more reminiscent of Scheffler's "Rule Model."[3]

The humanistic approach, with its motifs of "meaning-making" and its emphasis on personality and self-actualization, seems closest to the "Insight Model," which insists that human beings are "drawn out" in interaction with their environment. This approach has been traced back to the philosophy of Leibnitz.

The Leibnitz tradition . . . maintains that a person is not a collection of acts . . . the person is the source of acts. And activity itself is not conceived as agitation resulting from pushes by internal or external stimulation. It is purposive. To understand what a person is, it is necessary always to refer to what he may be in the future, for every state of the person is pointed in the direction of future possibilities.[4]

Experience is related to what happens in the objective world but is not *determined* by it. Consequently, the humanistic approach views psychology as ideally a descriptive science and not an explanatory one; it should describe what really happens in human experience. Humanistic psychologists therefore tend to favor a phenomenological approach, which can "take the wisdom and insights of the poets and give them precise expression and a rigorous, systematic grounding."[5]

The foregoing will suffice to indicate that the theories of humanistic psychology, especially those of its "existential" proponents, seem most relevant to the concerns of implicit religious educators[6] (while those of the behaviorists are clearly the least relevant). In the modern humanistic culture, in which the existential psychologists are often spiritual mentors, implicit religion is usually viewed as a higher stage of spiritual development than explicit "religiousness." Indeed, humanistic psychologists have sometimes commended implicit faith—which they juxtapose with the more primitive and (sociologically circumscribed) explicit patterns of authority and ritual.[7]

In fact, various psychologists who describe the "core" of human existence and development have been so frequently cited by religious thinkers and have themselves referred so positively to contemporary religious and theological conceptions that religious educators, even as they take heart, had better (also) take heed. For the psychologist, more than the sociologist, often rules on the quality and value of specific expressions of the religious sentiment—after all, a psychologist is considered competent to determine what mental health is and, sometimes, to gauge moral maturity. We can expect, therefore, that the problem of differentiating between (religious) model and (scientific) theory will be more difficult on this level of educational theory building and theological "translation" than on the sociological one.

Of course, as we saw, sociological theories also intimate prescriptive preferences. "Alienation" is, for Berger, "not doing" social reality, and this implies a stamp of disapproval upon blatantly explicit religion. Gellner has pointed out that the sociologist has a Platonic "working concept" of ethical knowledge in which given general terms do not merely class things together but also set standards for what is acceptable; in his words, "the classification incorporates a norm."[8] But the psychological way of being prescriptive, given the modern view that religion is primarily a matter of the individual and the negotiation of the self with the world, is prone to be more persuasive and more pervasive. Gellner has noted that from the psychological perspective, ethical knowledge is likely to be seen as basically internal and individualistic; this perspective suggests "the Hidden Prince" model, the good man struggling to "get out" from underneath the bad kernel—represented by neurosis or, perhaps, immaturity.[9] Expressions such as "self-realization" and "true identity" are characteristic of this perspective, and we may expect educational theory to incorporate these concepts of knowledge and being whenever humanistic psychologies (whether post-psychoanalytic or existential) are brought into play.

Lamm has clearly stated what is prescribed by the "development model" of education, which strives for autonomy and self-realization, and the ways in which it relies on psychological theory. In this model,

> criteria for measuring the content and direction of development are intrinsic. . . . [T]he individual does not become human by virtue of the fact that he has learned to function according to models of social roles or internalized cultural norms and values. His humanity is innate. The function of teaching and education is not to teach him to be human, but to enable what is human in him to be realized. Humanity is not standard; every individual is human in his own way.[10]

The goal is maximal individuation; the value of knowing things, acquiring cultural goods, is measured by their ability to enhance the development of those who have acquired this knowledge. The teacher in the "development model" is neither an agent of society nor a philosophically competent agent of culture, but an *expert,* knowledgeable about and sensitive to the patterns of psychological learning and development.[11]

From this discussion it will be obvious why implicit-minded religious educators will seek support and theoretical tools for their theory of religious education in a phenomenologically grounded psychology and will look to the cognitive models provided by developmental, or "stage," theorists. In the humanistic schools of psychology they will find a concern with universal tendencies of "growth" and development, of an apparent movement from social to individual forms of spiritual expression. Through such psychologies, religion can be linked in educational theory to creativity, spontaneity, and choice; self-discovery can be interpreted as a religious process and event. Likewise, the descriptions of developmental, or "stage," psychologists, who speak of *higher* stages of development in terms of autonomy (rather than heteronomy) or of ethics (as more "advanced" than morality), can be used to show how implicit religiosity corresponds to a more mature sensibility.

## A PSYCHOLOGICAL THEORY

An interesting and instructive theological use of such psychological categories is Richardson's essay "Three Myths of Transcendence."[12] We shall discuss this essay at some length, for it points both to the theoretical utility of such categories for religious understanding and education and to the possibility of using a psychological *theory* to demolish unworthy or "immature" religious models.

Richardson finds a consensus among modern theologians that "an irreducible element in 'true religion' is a certain feeling." These feelings are conveyed through myths and story images; through them children "see the point," learn the meanings, of religion. Richardson posits that there are three basic myths, representing three stages of personal, as well as historical, development.

The first is the primitive odyssey of *separation and return*, and it is spelled out in such stories as Hansel and Gretel. The theme of these myth-stories is "the resolution of the crisis created by a person's separation from his true home, from the abode of his real identity and well-being." Hansel and Gretel learn of their utter dependence upon the parent, for separation is danger and return means safety. "Stay away from the dark forest and close to Mother" is a myth that would seem (though Richardson does not use this word) to demand the child's obedience; in the author's words, the stories "objectify" the feeling "that his identity (his wholeness) is established in dependence upon the mother from whom he is separated by birth, that his happiness is in returning to and being fed and held by her and that it is right to call upon her and wrong to stray away from her. . . . " Such stories bespeak a pre-adolescent stage of development; historically they are equated with "early" religion.

The second group of stories, historically characteristic of "Christianity and post-prophetic Judaism," represents the displacement of the separation-and-return stories by the myth of *conflict-and-vindication.* These stories, illustrated by such characters as "Batman" (and, we may add, such stories as *Star Wars*), describe the hero's moving away from limitation, oppression, and suffering. "Through a testing, man attains to the vindication of his personhood, his independent being." Stories of "conflict and vindication" include the exodus from Egypt, the conflict between David and Goliath, and the crucifixion and resurrection of Jesus. These stories "inculcate a sense of reality as a structure of overagainstness experienced through conflict and formed in the person through his triumphal suffering." In the conflict-and-vindication myth, a man's identity is still established in relation to another—but now through " 'overagainstness' rather than through the participation characteristic of the separation-and-return orientation." Identity is gained through being *against* something; one *becomes* good through the struggle with evil; one *needs* the opposite in order to become and maintain one's own (contra-)identity. For Richardson, this stage in psycho-social development corresponds to adolescence.

A positive identity requires a third myth, the myth of adulthood—*integrity and transformation.* In this myth, the hero is no longer fearful "of those who would take away his enemy," and he need not "invent enemies to destroy."

Thus, in the new myth, exemplified by Kubrick's *2001: A Space Odyssey,* "the end of the space man is not some 'goal' in terms of which he either 'cyclically' or 'linearly' defines himself. It is, rather, his own self-transformation into a higher being, his spiritual rebirth, his divinization."[13] This man of integrity needs nothing except the demand or requirement rooted in himself to be true to those tendencies that make him unique. "In our integrity we can experience transcendence as our own potentiality to become more, as the demand for self-transformation."[14]

Richardson's use of developmental psychology obviously illuminates aspects of religious educational theory. This theory gives us a conception, however partial, of what being part of and obedient to a world of adults means to a child and how this world is transmitted to and comprehended by the child at a particular stage of development. Furthermore, we see how stories help children and adults "handle" conflicts and desires at various stages of life and, finally, how stories convey spiritual achievement. From the vantage point of theology—and the theology of education—we have here a conception of religious development as proceeding from the most explicit, in which God (like Mother) signifies the security-bestowing but sternly demanding parent, to the most implicit, in which an individual's spirituality is indivisible from the sum of his or her own potential. In terms of religious experience, we are given a new way of seeing, for educational use, such concepts as sin and repentance. These concepts can be variously understood as disobedience and "return"— the unwillingness to fight evil and the resolution to join the ranks of those fighting it, and the refusal to be responsible for one's existence and a "return" to one's potential. (This potential is characterized by opportunities granted every person to be "more human"—in knowledge, love, feeling, action, and understanding.) Thus, Richardson, through a theological interpretation of a certain developmental-psychological scheme, helps the educator to conceive more broadly what religious terms may mean to emerging personalities seeking themselves.

Yet, at the same time, it is clear that Richardson is using a developmental (anthropological and psychological) paradigm to develop a particular conception of religious and spiritual self-realization. Theory of human growth, anthropologically and psychologically conceived, has become a religious model. In this model, the "development" of personality is patterned on stages to be outgrown as well as stages to be reached; the underlying assumption is an evolutionary one, which points toward a consummation that is potentially pagan. A person's highest stage of development is his or her "divinization." Faith, which begins "childishly" with dependence and obedience, moves toward an absolute spiritual autonomy. This development may be described as "saintly" by enthusiasts of Ayn Rand's fictional heroes but will be disturbing to adherents of such religious traditions as the Jewish one, which insist on distinguishing between descriptive and normative statements.

In Judaism, as we have seen, there are explicit as well as implicit religious dimensions. If the explicit element is "for real," then one can learn much from psychological theories about empirically observed sequence in moral development but very little about religious moral norms. Religious traditions such as Judaism, which are explicit as well as implicit, teach that obedience and "returning home" are not childish but inherent in the human situation, which, upon reflection, is recognized as one's "finding" oneself and accepting one's limitations.[15] In this situational framework the religious Jew "places" such concepts as *mitzvah,* sin, *Galut* [exile], "nearness to God," and atonement.

Furthermore, "adolescents" are not the only ones who are constantly called upon to define and assert their moral identities by their choices of reference groups and by their decision not to acquiesce to injustice but rather to join those who combat it. "Those who have no enemies don't deserve any friends." As for the myth of transformation: In Judaism, the realization of the highest ideal of self-actualization is not attained when the commandments have been transcended or when battling evil is considered outlandish or trivial.

Abraham, whom the Midrash calls the archetype of the whole man "for whose sake the heavens and the earth were created,"[16] is a model personality of the Jewish religious tradition. Abraham "feared God" to such an extent that he was ready to sacrifice his son Isaac; he fought invading kings fearlessly and thus scrupulously defended his kinsman Lot, yet he dared to demand of the Judge of all the earth that He do justice. He surrendered to God, and yet it was he who "brought Him down into the world." He "stood before God" and he "walked before Him."[17] All three of these "moments"—obedience, self-vindication, and integrity—are problematic because of the existential commitment to, and the normative presence of, the others, and Midrashic literature reflects this problem without solving it.[18] Abraham always knew that God is "higher," and yet there are times when he had to "forget" this in order not to betray his moral sense; like Moses, Abraham "learned halakhah" from God, and yet he was ready to propose ethical norms that would oblige the Author of moral truth Himself. And the "movement" between these aspects of religious experience and norms constitutes the ongoing conversation into which the Jewish teacher wishes to initiate the pupil.[19]

Clearly, the humanistic psychological tradition can easily be applied to religious education in improperly normative ways. At the same time, it can shed light on aspects of the tradition that are neither doctrinal nor halakhic but are woven into its fabric, like the dialectic among obedience, self-vindication, and integrity or that between stages of development and of the life cycle, which are alluded to by Scripture and Sages. These aspects of the tradition are features of a Jewish anthropology, recommending on the basis of theo-psychological description. Psychological theory *draws them out,* inviting the educator to a closer look and to a more judicious selection.

## COMMUNICATION WITH COGNITIVE ALIENS

If the major educational problem engaging the sociologist who is asked to contribute to educational theory is that of *initiation* (socialization and acculturation), the psychologist is called upon to contribute to the enhancement of *communication.* In the former case, the theory is designed to help the teacher get young people "on the inside" of a cultural language; in the latter case, it is to make the educator appreciate and consider to what extent children, *because they are children,* live in a different cognitive or affective world.[20] The developmental psychologists whose theories and findings have been most influential in educational theory in recent years, and particularly in religious education, are Piaget, Kohlberg, and Erikson. Speaking of Piaget's findings, Elkind writes:

. . . the image of the child suggested by these discoveries is that of a person who, relative to adults, is a *cognitive alien.* That is to say, the child, like the person from a foreign country, thinks differently and, figuratively, at any rate, speaks a different language.[21]

According to Piaget, certain kinds of thinking are impossible until the child has reached adolescence, for thinking develops in stages. First, there is the sensory-motor period (from birth to the age of approximately two years), in which children acquire the abilities necessary to construct "rudimentary schemata of space, time, causality, and the permanence of objects,"[22] In the second stage, "the pre-operational stage," there is a development of the symbolic function; children learn to represent things. We have here "the gradual acquisition of language, the first indications of dreams and night terrors, the advent of symbolic play . . . and the first attempts at drawing and graphic representation."[23] At the beginning of the stage, children tend to identify words and symbols with the objects they are intended to represent; by the end of this period children understand that names are arbitrary designations.

At the next stage (usually from the age of seven to eleven years), children acquire concrete operations, which permit them to "do in their heads" what they formerly had to do through real actions. Children can count things men-

tally, they can deal with the relations between classes of things and thus make
differentiations between different kinds of categories. Thus, whereas a child
before this age is likely to say that one can be both a Protestant and an American "only if you move," during the concrete operational stage the child will
understand that Americans live in America and Protestants go to church.[24]

The last stage, usually reached between the ages of twelve and fifteen
years, is the stage of formal operations. In this stage it becomes possible "to
think about thought," to construct ideals, to understand metaphors (and so, to
grasp the "idea" of political and satirical cartoons), and to understand books
such as *Alice in Wonderland* as signifying rather than describing. After the
achievement of formal operational thinking, one can continue to hope for ever-
increasing understanding and depth, but the formal manner of thinking constitutes the final "stage" insofar as no further mental tools will develop.

In Piagetian theory, the kinds of questions children ask have to be understood in terms of the cognitive world of the child before they can be answered.
For example, "Why do leaves fall?" or "Why do we have to die?" are not,
for the child of four, questions that invite scientific answers. To the child such
answers are irrelevant and incomprehensible, for the four-year-old is interested
in purpose, not in cause. Thus, the latter question can be satisfactorily
"fielded" by an answer such as, "To make room for other people, for all the
new babies that are being born."[25]

As Elkind interprets Piaget, the development of thought takes place
through either *substitution* or *integration*. In substitution, a more mature idea
replaces a less mature one, but the earlier idea remains available for potential
use; it is not eradicated. For example, children substitute the idea that all things
have "spirit" with the idea that only things that move do, and then with the
idea that only conscious beings have "spirit." Young children, therefore,
speak to dolls, although they are destined to learn that dolls are merely lifeless
cloth. Yet, "the father who is quietly amused by his little daughter when she
speaks to and feeds her toy animals and dolls, nevertheless secretly thanks his
car for starting on a particularly cold and wintery morning."[26]

Piaget has written extensively on moral development, which belongs to this
"substitution" category. He traces moral maturation from concern with consequences to focusing on intentions. Thus, a child who broke twelve cups
while helping Mother to set the table is considered more blameworthy by a
young child than the one who broke one cup trying to get some jam that he had
been forbidden to have; the older child, evaluating the good intentions of the
first youngster, finds the boy breaking one cup more culpable. The "substitution" nature of this development is illustrated by Elkind as follows:

A child who breaks his mother's best lamp by accident is likely to be more severely punished than if he breaks an old cup on purpose . . . as adults dealing with children, we often revert to our earlier moral conceptions and gear our reactions to the amount of material damage done by the child rather than to his intentions.[27]

Religious understanding and identity also fall within the "substitution" framework. There is a development "from an initial primitive notion of religion as a kind of name, to an intermediary notion of religion as a kind of action, to a final conception of religion as a set of particular beliefs."[28] Here too, because the growth is by "substitution," the earlier ideas persist even when the more "advanced have already been accepted."

In *"integration,"* as Elkind explains it, immature ideas are brought together to arrive at more complex and abstract conceptions. For example, a child learns that higher is not necessarily bigger, because the category of size takes in both height and width. Though integration, like substitution, tends to follow a developmental timetable that is only partially modifiable by experience, it is different in that integration is more stable and irreversible than substitution. Once children have integrated height and breadth into their concept of size, they are not likely, barring mental disturbance or dysfunctioning, to think of size in one-dimensional terms again. Moreover, most of the ideas that develop by integration have something logical or quantitative about them; substitution deals more with such matters as religion and moral judgment and such fields as sociology and psychology.

Elkind points out another crucial Piagetian distinction having to do with two types of learning experience: We learn a body of knowledge, say, geography; we also must learn general categories of space, time, causality, and number. The former, "P," remains basically unaltered by mental growth, whereas the latter, "LM," is conceived differently at discrete stages. "The child has P content or he does not—either he knows that Independence Day is celebrated on the 4th of July, or he does not."

With LM contents, however, the situation is different . . . even the infant has a global conception of "right" and "left." [But] what is important about LM contents is that the child has a *different* conception of right and left at successive age levels. LM contents can, then, never be evaluated as present or absent or as right or wrong. In evaluating LM contents all we can say is that the infant's concept of right and left is *different* from that of the young child, whose conception is *different* from that of the adolescent and the adult.[29]

That the thrust of development is in the direction of what we have called (for religious education) implicitness is clear from the Piagetian distinction between heteronomous and autonomous stages of moral growth. As Sholl has summarized these stages:

At the heteronomous stage, the child is "subject to the rule of another." Authority and performance are emphasized. Duty is thought of in terms of obedience to authority which . . . is determined by adults. Rules are regarded as sacred and unchangeable.[30]

We are reminded, says Sholl, of Freud and Durkheim's discussions of morality, in which "imitation or learning by identity occur via select reinforcement and presentation of a model. Internalization of the parent's superego or of group norms and sanctions completes the process." Clearly a description, in our religious educational terms, of an *explicit* approach.

But this heteronomous stage is followed in development by autonomous morality, which originates with "cooperation and the idea of justice" and which is characterized by the person's being subject to his own law.

Here rules are digested rather than ingested or internalized. Moral conceptions become psychological rather than objective . . . Rules are conceived as "elaborately articulated social games". . . . Justice is thought of in terms of reciprocal rights.[31]

Clearly, it is the advanced stage that corresponds to the implicitly religious sentiment.


## FROM EXPLICIT TO IMPLICIT PERSONALITY

In the work of Kohlberg, the cognitive stages of Piaget are basically maintained, but interest is focused on moral-structural development, which runs parallel to the growth of cognitive understanding. And, as we shall see, the implicit orientation (to reality if not to religion) is unequivocally viewed as a higher stage than the explicit one.

Defining moral development in terms of levels of moral judgment, Kohlberg delineates three basic levels: the "pre-conventional," the "conventional," and the "post-conventional."[32] At the pre-conventional level, there are two stages: Stage One, "punishment and reward," is characterized by the view that the physical consequences of action, rather than human meaning or value, determine what is good or bad. In Stage Two, reciprocal fairness or instrumental hedonism prevails. Right action here consists of what satisfies the self's needs. Reciprocity is a matter of "you scratch my back and I'll scratch yours."

The conventional level also has two planes. Stage Three morality has to do with "good behavior" and acting in a socially approved way—which is largely dependent on stereotyped images of socially approved behavior. Stage Three behavior is concerned with "meaning well," being seen to be "good." In Stage Four, the orientation is toward authority, fixed rules, and the maintenance of social order. One does one's duty and earns respect by accepting the discipline of authority and rules.

At the post-conventional level, we have Stages Five and Six. The former is characterized by a social-contract orientation; "right action tends to be defined in terms of general rights and . . . standards which have been critically examined and agreed upon by the whole society." Emphasis is placed on rules of procedure, although the possibility of changing law in terms of rational considerations of social utility is considered. This, states Kohlberg, "is the 'official' morality of American government and finds its grounds in the thought of the writers of the Constitution." Finally, in Stage Six conscience and "self-chosen *ethical principles* appealing to logical comprehensiveness, universality, and consistency" are determinative. The principles of Stage Six are abstract and universal; "they are not concrete moral rules like the Ten Commandments. Instead, they are universal principles of *justice,* of the *reciprocity* and *equality* of *individual persons.*"[33]

Kohlberg summarizes the three levels (with their six stages) as follows: At the first level, "moral value resides in external, quasi-physical happenings, in bad acts, or in quasi-physical needs, rather than in persons or standards." At the second level, "moral value resides in performing good or right roles, in maintaining the conventional order and the expectancies of others," and at the third level, "moral value resides in conformity by the self to shared or shareable standards, rights or duties."[34]

Like Piaget, Kohlberg believes that children think differently from adults and that movement through stages is always upward and one step at a time. A child may stop at any stage but cannot reach a higher stage without having gone through the lower ones.

Kohlberg does not see a necessary connection between moral development and religious faith, although he does suggest, as a "metaphor," a "Stage Seven" in which the universal principles of Stage Six are integrated with a perspective on life's ultimate meaning. But it is interesting to note that Kohlberg's example of a "Stage Seven" personality, an individual who moves beyond existential despair to an ultimate stage of "integrity," is Marcus

Aurelius. The influence of Erikson here is clear and admitted; Marcus Aurelius is chosen partly "because he is outside the Judeo-Christian tradition, a helpful element in defining universals in faith."[35]

This "perspective of integrity," which is said to develop with the growth of "a mature psychosocial identity," is variously discussed and explained by Erikson in his description of the stages of life.[36] These stages have been called "a program of ego development . . . from birth to death"; the individual passes through the phases of the life cycle by meeting, and, it is hoped, resolving, a series of developmental psychosocial crises. Meissner has summarized these stages:

In the earliest stage of infancy, at the mother's breast, the child developed either a sense of basic trust or a sense of mistrust. In later infancy the child had to achieve a sense of autonomy, or failing that, he would be left with some degree of shame and doubt. In early childhood the child developed a sense of initiative hopefully without guilt. In latency, the issue was a sense of industry without a sense of inferiority. The adolescent crisis was the crystallization of the residues of preceding crisis into a more or less definitive sense of personal identity, as opposed to a diffusion of identity and a confusion of roles. For the young adult the question was the development of a sense of intimacy rather than isolation. For the older adult the issue was generativity, as a concern for establishing and guiding the next generation. And finally, in the twilight of life, the crisis to be resolved is that of ego integrity in the face of ultimate despair.[37]

Erikson has traced ethical development from this psychoanalytic perspective; he insists that a person's ethical sense is contingent on the inner strengths that support and sustain it. Like Piaget, Erikson draws a distinction between heteronomous and autonomous ethics, or what he calls morality and ethics. The former ("morality") flows from fear and is based on threats of abandonment or inner dread of guilt or isolation, whereas the latter ("ethics") is built upon ideals to which one aspires.[38] Like Piaget and Kohlberg, Erikson agrees that the higher cannot bypass the lower; furthermore, "ethics" always retains remnants of earlier stages of development, like growth by "substitution" as explained by Elkind.

Erikson has himself dealt extensively with the relationship of ego development and psychosocial growth to religion. This is a central theme in his classic study, *Young Man Luther*.[39] As in the theories of Piaget and Kohlberg, religious and moral development in Erikson's thought is more *mature* to the extent that it is more *implicit*. Piaget's "cooperation and justice," Kohlberg's "Stage Six," and Erikson's "ethics," while assuming that the hallmarks of explicit religiosity are requisite to mature personality development, all envision an ideal movement toward a more spiritual, autonomous personality.

This tendency of the psychologists themselves to make moral evaluations on the basis of their theoretical descriptions has been criticized by philosophers and educators. For example, Peters has argued that, although Kohlberg's findings are of unquestionable importance, "there is a grave danger that they may be exalted into a general theory of moral development." He reminds his readers that "any such general theory presupposes a general ethical theory," which would tell us whether "Stage Six" justice is indeed a more important and "higher" virtue than, say, courage, integrity, or autonomy. Speaking from a religious perspective, Dykstra points out that the philosophical foundations of the developmental view are not necessarily congruent with religious "immediacy" as actually experienced. And Egan insists that educational theory, concerned with what ought to be done to move children to desirable goals, can benefit more from the prescriptive "stages of development" proposed by Plato than from the theoretical and seemingly culture-free theories of developmental psychology.[40]

Formally, a "higher stage" in Kohlberg's theory is determined not by its greater moral rectitude but by the irreversibility of sequence in stages and by the fact that each stage presumably resolves conflicts that remain unresolved at earlier and lower stages. Yet, Levin notes that Kohlberg himself agrees that there is no "scientific" Stage Six"; it is "less a statement of an attained psychological reality than the specification of a direction in which, our theory claims, psychological reality is moving."[41]

The philosophy of growth and development, of ethics as ideally autonomous, and the centrality of living experience rather than of "bookish" tradition may, of course, constitute the backbone and essence of an educational theory; it may be stated by philosophers and educators prescriptively. This was done, comprehensively and very influentially, by John Dewey in the early years of the century. As Hofstadter has remarked, the concept of the growing child in the center of educational concern, of the child as "a phenomenon at once natural and divine," reflected both post-Darwinian naturalism and the romantic heritage. It assumed a " 'natural' pattern of . . . needs and instincts" and fostered the educational ideal of honoring this natural pattern. Dewey insisted that "the child's own instincts and powers furnish the material and give the starting point for all education. . . . "[42] This psychology-belief is, of course, congenial to much in the implicit religious orientation, but it is a distinct theory of education that looks to the scientific enterprise for a metaphysical model. It should not be confused with the psychological theories that are required by theology of education in its venture of becoming useful to religious educational theory. This distinction bears reiteration not only to protect theology of education against corruption but also to maintain the integrity of religious education itself. For the educator must be enabled to use psychological theory eclectically, to turn to various and opposing theories when, for religious or educational reasons, the contribution of one school of thought is seen as not comprehensive enough or *as too comprehensive*. We shall return to this problem and this procedure.


## STAGES OF RELIGIOUS DEVELOPMENT

What can be learned from the psychological theories of Kohlberg and other developmentalists who draw on a humanistic psychological tradition is well illustrated in the work of Fowler. In his *Stages of Faith*,[43] Fowler engages these psychologists in discourse and constructs a conception of religious development, which moves from "intuitive-projective" to "mythic-literal" and "synthetic-conventional" phases (which are lower) to stages that are "individuative-reflective," "conjunctive," and "universalizing." The first stage is dominated by religious imagination and fantasy; in the second the person appropriates—very literally—the stories, beliefs, and observances that symbolize belonging to his or her community; the third stage is characterized by unreflective acceptance of norms and values and an identification with "our kind of" (believing) people. Stage Four brings the individual to reflection about himself or herself and the distance between the self and society; the person "must begin to take seriously the burden of responsibility for his or her own commitments, lifestyle, beliefs, and attitudes."[44] In Stage Five, one discovers "the sacrament of defeat and the reality of irrevocable commitments and acts." One becomes alive to paradox and "the truth in apparent contradictions"; one appreciates symbols, myths, and rituals because of "the depth of reality to which they refer."[45] Finally, in Stage Six, an ideal type is portrayed. Paradox no longer has the power to paralyze the individual. Apparent contradictions no longer create a sense of conflicting loyalties. Stage Six is active, engaged "in spending and being spent for the transformation of present reality in the direction of a transcendent actuality." The particular communities of faith are no longer dialectically opposed to the universal but are "cherished because they are vessels of the universal."[46]

Fowler here presents an educational ideal that is normative yet uses psychological theories, in terms of what they suggest as well as how they constrain. "Stage Six" (and, for that matter, "Stage Five") is a typology, a recommended way to move, which reflects an understanding of a religious tradition that has been clarified and made more responsible by the use of psychological theory. One need not agree with Fowler's Stage Six theology; it is not "scientific," but a particular Christian view that seeks to identify and illuminate saintliness in other faiths as well.[47]

## SOME CONTRIBUTIONS OF PSYCHOLOGY TO RELIGIOUS TEACHING

What, then, can the religious educator, loyal to the "model" of his or her religious community and faith, learn from psychological theories of personality and growth? The following are some potential contributions of psychology to the educator's conceptions and practice:

1. The world of the child can be empirically shown to be substantially different from that of the adult. The teacher must know this in order not to misunderstand the child and not to be misunderstood by him or her. Children have a "theology" of their own, but they cannot "theologize" as the teacher can, although they may sometimes verbalize adult conceptions in a polished and misleading way. The child may get to know "P" (e.g., "the Torah was given by God"), but his or her understanding of God, Revelation, and Torah belongs to the domain of "LM" and will change with time and enlarged capacity and experience. This is not a new discovery; Maimonides, for example, addressed himself to this matter at length.[48] But it is often forgotten. Contemporary psychological research not only reminds us of it but also gives us detailed and variegated data on how children's minds move through different phases of perceiving and acquiring bodies of knowledge and stores of understanding.

2. Elkind's discussion of substitution (and the theories of Erikson and Fowler are germane here as well!) suggests that, as a child's religious understanding "grows," the child is not precluded thereby from drawing on previous stages and understandings. They remain available. "Substitution" suggests that one need not necessarily *outgrow* when one *grows*. The relationship between myth and metaphor need not be a one-way street. (The religious believer and the psychologists may evaluate this fact about "substitution" differently, but that does not affect its empirical basis.)

3. Kohlberg's findings, especially, suggest that thinking on issues relevant to religion—unless moral cognitive development is considered irrelevant to religion, which no religious person will admit unless he or she is tendentiously explicit—can be fostered by deliberation and discussion. One of Kohlberg's findings that is most relevant to educational theory and practice is that children seem to understand moral questions characteristic of one "stage"

above their own. Therefore, he posits, the presentation of dilemmas focal in that (higher) stage can be useful in stimulating moral development.[49]

This was also known in the religious tradition, and much of the process of Jewish learning was based on the assumption that deliberation was essential to capturing its "language."[50] But this too was often neglected or forgotten under the influence of overly explicit theology in situations of cognitive insecurity. Sosevsky, on the basis of his study of Kohlberg's theory, suggests that discussion of moral-religious issues will facilitate not only moral development but also the "recall" of often neglected aspects of Judaism. Kohlberg's method of deliberation, Sosevky argues, should be used in teaching even halakhic sources:

> . . . it is generally the fact that there is rarely clear-cut halakhic consensus on complex ethical issues, and (since) . . . in fact different halakhic authorities using the same basic sources may nevertheless disagree as to what constitutes proper conduct in a given situation, one will find that there is a great deal of room for heteronomous application of even Judaism's autonomous principles. The . . . principles [of Judaism] supply the parameters of an issue, while it is the role of the halakhists to determine which of these principles are relevant to any given situation.[51]

4. There seems to be something sequential about heteronomy and autonomy in moral development. Furthermore, it appears that the growth of the autonomous faculty involves a movement from the authority of parents and adult authorities to cooperation and inter-relationships with peers. Although this "movement" must be qualified by the evidence of children's cognitive egocentrism, which makes adults appear to be stupid and their norms the object of scorn,[52] the educator may draw the conclusion that the socializing activities and identity-forming functions of education associated with rules and role models must generally precede deliberation. Eventually, when there is a search for self, an identity crisis, there will be a greater need to "trust the child." But this trust will be easily granted and gratefully acknowledged only if the autonomous development rests on social foundations. Erikson has explained this cogently. Describing Freud's sense of "inner identity" with Jewry, he states, "The gradual development of a mature psychosocial identity . . . presupposes a community of people whose traditional values become significant to the growing person even as his growth assumes relevance for them."

> Societies require that, in each generation young people develop such identities. . . . [T]o remain vital, societies must have at their disposal the energies and loyalties that emerge from the adolescent process [and identity crisis]: as

positive identities are "confirmed," societies are regenerated. Where this process fails in too many individuals, a historical crisis becomes apparent.[53]

Each of these factors, and others of concern to the psychologist and to the educator, may enter into curricular planning and presentation and can aid in negotiation between the teacher armed with subject matter and the pupil coming into the school with an internal environment and moving in the midst of a particular social landscape.

Yet the "translation" from psychology into education, and religious educational theory especially, is always ambiguous. Too facile applications may be religiously destructive. Let us examine this point, with reference to the psychological concept of *readiness* and to the concept of *growth*.

1. *Readiness:* The difference between the cognitive "world" of the child and that of the adult has drawn the attention of educators to the idea of "readiness." Goldman, for example, argues against indiscriminate use of the Bible in religious education before children are ready for it.[54] The Bible, he states, is not a children's book, and to make children familiar with it too early "is to invite boredom and confusion, and even the most enthusiastic religious educator would not wish for this result to occur." In Goldman's view, therefore, there must be "a severe pruning of Bible content in the early years, for it is only later that an understanding and appreciation develops of what the Bible has to say."[55] Yet, and with equal cogency, one may advance the unabashedly explicit view (say, of Leibowitz) that since children can understand "P" (e.g., God wants us to observe *mitzvot*), they should be taught the religious truth of "P"; their understanding ("LM") will develop (with little assistance from teachers) as *they* develop. In other words, we should teach the child "to believe in God" and leave "knowledge of God" to his or her later development.[56] In this view, the Bible is a book for everyone, although children will understand it childishly.

2. *Growth:* Determining whether a child's understanding is less religiously advanced or pure than an adult's is, of course, dependent on a theological value judgment. Buber, we saw, considered the child more in tune with "I-Thou" realities than the adult, whereas Breuer has insisted that the child cannot understand religious truth intrinsically until "the nation" has educated him or her.[57] The question of whether children can or cannot understand the Bible "correctly" until they have reached a "higher" stage is also linked to the theological question of whether biblical stories are "really" only symbols of religious truth or whether they are also to be understood historically, "as something having happened."[58] In addition to this, of course, there is the question of how children understand that something "really happened."

Beilin, in conversation with Jewish teachers, was quite right in stating that religious education requires a knowledge of psychology—and of particular controversies within the field of psychology—but that the psychologist cannot make religious educational decisions. "Ultimately . . . the problems that are posed by the psychologists and by the scientists have to be interpreted in terms of some kind of ethic and some kind of religious and philosophic framework. The ultimate questions that we ask have to be interpreted in the sense in which we ask them."

. . . . Even if a scientist tells you that Bible instruction is not terribly important to young children because they really can't comprehend it, you are going to do it anyway because you know it is right.

This creates something of a problem for you; it also creates something of a problem for me. In trying to come to grips with the issue here . . . it does not turn out to be a question of simply defining the conditions under which children develop. Nor is it simply a question of fulfilling certain kinds of moral, ethical, or philosophical objectives. There has to be some kind of dialogue between what the scientists have to say and what the moralists have to say.[59]

We began our discussion of psychological theory in religious education as clarifying diverse aspects of implicit religious concerns, or, more precisely, the development of an integrated personality capable of having "ultimate concern." We have seen that contemporary psychological theories can indeed make important contributions with regard to what is happening in the cognitive, moral, and emotional development of a child and that they are particularly congenial to implicit religiosity. Developmental psychologists stress the uniqueness of each age; they conceive of development as advanced through thought and deliberation, and they insist that the child as he or she is and his or her inner motivations be taken as seriously as "culture." They suggest that the "initiating" adults are, in a sense, incomprehensible strangers to the emerging personality; they stress the limitations placed on adults who wish to initiate and impose. To this the humanistic psychologists add that each individual is unique, that the human being is characterized by a desire for a constant growth of selfhood.

Yet they agree that the individual develops within society. No matter how urgent the insistence that the thrust of education is the development of "subjecthood"—the development of a self-understanding that, in theological terms, sees the singular individual in his or her transcendental relationship to God—nevertheless it is not questioned that the development of every personal identity takes place within a social framework.

It is hoped that the tasks of sociology and psychology in religious educational thought will now be clearer to us. Various approaches within these disciplines aid us in understanding what religious commitment and "encounter" look like educationally—in terms of socialization and initiation and of development and individuation. Furthermore, these fields not only expose to view and illuminate an internal "Jewish theory of education"—as the explicit-minded educator will be pleased to note—but also help us to expand and shift emphases in it, as the implicit religionist will understandably demand.

Nevertheless, psychological or sociological theories should not be applied in the classroom as though they (singly or in some combination) constituted the essence of educational wisdom and standards. This is probably true in all education, in which theorists should be wary of making the fallacious move from *is* to *ought;* it is certainly true of religious education, which cannot promote scientific theories to the level of faith models.


## "IRONY" AND HUMILITY

At the beginning of this chapter, we discussed Richardson's conception of transcendence as a developing personal enterprise that led from (childish) "separation-and-return" through (adolescent) "conflict-and-vindication" to the goal of (adult) "integrity-and-transformation." The theology of psychological development that emerged was that of *the* completed saint. This saint, because he is more than human, therein representing an idolatrous ideal, is also less than human—because he has "outgrown" self-limitation, allegiance, social discipline, and idealism. He thus embodies a conception of implicit religiosity "run wild." We noted that this illustrates why the educational theorist—certainly the religious one—must be careful about belief systems that appear to be scientific theories.

Now, after having shown how explicit and implicit religiosity are themselves *partial* and must be brought into confrontation in order for a comprehensive theology of education to be constructed and how even an integrated theology of education is only *partially* capable of answering by itself the questions that arise in educational theory, and how both sociology and psychology can only *partially* deal with this lacuna, we may formulate our critique in religious-educational terms.

Theories that are only implicit-psychological, *or* only explicit-sociological, *or,* for that matter, only based on a theological conception of subject matter *or* a sociological conception of the environment *or* a psychological conception of the learner attempt to reduce the complexity of experience to manageable proportions. They seem to make the claim, whether scientifically or theologically, that one can know the whole truth—at least in principle—and package it educationally. But the religious teacher who affirms that truth is *given* to us and obliges us—an explicit axiom—but that it never *belongs* to us and that it is never quite packageable—an implicit insight—cannot accept that. If the religious teacher's theology of education is nourished by both explicit and implicit sources, he or she believes that the truth can be well enough known to make religious standards and religious initiation possible and justified but never known enough to make new insight redundant, certainly not in new situations.

In religious education, no social conception and no personality theory is *the* blueprint for education, because religious educators insist that sociology and psychology be used in a way that is responsible to theological principle. But religious educational theory cannot restrict itself to a given theology either; religious experience testifies that a theology that explains everything and contains everything impedes the service of God and the search for meaning. Such a "definitive" theology does not acknowledge its debts to the various philosophical and scientific discoveries of its age and thus does not recognize its limitations. It is either more normative than is humanly possible (and not only in this modern age) or so "open" that it loses its meaning in the human world that requires self-limitation.

Egan, from a philosophical educational standpoint, has suggested how to move beyond conceptual and intuitive certainties without "outgrowing" them.[60] He posits four stages of human development that incorporate expanding experience and meaning: the *mythic*, the *romantic*, the *philosophic*, and the *ironic*.

The mythic stage is similar to Richardon's "separation-and-return"; the romantic stage is reminiscent of his "conflict-and-vindication." The philosophic stage, characteristic of upper high school and undergraduate university students, arises out of the need to draw the "endless particulars" that were previously learned into a meaningful general scheme; thus, students at this stage organize reality into broad and all-encompassing categories. Concepts like "society," "culture," and "human nature" are the hallmarks of thinking and speaking, and people are seen as "types" who represent ideas. At the philosophic stage, one does not have "storytelling" in the (previous) mythic or romantic forms, but the stories are still present as philosophic certainty imposed upon reality. The "philosophic" student who is, say, a Marxist, *knows* the true meaning of the class struggle, past and present; he or she also *knows* how it will all turn out—and why. We may comment here that many enthusiasts of social scientific theories are "philosophic" in this sense, and so are adherents of theologies that are one-sidedly explicit or implicit.

As for the ironic stage, Egan suggests that it should emerge from the eventual understanding of learners (cultivated by the gentle prodding of teachers) that no general scheme can adequately reflect the richness or complexity of reality. The ironic stage "represents a clear appreciation of where we end and the world begins."

The ironic stage is not, however, "above" reality in the sense that the other stages have been outgrown.

Childhood, immaturity, childish thinking, adolescence, are typically seen as things we grow *out of*. The notion of educational development I am presenting here suggests rather that these be seen as things we grow *with* and *on*. It considers the continuities between childish and adult thinking much more significant than any discontinuities. It represents educational development as a process of accumulation, the characteristics of the stages not as things we grow out of but as things we elaborate on; not as things we discard on entering later stages but as things that become more disciplined and controlled.[61]

Egan's perspective is not specifically religious. But if theology of education is as dialectical as we have suggested, and if the theories that are useful to religious education are as variegated (and as problematic!) as we have indicated, then religious education too requires a conception of accumulating knowledge that does not outgrow the Torah of yesteryear but, in commenting, elaborating, and innovating, re-affirms its truth by retaining its accessibility, which is never *final*. In such an *ironic* religious theory, one is initiated into a community that is replenished in maturity rather than outgrown; one is taught belief in God, which becomes, in the course of a life of study, a search for the knowledge of God. And one never wholly "has" it.

"Ironically," Buber was perhaps correct, from his implicitly religious perspective, in pointing out that Judaism has no word for religion because God is not content with part of human life. And Breuer, from his explicit standpoint, was not unjustified in "ironically" considering the initiation into the "Torah community" as national education, because its religious significance so depends on what *could* happen in the life of the individual.

In religious language, this irony is called humility. The command to "walk humbly with thy God" is addressed to everyone; the model for such humility is our teacher, Moses. Moses, who spoke to God "face to face," knew too much to know everything. Therefore, the Torah says of him that "the man, Moses, was very humble, more than any man on the face of the earth" (Num. 12:3).

# 13 The Elements of Religious Jewish Education

## COMPONENTS OF THE EDUCATIONAL THEORY

Our discussion of religious educational theory has taken us through various domains. We have dealt with the classic, "normative" features of education, which have perennially served to inform civilizations, societies, and individuals about what "being truly educated" means. We saw how deliberation, always needed to correct distortions in the application of normative philosophy of education, became a replacement for such a normative framework as a result of cultural and religious crisis.

Moving to specifically religious educational norms, we discovered that the particular content of religious philosophy of education is to be found in religious teaching as experienced and recorded and as systematically stated in theology. It became clear that the most normative elements for education were formulated in what we termed explicit theology, whereas the more fluid elements, inviting deliberation in education, were characteristic of implicit theology.

As our discussion proceeded, we came upon the problem of non-normative aspects of educational theory, which directed our attention to *processes* in education: specifically, what is actually involved in initation into culture and in the individual development and "self-actualization" of the child. At this point, we had to examine how certain sociological and psychological theories and conceptions play a role in religious education.

Our discussion throughout was informed by the fact of crisis: the disintegration of religious norms in secular society, the distance created in modern society between the subject matter of Jewish tradition and contemporary culture, the alienation of teachers from either tradition or pupils and society, the accumulating evidence that, for many or most Jews, religious education is a problem rather than a way of grappling with life (people and culture—and cosmos).

## DISTORTIONS IN AN AGE OF CRISIS

We examined—in thought, theory, and texts—various tendencies that were one-sided, extreme, and partial, tendencies that could be laid at the door of this crisis of religion in secular society. Thus, we saw that religious education is characterized by numerous distortions. For example:

1. Although under "normal" circumstances subject matter is reflected in the life of society, and teachers are agents of society and culture in shaping pupils in light of subject-matter prescriptions, the religious tradition does not function in this way for most contemporary Jews. The subject matter appears to stand not only opposite children "waiting to be shaped" by transmitted truths, but also opposite society itself. The environment is uncomprehending or hostile. The explicit theologian, who has developed an explicit approach in response to this situation, attempts to mobilize the teacher for the cause of the (traditional) subject matter, in an assault on the child and his or her community. The implicit thinker, on the other hand, champions the child and the environment and tries to enlist the teacher to help cope with the "problems" inherent in the religious (subject matter) tradition. The gap between explicit and implicit religious orientations in education may therefore be seen as aspects of the alienation perceived between "religious subject matter" and society.

2. Religious educational thought, consequently, can be tendentious in various ways. In some cases, the tendency is to ignore the child for the sake of tradition. In such cases, the tradition is viewed as objectively outside the child in its totality, inviting some externalization but, except for an elite, no internalization. In other cases, religious education is considered simply an aid in fostering the moral development of the child, and the imposed dimension of religious life is ignored. Sometimes, theology will be limited to explicit prescriptions for achieving initiation; at other times, it will consist simply of implicit insights on how to use gleanings from tradition for spiritual enhancement. Often, especially if the orientation is implicitly religious, theology will be subjugated to human sciences, particularly psychology, and religious teachings will be reduced to intimations—or techniques—of self-realization. Conversely, if the orientation is explicitly religious, the sciences

will sometimes be ignored and prescriptions of educational procedures will be arbitrarily lifted from the religious tradition, as though the tradition did not "say" many different things about these procedures.

3. Teachers are sometimes tradition people, bearing texts that are, by certain explicit criteria, very authentic but hardly communicative with children. At other times, they are persons of social and psychological expertise who may meet certain very implicit standards of religiosity but who have sacrificed the authenticity of the religious teaching on the altar of relevance and communicability.

We have attempted to deal with this overriding problem of religious education in secular society on several levels, for we saw our task as a three-fold one.

First, we addressed ourselves to the *classic normative* aspect of all historical "philosophies of education." This involved establishing that educational theory requires a prescriptive philosophy that informs the educator about what is desirable and on what foundation of principles and ideals certain ends are deemed more worthy than others. Since we were concerned with religious education, we examined the axiom that religious doctrines and norms supply the substance of religious "philosophy of education." This led us to the theologians, whose enterprise was the systematic statement of these beliefs and standards, to see how their claim to supply a philosophy of religious education was defended.

Second, our philosophical task was *analytical*. Discovering that the practical enterprise of education involves the application of norms prescribed by philosophers and theologians to given human situations and children, we had to examine the contours and dynamics of "normative breakdown" in modern society. This analysis obliged us to look not only at secular alternatives to religious education being offered in modern society but also at new attempts to understand which phenomena of human life have been dealt with by religion and religious education. It also obliged us to examine diverse theological interpretations of what can be universally and Jewishly regarded as religious experience and expression. Our analysis led us to typologies of religious approaches. These were convenient for analytical purposes, for they could be shown to represent directives of response to the challenge of secular modernity. In addition, our analysis indicated the need to examine the uses of scientific theory in areas in which, it could be shown, theological discourse was educationally incompetent or incomprehensive.

Third, our task was a *regulative* one. Finding that religious thought tended to prescribe in diverse directions and led to conflicting curricular conceptions, we sought to show how both the explicit and the implicit features of religion might receive their due in educational thinking and how each could be kept from encroachments on the other in the educational arena. Moreover, we indicated how sociology and psychology might overstep their bounds within a theory of religious education that, as a theory of *religious* education, must in principle consider norms as deriving from religious teaching rather than from theoretical scientific descriptions. The analytical function of our "philosophy of religious Jewish education" made us sensitive to possible overly ambitious alliances between sociology and explicit theology on the one hand and psychology and implicit theology on the other. Our regulative task was to contrast the need of one discipline for another with the necessity of setting limits and priorities.

In the setting of priorities, the normative feature of religious educational philosophy again came to the fore. Normatively, this philosophy must defend the domain of religious teaching as providing the substance of educational norms and providing the apparatus for interpreting them so they can be applied in new circumstances. In the analytical sphere, the philosopher of education examines why this does not always happen; why, in some situations—like the modern one—it is even *unlikely* that the explicit-implicit dialectic of religion will be clearly understood. But the philosopher *does* take the model of religion and its theory-producing (i.e., theological) apparatus as a basic datum of religious education. This stems from the philosophical conception of norms as being both imposed and chosen and from the philosopher's analysis of religion as a domain of norms and existential "choice of being." The normative and analytical features of the philosopher's work thus serve as guides in regulating the relationship among diverse theological approaches and the relationship of theology and science.

## THE PHILOSOPHER IN THE CLASSROOM

What actually happens when the norms are "brought down" into practice is, of course, a basic datum of the analytical and regulative functions of philosophy of religious education. Let us illustrate this.

1. A situation in which teachers constantly refer to "we" (and how "we" believe and practice) but one in which a norm-bearing community is conspicuous in its absence is too normative for that particular social reality to bear. In such a teaching situation, the crisis of credibility will deepen unless a commitment is made to community, even though the price may be to withdraw partially from secular society. The philosopher, together with the sociologist, will point out that without community there is explicit religion but no (sociological) plausibility structure. Here, explicit religion will be, quite simply, *implausible*.

2. A curriculum that is all themes and no (complete) text should be recognized as making unambiguously implicit assumptions about religious instruction. Themes are universal, and a particular tradition may illuminate and illustrate themes, but it is unlikely that the specific teaching of the tradition will be discovered unless the curriculum writers and teachers balance thematic learning with textual study. Conversely, a curriculum of texts, at times even chosen for their "irrelevance" to everything the "others" engage in and value, must be seen to be thoroughly explicit. It is likely to be all ritual and no new art. It is liable to ignore the insights of "the others"—and of the child—concerning truths that can be shown to be universal. Here the philosopher, while esteeming the search for Jewish truth in the text, must point out the potential corruption of this procedure. A philosopher may suggest some comparative study of Jewish and other sources— and not merely for polemical purposes—and the desirability of fostering self-expression *as well as* classic competence.

3. The philosopher may find that basic doctrines (and traditional facts and events) are not taught because children are deemed not "ready" or teachers do not really believe them. Here, one must note that basic doctrines are never taught as existential insights but as socially endorsed knowledge, as "P" and not as "LM" (to use the psychological idiom); as the "objective" moment of plausibility (in sociological terms). A philosopher will point out that the doctrines are aspects of the explicit pole of religion. If teachers do not believe them, it may be because they have not worked on them implicitly, have not appropriated them in their own way—have not understood "P" as inviting them to "LM" understandings—or cannot find a way to take this particular tradition, or, perhaps, any religious tradition, seriously. In the first case, the philosopher will suggest, teachers must become more conversant with religious thought in order to become better teachers. In the second case, they perhaps should not be teaching in a religious framework.

Analytically, of course, the philosopher will point out that *any* decision— whether leaning in a more implicit or a more explicit direction, making greater use of sociological or of psychological knowledge or insight—will involve dangers and distortions. This is especially true in a secular society that puts religious education on the defensive no matter which policy is adopted.

## THE ELEMENTS OF THEORY IN THE CURRICULUM

We have already alluded to the curricular implications of various elements: explicit and implicit, normative and deliberative, social and existential. Here we must elaborate on several issues that arise as a result of what might be inadequate negotiation between diverse elements in religious educational theory.

Explicit dimensions of religious education, we have seen, initiate into the tradition. This is done largely through the tradition's sacred texts, which were "there" before the pupil and which oblige him to knowledge and practice. This explicit educational axiom can be sociologically corrupted in two ways. The secular corruption is to neutralize the norms of the text by placing it within a historic context, as though the only truth in it were the sociology of religion. Taught in this way, the text is never understood in its own terms but always in a reductionist way. For example, the prophets spoke "in the name of God" because that's "the way they did it" in benighted and superstitious epochs. Or, the rabbis "thought up" the halakhic regimen of the Talmud to protect the Jewish people's survival in the Diaspora. Here we have explicit theology for secularists; sociology becomes the message, and only the letters on the religious parchment remain (cognitively) imposed, without meaning, without the power to generate enchantment.

The converse corruption is religious: The educator wishes to learn from sociology how to socialize children into Judaism under present circumstances but without confronting the problems characterizing these circumstances. The text is therefore taken with apparent seriousness, but the learner and the university world of the teacher and modern culture are not. Socialization is into a context that no longer exists; it is effected either by denial of the present situation entirely or by making the text a-historical *in toto*. (For example, Moses reminds the "businessmen" in the desert that they too have a stake in the Torah, for they will support yeshivot.[1] This approach, while Midrashically valid, is problematic today when the Midrash too is seen to have a historical context, and therefore must be stated to *be* Midrash.) Although this approach appears to be reverent to the text, the philosopher of religious education must ask whether it is indeed so, given the valid insistence of the implicit theologian that the Torah is meant to constitute *teaching* in all situations, for all people.

The philosopher of Jewish education has thus carried out a regulative function. Addressing constructive proposals, he or she interprets the relationship of the various disciplines in a more normative mode. For example, in analyzing the central religious educational activity of "learning Torah" as explicitly understood and sociologically enriched, the philosopher may suggest that:

1. "Learning" (Torah) must be seen as a community-delineating activity. It must be celebrated. There are various ways of doing this. The traditional reading of the Torah is a form of celebration; so is conducting a *siyyum*—a concluding festivity—upon reaching the end of one section of study. Another way is to conduct seminars and weekend retreats that are built around study

but that obviously include practical-religious and communal-recreational activities as well.

2. The texts should be taught as having a normative message. The learner should be introduced to the question: What is the text saying and what obligation does it impose? Clearly, this question arises in the context of socially authorized habits and skills that the child observes and that the teacher embodies in one way or another.

3. The text, in order to invite externalization and internalization on the part of the learner, must also be addressed in the context of *our* understanding, what it says to us. Since we are here concerned with the explicit thrust, of "teaching Torah" and learning from *it* what we have to know, the philosopher may note that, in *this* context, we are more concerned with present-day implementation of halakhah than with the contemporary application of its principles. Of course, through an implicit prism, it will look somewhat different.

Let us turn now to regulative and normative aspects of philosophy of religious education, as they address themselves to implicit dimensions. How implicit orientations to religious education can be corrupted by psychology has already been dealt with in the previous chapter. Yet, something more must be said about the precarious relationship between explicit and implicit theology, in the context of the total educational theory. Here, after analyzing and regulating, let us engage in unabashed normative search.

## BEING BOTH LOYAL AND OPEN: SEEKING THE ELUSIVE NORM

It is quite simple to reiterate that a religious education that is all imposed, that is all explicit and socializing, is religiously flawed. It is all too easy to repeat that religious education may not deny the (implicitly religious) gifts and aspirations of the child nor the realities of individual development and temperament. We all know, theoretically and from practical experience, that narrow explicit education, except in situations of extreme ghettoization, will rarely cultivate individuals who can learn from their environment or contribute to it. Indeed, such an education will encourage young people to choose for their own a secular or pagan world as an alternative to a seemingly deadening and dull Jewish one.

And yet, in fact, the problems raised by the theologically implicit demand for openness and innovation and its expressions in the psychological terms of autonomy and personal development have always been extremely serious, most especially in modern society. For the explicit element is no less intrinsic to religious education than the implicit one. How *does* one really educate a young person, really *help* a young person to become loyal, disciplined by the regimen of revealed norms and, at the same time, curious, open and endowed with an expansive spirituality? What is the ''recipe'' for blending piety and humility with a more-than-scholastic intelligence and faculty of criticism?

The number of religious and secular thinkers who have suggested ideological and educational solutions to overly explicit conceptions of tradition is legion. Usually, however, they have discovered that an emphasis on the innovative leads quickly to overly implicit and, finally, vacuous relationships to religious tradition and experience. The secular Ahad Ha-Am, despite his inability to ''believe'' in the religious normativeness of Judaism, had a clearly explicit and conservative temperament and wished desperately to find a new ''national'' understanding in which nationally revered forms would contain ever renewed and new content.[2] But his educational critics, even friendly ones, sensed that these ''holy'' forms were at best public and usually empty.[3] The national spirit, reaching out for meaning and morality and looking within for spiritual commandments, never ''added up'' to the authentically explicit—to ''the Word of our God'' descending from above.

In discussing Samuel Hugo Bergman and other implicit religious thinkers, we noted that the problem of the text and its inner meaning for the reader, of the tension between the potentially deadening routine and the vital need for roots—in short, the problem of inspired change in a framework of sacred stability—is the central problem of religious life and education.

But perhaps the problem has been misrepresented. Perhaps, the norm of *learning* has been mis-taken as bespeaking the explicit role of Jewish religiosity, rather than only one side of the coin *of Torah itself.*

Let us illustrate. The problem of how the implicit religious sensibility may inform the human soul without undermining the explicit demand enters human history and understanding with the biblical words that describe ''the beginning ''  For the unending dominion of God, as reflected by the majesty of His being and the eternity of His law, is only one side of the coin. The ''imposed'' tradition begins with the (implicit) question of how the world came into existence. Later, it describes, through biblical narrative and Midrashic elaboration, how Abraham rebelled against the traditions of his father, Terach, and *returned* to the ways of his forefathers Noah and Shem, even while he went far beyond them.[4]

It is the Torah itself that introduces the child to interesting changes, some cosmic, some ''developmental'': The serpent, which originally walked like a person, came to crawl on its belly; a pampered young man, Joseph, became an exemplar of righteousness. The pupil will learn, while *learning Torah,* that, in one view, God commanded the building of the Tabernacle only because He realized, after the episode of the Golden Calf, that Israel required a concrete symbol of the Divine Presence—as well as a religiously acceptable use of their wealth and building talents. And, of course, the prayers of Moses made God change His mind—sometimes.[5]

Children studying the tradition under the guidance of teachers who can reflect on the enterprise of teaching through the prism of religious educational theory will discover in the Torah the tension between authority and autonomy, between the majestic word of God and the overflowing spirit of God everywhere. They will learn that Joshua, in distress at the men "prophesying in the camp," urged Moses to imprison them and that Moses not only refused to imprison them but also uttered the bemused wish, "If only all the people of God were prophets!" And this the same Moses who solemnly told Korah and his congregation that "the Lord will make known who are His and who is holy. . . ."[6] Examining the famous debate about Achnai's stove and its ritual purity,[7] pupils will have to comprehend not only that the rabbis "outvoted" Rabbi Eliezer and God in a halakhic dispute but also that God "laughed" happily at their decision, *and* gave evidence of dissatisfaction with it. These and other examples illustrate, as we have argued earlier, not only that Jewish religiosity (as that of every other religious faith) is both explicit and implicit, but also that the educational problem for religious educators is taxing indeed. This is true not only because religious truth becomes accessible through reflection upon valuative issues and options but also because of the "situation" of religious education in our time, when there is a tendency to present change itself as *the* norm (and thus to destroy the experience of norm) or the reverse: to combat that tendency by illicitly concealing the religious dimension of innovation.

The religious tradition, of course, "mediates" the relationship between norms and innovation in various ways. On the one hand, one who denies the revealed character of a single letter of the Torah is charged with apostasy, yet this explicit statement is modified by implicit exegesis.[8] Such concepts as *"dibra Torah neged yetzer ha-ra"* ("the Torah takes human impulse into account") suggest eventual "refinement" of God's law when human "impulse" is refined through the regimen of Torah itself. Similarly, the principle of *"eit la'asot la-Shem"* ("it is time to act for God's sake") justifies actions that are traditionally forbidden, "for the sake of Heaven."[9] The principle of *Torah she'b'al peh* ("Oral Torah") is innovative, but this innovative thrust is countered by the rabbinic view, itself a part of the Oral Torah, "that whatever will be innovated by the last pupil in the last generation was given at Sinai."[10]

## A QUESTION OF PRIORITIES

For the educator, a philosophical yet all-too-practical question looms large: namely, what comes first? Does one begin with explicitly religious imposition and socialization, with loyal participation and normative "self-understood-ness," or with implicitly religious "outreach" and spiritual discovery? For the truism that both can be discovered in the sources does not give the teacher direct pedagogical or didactical guidance.

We may recall that the implicit religious thinker Martin Buber extolled "the total openness" of youth, which "has not yet sworn allegiance to any one truth for whose sake it would close its eyes to all other perspectives."[11] His answer would seem to be clear: The implicit, the "open," approach is the natural path to the divine. But Buber too scorned an education that is *all* letting children become themselves, what he termed the "gardener" approach, and this despite his solemn reservations about the "sculptor" approach, which shapes the child into a pre-conceived form. Not incidentally, these reservations about both "gardening" and "sculpturing" in education are articulated in an essay entitled "On National Education."[12] For Buber considered the restored national Jewish life that he envisioned for *Eretz Yisrael* as the framework for the *explicit* spirit of Israel that will again regain, there, its *implicit* religious content. Zionism, in one sense, is the religious solution of an educational problem: how to assure a community for a religious sensibility that is ontologically individual and, in this historical era, isolated. Buber too knew that Judaism did not begin with the implicit, even though his theology considered the implicit most essential and sublime.

That there is a problem of "how to be explicit before you develop implic-itness" in a society in which the ideals of Judaism are alien and in which re-ligion is privatized is, of course, admitted even by thinkers whose understanding of Jewish religion is that it *is* explicit before it is implicit. They tend to see this, however, as arising out of the consciousness of modern secular society that we and our children share. Thus, Fackenheim, whose theology is revelation-centered (and may be categorized as "explicit-liberal"), agrees that the contemporary failure of the traditional way has theological ramifications as well:

The method of modern Jewish theology must differ from that of classic theology. The latter "worked its way down," i.e., assumed from the start what to modern man is the thing most in question: the actuality of a divine revelation given by man and Israel. Modern theology must "work its way up," i.e., show by an analysis of the human condition that man's existence, properly under-stood, forces him to raise the question of the Supernatural and the existential problem of the "leap into faith." . . . The analysis of the human condition constitutes the necessary prolegomenon for all modern Jewish, and indeed, all modern theology.[13]

However, the sociologist will remind us that this modern situation, which requires beginning religious education implicitly, is first and foremost the consequence of life in modern *society,* whose assumptions and patterns, whose "plausibility structure," are alien to Judaism. And if we listen attentively to philosophical theorists who integrate psychological and sociological theories of learning, development, and initiation, we hear them saying that individuation must be—*is always*—built on socialization of some kind. They instruct us that children do speak their own language but become communicative and society-shaping when they become capable of generating their own *literature* in a *language that they have learned.* Peters, we recall, reminds the educator that, however paradoxical it may be, moral habits must precede moral reasoning. Scholars representing widely ranging vantage points have discussed how the self and its "emergence" are a matter of initiation *and* encounter. The human self evolves out of confrontation with the "non-self" in various manifestations (the world, others, one's own subconscious).[14] That self must be found by those who have perceived tasks and have been given tools by others. It must be found, to a large degree, through others.

For religious Jews, then, the problem is to a large extent the non-religious "other" society. If socialization indeed precedes individuation, we must ask to which extent Jews will create community to allow explicit religion to be constructed educationally and to function plausibly in such a way that habit, participation as self-understood, cognitive competence, and skills of communication are publicly esteemed and enjoyed—and collectively perceived as meaningful.

For, of course, the primacy of the explicit in development and culture is not only a sociological finding or a datum of identity formation. It is first and foremost a prescription of the Jewish religious tradition itself, which places the duty of doing before the experience of understanding.[15] In this sense, it is no canard to say that Judaism is a "religion of law" because it imposes obligations and a social framework before it promises individual self-actualization. Thus, the archetypal convert, Ruth the Moabite, places her acceptance of the people and its norms even before her faith in the God of Israel. Even more blatantly, the talmudic Midrash states that, when Israel left Egypt and arrived at Mount Sinai, "the Holy One, Blessed be He, suspended the mountain over their heads like a barrel and said to them: 'If you accept the Torah, well and good; and if not, here will your graves be.' '"[16] Surely this is an explicit statement of beginnings.

And yet, we must return to our problem, which was not solved by pointing out the valuative ("theoretical") priority of explicit teaching (whatever the practical difficulties in a given situation). For implicit religion is a part of religion itself; as we have shown previously, albeit in a cursory way, it is a constituent element of the Torah. It is a principle of the model itself, for it gives the unchanging, the majestically divine, a perspective and a situational context.

As the philosopher may analytically note, the predicament of religious education is that, whereas the tradition is founded on the assumption that the explicit precedes the implicit in religious teaching, modern society and its plausibility structure are congenial only to the implicitly religious. So, if one wants to be explicit—and thus traditional—one tends to give up most of modern society and its resources for fostering the implicit religious development of children. Conversely, if one "gives in" to modern society, the implicit tends to become the norm itself, and it becomes virtually impossible to move to the explicit dimension.

Our theory of religious education, in all of its elements, has informed us that we must deal with three issues if religious education is to have religious integrity, no matter how difficult this will be in given circumstances (such as those just described). (1) Religious education must effect the socialization of the child into a religious community that is explicitly "there," visible; (2) it must foster the child's individuation as an implicitly religious person; and (3) it must negotiate the tension between religious belonging and reliability, on the one hand, and religious "becoming" and spiritual autonomy, on the other.

The religious tradition would seem to indicate, as noted earlier, that before the "existential threshold" of early adolescence education should deal primarily with the first issue mentioned in the previous paragraph; it should generally be socializing. (This religious prescription, as we have seen, corresponds to sociological and psychological theories of initiation and growth; indeed, these theories provide important guidelines for educational process.) Then, after the threshold of adolescence, there must be a progressively greater demand made on the child for decision and responsibility. For children are not robots and commandments are *addressed* to them and predicated on choice. In theological terms, we may say with Simon that the child who had been *given* Torah must be helped and enabled to *accept* it.[17] In theoretical socio-psychological terms, a child moves, in the religious life, from an avoidance of guilt to commitment. The youngster makes choices that he or she believes are required to "become himself or herself" and to make the community to whose integrity he or she is committed closer to the ideal that alone renders the commitment wholehearted. In educational terms, the child moves from socialization to individuation, to a psycho-social identity that is rooted in the community of Israel but that is uniquely the individual's own.

Yet, this must be qualified. Under no circumstances may socialization and individuation be simply or mechanically sequential. Even the early teaching of habit must be conducted in a manner that facilitates the development of powers of reasoning and individual self-esteem. There must be an aspect of implicit religion at every phase, because the child, although a "cognitive [and affective] stranger" to the adult, *does* have a world. Likewise, there must be explicit teaching at every age; community is not simply a psychological crutch on the road to maturity but is intimately and organically "present" in responsible and meaningful existence. Freedom should never be perceived as antithetical to community and commitment.

For the element of change to be inherent in religious education without collapsing the sacred "model," what can the educational theorist put on the agenda?

First, he or she must insist that there actually be a religious community in which children and, it is hoped, their parents, live. The theorist will ask how, under present circumstances, the maximal Jewish social structure can be constructed or maintained that does no violence to Jewish commitments to the wider society and its goods. For otherwise, the model will collapse—or will be placed in a straitjacket. Only when the question of what constitutes Jewish community and polity has been answered can the issue of change be addressed with psychic security and without semi-conscious reservations. *The more one can take for granted in terms of loyalty, the larger the scope for spontaneity and individuality within the parameters of religious education and life.* But this is true only if the implicitly religious demand to maintain responsible ties with the "general" world is respected.

The educational theorist will ask us to remember that, at every stage of learning, change is a personal-psychological phenomenon and not only an element of culture and history. In religious education there is usefulness in the psychological-implicit concept of readiness in the very midst of a social-explicit situation. Thus, although the explicit religious orientation will insist that the entire community must learn and experience things together—for example, the reading of the Torah on prescribed occasions and the shaking of the *lulav* on Sukkot—for these precede developing children and are designed to envelop them, yet not all will or must find the same meaning in the ritual. Adult meanings may not be imposed on those who neither want them nor (explicitly speaking) have "earned" them. Children should more readily and frequently be *asked* than *told* what the explicitly religious norm signifies.

Thus, the religious school or camp that takes individuality and development seriously may not deny the child's right to his or her chart of meaning-finding or program of meaning-making. In a sense, this seems antithetical to the (explicit) axiom that the sources of sacred knowledge provide all the "right" answers to every possible question. But if the theology of education discloses that the Jewish tradition itself—indeed, every religious tradition—is composed of implicit as well as explicit elements, then even the most "traditional" curriculum maker and teacher must (1) distinguish the sphere of "right" answers in the halakhah from the open questions (certainly and at least) in the non-halakhic dimensions of the religious tradition and (2) locate valuative questions in the tradition and make them accessible for deliberation and decision-weighing by the pupils.

This deliberation will be based on the premise that all values (and, prominently, those in religious teachings) co-exist not only with *existential* opposites—such as courage and fear—but with *valuative* opposites, such as courage and prudence. This means that, just as truth as a value stands against the existential opposite of falsehood, and peace must cope with the existential opposite of innate aggressiveness, so, in many situations, must truth and peace be seen as valuative opposites, as competing for priority and application.[18]

In the case of valuative opposites (such as truth versus peace, or the dignity of human life versus its sacredness), we have religious dilemmas and, therefore, the "ground" for moral and religious deliberation. The religious tradition often presents us, to paraphrase the talmudic Sage Rabbi Ishmael, with "two texts that contradict each other," and these impel us to look for "the third text that reconciles them."[19] More specifically, in different contexts, diverse values have priority. These contexts must be understood, and the priorities must be determined. Such understandings and decisions will never be finally or authoritatively concluded, for new contexts and situations arise continually. The question, "What is the right thing to do?" *in practice,* is thus implicit and open as well as, *in principle,* explicit and closed. It has to do with authority but also with deliberation. (Thus, where overly explicit educators will opine that "children don't know enough to discuss, let alone decide" such matters, the implicit colleague will argue that no one knows enough about the ultimate in a particular situation to be sure and that even children have ultimate concerns.) Here, the precariousness of the balance between the norm and the unease that it may generate is sharply brought into view. To maintain that balance, it may be religiously and educationally sound to juxtapose—or at least compare—the plurality of views among the children with the differing opinions on the issue at hand among recognized authorities whose controversies represent the diversity yet roughly mark the outer limits of religiously defined deliberation.

The educational theorist will insist that the ultimate commitments of the child must be related to the individual integration of his or her personality. These commitments are not only what the religious fellowship (the community) does, and what the member of the community does by virtue of belonging to it, but also how the life of commitment should be lived by him or her and how he or she may understand it. If a *mitzvah* is an ultimate act—that is, one that integrates people and tells them who they are—it must express them ("implicitly") as well as oblige—and shape them ("explicitly"). Eventually, if explicit education has succeeded and youngsters have been "brought under the wings of the Divine Presence" (i.e., into the *model* of Judaism), they will grope toward their own theology, their own *ta'amai ha-mitzvot* (intellectual understanding of the commandments)—i.e., a personally congenial *theory*. The "commanded life" that we live must be one that we can, in a comprehensive way and as whole persons, live *with*. For the explicit-implicit ideal is, for religiously educated persons, to live as committed participants in a faith tradition in which the participation is constantly re-enforced by moments of "absoluteness" experienced within that tradition. And, we may add, the religiously "whole" person "loyally" anticipates these experiences within his or her own community and recognizes them in *all* communities.

This means that children must learn not only to revere the tradition and be initiated into its holy (imposed and imposing) character but also to articulate their feelings and understandings of various aspects of the explicit substance of the tradition (e.g., the biblical verse or character, the rabbinic adage, the *mitzvah*). Non-conformism in expression or in interpretation (i.e., an image or an idea that the teacher has not imagined, learned, or thought of) should be looked upon with favor, if only to make it possible for the individual to appropriate the community's sacred text and to make it a source of inspiration— a "place" in which the individual may find himself or herself. The belief in the unfathomable richness of God's word is an implicit as well as an explicit concept, for the Torah not only "has" seventy "aspects" but also invites them; not only is "everything in it" but it is "like a hammer splitting rocks into many pieces."[20] At the same time, the teacher is right in pointing out when a certain understanding or metaphor is conspicuously not within the "language" of Judaism. Judaism is a particular religious-national culture. It has its value-commonplaces in which the discussion of Jewish meaning and substance is carried on. It is possible, therefore, to express existential insights in a manner that is not communicative in the dialogue as carried on by Jews "within the tradition."

The theorist will note that the implicit aspect of religious education, with its theological openness to all wisdom and to changing theories and conceptions as potentially contributing to human spirituality and "ultimate concern," requires that all bodies of knowledge and the ways they are best learned be treated with indigenous seriousness in the curriculum. This means that the child must learn *both* to distinguish among different kinds of inquiry and knowledge and to relate to diverse disciplines through appropriate methods and within their legitimate contexts *and* to see them in a manner that is religiously integrated. The first of these requirements even has an "explicitly" religious component; it signifies, in almost compartmentalized fashion, that one cannot, for "religious" reasons, disqualify biological theories (say, of evolution); only biologists are qualified to argue the worth or verity of biological theories. The second requirement means that children must be helped to relate what they learn Jewishly and what they learn in biology—religiously. The disciplines are diverse, but the personality should be one. This does not mean that all knowledge must be "explained" theologically; that is, apologetically and in pseudo-prophetic pronouncements, but that religious questions that arise in various fields of study, such as moral issues in social psychology or ecological questions in the study of natural science and technology, should be dealt with in an attitude of existential seriousness. In other words, although the discipline and the ways of discovery are, except in specific outrageous cases, indifferent to moral and human considerations, the ultimate divorce of theory from human significance and responsibility is religiously untenable and may be morally catastrophic.[21]

Finally, the theorist will suggest that the implicit element of religious educational theory, partially translated into educational theory by psychological conceptions of personality development, dictates that children be taught to take their own experiences seriously, just as they take seriously that cumulative experience that is transmitted to them. The Hasidic teachers, who have highlighted the implicit features of Jewish religiosity, pointed out that we pray to "the God of Abraham, the God of Isaac, and the God of Jacob" rather than to "the God of Abraham, Isaac, and Jacob" because each of the patriarchs found God in his own way.[22] A religious personality that is both loyal and spontaneous requires a community that makes some self-understood demands but that also tolerates idiosyncrasies and is hospitable to personal differences and controversies "for the sake of Heaven" (i.e., those that have a religious foundation). A religious curriculum must leave room for privacy—a privacy that is publicly acknowledged and even appreciated. For if all religious experience is confined to the community, to the existing social reality, not only the undisciplined but also the "Messianic" soul, which anticipates a more ideal reality, will rebel.

Conversely, the explicit dimension of religion reminds the individual not to take himself or herself too seriously, not to "refuse to play" in the here and now by protestations of Messianic idealism. For the religious person not only is commanded to authenticity but also must accept discipline and act responsibly within his or her limitations.

The explicit religious educator will object that the implicit aspects of the theory proposed previously, which seeks to do justice to the innovative and spontaneous aspects of the educational enterprise, enabling individuals to grow into a tradition and contribute to its growth, constitute a danger. The educator fears that the child will leave the community and may stop being "religious." However, the paradox of the religious situation is that where there is no such possibility (or danger) there is no hope of maintaining the religious community that attracts and holds the loyalty of men and women who constituted God's community in the first place. It becomes a refuge of the dull and the conventional. The "spirited" go elsewhere and take the spirit with them.

Conversely, the implicit religious educator will charge that the religious spirit is stifled by an imposed tradition and that the tradition itself is a problem. But people *are* born into community, into a historical and human situation not of their choosing. And this "situation" does impose specific demands and choices upon them. Therefore, education *is* initiation, for we must live with one another as well as "find" ourselves. And although prophets do say new things, they must speak a language that can be understood. For even they, in the very agony of their individuality, are charged with the command to address a community that seeks truth, accepts authority, and reveres (however ambivalently) the person bearing God's word. The issue is whether Jews will choose a community that is prepared to listen to such persons and to live by their teachings. The *problem* is that prophets are ignored or misinterpreted—and that it is difficult to distinguish between true and false ones.

Finally, a "word of Torah"—in the context of our discussion of religious education, and as a continuation of it.

Our text is one we have already mentioned: It is the talmudic Midrash that depicts God forcing the Torah on Israel as the people stood "under the mountain," offering them the alternatives of acceptance or instant death. No religious teaching could be more unambiguously explicit in its orientation than this one, more imposed and commanded, more impervious to freedom and meaningful choice.

But, as already noted in an earlier chapter, matters (and texts) are seldom as explicit or implicit as they seem. A citation from Scripture or Talmud that is all one or the other is either partial, wrenched out of its context, or not interpreted, detached from the understanding and circumstances of those who studied it with commitment and concern. So, instead of citing snatches of text, let us learn Torah, looking at that awesome mountain again, lifted over the heads of the Israelites "like a barrel." Let us try to scale it with the aid of Sages and under the guidance of that doyen of medieval commentators, Rashi.

"And they stood under the mountain" (Exod. 19:17). Said Rabbi Avdimi, the son of Hamma, son of Dossa: From this we learn that the Holy One, blessed be He, suspended the mountain over their heads like a barrel and said to them: "If you accept the Torah, well and good; and if not, here will your graves be." Rabbi Acha, son of Yaakov, said: Here there is a strong possible claim with regard to the Torah. [Rashi: For if the Torah takes Israel "to court" for not having observed its laws, Israel can counter that the Torah was forced upon them and that, therefore, its claim is not binding.]

Said Rabba: Nevertheless [though it was originally forced upon them] they [Israel] accepted it [the Torah, of their own free will] in the days of Ahashuerus [the Persian king of the Purim story; Rashi: Because of the miracle that had been performed for them], since it is written (Esther 9:27), "The Jews ordained and took upon themselves. . . . " They [themselves] ordained that which they had already taken upon themselves [against their will].[23]

Several questions arise: Why did God hold the mountain over their heads? Surely He knew, no less than Rabbi Acha, that a contract entered into under coercion is ultimately flawed or even, perhaps, invalid? Why does Rabba bring Purim into it? And why does Rashi consider the miracle of Purim as the cause for Israel's voluntary acceptance of the Torah? Weren't there enough—and greater—miracles in Egypt and at Sinai?

A good place to begin is with the seeming irrelevancy—Purim.[24] The miracle of Purim, unlike that of, say, Passover and the Exodus, is categorized as a "hidden miracle." The name of God, we recall, is not mentioned in the Book of Esther. Events seem to take their natural course, and the salvation of Israel appears to be simply the consequence of a happy chain of coincidences. One night the king could not sleep and had the royal book of records brought to him (Esther 6:1), Haman "happened" to be at court, and his diabolical plan to hang Mordecai "happened" not to please the king, who had just happened to discover how Mordecai had saved his life.

Nothing is said here about God. But believers who are also implicitly faithful search out the meaning of situations that "naturally" surround them and recognize the hand of God in circumstances and events in which He is seemingly absent, not "officially" mentioned. The implicit believer sees Him everywhere: in a conversation between friends, in liberated Jerusalem, even in the wakefulness of the foolish King Ahashuerus. [Thus it is that the Midrash on Esther 6:1 explains that it is the *King of kings* who does not sleep, as it is written: "Behold the Guardian of Israel neither sleeps nor slumbers" (Ps. 121:4).[25]] And having found Him in "the natural course of events," the implicit selves of all religious believers, out of spiritual need and concern, freely accept the Torah, which was previously forced on them, "explicitly." They discover the Torah as speaking to them, just as they have discovered the hidden miracle in which God spoke to those who seek and listen.

The "open miracle" of Exodus and Sinai does not await human discovery. It is dazzling, fearsome, unmistakable. Thus does the poet whose meditation introduces *Shofarot* in the Rosh Hashanah *Musaf* prayer describe it:

. . . The whole world trembled at Thy presence, and the works of creation were in awe of Thee, when Thou did reveal Thyself, our King, upon Mount Sinai to teach Thy people Torah and commandments, and did make them hear Thy majestic voice and holy utterances out of flames of fire. Amidst thunder and lightning Thou did manifest Thyself to them and while the *shofar* sounded Thou did shine forth upon them . . .

The open miracle is all thunder and lightning. The voice of God, coming to teach His people Torah and commandments, is as piercing as the sound of the *shofar,* heard by handmaidens as by prophets. Here the identity of the King is clear; nothing is hidden.

Such a miracle is overwhelming. Just as the outpouring of attention showered on a young and powerless child by his or her parents forces the child into a relationship of grateful dependence, so God, in His openly miraculous love, gave Israel no choice. He held the mountain over their heads by pouring love and attention and commandments upon them.[26]

The religious person who is overly implicit is bothered by that, but the one whose faith is both explicit and implicit is thrilled and moved by it. He or she knows that, had the mountain not been held over their heads, the Jews would have had no Torah to ordain freely. So too does the social scientist know that the free self emerges in an ordered "world" in which there is imposed lawfulness. And the educational philosopher will explain that, for the child as for the people, there is coercion, "situation," before there is conviction, even though ultimately, coercion will not hold up in court—or in conscience. The commandments held over our heads must be freely acknowledged and related to our concerns, even as they demand to shape us and inform our concerns.

Is the freely ordained Torah "that will stand up in court" exactly the same, for a given individual, for a given generation, as that forced upon the myriads of Israel? Or that given to children when mother and father and teachers "hold it over their heads" to bring them into the community? Yes and no, as Moses learned when he was allowed, according to a famous talmudic tale, to sit in on a lesson given by Rabbi Akiva, the renowned Sage who "deserved to be the one through whom the Torah be given." Moses, relates the Talmud, did not understand Rabbi Akiva's exposition. He became despondent, and "his strength left him."

Yet Moses was ultimately reassured when Akiva came to a certain point and his disciples asked him how he knew what he had just taught. He replied that it was a *halakhah l'Moshe mi-Sinai*, "a halakhah [ascribed] to Moses, [given] at Mount Sinai."[27]

# Conclusion

Let us return briefly to the several religious and non-religious Jewish publics with whom we began. Does theoretical discussion characterizing the philosophy of religious Jewish education help them? Does it clarify areas of agreement and of controversy? Does it aid in establishing criteria for success and suggest ways of dealing with partial failures? Does it illuminate various conceptions of authority and community of freedom and the individual—and of normative or achievable relationships between them? By the answers to such questions, the value of theoretical discussions of this kind may be tested.

If our theoretical examination of theology and theory of religious education is useful, it must raise questions for all of our Jewish publics. The Orthodox community must re-examine the question of whether Reform and Conservative education is legitimately excluded from the category of religious education. The Orthodox may, indeed, be expected to take issue with other groups when the non-Orthodox consider implicit religion as their starting point, whereas, they insist, with no little justice, that the Jewish religious tradition is founded on the principle that explicit precedes implicit religiosity. The non-Orthodox educators, in response, are likely to point out that Jewish religious education that does not begin with the implicit features of Judaism will be incomprehensible to the modern Jew. And the Orthodox will complain that the Conservative and the Reform, usually lacking "normative communities," have no way of proceeding from the implicit to the explicit, whereas the Orthodox themselves may be charged with often ignoring religion's implicit dimensions. Yet, it appears that the discussion must be conducted on these grounds; the customary name-calling in which Jews are simply denounced as "deviationists" or "fundamentalists," as "irreligious" or "benighted," while emotionally satisfying, does little to clarify or to illuminate.

The most consistently post-Emancipation "religiously" defined Jews, such as educators associated with radically Reform groups like the American Council for Judaism, may, in light of our discussion, better understand why they have trouble accepting even most Reform textbooks for use in their classrooms, and why their particular combination of thoroughly implicit religiosity and a denial of the national features of Judaism make most religious educational materials produced in the Jewish community unacceptable to them.[1] In re-examining their approach to Jewish religious education, they may come to re-evaluate their relationship to the Jewish community and people.

The non-religious educators, in Israel especially, may ask themselves whether basic existential questions asked in the Israeli "general" school are not, in fact, intrinsically tied to implicit religious assumptions and goals. They may examine whether the national entity—community, as it were—does not serve as a "non-religious" substitute for explicit religious normativeness. They may question whether it is fruitful to deny the religious dimension of existential issues and experiences because of the ideological axiom fostered by religious and anti-religious establishments and stereotypes that Jewish religion is almost exclusively implicit. These educators must confront the question of whether they have thrown out the baby with (what they consider) the bath water, thereby ironically leaving the responsibility for representing Jewish traditional spirituality to those whose theology they reject.

As for the ultra-traditionalists—who surely believe that implicit religion is part of Torah, since they never felt impelled to deal systematically with the problem of modernity and thus never had to be philosophically "consistent"— they might ask themselves whether the consciousness of siege that besets their community of commitment has not made them too explicit, even by their own lights. Even more important, they must consider whether the refusal to deal with modernity can be justified in the name of Religious Truth.

For all these publics there are certain questions on the agenda of Jewish education that may be raised in common, however much the various groups will differ in resolving them. And theorists can be helpful in formulating these questions.

Theories of religious Jewish education will not, of course, resolve all differences between Jews who categorize themselves as religious and non-religious, or among various groups of religiously defined Jews. But such educational theories may expose areas for discussion and fruitful controversy. And they are likely to disclose some commonalities that characterize diverse groups of Jews who are heirs to an acknowledged tradition and who are a community confronting a particular world—of culture and of nations.

On the basis of theoretically founded discussion, many issues can be clarified in the relationship of Jewish education to the tradition and to the modern world. For example, a distinction may be drawn between Judaism's attitude toward a humanistic and enhancing secularity—which is not foreign to the Jewish religious tradition—and its attitude toward a pagan and self-aggrandizing secularism, which is.[2] It is also important to examine the various "religious" and "national" viewpoints in contemporary Judaism and Jewish education and to disclose the "explicit" and "implicit" assumptions that inform them. Such discussions will indicate that some of the controversy has been misconstrued and that some philosophical and educational alliances are unfounded.

If a theory of religious Jewish education will help us discover some unsuspected affinities between "religious" and "non-religious" Jews, it will not create artificial harmony; at times, it will accentuate principled distinctions and disagreements. Yet, one must place near the top of any agenda for educational deliberation the question of how we can learn from those with whom we disagree and live with those from whom we do not particularly desire to learn anything, while yet maintaining our principles and testifying to our truth as we have experienced it.

To the very explicit-minded person the formulation of the issue is itself suspect; it sounds inconsistent or confused. To the very implicit-minded person; the answer and the question seem far simpler than they are. But in the modern situation, it is imperative to love both truth and peace, no matter how "ironic" this seems or sounds.

There are those who will say that such a "dialectical" approach to Torah and to modernity is impractical, for only a small, elite group can live with it. In fact, however, if there will be no "dialectics" in our education and lives, no commitment to both principle and pluralism, it is possible that there will soon be no human life on this threatened planet. If we cannot educate toward an existence in which there is ambiguity grounded in commitment to Transcendence, our species may soon cease to exist, or our children will witness the extinction of consciousness in a "brave new world." But even those who do not like their apocalypticism painted on such a broad canvas must agree that the much buffeted Jewish people cannot live as though the religious teachings of Judaism have no message or as though the present makes no demands. For if we try to live that way we prejudice our survival in free societies and undermine, perhaps decisively, the State of Israel—which was envisioned to represent both historical and spiritual continuity and modernity, and to construct a bridge between them.

Saying how to be principled and pluralistic, or pious and open, in education is harder than saying that it must be done. No "movement" has the whole answer, though probably none completely lacks clues waiting to be picked up and deciphered. What is certain is that finding answers, however tentative, will require sensitivity, practical knowledge, and a believing good sense, on the one hand, and some theoretical grounding that generates insight and organizes rationality, on the other.

I have tried to present some of the theory, in the hope that it will make a practical difference.

# Notes

The notes to this book are meant to serve the teacher as well as to engage the scholar. With regard to the former, I have made several assumptions in choosing bibliographical material:

1. The teacher may wish to "read up on" some issues, and I therefore suggest representative material that may give educational directions.

2. When possible, I have cited material in English, but I have assumed that Hebrew-reading (and -teaching) readers may wish to know of additional material that has not been translated.

3. To "back up" points being made with regard to the Jewish tradition, I cite illustrative texts, which, in my opinion, make the point being posited. Obviously, however, a Midrashic or exegetical comment is *not* cited to establish what "Judaism says" about the subject, but rather, that that particular aspect of Jewish teaching has already been highlighted by sages and scholars—and can be usefully introduced into instruction.

4. At times, I have added a paragraph to the text in the notes. These comments, I hope, give food for thought, but I feel that if placed in the text they would be detrimental to the flow of the discussion.

## *Chapter 1*

1. For a useful survey and discussion of contemporary schools of thought in education and pertinent biographical material, see Robert E. Mason, *Contemporary Educational Theory* (New York: David McKay Company, Inc., 1972).

2. Israel Scheffler, *Conditions of Knowledge: An Introduction to Epistemology* (Chicago: Scott, Foresman & Co., 1965), pp. 1–6. Scheffler, "Philosophical Models of Teaching," in Israel Scheffler, *Reason and Teaching* (London: Routledge and Kegan

Paul, 1973), pp. 67–81. Zvi Lamm, *Conflicting Theories of Instruction: Conceptual Dimensions* (Berkeley: McCutchan, 1976).

3. This differentiation has, of course, often been made in educational theory, with the former identified with educational conservatism and the latter with educational liberalism. Cf. James Bowen and Peter R. Hobson, *Theories of Education: Studies of Significant Innovation in Western Educational Thought* (Brisbane: John Wiley & Sons, 1974). See also P.H. Hirst and R.S. Peters, *The Logic of Education* (London: Routledge and Kegan Paul, 1970), chap. 2. A summary of the two views is succinctly given in T.W. Moore, *Educational Theory: an Introduction* (London: Routledge and Kegan Paul, 1974), pp. 20–21. For the realization of how this distinction may be viewed as crucial to Jewish education, I am indebted to the paper by Isa Aron, "Deweyan Deliberation as a Model for Decision-Making in Jewish Education," *Studies in Jewish Education II* ed. Michael Rosenak (Jerusalem: The Magnes Press, The Hebrew University, 1985), pp. 136–149, especially pp. 143–145. Shortly after Dr. Aron's paper (delivered at a conference at the Hebrew University in 1980) had suggested the centrality of this dichotomy for Jewish education, I saw the matter illustrated in a curricular controversy between Chanan Alexander and David Resnick on the issue of teaching Jewish Law in Conservative Schools. Cf. David Resnick, "Jewish Law in Conservative Schools," *Conservative Judaism* 34(1):55–62 (September-October 1980); and Chanan Alexander, "Halakhah and Aggadah in Conservative Curricula: A Response to David Resnick," *Conservative Judaism* 34(6):57–63 (July-August 1981).

4. See, for example, William K. Frankena, "A Model for Analyzing a Philosophy of Education," *Readings in the Philosophy of Education,* ed. Jane Martin (Boston: Allyn & Bacon, Inc., 1970), pp. 15–20.

5. For discussions of this concept, see Bowen and Hobsen, *Theories of Education,* pp. 10–11; Harry Schofield, *The Philosophy of Education* (London: George Allen and Unwin, 1972), chap. 1; Charles J. Brauner and Hobert W. Burns, *Problems in Education and Philosophy* (Englewood Cliffs, N.J.: Prentice-Hall, Inc., 1965), chap. 1.

6. Ralph W. Tyler, *Basic Principles of Curriculum and Instruction* (Chicago: The University of Chicago Press, 1949), p. 4.

7. *Ibid.*

8. Paul H. Hirst, "Philosophy and Curriculum Planning," in Hirst, *Knowledge and the Curriculum* (London: Routledge and Kegan Paul, 1974), p. 3. For his discussion of objectives in education, see *ibid.,* pp. 1–15.

9. For this distinction and Hirst's view, see Moore, *Educational Theory,* pp. 5–8.

10. This tendency is discussed and illustrated later, in Chapter 7.

11. An important study (and example) with regard to this expectation is Mordecai Bar-Lev, *"Bograi Ha-Yeshivot Ha-Tichoniyot B'Eretz Yisrael Ben Masoret Vichidush"* ("The Graduates of the Yeshiva High Schools in Eretz Yisrael Between Tradition and Innovation"). Ph.D. diss. (Bar Ilan University, 5737[1977]). In this example the criteria for success are blatantly behavioral (in terms of community expectations and institutional patterns of conduct). For the criteria of success in terms of doctrinal orthodoxy, see Yitzchak Meir Goodman, "A Correlation Study of Jewish Education and *Hashkafah* Among College-Age Jewish Students," *Studies in Jewish Education II,* pp. 299–315.

12. For models in the Orthodox community, see Charles Leibman, "Orthodoxy in American Jewish Life," *American Jewish Year Book 1965,* vol. 66 (Philadelphia and New York: Jewish Publication Society of America and American Jewish Committee, 1965), pp. 21–92. Reform *community* models are less common, for ideological as well as for sociological reasons; Kibbutz Yahel in the Negev is a prominent example. In the words of one Reform leader: " . . . if I were asked where in our entire world Progressive movement is the interdependence of the universal and particular impulses

most manifest and relevant, I would say that it is in our new small community in the Arava called Kibbutz Yahel . . . '' [Richard G. Hirsch, ''Jewish Peoplehood: Implications for Reform Judaism,'' *Forum* (37):125 (Spring 1980).]

13. Joseph B. Soloveitchik in ''The Lonely Man of Faith,'' *Tradition* 7(2):7–8 (Summer 1965) makes the distinction between the *ontological* loneliness and the *historical* loneliness of the man of faith, which may be said to correspond to these two types of unease in the soul of the normatively oriented educator.

14. John Dewey, *Democracy and Education* (New York: The Free Press, 1966), p. 160.

15. Joseph J. Schwab, *The Practical: A Language for Curriculum,* (National Education Association, 1970), pp. 3–4. See also John Dewey, *The Quest for Certainty* (New York: Minton, Balch and Co., 1929), chap. 10, for an earlier development of this concept.

16. Seymour Fox, ''The Vitality of Theory in Schwab's Conception of the Practical,'' *Curriculum Inquiry* 15(1):69–70 (Spring 1985).

17. John Dewey, *Human Nature and Conduct* (New York: The Modern Library, 1930, p. 179. Also see Isa Aron, ''Moral Philosophy and Moral Education II: The Formalist Tradition and the Deweyan Alternative,'' *School Review* 85(4):523–528 (August 1977).

18. Seymour Fox, in conversation with the author.

19. In conversation with the author.

20. ''The subject matter of the practical (unlike the theoretical) . . . is always something taken as concrete and particular and treated as indefinitely susceptible to circumstance, and therefore highly liable to unexpected change . . . '' Schwab, ''The Practical,'' p. 3.

21. Isa Aron, ''Deweyan Deliberation,'' pp. 141–142.

22. Abraham Joshua Heschel, *Torah Min Hashamayim B'Aspaklariya Shel Hadorot* II *(Theology of Ancient Judaism)* (London: Soncino Press, 5725[1965]), motto on unpaginated first page.

## Chapter 2

1. William K. Frankena, *Three Historical Philosophies of Education* (New York: Scott, Foresman & Co., 1965), p. 8.

2. For a discussion of *Weltanschauung,* especially in Dilthey's conception see Willson H. Coates and Hayden V. White, *The Ordeal of Liberal Humanism: An Intellectual History of Western Europe,* vol. 2 (New York: McGraw-Hill Book Co., 1970), pp. 256–262.

3. See Israel Scheffler, ''Justifying Curricular Decisions,'' *Readings in the Philosophy of Education,* pp. 23–31; Robert H. Ayers, ''Crypto-Theologies and Educational Theories,'' *Educational Theory* 15(4):282–292 (October 1965).

4. On this, see Samuel Sandmel, ''Reflections on the Problem of Theology for Jews,'' *Journal of Bible and Religion* 33(2):101–112 (April 1965); Monford Harris, ''Interim Theology,'' *Judaism* 7(4):302–308 (Autumn 1958). For discussions in Hebrew, see David Neumark, ''Hashkafat Chaim—Hashkafat Olam'' (Life View—World View'') *Hashiloach* 11(1–4):26–32, 129–139, 219–231, 418–432 (January-July 1903); Y. Jacobson, *Le-Baayat Hagmul Ba-Mikrah* (Tel Aviv: Sinai, 5709), pp. 42–59 (''Al Neumai Hashem Be-Sefer Iyov,'' ''On the Speeches of God in the Book of Job'').

5. In the words of John Dewey, ''The primary ineluctable facts of the birth and death of each one of the constituent members in a social group determine the necessity of education.'' (*Democracy and Education,* p. 3).

6. Ralph Barton Perry, "Education and the Science of Education," in *Philosophy and Education* 2nd ed., ed Israel Scheffler (Boston: Allyn & Bacon, Inc., 1966), p. 17.

7. Lamm, *Conflicting Theories of Education.*

8. Van Cleve Morris, "Is There a Metaphysics of Education?" *Educational Theory* 17(2):141–146 (April 1967). Also, Van Cleve Morris, *Existentialism in Education* (New York: Harper & Row, 1966).

9. See John Dewey, *Experience and Education* (New York and London: The Free Press and Collier-Macmillan Ltd., 1966), especially chap. 2.

10. Thomas F. Green, "Teaching, Acting and Behaving," in Scheffler, *Philosophy and Education,* pp. 115–135.

11. For a discussion of continuity within Judaism, see Nathan Rotenstreich, "Historical Viewpoints in Judaism," *Conservative Judaism* 28(3):3–12 (Spring 1974).

12. BT Megillah 31b.

13. For the terms "language" and "literature" see R.S. Peters, "Reason and Habit: The Paradox of Moral Education," in Scheffler, *Philosophy and Education,* pp. 252–253, and Michael Oakeshott, "Learning and Teaching," in *The Concept of Education,* ed. R.S. Peters (London: Routledge and Kegan Paul, 1967), pp. 160–161.

14. Cf. Schofield, *The Philosophy of Education,* chaps. 2–4.

15. See the discussion in R.S. Peters, "Freedom and the Development of the Free Man," *Moral Development and Moral Education,* (London: George Allen & Unwin, 1981), pp. 116–139.

16. Perry, "Education and the Science of Education," pp. 26–27, 34–35.

17. Cf. Jacques Maritain, *Education at the Crossroads* (New Haven: Yale University Press, 1943), especially pp. 1–28.

18. James W. Fowler, *Stages of Faith: The Psychology of Human Development and the Quest for Meaning* (San Francisco: Harper & Row, 1976), pp. 3–8.

19. For a Reform view, see Emil L. Fackenheim, "Apologia for a Confirmation Text," *Quest for Past and Future* (Bloomington: Indiana University Press, 1968), chap. 9. For a Conservative view, see Seymour Siegel, "The Meaning of Jewish Law in Conservative Judaism: An Overview and Summary," *Conservative Judaism and Jewish Law,* ed. Seymour Siegel (New York: The Rabbinical Assembly, 1977), pp. xiii–xxvi. For an Orthodox approach that maintains that theology is "literature," see Eliezer Berkovits, "What is Jewish Philosophy?" *Tradition* 3(2):117–130 (Spring 1961).

20. Generally, we may expect the more "traditional" exponents of Judaism to be correspondingly more normative. But normativeness as an integral aspect of religion and religious education has also been addressed by "liberal" thinkers. See, for example, Jakob Petuchowski, "The Limits of Liberal Judaism," *Judaism* 14(2):146–158 (Spring 1965).

21. Leibman, "Orthodoxy in American Jewish Life," especially pp. 38–51, 89–92.

22. Marshall Sklare, *Conservative Judaism: An American Religious Movement,* augmented ed. (New York: Schocken Books, 1972), pp. 154–158; also, Emil L. Fackenheim, "The Dilemma of Liberal Judaism," *Quest for Past and Future,* pp. 130–147.

23. Samuel C. Heilman, *Synagogue Life: A Study in Symbolic Interaction* (Chicago: University of Chicago Press, 1976), especially summation comments, p. 266.

24. Joseph B. Soloveitchik, *Halakhic Man,* trans. Lawrence Kaplan (Philadelphia: Jewish Publication Society of America, 1983), pp. 128–131.

25. Ahad Ha-Am, "Priest and Prophet," in Ahad Ha-Am, *Selected Essays,* trans. Leon Simon (Philadelphia: Jewish Publication Society of America, 1944), pp. 125–138.

26.  Walter I. Ackerman, "Jewish Education—For What?" *American Jewish Year Book 1969,* vol. 70, pp. 3–36. Harold S. Himmelfarb, "Jewish Education for Naught: Educating the Culturally Deprived Jewish Child," *Analysis* (51):1–11 (September 1975).

27.  Leonard Fein, "Suggestions Towards the Reform of Jewish Education in America," *Midstream* 18(2):42 (February 1972).

28.  David Schoem, "Ethnic Survival in America: An Ethnography of a Jewish Afternoon School." Ph.D. diss. University of California, Berkeley, 1979.

29.  David Schoem, "Inside the Classroom: Reflections of a Troubled People," *Jewish Education* 48(1):38 (Spring 1980).

30.  *Ibid.,* p. 39.

## Chapter 3

1.  Schwab, *The Practical: A Language for Curriculum,* pp. 17–18.

2.  For an analysis of various approaches along the Zionist spectrum, including those that are centered on the political, social, and psychological problems related to an exilic or "abnormal" national existence, see Arthur Hertzberg, *The Zionist Idea,* ed. Arthur Hertzberg (New York: Doubleday & Co., and Herzl Press, 1959), pp. 15–100. An outspoken exposition of the "socio-psychological problem approach" to education for Zionism and Israel is David Kuselewitz, *Teaching Israel* (New York: Herzl Press, 1964).

3.  For an illustrative Jewish anti-Semitic "self-analysis," see Otto Weininger, "The Jew Must Free Himself from Jewishness," in *The Jew in the Modern World: A Documentary History,* ed. Paul R. Mendes-Flohr and Jehuda Reinharz (New York and Oxford: Oxford University Press, 1980), pp. 233–236.

4.  Aron, "Moral Philosophy and Moral Education II," *School Review* 85(4):525 (August 1977), where this Deweyian position is succinctly stated (p. 525): " . . . the deliberator must bear in mind the possibility that conditions have changed. Principles and ideals too are useful tools for deliberation, *for they represent the results, in summary form, of age-old deliberations* [emphasis added]. Precisely because of their long history, however, certain principles or rules may be outdated, not suitable for current situations."

5.  For definitions of sects and sectarianism, see J. Milton Yinger, *The Scientific Study of Religion* (London: The Macmillan Co., 1970), pp. 252–279, esp. pp. 277–278.

6.  For a discussion of halakhic deliberation that relates to modern consciousness and religious disbelief or laxity in terms of the modern (secular) situation, see Zvi Yaron, *Mishnato Shel Ha-Rav Kook (The Teachings of Rabbi Kook)* (Jerusalem: The Jewish Agency for Israel, 1974), chap. 6.

7.  Cf. Emil L. Fackenheim, "On The Eclipse of God," in *Quest for Past and Future,* pp. 229–243.

8.  Cf., for example, John E. Smith, *Experience and God* (New York: Oxford University Press, 1968), especially pp. 187–190; John H. Randall, "The Conflict of the Religious Tradition with Science," in Randall, *Philosophy After Darwin* (New York: Columbia University Press, 1977), pp. 3–21.

9.  H.J. Paton, *The Modern Predicament* (London: George Allen & Unwin, 1955), chap. 7.

10.  Franz Rosenzweig, "The Commandments: Divine or Human?" in Rosenzweig, *On Jewish Learning,* ed. N.N. Glatzer (New York: Schocken Books, 1955), p. 121.

11.  Bertrand Russell, *My Philosophical Development,* cited in Fackenheim, "On the Eclipse of God," p. 239.

12. For educational expressions and ramifications of these diverse national views, see Zvi Adar, *Jewish Education in Israel and in the United States*, trans. Barry Chazan (Jerusalem: The Samuel Mendel Melton Centre for Jewish Education in the Diaspora, Hebrew University, 1977), chaps. 4–6; J. Schoneveld, *The Bible in Israeli Education* (Amsterdam: Van Gorcum, 1976), chaps. 4–6, 13.

13. *Hamadrich Hashomeri* (5 December 1954), p. 79.

14. Nathan Rotenstreich, "Secularism and Religion," *Judaism* 15(3):261 (Summer 1966).

15. Ahad Ha-Am, "Slavery in Freedom," *Selected Essays*, pp. 171–194.

16. Cited by Saul L. Goodman in *The Faith of Secular Jews*, ed. Saul L. Goodman (New York: Ktav Publishing House, Inc., 1976), p. 14. For a lengthier exposition see Simon Dubnow, "Jewish History: An Essay on the Philosophy of History," in Dubnow, *Nationalism and History* (Cleveland: Meridian Books, 1961), pp. 266–267.

17. As, for example, Ahad Ha-Am, "Slavery in Freedom." For a particularly sharp critique of this kind, see Gershom Scholem, "The Politics of Mysticism: Isaac Breuer's New Kuzari," in Scholem, *The Messianic Idea in Judaism and Other Essays on Jewish Spirituality* (New York: Schocken Books, 1971), pp. 325–334, esp. n. 5, p. 364.

18. A classic and oft-cited example is the historical ballad of Judah Leib Gordon, "Zidkiyahu Be-Bet Ha-Pekudot" ("Zedekiah in Prison"), in which the Judaean king conducts a tirade against the prophets, especially Jeremiah, who are accused of wishing to convert a nation into bands of passive pietists. For a discussion of this literary genre, see Simon Halkin, *Modern Hebrew Literature: Trends and Values* (New York: Schocken Books, 1950), chaps. 1–3.

19. BT Sanhedrin 44a. For a talmudic exposition on the parameters of apostasy, see Aharon Lichtenstein, "Brother Daniel and the Jewish Fraternity," *Judaism* 12(3):260–280 (Summer 1963).

20. Ben-Zion Mossenson, "Ha-Tanakh Be-Bet Ha-Sefer" ("The Bible in the School"), *Hachinuch* 1(1):23–32; 110–119 (5670).

21. Mordecai Segal, *Erkai Mikra, Erkai Adam (Biblical Values, Human Values)* (Tel Aviv: Seminar Hakibbutzim, 1959), p. 166.

22. Ahad Ha-Am's disagreement is carefully but unmistakably expressed in his letter-essay, "Divrai Shalom" ("Words of Peace"), *Kol Kitvai Ahad Ha-Am (Collected Writings of Ahad Ha-Am)* (Tel Aviv: Dvir, 5707 [1954]), pp. 56–60. For Zuta's approach, see H.A. Zuta, *Darko Shel Moreh: Pirkai Zichronot (The Way of a Teacher: A Memoir)* (Jerusalem: Reuven Mass, 1938) and Schoneveld, *The Bible in Israeli Education*, pp. 41–46.

23. Ahad Ha-Am "Torah She'Balev" ("The Torah of the Heart"), *Kol Kitvai Ahad Ha-Am,* pp. 51–55.

24. Ahad Ha-Am expresses this in educational terms in "Ha-Chinuch Ha-Leumi" ("National Education"), *Kol Kitvai Ahad Ha-Am,* pp. 410–414. As Schweid summarizes this national-educational ideal: "This (Jewish literature) in all its contents is ours and the teaching that Ahad Ha-Am intends is the cultural one . . . How will this teaching express itself in the climate of the school and in the life style of pupils? Ahad Ha-Am does not answer this question and apparently does not consider himself bound to answer it. In the framework of a secular-national world view, the answer is entrusted to each individual, as long as he does not cut himself off from the public realm of the Jewish collective-community." Eliezer Schweid, *Ha-Yahadut V'Ha-Tarbut Ha-Chilonit (Judaism and Secular Culture),* (Tel Aviv: Hakibbutz Hameuchad, 1981), pp. 40–41.

25. Yudel Mark, "Jewishness and Secularism," in Goodman, *The Faith of Secular Jews,* p. 99.

26. Mordecai M. Kaplan, *The Meaning of God in Modern Jewish Religion* (New York: Behrman House, 1937) and *Judaism as a Civilization* (New York: Schocken Books, 1967), Parts 5 and 6. For a discussion of Kaplan's theology, see Henry N. Wiemann, "Mordecai M. Kaplan's Idea of God," in *Mordecai M. Kaplan: An Evaluation,* ed. Ira Eisenstein and Eugene Kohn (New York: Jewish Reconstructionist Foundation, Inc., 1952), pp. 193–210.

27. Harold Schulweis, "Like All Other Religions," in *Varieties of Jewish Belief,* ed. Ira Eisenstein (New York: Reconstructionist Press, 1966), p. 240.

28. Goodman, "The Credo of a Jewish Educator," in *The Faith of Secular Jews,* p. 119.

29. For a radical expression of this view, see Richard L. Rubenstein, "Jewish Theology and the Current World Situation," *Conservative Judaism* 28(4):3–25 (Summer 1974).

30. Richard L. Rubenstein, *After Auschwitz: Radical Theology and Contemporary Judaism* (Indianapolis: The Bobbs-Merrill Co., Inc., 1966), esp. chaps. 1, 7, 13.

31. " . . . the Messianic idea has compelled *a life lived in deferment,* in which nothing can be done definitively, nothing can be irrevocably accomplished." Gershom Scholem, "Towards an Understanding of the Messianic Idea," *The Messianic Idea in Judaism,* p. 35.

32. See A.B. Yehoshua, *Between Right and Right,* trans. Arnold Schwarz (Garden City, N.Y.: Doubleday & Co., Inc., 1981), chap. 2.

33. For a prominent exposition of this view, see Gershon Weiler, *Medinah V'Chinuch: Iyyunim Philosophiim (State and Education: Philosophical Explorations)* (Tel Aviv: Papyrus Publishing House, 1979).

34. This was adduced as a ground for negotiation between halakhah and the new reality of the State of Israel even by some religious thinkers, notably, Isaiah Leibowitz, in his early writings. See his "Ha-Mitziut Ha-Chevratit-Medinit Ke-Baayah Datit" ("The Socio-Political Reality as a Religious Problem") and "Ha-Shabbat Ba-Medinah Ke-Baayah Datit" ("The Sabbath in the State as a Religious Problem") in Leibowitz, *Yahadut, Am Yehudi U'Medinat Yisrael (Judaism, the Jewish People and the State of Israel* (Jerusalem: Schocken, 1975), pp. 98–120.

35. Although this type of polemic has become especially widespread since the rise of religious nationalistic sentiment, especially in the Gush Emunim movement (for example, Amnon Rubenstein, *Mi-Herzl Ad Gush Emunim V'Chazarah [From Herzl to Gush Emunim and Back]* [Tel Aviv: Schocken, 1980]), it has been a long-standing concern of secular Zionists that a normative religiosity will weaken the Zionist ethos they represent. See, for example, Yitzchak Tabenkin, "A People, Not a Faith," in *Forum for the Problems of Zionism, Jewry and the State of Israel IV* (Proceedings of the Jerusalem Ideological Conference 1957) (Jerusalem: The World Zionist Organization, 1959), pp. 187–194.

36. Adar, *Jewish Education,* p. 96.

37. John Dewey, *A Common Faith* (New Haven: Yale University Press, 1934), pp. 21–22; 41–42.

38. See John Wilson, et al., *Introduction to Moral Education,* (Middlesex, England: Penguin Books, 1967), pp. 176–183. See also Milton Rokeach, *Beliefs, Attitudes and Values* (San Francisco: Jossey-Bass, Inc., 1968), pp. 189–196.

39. On such problems as verbalization (in which a "rote" attitude toward the Bible that is unrelated to the lives and beliefs of the pupils is developed in school), see Avraham Minkowitz, "Ba-Ayot Psychologiot B'Hora-at Ha-Tanakh," ("Psychological Problems in Bible Instruction"), in *Da-at U'ma'as Bichinuch: Sefer Zikaron L'Avraham Arnon (Abraham Arnon Memorial Volume)* (Tel Aviv: Ha-Va'ad Ha-Tziburi, 1960), pp. 305–325.

## Chapter 4

1. Franz Rosenzweig, in a letter to Gertrud Oppenheim dated May 1, 1917, speaks of "the dangers of assimilation," which he dismisses as not serious, "for in this Europe replete with history the past cannot be simply dismissed." He continues: "But the second danger (i.e., Zionism) holds a serious threat, for Asia is today relatively unpopulated. It is for this reason that Herman Cohen, with absolutely trustworthy instinct, hates the Zionists. He once said to me something he has never put on paper . . . 'These bums want to be happy.' " (Source: Nahum N. Glatzer, *Franz Rosenzweig: His Life and His Thought,* 2nd ed. [New York: Schocken Books, 1961], pp. 53–54.)

2. Yechezkel Kaufmann, "The National Will to Survive," *Sources of Contemporary Jewish Thought II,* ed. David Hardan (Jerusalem: World Zionist Organization, 1970), p. 121.

3. Yaakov Klatzkin, "The Galut Cannot Survive," *Sources of Contemporary Jewish Thought I* (Jerusalem: World Zionist Organization, 1970), pp. 75–92.

4. Kaufmann, "The National Will to Survive," pp. 118–119.

5. See, for example, Immanuel Jakobovits, "The Cost of Jewish Survival," *Judaism* 15(4):426–436 (Fall 1966).

6. Emil L. Fackenheim, "Judaism, Christianity and Reinhold Niebuhr," *Judaism* 5(4):321–324 (Fall 1956).

7. Cf., for example, *Conceptions of Inquiry,* ed. Stuart Brown, John Fauvel, and Ruth Finnegan (London: Methuen, in association with the Open University Press, 1981), esp. Part 4, "Conceptions of Inquiry."

8. Compare Thomas F. O'Dea, "The Crisis of the Contemporary Religious Consciousness," *Daedalus,* 96(1):116–134 (Winter 1967) and Mary Douglas, "The Effects of Modernization on Religious Change," *Daedalus* 3(1):1–19 (Winter 1982).

9. C.G. Jung, *Psychology and Religion* (New Haven: Yale University Press, 1938). For a sympathetic treatment of Jung's conception of religion and its ramifications, see Werner Stark, *The Sociology of Religion: A Study of Christendom,* vol. 4 (London: Routledge & Kegan Paul, 1972), pp. 409–420.

10. Sigmund Freud, *Civilization and Its Discontents* (New York: W.W. Norton & Co., 1961), chap. 1.

11. Karl Popper, "Conjectures and Refutations," in *Conceptions of Inquiry, op. cit.,* pp. 100–106. Erich Fromm, *Psychoanalysis and Religion* (New Haven: Yale University Press, 1950), chap. 1.

12. For a discussion of this, see Roger Lincoln Shinn, *The Existentialist Posture* (New York: Association Press, 1970).

13. Cf. Ian T. Ramsey, *Religious Language: An Empirical Placing of Theological Phrases* (New York: Macmillan, 1963).

14. George F. Thomas, *Religious Philosophies of the West* (New York: Charles Scribner's Sons, 1965), chap. 9.

15. Emil L. Fackenheim, *The Religious Dimension in Hegel's Thought* (Bloomington: Indiana University Press, 1967), pp. 223–242.

16. John Macquarrie, *Twentieth Century Religious Thought: The Frontiers of Philosophy and Theology* (New York: Harper & Row, 1963).

17. Walter Kaufmann, *Critique of Religion and Philosophy* (Garden City, New York: Anchor Books–Doubleday & Co., 1961), pp. 258–368.

18. Aharon Lichtenstein, "Brother Daniel and the Jewish Fraternity," 268–269.

19. Kaplan, *Judaism as a Civilization,* pp. 313–331.

20. Milton Himmelfarb, *The Jews of Modernity* (Philadelphia: Jewish Publication Society of America, 1973), chap. 1, pp. 3–21.

21. *Ibid.*, pp. 20–21.

22. The issue has been shown to be a central one in the thought of modern Jewry by Max Weiner in his *Jüdische Religion in Zeitalter Der Emanzipation.* Hebrew edition, *Ha-Dat Ha-Yehudit Be-Tekufat Ha-Emancipatzia,* trans. Leah Zagni (Jerusalem; Mossad Bialik and the Leo Baeck Institute, 1974).

23. See *Textbook Analyses* (American Council for Judaism, undated, stencil). The writers find that the vast majority of *Reform* Jewish textbooks examined for possible use in schools and associated with the American Council for Judaism were either unacceptable or accepted with reservations. (Forty-six out of a total of 73 were found completely unacceptable.) Offensive terms in unacceptable books included "the Jewish people" and other "nationalistic" expressions. The "tragic absence of spirituality" in most Jewish texts was contrasted with the religious texts of Protestant groups that publish educational materials (p. 12).

24. *Ha-Amakat Ha-Toda-ah Ha-Yehudit Be-Vait Ha-Sefer Ha-mamlachti: Ha-Nachot Ve-Tochniyot Limudim (Strengthening Jewish Consciousness in the State Schools: Directives and Syllabi* (Jerusalem: Ministry of Education and Culture, 1959), p. 8.

25. For example, Adar, *Jewish Education,* chap. 7.

26. Aharon Yadlin, "Chinuch Ha-Dor Ha-tzair Le-Achar Ha-Milchamah" ("The Education of the Young Generation After the War"), in *Hizdahut Ha-Umah im Ha-Medinah (Israel and the Jewish People During and After the Yom Kippur War),* ed. Moshe Davis (Jerusalem: Hasifriyah Ha-Tzionit 5736 [1975]), pp. 292–293.

27. See Baruch Kurzweil, "The New Canaanites in Israel," *Judaism* 2(1):3–15 (January 1953).

28. Yonatan Ratosh, "The New Hebrew Nation (The Canaanite Outlook)" in *Unease in Zion,* ed. Ehud ben Ezer (Jerusalem: Quadrangle—The New York Times Book Co., Jerusalem Academic Press, 1974), pp. 201–234.

29. See Gershom Scholem, "Zionism—Dialectic of Continuity and Rebellion," in *Unease in Zion,* pp. 263–296.

30. Meir Ben-Horin, "Judea-Zionism: Meaning Old and New," *Judaism* 20(3):295–305 (Summer 1971).

31. Yaakov Herzog, *A People That Dwells Alone,* ed. Misha Louvish (London: Weidenfeld & Nicolson, 1975), especially pp. 48–59 and pp. 124–129.

32. Thomas S. Kuhn, *The Structure of Scientific Revolutions,* 2nd ed. (Chicago: University of Chicago Press, 1970), esp. chaps. 3 and 8. For examples of "counterinstances," see pp. 79–80.

33. Leo Strauss, preface to [the English edition of] *Spinoza's Critique of Religion,* in *The Jewish Expression,* ed. Judah Goldin (New York: Bantam Books, Inc., 1970), p. 375.

34. Pesach Schindler, "The Holocaust and Kiddush Ha-Shem in Hassidic Thought," *Tradition* 13(4) and 14(1):88–104 (Spring-Summer 1973).

35. Yona Ben-Sasson, "Mashmaut Ha-Datit Shel Ha-Shoah" ("The Religious Significance of the Holocaust") in *Emunah Bashoah (Faith During the Holocaust)* (Jerusalem: Ministry of Education and Culture, Department of Torah Culture, 5740), pp. 47–50.

36. R.J. Zwi Werblowsky, "Crises of Messianism," *Judaism* 7(2):106–120 (Spring 1958).

37. Abraham Isaac Kook, "Fragments of Light: A View as to the Reason for the Commandments," in *Abraham Isaac Kook: The Lights of Penitence, The Moral Principles, Lights of Holiness, Essays, Letters and Poems,* trans. Ben Zion Bokser (New York: Paulist Press, 1978), pp. 303–323. This essay illustrates what Rabbi Kook emphasized in many of his writings: that the concrete framework is the necessary context of spirituality, which is distorted when it is disembodied.

38. A prominent example is the stricture in medieval halakhic rulings against "immoderate" public appearances by women, according to the rule that "the glory of the king's daughter is within [the gates]." This is no longer normative even within the ultra-Orthodox community, wherein women work in offices, shops, and schools. This issue is discussed, with relevant halakhic references from codes and responsa, in Amnon Shapira and Yechezkel Cohen, *Ha-Isha B'timurat Ha-Zman (The Status of Women in Historical Perspective)* (Ha-Kibbutz Ha-Dati, Jerusalem: Ne'emanai Torah V'avoda, 5744.

39. For an important non-Orthodox expression of the individual-existential dimension of the teaching of tradition, see Aryeh Simon, *"He-Arot Le-Erech Ha-Tanakh Be-Chinuchainu"* ("Comments on the Value of the Bible in our Education"), *Urim* 9 (4–5):275–280 (5712). For an Orthodox view, see Simcha Friedman, "Samchutiut V'Demokratia Be-Chinuch Ha-Dati" ("Authoritarianism and Democracy in Religious Education"), address delivered at a conference of religious educators at Kfar Batya, 8 Nissan 5734, stencil distributed by Ministry of Education and Culture, Youth Department. See also Z'ev Falk, *Law and Religion: The Jewish Experience* (Jerusalem: Mesharim Publishers, 1981), chaps. 5–7; Eliezer Berkovits, *Not in Heaven: The Nature and Function of Halakha* (New York: Ktav Publishing House, Inc., 1983).

40. Falk, *Law and Religion*, chap. 10.

41. Ayers, "Crypto-Theologies and Educational Theologies."

42. Perry, "Education and the Science of Education," p. 27.

43. Philip H. Phenix, *Religious Concerns in Contemporary Education* (New York: Teachers College, Columbia University, 1959). "Religion as ultimate concern . . . provides the large framework within which education occurs" (p. 19).

44. Moreover, to argue, as some educators do, that all education is indoctrination is to ignore descriptive and normative differentiation that have carefully been drawn between the two. Cf. I.A. Snook, *Indoctrination and Education* (London: Routledge & Kegan Paul, 1972).

45. Ernest Becker, *Beyond Alienation* (New York: George Braziller, 1967), chap. 9, esp. pp. 200–206.

46. Falk, *Law and Religion*, pp. 66–68; Berkovits, *Not in Heaven*, chap. 1.

47. For examples of theoretical writers who "re-open" the discussion, see Joseph J. Schwab, "On the Corruption of Education by Psychology," *The School Review* 60(2):169–184 (Summer 1958); Richard Hofstadter, "The Child and the World," *Daedalus* 91(3):501–525 (Summer 1962).

48. Naphtali Herz (Hartwig) Wessely (Weisel), "Words of Peace and Truth," in Mendes-Flohr and Reinharz, *The Jew in the Modern World*, p. 63.

49. See, for example, Michael Polanyi, *Personal Knowledge: Towards a Post-Critical Philosophy* (New York: Harper Torchbooks, 1958).

50. Franz Rosenzweig, "Towards a Renaissance of Jewish Learning," *On Jewish Learning*, pp. 55–71; Avraham Chein, *B-Mamlechet Ha-Yahadut (In the Kingdom of Judaism)* vol. 3 (Jerusalem: Mossad Harav Kook, 1970), pp. 45–48.

## Chapter 5

1. J. Schoneveld, *The Bible in Israeli Education*, considers this tendency in his discussion of several educators and of the "tradition-oriented" approach in the Labor Stream (i.e., schools associated with the Labor movement) in pre-Liberation Palestine, pp. 100–105.

2. Mordecai Bar-On, "Emunato Shel 'Bilti-Ma'amin' " ("The Faith of a 'Non-Believer' "), *Petachim* 1(2):3–10 (Kislev 5728).

3. See, for example, Fromm, *Psychoanalysis and Religion*, chap. 2.

4. Joachim Wach, *The Comparative Study of Religions* (New York: Columbia University Press, 1958), p. 24.

5. *Ibid.*, p. 28.

6. William James, *The Varieties of Religious Experience* (New York: The Modern Library, 1902). For James's definition of "personal" (as opposed to "institutional") religion, see pp. 29–32.

7. Wach, *Comparative Study*, p. 121.

8. Yehuda Ha-Levi, *The Kuzari: An Argument for the Faith of Israel* (New York: Schocken Books, 1964). See especially Part I, 10–27, 101–103; Part II, 32–44; Part III, 15–17. Moses Maimonides, *Guide to the Perplexed*, III, 27.

9. For a brief exposition of the Noachide Laws, see *Encyclopaedia Judaica*, Vol. 12 (Jerusalem: Keter Publishing House, 1972), pp. 1189–1191. On spirituality among the nations, the biblical books of Jonah and Ruth and their rabbinic-Midrashic commentaries contain much material. Two prominent rabbinic sources are the aggadic *Tanna Debai Eliyahu Rabba,* which proclaims that any person, Jewish or Gentile, who "engages in Torah" merits to have the Divine Spirit dwelling upon him, and the earlier talmudic passage (BT Sukkah 52) that places the Gentile King Malchizedek among four "craftsmen" who will play an important role in the final redemption.

10. One of the Noachide commandments forbids idolatry, but there is no Noachide law requiring doctrinal affirmations about God. With regard to permissive attitudes concerning "other gods," see Deut. 4:19.

11. "The fool has said in his heart, there is no God." Ps. 19:1.

12. On the views of Rabbi Menachem Ha-Meiri, who ruled that the talmudic condemnations and discriminations imposed upon idolators do not apply to the Christians and Moslems of his time (thirteenth century), see Jacob Katz, *Exclusiveness and Tolerance* (New York: Schocken Books, 1962), chap. 10.

13. Cf. Jacob Katz, "Kavin L'Biographia Shel Ha-Chatam Sofer" ("Guidelines to a Biography of the Chatam Sofer"), *Mechkarim L'Gershom Scholem B'Kabbala U'Btoldot Ha-Datot (Studies in Honor of Gershom Scholem)* (Jerusalem: Magnes Press, 1967), 143–144.

14. The definition of religion as "belief in an ever-living God" is that of James Martineu; his definition and that of Schleiermacher (and others) are cited by William P. Alston in "Religion," *The Encyclopedia of Religion*. Major portions of the essay are found and discussed in Elliot N. Dorff, *Jewish Law and Modern Ideology* (New York: United Synagogue Commission on Jewish Education, 1970), chap. 1. The definitions of Whitehead and MacMurray are also stated, and a reading from MacMurray's *The Structure of Religious Experience* is given, as well as discussion questions for teachers. For Gordon Allport and his conception of religious intention, see Allport, *The Individual and His Religion* (New York: Macmillan and Co., 1952), pp. 127–128.

15. In Dorff, *Jewish Law and Modern Ideology*, pp. 5–8.

16. *Ibid.*, pp. 8–9.

17. Paul Tillich, *Systematic Theology I* (Chicago: University of Chicago Press, 1951), pp. 11–12.

18. J. Milton Yinger, *The Scientific Study of Religion* (New York: The Macmillan Co., 1970), p. 14.

19. *Ibid.*, p. 15.

20. Paul Tillich, *Dynamics of Faith* (New York: Harper & Row, 1957), pp. 2–4.

21. For a philosophical discussion of "situation" as relevant to religious sensibilities, see Emil L. Fackenheim, *Metaphysics and Historicity* (Milwaukee: Marquette University Press, 1961).

22. Thus the statement by Russell cited previously (Chapter 3, n. 11) is thoroughly secular although it deals with a religious "experience."

23. Sigmund Freud, *The Future of an Illusion* (New York: Anchor Books, 1964), chap. 6.

24. See Leo Baeck, "Two World Views Compared," in Baeck, *The Pharisees and Other Essays* (New York: Schocken Paperback, 1966), pp. 125–145.

25. Phenix, *Religious Concerns in Contemporary Education.*

26. *Ibid.*, pp. 9–11.

27. See, for example, Sidney Hook, *Education for Modern Man* (New York: Alfred A. Knopf, 1963), pp. 107–111.

28. Genesis Rabbah 1:4.

29. Abraham Joshua Heschel, *God in Search of Man: A Philosophy of Judaism* (New York: Harper Torchbooks, 1955). "And God said, 'Let there be light' is different in spirit from a statement such as 'And Smith said, 'Let us turn on the light.' " p. 185.

30. Charles S. Leibman, "The Sociology of Religion and the Study of American Jews," *Conservative Judaism* 34(5):23 (May-June 1981). See also n. 23, p. 33.

31. R. Stark and C.Y. Glock, "Dimensions of Religious Commitment," in *Sociology of Religion,* ed. Roland Robertson. (Middlesex, England: Penguin Books, 1969), pp. 253–261.

32. Heschel, *God in Search of Man,* p. 3, posits that "the moment we become oblivious to ultimate questions, religion becomes irrelevant and its crisis sets in." His argument is that religion is an answer to such ultimate questions and that when the questions are forgotten, the answers become "empty."

33. Joachim Wach, *Types of Religious Experience* (Chicago: University of Chicago Press, 1951), p. 43.

34. Victor Turner, *The Ritual Process,* cited in Leibman, "The Sociology of Religion," p. 24.

35. For a definition of "non-propositional faith," see John H. Hick, *Philosophy of Religion* (Englewood Cliffs, N.J.: Prentice-Hall, Inc., 1973), pp. 59–63. In Hick's words: " . . . the content of revelation is not a body of truths about God, but God Himself coming within the orbit of man's experience by acting in human history. From this point of view, theological propositions, as such, are not revealed, but represent human attempts to understand the significance of revelatory events . . . " (p. 60). Hick contrasts this with the "propositional view of faith" and of revelation, which maintains that "the content of revelation is a body of truths expressed in statements or propositions. Revelation is the imparting to man of divinely authenticated truths. . . . Corresponding to this conception of revelation is a view of faith as man's obedient acceptance of these divinely revealed truths (p. 52). These two concepts are closely related to the terms *explicit religion* and *implicit religion,* which we shall be using frequently in our discussion of the dimensions of religious education.

36. Ahad Ha-Am's attempt to do so systematically is reflected in such essays as "Sacred and Profane," *Selected Essays of Ahad Ha-Am,* pp. 41–45. Secular Zionism in its cultural manifestations is, of course, predicated on this possibility and on the legitimacy of using sacred Jewish symbols and concepts in secularized contexts. See Charles S. Leibman and Eliezer Don Yehiya, *Civil Religion in Israel: Traditional Judaism and Political Culture in the Jewish State* (Berkeley: University of California Press, 1983). On secular uses of traditional symbols, see especially chap. 1.

37. Simon Rawidowicz, "On Interpretation," in Rawidowicz, *Studies in Jewish Thought,* ed. Nahum N. Glatzer (Philadelphia: The Jewish Publication Society of America, 1974). Rawidowicz states that interpretation is characterized by "a tension between continuation and rebellion, tradition and innovation. It derives its strength both

from a deep attachment to the 'text' and from an 'alienation' from it, a certain distance, a gap which must be bridged'' (p. 47).

38. Joseph J. Schwab, "Problems, Topics and Issues," in *Education and the Structure of Knowledge,* ed. Stanley Elam. (Chicago: Rand McNally, 1964), pp. 5–6.

39. Max Kadushin, *The Rabbinic Mind,* 3rd ed. (New York: Bloch Publishing Co., 1972), chaps. 2–3.

40. Yet the differentiation is problematic. See the discussion in Chapter 9, herein.

41. On the special Providence resting on *Eretz Yisrael,* cf. Deut. 11:12; on commandments observed only in *Eretz Yisrael,* cf. Mishnah Kelim, Chap. 1:6; BT Kiddushin 37a. On prophecy "only in *Eretz Yisrael,*" see Mekilta, Pischa 1; on the ascent of the nations to Jerusalem, Mic. 4:1–2 and Isa. 2:2–3; on the "assignment" of *Eretz Yisrael* to Israel, see Rashi on Gen. 1:1.

42. Franz Rosenzweig, *The Star of Redemption,* trans. William H. Hallo (Boston: Beacon Press, 1964), Part 2. Martin Buber, "The Man of Today and the Jewish Bible," in Buber, *Israel and the World* (New York: Schocken Books, 1963), pp. 96–102.

43. Eliezer Schweid, "A Secondary Relationship to Tradition: A Study of One Particular Aspect of Ahad Ha-Am's Doctrine," in Schweid, *Israel at the Crossroads,* trans. A.M. Winters (Philadelphia: The Jewish Publication Society of America, 1973), pp. 69–83.

44. Heschel, *God in Search of Man,* chap. 10. For a discussion of Gabriel Marcel's distinction, see Craig Dykstra, *Vision and Character: A Christian Educator's Alternative to Kohlberg* (Ramsey, N.J.: Paulist Press, 1981), pp. 35–36.

45. Schweid, "A Secondary Relationship to Tradition," pp. 82–83.

46. See Emil L. Fackenheim, *God's Presence in History: Jewish Affirmations and Philosophical Reflections* (New York and London: New York University and University of London Press, 1970), chap. 1.

## *Chapter 6*

1. Fowler, *Stages of Faith,* p. 277.

2. BT Berakhot 61b.

3. The recitation of the first paragraph of the *Shema* is often termed "accepting the yoke of the kingdom of Heaven" in rabbinic literature. See Rashi on Berakhot 61b.

4. Eliezer Berkovits, *Faith After the Holocaust* (New York: Ktav Publishing House, Inc., 1973), pp. 80–85.

5. Abraham Joshua Heschel, *Man's Quest for God* (New York: Charles Scribner's Sons, 1954), p. 96.

6. From *Amudim* (Journal of the Religious Kibbutz Movement), July-August 1967, p. 363. Cited and translated in my article, "Moments of the Heart," *Judaism* 17(2):217 (Spring 1968).

7. Sanhedrin Chapter 4; Mishnah 5.

8. *The Seventh Day: Soldiers Talk About the Six Day War,* ed. Avraham Shapiro et al. (New York: Charles Scribner's Sons, 1970), pp. 235–236.

9. Martin Buber, *Eclipse of God* (New York: Harper Torchbooks, 1952), pp. 7–9.

10. Paul Tillich, "The Two Types of Philosophy of Religion," in Tillich, *Theology of Culture* (Oxford: Oxford University Press, 1959), pp. 10–29; Martin Buber, *On Judaism* (New York: Schocken Books, 1972), especially "Jewish Religiosity," p. 80; William James, *The Varieties of Religious Experience,* pp. 29–32; Peter L. Berger, *The Heretical Imperative: Contemporary Possibilities of Religious Affirmation* (Garden

City, N.Y.: Anchor Press–Doubleday, 1980), chaps. 3 and 5; Wilfred Cantwell Smith, *The Meaning and End of Religion* (New York: Harper & Row, 1962), chaps. 6 and 7.

11. We are considering explicit and implicit religion as *dimensions* and shall argue for the desirability and necessity of bringing about an interaction between them in education. The terms are taken from *Religious Education in Secondary Schools: Schools Council Working Paper 36* (London: Evans and Methuen, 1971), where the distinction is made between "neo-confessional," "implicit" and "explicit" types of religious education. Our use of the term "implicit" is very similar to that of the Working Paper. What there is called "neo-confessional" is close to what we are calling "explicit." See pp. 30–42 of that document.

12. For the episodes of the Gentiles who came before the Sages Shammai and Hillel to be converted to Judaism, see BT Shabbat 31a. For an educational discussion of these episodes, see Edward M. Gershfield, "Hillel, Shammai and the Three Proselytes," *Conservative Judaism* 20(3):29–39 (Spring 1967).

13. For "propositional" truth, as defined by Hick, see Chapter 5, n. 35, herein.

14. The significance of the study of Torah in this process is especially evident in the case of the third proselyte, the most "simple" of the three, who is described as "explaining his status to himself" by the use of talmudic logic. (Shabbat 31a).

15. Emanuel Rackman, *One Man's Judaism* (New York: Philosophical Library in association with Jewish Education Committee, 1970), p. 48.

16. Martin Buber, "Herut: On Youth and Religion," in *On Judaism*, p. 150.

17. J.B. Soloveitchik, "The Lonely Man of Faith," pp. 62–63.

18. For a theoretical statement that constitutes an important modern basis for this, see Samson Raphael Hirsch, *The Nineteen Letters of Ben Uziel*, trans. B. Drachman (New York: Bloch Publishing Co., 1942), pp. 146–147.

19. Aaron Soloveitchik, "Standards for Achievement in the Day School," *Hebrew Day School Education: An Overview*, ed. Joseph Kaminetsky (New York: Torah Umesorah, 1970), pp. 27–28.

20. Shirley Newman, *A Child's Introduction to Torah* (New York: Behrman House, Inc., for the Melton Research Center of the Jewish Theological Seminary of America, 1972), p. 9.

21. Joseph B. Soloveitchik, "Confrontation," *Tradition* 6(2):19 (Spring-Summer 1964).

22. J.B. Soloveitchik, in *Halakhic Man*, insists that "halakhic man" differs in his world view from the universal *homo religiosus* (p. 17), and it is questionable whether one can be anything like the human type, called "halakhic man," outside the framework of traditional Judaism. Moreover, a careful reading of Soloveitchik's "Confrontation" and "The Lonely Man of Faith" suggests that the pious Jew is a willing partner of modern secular man in his scientific and technological enterprises but takes issue with the allegedly man-made religions, which, being an aspect of human culture, falsely make claims to redeem human beings. Conversely, Buber, in his essay "Herut: On Youth and Religion," can speak of religion as an orientation, an "openness."

23. Jacob Katz, *Tradition and Crisis* (Glencoe, Ill.: Free Press, 1961), chap. 23.

24. Cf. Peter L. Berger, *A Rumour of Angels* (Garden City, N.Y.: Doubleday, 1970), chap. 1.

25. Cf. Thomas F. O'Dea, *The Sociology of Religion* (Englewood Cliffs, N.J.: Prentice-Hall, Inc., 1966), pp. 13–18.

26. Cf., for example, Horace M. Kallen, *The Education of Free Men* (New York: Farrar, Straus and Co., 1949), chap. 13, especially pp. 228–229.

27. Ward Maddon, *Religious Values in Education* (New York: Harper & Brothers, 1951), pp. 14–15.

28. Becker, *Beyond Alienation,* chap. 9.

29. Buber, "Teaching and Deed," *Israel and the World,* p. 142.

30. See, for example, Will Herberg, *Protestant, Catholic, Jew* (Garden City, N.Y.: Doubleday, 1955) in which the three faiths are studied as the "three religions of democracy" through which American religious identity is established. Yet, Marty has suggested that the contemporary pattern may have shifted and that "old-time religion," even when idiosyncratic, may have been prematurely dismissed by academic and liberal elites. See Martin E. Marty, "Religion in America Since Mid-Century," *Daedalus* 3(1):149–163 (Winter 1982).

31. Berger, *The Heretical Imperative,* p. 85.

32. Baruch Kurzweil, "Al Ha-Toelet V'Al Ha-Nezek Shel Mada-ai Ha-Yahadut" ("On the Benefits and the Damage of Jewish Science"), in Kurzweil, *Be-ma-avak al Erkai Ha-Yahadut (In the Struggle Concerning the Values of Judaism)* (Jerusalem and Tel Aviv: Schocken, 5730[1969]), pp. 184–193. The extreme polemical nature of Kurzweil's approach, tinged with profound ambivalence, appears itself to be one of the characteristics of modern "return" to explicitly religious concerns. See Fackenheim, "Apologia for a Confirmation Text," pp. 148–152.

33. See Kurzweil's critique of Buber on this issue in Kurzweil, *L'Nochach Ha-Mevuchah Ha-Ruchanit Shel Dorainu (Facing the Spiritual Perplexity of Our Generation* (Ramat Gan: Bar Ilan University, 1976).

34. See my discussion on this point in "The Tasks of Jewish Religious Educational Philosophy," *Religious Education* 73(5):513–528 (September-October 1978) and in Chapter 10, herein.

35. Isaac Breuer, "Religion and Nation," in *Concepts of Judaism,* ed. Jacob S. Levinger (Jerusalem: Israel Universities Press, 1974), p. 33.

36. Buber, "Herut: On Youth and Religion," p. 152.

37. Isaiah Leibowitz, "Chinuch L'Mitzvot," ("Education for [Observance of] the Commandments), in *Yahadut, Am Yehudi U'Medinat Yisrael,* pp. 57–67.

38. Marvin Fox, "The Case of the Day School," in *Judaism and the Jewish School,* ed. Judah Pilch and Meir Ben-Horin (New York: Bloch Publishing Co., for the American Association for Jewish Education, 1966), pp. 212–213.

39. Harold S. Kushner, *When Children Ask About God* (New York: Schocken Books, 1976), p. 16.

40. Jack Cohen, *Jewish Education in Democratic Society* (New York: The Reconstructionist Press, 1964).


*Chapter 7*

1. BT Megillah 14a.

2. According to Rabbi Menachem Ha-Meiri, *Bet Ha-Bichirah* on Megillah 14a, p. 42. I am grateful to Ms. Beverly Grivetz-Greenstein for this reference.

3. Leibowitz, "Chinuch L'Mitzvot," *Yahadut, Am Yehudi U'Medinat Yisrael,* p. 57.

4. Leibowitz, "Mitzvot Ma-asiyot: Mashmauta Shel Ha-Halakhah" (The Practical Commandments: The Significance of the Halakhah"), *Ibid.,* pp. 13–36.

5. Leibowitz, "Chinuch L'Mitzvot," pp. 58–59.

6. *Ibid.,* p. 59.

7. On deontological theory, see William K. Frankena, *Ethics* (Englewood Cliffs, N.J.: Prentice-Hall, Inc., 1963), chap. 2. Leibowitz appears to hold to a "rule-deontological" position; namely, that the standard of right and wrong consists of rules that are independent of whether or not they promote some "good" external to them. Rather

they are to be obeyed because they are revealed, or inherent in human spirituality, or for some similar reason. On Leibowitz as applying a Kantian conception of deontological ethics to Judaism, see Naomi Kasher, "T'fisat Ha-Dat Shel Leibovitz L'umat T'fisat Ha-Mussar Shel Kant" ("The Religious Conception of Leibowitz as Against Kant's Conception of Morality") in *Sefer Yeshayahu Leibovitz,* ed. Assa Kasher and Ya'akov Levinger (Tel Aviv: Student Union of Tel Aviv University, 5737[1977], pp. 21–34.

8. Leibowitz, "Chinuch L'Mitzvot," pp. 59–61; also, "Emunah, Daat U'mada" ("Faith, Religion and Science"), *Yahadut, Am Yehudi U'Medinat Yisrael,* p. 359.

9. Isaac Breuer, "Religion and Nation," p. 35. All citations from Breuer in this chapter are from this essay, pp. 33–36.

10. Soloveitchik, "The Lonely Man of Faith," in *Halakhic Man, op. cit.*

11. *Ibid.*, pp. 51–52.

12. Soloveitchik, "His Creative Capacity," *Halakhic Man, op. cit.*

13. Soloveitchik, "The Lonely Man of Faith," pp. 63–65.

14. See Chapter 2, herein, and n. 7 of that chapter.

15. Significantly, Soloveitchik connects the concept of "holiness of place" with the idea of a person "finding his place" within the normative-covenant community. This belongingness and sense of "holy place," *kedushat makom,* integrates knowledge and commitment—and it is in this "place," of Torah, and through it, that the Jew finds God. "Holiness of place," of belonging, precedes and underlies the development of "holiness of time," *kedushat hazman:* the conquest by the individual of casualty and mortality—i.e., the achievement of a free and unique (prophetic) status. This progression is described in detail in *Halakhic Man;* the concept of "place" as belonging and commitment is found in Joseph B. Soloveitchik, "Sacred and Profane: *Kodesh* and *Chol* in World Perspective," *Gesher* (publication of Student Association of Yeshiva University) 2(1):13.

16. This, too, is deduced from the revelation to Israel, which posits the "seven Noachide commandments" through which non-Jews achieve the status of "the righteous of the nations of the world." These people, like Jews observing the entire Torah, have "a share in the world to come."

17. This is so because religion is only an end in itself and is not designed to serve purposes external to itself, valuative or otherwise, that can be perceived and implemented without benefit of revelation. Thus, Leibowitz insists that there is no necessary connection between religion "for its own sake" and humanistic values. Breuer declares that Judaism is first and foremost God's law and not religious sentiment, and Soloveitchik agrees that "Adam the first," the man of culture described in "The Lonely Man of Faith," pp. 18–23, can achieve everything *except a redeemed existence,* which may be anticipated only through allegiance to the covenant community.

18. Theology is thus, at least for explicit thinkers whose orientation is Orthodox, the "literature" rather than the "language" of Judaism. (See herein, Chapter 2, n. 13). Religious explicit thinkers who are non-Orthodox and who do not consider the traditional halakhah to be synonymous with the "language" of Judaism may consider the *principle* of halakhah or theological doctrines to be the revealed "essence" of Judaism. In the latter case, they may appear doctrinally "dogmatic" to the extent that they insist on the absolute and singular obligation imposed by Judaism to maintain and further beliefs and attitudes that embody the truth of Judaism. Cf., for example, Fackenheim, "An Apologia for a Confirmation Text," *op. cit.*

19. For this translation threatens the autonomy of the revealed truth, invites the application of external criteria, and seems to open the door to distortions and corrup-

tions. The consistently explicit community tends to shrug at the incomprehension of the "outside world": The explicit *thinker* is impelled to interpret and to provide a rationale even for that shrug.

20. Seymour Fox, "Towards a General Theory of Jewish Education," in *The Future of the Jewish Community in America,* ed. David Sidorsky (Philadelphia: Jewish Publication Society of America, 1973), pp. 260–270. Fox points out what happens to conceptions for education that are both unclear to begin with and haphazardly negotiated for practical use. For further discussion of this, see Seymour Fox, "Theory into Practice," in *Philosophy for Education,* ed. Seymour Fox (Jerusalem: The Van Leer Jerusalem Foundation, 1983), pp. 91–97. Also see the discussion in Chapter 10, herein.

21. Walter Orenstein and Hertz Frankel, *Torah as Our Guide,* (New York: Hebrew Publishing Co., 1960).

22. On this point, see R.S. Peters, "Reason and Habit: The Paradox of Moral Education."

## Chapter 8

1. Martin M. Buber, "The Holy Way: A Word to the Jews and to the Nations," *On Judaism,* pp. 136–137.

2. *Ibid.,* pp. 137–138.

3. Buber, "Jewish Religiosity," *On Judaism,* p. 80.

4. Buber, "Herut: On Youth and Religion," pp. 162–163.

5. *Ibid.,* p. 151.

6. Martin Buber, "Education," in Buber, *Between Man and Man,* trans. Ronald Gregor (New York: The Macmillan Co., 1965), p. 101.

7. *Ibid.,* p. 89.

8. Samuel Hugo Bergman, "Can Transgression Have an Agent?" in Bergman, *The Quality of Faith: Essays on Judaism and Morality,* trans. Yehudah Hanegbi. (Jerusalem: The Youth and Hechalutz Department of the World Zionist Organization, 1970), p. 19. pp. 19–20. The use of this verse for innovation suggests that it be translated as: "This is a time to serve the Lord [even] by going against Thy Torah."

9. Bergman, "The Sacrifice of Isaac and Contemporary Man," *The Quality of Faith,* p. 29.

10. *Ibid.,* pp. 29–30.

11. Bergman, "Expansion and Contraction in Jewish Ethics," *The Quality of Faith,* p. 39.

12. Bergman, "Two Letters to a Young Woman in a Kibbutz," *The Quality of Faith,* pp. 44–45.

13. Kook, "The Road to Renewal," p. 296.

14. *Ibid.,* p. 297.

15. *Ibid.,* pp. 301–302.

16. Abraham Joshua Heschel, "Depth Theology," in Heschel, *The Insecurity of Freedom* (New York: Schocken Books, 1977), pp. 115–116.

17. *Ibid.,* pp. 118–119.

18. Heschel, "Jewish Education," *The Insecurity of Freedom,* p. 233.

19. *Ibid.,* p. 237.

20. Leonard Gardner, *Genesis: The Teacher's Guide,* ed. Louis Newman (New York: United Synagogue Book Service, 1966); Ruth Zielenziger, *Genesis: A New Teacher's Guide,* ed. Barry W. Holtz (New York: The Melton Center, The Jewish The-

ological Seminary of America, 1979). We shall also refer to the Student's Guide prepared for this volume.

21. *Genesis: The Teacher's Guide,* pp. iii–iv.

22. *Genesis: A New Teacher's Guide,* p. 1.

23. *Ibid.,* p. 8.

24. *Ibid.,* pp. 10–13.

25. *Ibid.,* pp. 13–14.

26. *Ibid.,* p. 44.

27. Leibowitz, "Ha-Moreshet Ha-Yehudit-Notzrit Ha-Mishutefet" ("The Common Jewish-Christian Heritage"), *Yahadut, Am Yehudi U'Medinat Yisrael,* p. 330. The fact that the central symbol of Christianity is the cross signifies to Leibowitz that Christianity is an *anthropocentric* faith; he claims that the Binding of Isaac is the central religious symbol of Judaism, which points to Judaism's *theocentric* character.

28. *Genesis: A New Teacher's Guide,* p. 248.

29. *Ibid.,* p. 241.

30. *Ibid.,* p. 242.

31. *Genesis: The Teacher's Guide,* pp. 100–106, and in subsequent lesson units. These dilemmas are explained and given theoretical bases in Burton Cohen and Joseph Schwab, "Practical Logic: Problems of Ethical Decision," reprinted from *The American Behavioral Scientist,* vol. VII, no. 8 in *Ibid.,* pp. 492–497.

32. Louis Newman, ed. *Genesis: The Student's Guide,* Part I. (New York: United Synagogue Book Service, 1967), pp. 85–86.

33. *Ibid.,* p. 88.

34. *Ibid.,* pp. 89–92.

35. *Genesis: A New Teacher's Guide,* p. 396.

36. See the discussion in Chapter 1 of the normative-ideational orientation in contra-distinction to the deliberative-inductive one.

37. Such as Leibowitz's position that religious education is "education for the observance of the commandments" and it would be presumptuous to expect or demand more from education, "though it is clear and obvious that . . . the core and essence of religion are expressed in 'Thou shalt love [the Lord thy God]' . . . this depends on the internal-individual determination of the person after he received his educational training [in the observance of the commandments]," "Chinuch L'Mitzvot," p. 59.

38. Berger, *The Heretical Imperative,* chap. 5.

39. Avraham Y. Karelitz ("Hazon Ish"), "Emunah U'Bitachon" ("Faith and Trust") in *Hagut B'Machshevet Yisrael Ha-Mikorit (Essays in Traditional Philosophy of Judaism),* ed. Avraham Bick (Jerusalem: Mossad Harav Kook, 1983), pp. 227–229.

40. Avraham Isaac Kook, *Orot Ha-Kodesh (The Lights of Holiness),* vol. 3 (Jerusalem: Mossad Harav Kook 5724 [1973]), Introduction, Section 11, p. 27.

## Chapter 9

1. On the "temperaments" and styles of conservative- and liberal-minded individuals, see Karl Mannheim, *Essays in Sociology and Social Psychology,* ed. Paul Keeskemeti (London: Routledge and Kegan Paul, Ltd. 1953), chap. 3. On the problematics of such sociological categories for religious educational theory, see our discussion in Chapter 12, herein.

2. Heschel, *God in Search of Man,* p. 337. See entire Chap. 37 for a detailed exposition.

3. Hayyim Nahman Bialik, "Halakhah and Aggadah," in *Modern Jewish Thought: A Source Reader,* ed. Nahum A. Glatzer (New York: Schocken Books, 1977), p. 61.

4. Cf. Solomon Simon, "Stringent Aggadah—Lenient Halachah," *Judaism* 12(3):296–306 (Summer 1963), which cites interesting sources to establish this thesis.

5. Cf., for example, Leo Baeck, *The Essence of Judaism* (New York: Schocken Books, 1948).

6. See Chapter 8, herein.

7. David Novak, *Law and Theology in Judaism* (New York: Ktav, 1974), p. 3.

8. *Ibid.,* p. 1.

9. *Ibid.,* pp. 1–2.

10. *Ibid.,* pp. 4 and 12.

11. Walter S. Wurzburger, "Meta-Halakhic Propositions," *The Leo Jung Jubilee Volume* (New York: The Jewish Center, 1962), pp. 213 and 218.

12. Rosenzweig, "The Commandments: Divine or Human?" *On Jewish Learning,* p. 117.

13. Frederick Ferre, "Mapping the Logic of Models," in *New Essays on Religious Language,* ed. Dallas M. High (Oxford, Clarendon Press, 1969).

14. *Ibid.,* p. 90.

15. *Ibid.,* p. 91.

16. Berkovits, "What is Jewish Philosophy?" p. 120.

17. *Ibid.*

18. Saadya Gaon, *Emunot V'Daot (Book of Doctrines and Beliefs),* abridged and translated by Alexander Altmann in *Three Jewish Philosophers* (New York, Atheneum, 1979), pp. 44–45. Altmann's translation: " . . . in order that we may find out for ourselves what we know in the way of imparted knowledge from the prophets of God."

19. For an explanation of this rabbinic decision, see Berkovits, *Not in Heaven,* pp. 14, 75, and 96.

20. Cf. Exodus Rabbah 28:6. This Midrashic position can, of course, be interpreted both explicitly and implicitly—explicitly in the sense that everything is imposed and was always "given," and implicitly in the sense that new things are given revelatory legitimation and are to be transmitted in their proper time and in the relevant generation.

21. See Berkovits's discussion, *Not in Heaven,* pp. 77–78, on whether sages have the right to "uproot" a law from the Torah and on the need to abide by its principles. Also see Boaz Cohen, *Law and Tradition in Judaism* (New York: The Jewish Theological Seminary of America, 1959), chap. 1.

22. Fritz A. Rothschild, "Truth and Metaphor in the Bible," *Conservative Judaism,* 25(3):15–22 (Spring 1971) on the issue of proper versus misleading or unacceptable metaphors.

23. For an educational discussion on how to "do" that into which one has been "initiated" via the particular heritage, or "field," and its methods, see Joseph J. Schwab, "Eros and Education: A Discussion of an Aspect of Education," *Journal of General Education* 7:51–71 (October 1954).

24. See Gershom Scholem, "Revelation and Tradition as Religious Categories in Judaism," *The Messianic Idea in Judaism,* pp. 282–303. Baeck has suggested that the idea of perfection (of God's teaching, of truth, and so forth) signifies "unchanging" in Greco-Western thought, whereas the Jewish tradition views perfection as dynamic. "Nothing is fixed." (Baeck, "Two World Views Compared," *The Pharisees and Other Essays,* pp. 136–145). Thus, the "wholeness" of the Torah (Psalm 19) can be understood to mean: always adequate, always authoritative, always supplying norms for the particular situation.

25. See Chapter 6, herein.

26. I.e., in Kuhn's terminology, they may have been saying that the death-by-torture that their master was suffering was a "counter-instance" to the model of Judaism, which was demonstrated to be false or useless by this situation. See Chapter 4, n. 31, herein.

27. "Rabbi Akiva says . . . 'With all thy soul'—even if he takes thy soul from thee . . . ' " BT Berakhot 61b. On Rabbi Akiva's mode of interpretation, see Louis Finkelstein, *Akiba: Scholar, Saint and Martyr* (New York: Atheneum, 1964), pp. 308–312.

28. Buber, "The Man of Today and the Jewish Bible," p. 98.

29. Fackenheim, *God's Presence in History,* pp. 75–78.

30. S.Y. Agnon, "Before the Kaddish: At the Funeral of Those Who Were Killed in the Land of Israel," in Goldin, *The Jewish Expression,* pp. 484–485.

31. *Siach Lohamim (The Seventh Day),* cited as in my translation in Rosenak, "Moments of the Heart," p. 220.

32. Joseph B. Soloveitchik, *Chamesh Drashot (Five Homiletic Addresses)* (Jerusalem: Machon Tal Orot, 5734), pp. 17 and 25.

33. Schindler, "The Holocaust and Kiddush Ha-Shem in Hassidic Thought," p. 90. Schindler points out, however, that even in the traditional rabbinic Hasidic community, pleas for resistance to the Nazis could be heard. Thus, R. Menachem Zemba, in urging resistance in the Warsaw Ghetto, states: "Thus by the authority of the Torah of Israel, I insist that there is absolutely no purpose nor any value of *kiddush ha-Shem* in the death of a Jew. *Kiddush ha-Shem* in our present situation is embodied in the will of a Jew to live. . . . " (p. 94)

34. Sanhedrin, Chapter 4, Mishnah 5.

35. BT Makkot 7a.

36. Alexander Carlebach, "Autonomy, Heteronomy and Theonomy," *Tradition* 6(1):37 (Fall 1963).

37. Maimonides, *Hilchot Melachim* 8:11.

38. For a further discussion of this, see Chapter 12, herein.

39. Compare the Torah reading describing the service of the High Priest on Yom Kippur (Leviticus 16) with the Haftarah's rebuke to those who delude themselves into thinking that mechanical and rote atonement can be a substitute for compassion and moral concern (Isaiah 58). Likewise, the afternoon Torah reading (Leviticus 18), warning against the punishment for transgressors against the stern sexual code, can be readily contrasted with the compassionate prophetic reading for that sevice, the Book of Jonah.

40. Some prominent examples of implicit "readings" of explicit texts: Rabbi Meir's interpretation of the law of *sotah* (in which a woman suspected of illicit sexual relations is tied by ordeal) as intending to make peace between husband and wife (Leviticus Rabbah 9) and the traditional belief that the biblical affliction of leprosy is occasioned by tale-bearing and slander (cf. Deut. 24:8–9). Examples of explicit readings of implicit texts: That Jacob was "a dweller of tents" is understood by the Sages as signifying that he studied at the "Yeshiva of Shem and Ever" (Rashi; Gen. 25:27); Naomi, seeing that her daughter-in-law insisted on joining her (saying "where thou dwellest I shall dwell") is said to have begun to teach her the laws of houses, such as the halakhah of *mezuzzah* (Ruth Rabbah 2:22).

41. Maimonides, *Guide of the Perplexed* 3:27.

42. See Nahmanides' commentary on Lev. 19:2.

43. Cf. the tale of Kamza and Bar Kamza, BT Gittin 55b–56a, especially the comment of R. Jochanan (56a).

44. Exod. 13:14; Num. 19. The fact that it was extraordinarily difficult to impose capital punishment in Jewish law and the fact that the Sages had difficulty in explaining

the law of the red heifer perhaps testify to the implicit features of Judaism but do not remove the explicit data of the commandments from Judaism.

45. For such an implicit conception, anchored to a secular model of inquiry, see Joseph J. Schwab, "The Religiously Oriented School in the United States: A Memorandum on Policy," *Conservative Judaism* 18(3):1–14 (Spring 1964). Schwab legitimates the teaching of tradition in contemporary society by arguing that tradition is "past inquiry."

46. Morris, *Existentialism and Education,* p. 114.

47. BT Berakhot 64a.


## Chapter 10

1. For example, Lukinsky argues that recent curricular materials suggested for the afternoon school convey the "message" to students that if their parents really cared about their Jewish education, they would have sent them to a day school. Since, however, the children were sent to an (inferior) afternoon school, the most that can be done for them is to assure that they will not be totally ignorant with regard to Jewish subjects. Joseph Lukinsky, "Let's Not Give Up Yet," *Conservative Judaism* 31(2):90 (Winter 1977).

2. See, for example, Jay B. Stern, "Losing One's Faculties in Jewish Education," *Conservative Judaism* 18(3):1–23 (Spring 1964).

3. Michael Rosenak, "The Tasks of Jewish Religious Educational Philosophy," p. 518.

4. Moore, *Educational Theory,* pp. 5–7.

5. *Ibid.,* p. 16.

6. Charles D. Hardie, *Truth and Fallacy in Educational Theory* (New York: Teachers College, Columbia University, 1962), p. 73.

7. See Chapters 11 and 12, herein.

8. Although, as already noted, his *community* may consider this to be the task of rabbis, interpreters of halakhah.

9. On the place of means in normative education, see Frankena, *Three Historical Philosophies,* p. 8. On the non-neutrality of means in Jewish education, see Seymour Fox, "Prolegomenon L'Philosophia shel Chinuch Yehudi" ("Prolegomenon to a Philosophy of Jewish Education"), *Kivunim Rabbim: Kavvanah Achat (Many Directions: One Intention)* (Jerusalem: School of Education, Hebrew University, 5729[1968]), p. 148.

10. Aron, "Deweyian Deliberation," p. 142.

11. The reference is to the Mishnaic adage of Ben Bag-Bag (Avot 5:25): "Turn it (the Torah) and turn it (again) for everything is in it."

12. See Chapter 8, n. 37.


## Chapter 11

1. Plato expressed and developed his thesis that "there is no teaching but only recollection" particularly in *Meno.* For a talmudic explication of the theory of recollection, see BT Niddah 30b.

2. Rashi on Exod. 31:3.

3. Scheffler, "Philosophical Models of Teachings," *op. cit.*

4. Richard Peters, "Moral Education—Tradition or Reason? in *Let's Teach Them Right,* ed. Christopher Macy (London: Pemberton Publishing Co., Ltd., 1969), p. 104.

5. Peters, "Reason and Habit," pp. 261–262.

6. *Ibid.*, p. 252.

7. Cf. John Dewey, "Ethical Principles Underlying Education," in *John Dewey on Education: Selected Writings,* ed. Reginald D. Archambaullt (New York: The Modern Library, 1964), pp. 108–138. An important discussion on this, in Hebrew, is Carl Frankenstein, "Ha-Chvanah Ve'kfiyah Be-Chinuch" ("Some Remarks on the Meaning of Directive Education"), *Megamot* 1(3):239–245 (April 1950).

8. Émile Durkheim, *Education and Sociology,* trans. Sherwood D. Fox (New York and London: The Free Press and Collier-Macmillan Ltd., 1956), p. 67.

9. *Ibid.*, p. 71.

10. *Ibid.*, pp. 71–72.

11. Émile Durkheim, *Moral Education: A Study in the Theory and Application of the Sociology of Education* (New York and London: The Free Press and Collier-Macmillan Ltd., 1961), p. 52.

12. Jean Piaget, *The Moral Judgment of the Child* (Glencoe, Ill.: The Free Press, 1932), p. 346.

13. We shall refer below specifically to Peter L. Berger, *The Sacred Canopy: Elements of a Sociological Theory of Religion* (Garden City, N.Y.: Doubleday & Co., Inc., 1967). I have previously discussed the uses of Berger's sociology of knowledge in my *Tifkudim Shel Theologia Yehudit Bat Zmanainu B'chibur Teoria Chinuchit Datit Batfutzot (Tasks of Contemporary Jewish Theology in the Construction of Religious Educational Theory in the Diaspora),* Ph.D. diss., Hebrew University, 1975, Chap. 11.

14. Berger relates specifically to the tension between the sociological discipline and theological discourse, occasioned by the fact that the former operates on the basis of "methodological atheism," which can be misinterpreted. Nevertheless, Berger posits that sociology as a discipline has ramifications that the theologian may not ignore and that *will* affect his or her theological options. See Berger, *The Sacred Canopy,* Appendix II: "Sociological and Theological Perspectives," pp. 179–185.

15. Berger, *The Sacred Canopy,* p. 4.

16. *Ibid.*, p. 5.

17. *Ibid.*, p. 6.

18. *Ibid.*, p. 7.

19. Miller distinguishes between the core and the sub-identities as general regions in the total identity. The core is the primary self, formed earliest and most difficult to change (including such components as sexual identity or, for example, one's identity as "the only child in the family"). Between the "core" and the "sub-identities" is the periphery (Goffman's "presented self"), a compromise between the ideal identity and pressures of the social situation: what Miller terms *roles,* namely, "the minimum of attitudes and behavior required for participation in the overt expression of the social position." A sub-identity represents the cluster of all the attributes manifested by a person, *not* "minimal requirements" alone. A sub-identity of a person does not connote merely the fact that he is and acts like a father but indicates what *kind* of parent he is. Daniel R. Miller, "The Study of Social Relationships: Situation, Identity and Social Interaction," in *Psychology: A Study of a Science,* vol. 5, ed. Sigmund Koch (New York: McGraw-Hill Book Co., 1963), pp. 672–673. The sub-identity concept is useful not only in distinguishing between correct social action and internalization but also in distinguishing between what a person *accepts as his or her role* as a group member and what he or she considers to be his or her unique self. It suggests the implicit dimension of religion as expressing an individual character without relinquishing the social role. This will figure prominently in our subsequent discussion of the religiously educated personality.

20. Berger, *The Sacred Canopy,* p. 16.

21. *Ibid.,* p. 19.

22. *Ibid.,* pp. 21–28.

23. *Ibid.,* p. 33 and pp. 42–44.

24. Jacob Jay Lindenthal, "Some Thoughts Regarding the Influence of Traditional Judaism on the Work of Emile Durkheim," *Tradition* 11(26):41–50 (Summer 1970).

25. *Ibid.,* p. 45.

26. Soloveitchik, "The Lonely Man of Faith," pp. 58–59.

27. *Ibid.,* p. 59.

28. Allport, *The Individual and His Religion,* p. 24.

29. See Chapter 5 herein.

30. Cohen and Schwab, in "Practical Logic: Problems of Ethical Decision," p. 497, speak of "translating 'felt' goods into formulated precepts." "Felt goods" are perceived in "the immediate experience of one's own or another's behavior." Only after it is "felt" can it be formulated. (For example, "I want to be as charitable as my father was.") We may say that the indirect teaching of beliefs is achieved by model personalities who evoke a desire to make their ways habitual; i.e., to appropriate them and to gain competence in doing and understanding them.

31. David Elkind, *Children and Adolescents: Interpretative Essays on Jean Piaget* (New York: Oxford University Press, 1970), pp. 56–57.

32. Alexander, in a documented paper, has argued that denying children a world of religious and symbolic expectability and participation may well lead to the inability of these individuals, as adults, to find meaning and order in their world, with fateful consequences, including such phenomena as "insane" religious sects. Chanan Alexander, "Schools Without Faith," *Religious Education* 76(3):307–321 (May-June 1981).

33. Robert A. Nisbet, *Tradition and Revolt: Historical and Sociological Essays* (New York: Vintage Books–Random House, 1970), chap. 4.

34. Piaget, *The Moral Judgement of the Child,* p. 346.

35. Durkheim, *Moral Education,* p. 120.

36. Robert A. Nisbet, *Emile Durkheim* (Englewood Cliffs, N.J.: Prentice-Hall, Inc., 1965), p. 42.

37. Durkheim, *Moral Education,* p. 120.

38. " . . . alienation is the process whereby the dialectical relationship between the individual and his world is lost to consciousness. The individual 'forgets' that this world was and continues to be co-produced by him." Berger, *The Sacred Canopy,* p. 85.

39. *Ibid.,* pp. 87–98. Berger's description of religion as a "powerful agency of alienation" (p. 87) is clearly directed at what we are calling explicit religion. But see also *Ibid.,* pp. 98–101, where religious de-alienating possibilities are discussed.

40. Indeed, he will have a "religious urge" to demonstrate that religion is *not* alienating and that it requires commitment and responsibility. Thus, the demand for individual self-expression is seen to sanctify the collective tradition itself.

41. I.e., since the scientist is competent to describe processes and to develop theories, he or she is competent to portray social realities, to diagnose problematic situations, and to anticipate consequences of available responses (solutions). But the decision of how religious purposes are to be translated into reality via guidelines of normative prescriptions is a task for the religious thinker and teacher.

42. The Midrash (Genesis Rabbah 38:13) relates that Abraham smashed his father's idols. When Terach came upon the scene, Abraham explained that a woman had come to sacrifice meal to the idols and that each of them had demanded to be the first to eat; subsequently, the senior idol broke all the rest. Terach responded angrily: "Why are you making a fool of me? Are they capable of doing this (i.e., hitting and breaking one another)?" Abraham replied: "Are your ears hearing what your mouth is saying?"

43. The relationship of many secular Israeli Jews to religion appears to be this kind of alienation. "Judaism" is the province of "the religious," who neither solicit nor need the intervention or intense interest of the "non-religious." Both groups gain certain benefits from this alienation: "the religious" by maintaining complete control of "Judaism," the "non-religious" by being freed from responsibility for the maintenance of something that is presented (and accepted) as being an "objective datum" that requires (and brooks) no cultural and spiritual initiative. Since this "religion" thus manifests itself to both groups, the religious and the non-religious alike, as only *explicit,* the implicit elements of Jewish religiosity are often viewed as unrelated to Judaism. Traditional Jewish "cumulative tradition" is therefore seen as irrelevant to "spirituality." In educational terms, this situation invites what Buber has called a "fictitious" approach to tradition. "Those who follow it exalt the works and values of national tradition . . . and point to them with the mein of collectors and owners, as though they were coronation robes in a museum, not, of course, suitable apparel for a living sovereign. While they boast of their tradition, they do not believe in it. . . . " Buber, "On National Education," in *Israel and the World,* p. 161.

44. Karl Mannheim, *Ideology and Utopia: An Introduction to the Sociology of Knowledge,* trans. Louis Wirth and Edward Shils (New York: Harcourt Brace, 1936).

45. *Ibid.,* p. 297.

46. *Ibid.,* pp. 281–282.

47. Keith Dixon, *The Sociology of Belief* (London: Routledge and Kegan Paul, 1980), p. 17.

48. Ahad Ha-Am, to whose thesis concerning "the national will to survive" this attitude is often traced, was actually rather ambivalent about the negative "fruit" borne on the "tree" of Jewish culture in the Diaspora. The fruit may indeed be blemished by conditions of exile, but the essential nature of the tree remains the same. See Ahad Ha-Am, "The Spiritual Revival," *Selected Essays of Ahad Ha-Am,* pp. 263–264. He did, however, speak of the adaptation of the "organism" to its environment which, in Exile, "when we were slaves," led to "the teachings of the Talmud and the Shulchan Arukh, with its equally extreme insistence on practice" (p. 264).

49. Mannheim, *Ideology and Utopia,* p. 283.

50. *Ibid.*

51. *Ibid.,* pp. 283–284.

52. *Ibid.,* p. 284.

53. Dixon, *The Sociology of Belief,* p. 213.

54. See our previous discussion in Chapter 7.

55. Amos 9:7. In terms of our thesis, we find it noteworthy that on the Sabbath when the Haftarah introduced by this verse is read, the corresponding Torah portion begins with a declaration of the unique holiness of the community of Israel. (Lev. 19).


## Chapter 12

1. In addition to the articles of Schwab and Hofstadter already noted in this context (see Chapter 4, n. 46, herein), see also Kieran Egan, *Education and Psychology: Plato, Piaget and Scientific Psychology* (New York: Teachers College, Columbia University, 1983). It is noteworthy that Kohlberg and Mayer, from a psychological standpoint, also remark upon the "psychological fallacy . . . (as) a form of the naturalist fallacy. As practiced by psychologists the naturalist fallacy is the direct derivation of statements about what human nature, human values and human desires ought to be from psychological statements about what they are." Lawrence Kohlberg and Rochelle Mayer,

"Development as the Aim of Education," *Harvard Educational Review* 42(4):466 (November 1972).

2. Scheffler, "Philosophical Models of Teachings," *Reason and Teaching,* pp. 68–71.

3. *Ibid.,* pp. 76–79. On the "insight model" (discussed in the following paragraph), see *Ibid.,* pp. 71–76.

4. Gordon W. Allport, *Becoming: Basic Considerations for a Psychology of Personality* (New Haven: Yale University Press, 1955), p. 12.

5. Frank Milhollan and Bill E. Forisha, *From Skinner to Rogers: Contrasting Approaches to Education* (Lincoln, Neb.: Professional Educators Publications, Inc., 1972), p. 88.

6. For an example of how a traditionalist Jewish rabbi-educator relates theological and philosophical issues to such a psychological school, see Reuven P. Bulka, *The Quest for Ultimate Meaning: Principles and Applications of Logotherapy* (New York: Philosophical Library, 1979).

7. Cf., for example, Erich Fromm, *Psychoanalysis and Religion,* chap. 3; Rollo May, *Man's Search For Himself,* (New York: Delta, 1953), pp. 193–222.

8. Ernest Gellner, *Thought and Change* (London: Weidenfeld & Nicolson, 1964), p. 84.

9. *Ibid.,* pp. 86–88.

10. Lamm, *Conflicting Theories of Instruction,* pp. 27.

11. *Ibid.,* pp. 168–172.

12. Herbert W. Richardson, "Three Myths of Transcendence," in *Transcendence,* ed. Herbert W. Richardson and Donald R. Cuttler. (Boston: Beacon Press, 1969), pp. 98–113.

13. On "separation-and-return," see *Ibid.,* pp. 107–108; on "conflict-and-vindication" myths, see pp. 108–111. For the "integrity-and-transformation" model, see pp. 111–112.

14. *Ibid.,* p. 112.

15. I.e., one "belongs" to an order of things; despite his or her individuality and uniqueness as created in God's image, the human being is *not* and never can become God.

16. "Who walks in righteousness—that is Abraham." BT Makkot 24a.

17. See Gen. 22; Gen. 14; Gen. 18:24–25. On Abraham's "bringing God down into the world," *Sifre* (cited in) H.N. Bialik and W.H. Ravniyzki, *Sefer Ha-Aggada* (Tel Aviv: Dvir, 1955), p. 26; Gen. 18:22; Gen. 24:40.

18. Cf. Fackenheim, *God's Presence in History,* pp. 20–21.

19. For instance, a crucial question asked by Bergman in "The Sacrifice of Isaac and Contemporary Man," pp. 24–31, is whether Abraham had the right to obey God unquestioningly when He demanded the sacrifice of his son, a question intimated by the Midrash itself. The fact that Abraham demanded that "the Judge of all the earth do justice" in the case of the wicked cities of Sodom and Gomorrah, where he *did* argue with God, adds a paradoxical dimension to the discussion.

20. Elkind, "Children's Questions," in *Children and Adolescents,* pp. 26–33.

21. Elkind, "Piaget and Education," *Ibid.,* p. 83.

22. Fowler, *Stages of Faith,* p. 54.

23. Elkind, "Jean Piaget," *Children and Adolescents,* p. 19.

24. Elkind, "How the Mind Grows," *Ibid.,* p. 42. See also David Elkind, "The Development of Religious Understanding in Children and Adolescents," in *Research on Religious Development,* ed. Merlon P. Stromner (New York: Hawthorn Books, Inc., 1971), pp. 677–678.

25. Elkind, "Children's Questions," p. 30.

26. Elkind, "How the Mind Grows," p. 35.

27. *Ibid.*, p. 39.

28. *Ibid.*, p. 42.

29. Elkind, "Piaget and Education," p. 93.

30. Doug Sholl, "The Contributions of Lawrence Kohlberg to Religious and Moral Education," *Religious Education,* 66(5):365 (September-October 1971). For Kohlberg's exposition of these stages, Lawrence Kohlberg, "The Child as Moral Philosopher," in *Moral Education,* ed. Barry I. Chazan and Jonas F. Soltis (New York: Teachers College, Columbia University, 1973), pp. 131–143.

31. Sholl, p. 365.

32. Kohlberg, "The Child as a Moral Philosopher," *Moral Education,* pp. 133–134.

33. *Ibid.*, p. 134.

34. Lawrence Kohlberg, "Education for Justice: A Modern Statement of the Platonic View," *Moral Education: Five Lectures* (Cambridge, Mass.: Harvard University Press, 1970), pp. 71–72.

35. Kohlberg, "Education, Moral Development and Faith," *Journal of Moral Education* 4:15 (1974).

36. Erik H. Erikson, *Childhood and Society* (Middlesex, England: Penguin Books, 1950), chap. 7; Erik H. Erikson, *Identity: Youth and Crisis* (New York: W.W. Norton and Co., 1968), chap. 3.

37. William Meissner, "Erikson's Truth: The Search for Ethical Identity," *Theological Studies* 31(2):311 (June 1970).

38. Erikson, *Identity,* p. 259.

39. Erik H. Erikson, *Young Man Luther* (New York: W.W. Norton and Co., 1958).

40. R.S. Peters, "Moral Development: A Plea for Pluralism," in T.M. Mischel, *Cognitive Development and Epistemology* (New York: Academic Press, 1971), pp. 263–264; Dykstra, *Vision and Character,* pp. 23–28; Egan, *Education and Psychology, op. cit.*

41. Michael Levin, "The Stages of Man?" (Review Essay), *Commentary* 73(1):85 (January 1982). One should be aware, however, that Kohlberg himself has expressed concern about the naturalist fallacy. See n. 1 to this chapter.

42. Hofstadter, "The Child and His World," p. 509.

43. Fowler, *Stages of Faith, op. cit.*

44. *Ibid.*, p. 182.

45. *Ibid.*, p. 198.

46. *Ibid.*, pp. 200–201.

47. Fowler declares that Stage Six consists of "normative images" that are "strongly influenced by H. Richard Niebuhr's description of radical monotheistic faith." *Ibid.*, p. 204. For his answer to critics who are not situated within his particular normative framework, see *Ibid.*, pp. 206–207.

48. See, for example, Maimonides' Commentary (or Introduction) to Helek: Sanhedrin in *A Maimonides Reader,* ed. Isadore Twersky (New York: Behrman House, Inc., 1972), pp. 401–423.

49. Kohlberg, "The Child as a Moral Philosopher," p. 142.

50. Thus, Talmud study was so esteemed because the deliberation there appears as the central feature of "acquiring Torah" rather than a knowledge of facts or decisions. The idea is succinctly expressed in the Talmud (BT Hagigah 3b) in the commentary to the verse "And God spoke all these words, saying . . . " (Exod. 20:1): "To teach you about the sages who sit in assembly and occupy themselves with the Torah: though these (i.e., some) declare (a particular thing) unclean and those (i.e., others) declare (it) pure; these declare it unfit and those declare it fit, these permit and those

forbid, nevertheless, all were given by one God, as it is said, 'And God spoke all these words . . . ' "

51. Moshe Chaim Sosevsky, "Kohlberg's Moral Dilemmas and Jewish Moral Education," *Jewish Education* 48(4):12 (Winter 1980).

52. Elkind, "Egocentrism in Children and Adolescents," *Children and Adolescents,* pp. 50–71.

53. Erik H. Erikson, "Identity, Psychosocial," in *International Encyclopedia of the Social Sciences,* Vol. 7, ed. David L. Sills (New York: Macmillan and Free Press, 1968), col. 61. For a further discussion of this, see Walter E. Conn, "Erikson's 'Identity': An Essay on the Psychological Foundations of Religious Ethics," *Zygon* 14(2):126 (June 1979).

54. Ronald Goldman, *Readiness for Religion: A Basis for Developmental Religious Education* (London: Routledge and Kegan Paul, 1965).

55. *Ibid.,* p. 71.

56. Cf. David Novak, *Law and Theology in Judaism,* chap. 15 ("Belief in God"), for a treatment of the controversy between Maimonides and Nahmanides as to whether belief in God is to be counted as a *mitzvah* (commandment). The question of whether one can be commanded to believe in the existence of the One Who commands is answered by Maimonides in the affirmative (as Novak explains it) insofar as the commandment is perceived as a demand upon the community to teach belief as an aspect of community obligation. Though the individual is duty-bound to strive for a *knowledge* of God, this is not what the community is either required or capable of giving the individual. The similarity to Leibowitz's conception of "Education for the Observance of the Commandments" is striking.

57. Breuer, "Religion and Nation," *op. cit.*

58. See Edwin Cox, "Honest to Goldman: An Assessment," *Religious Education* 53(6):427 (November-December 1968).

59. Harry Beilin, "The Cognitive Basis for Development of Moral Concepts," in *New Insights into Curriculum Development,* Part I, ed. Walter Ackerman and Norman Schanin (New York: Educators Assembly of the United Synagogue of America, 1965), p. 23.

60. Kieran Egan, "Towards a Theory of Educational Development," *Educational Philosophy and Theory* 11(2):17–36 (November 1979). See also Egan, *Educational Development* (New York: Oxford University Press, 1979).

61. Egan, *Educational Philosophy and Theory,* p. 32.

## *Chapter 13*

1. Orenstein and Frankel, *Torah as our Guide,* p. 180. See the discussion in Chapter 7, herein.

2. Ahad Ha-Am, "Sacred and Profane," *op. cit.*

3. Cf., for example, the discussion in Schweid, *Ha-Yahadut V'Ha-Tarbut Ha-Chilonit,* pp. 32–36.

4. The tradition of a "yeshiva," founded by Shem and Ever, where Jacob studied Torah (Genesis Rabbah 63:8) illustrates the relationship between the innovative and the "given" resources of continuity that embody the explicit "normative order of things."

5. BT Berakhot 71.

6. Num. 16:5.

7. B.T. Bava Metzia 59b.

8. See Deut. 21:11, which permits marrying the captive woman, and the commentary of Rashi on this verse; BT Sanhedrin 99a–100a, where the belief in the rev-

elation of every letter of the Torah is mandated, and the explication of the Sages of the Torah is endowed with authority.

9. See Berakhot, chap. 9, Mishnah 5, and the commentary of Rashi.

10. See Ephraim E. Urbach, *Hazal (The Sages: Their Concepts and Beliefs)* (Jerusalem: Magnes Press, 1969), chap. 12.

11. Buber, "Herut," p. 149.

12. Buber, "On National Education," in Buber, *Israel and the World* (New York: Schocken Paperback, 1963), pp. 149–150.

13. Emil L. Fackenheim, "An Outline of a Modern Jewish Theology," *Quest for Past and Future,* p. 101.

14. See Bruno Bettelheim, *The Uses of Enchantment: The Meaning and Importance of Fairy Tales* (New York: Vintage Books–Random House, 1977), particularly the analysis of "The Three Feathers," pp. 102–111. For a religious Jewish discussion of the confrontation with the non-self and the development of the self within the framework of that confrontation, from the perspective of a talmudic scholar, see David Weiss, "Towards a Theology of Rabbinic Exegesis," *Judaism* 10(1):13–20 (Winter 1961).

15. For example, the talmudic sage R. Simai related that Israel was rewarded for declaring that "we shall do" before "we shall hear" (BT Shabbat 88a).

16. *Ibid.*

17. Ernest A. Simon, "Chinuch," *Encyclopedia Chinuchit (Educational Encyclopedia),* Vol. 1 (Jerusalem: Ministry of Education and Culture and Mossad Bialik, 1961), p. 131.

18. On this, see Carl Frankenstein, "Al Amitut Ha-Arachim V'Ha-Hora-a" ("On the Truthfulness of Values and Instruction"), *Shdemot* (57):38–45 (5735).

19. One of the thirteen modes whereby Rabbi Ishmael explains that the Torah is to be interpreted *(Braita of Rabbi Ishmael,* included in the morning service of the traditional *siddur).*

20. "Is not My world like . . . a hammer that breaketh the rock in pieces? (Jer. 23:29). As the hammer splits the rock into many splinters so will a scriptural verse yield many meanings," BT Sanhedrin 34a.

21. On the dangers and possible corruptions related to the teaching of scientific disciplines with explicit "prophetic" insights and "guidelines," see George R. La Noue, "Religious Schools and 'Secular' Subjects," *Harvard Educational Review* 32(3):255–291 (Summer 1962). Yet, the Jewish educator must also be sensitive to the comment of Franz Rosenzweig in "Believing Science" that while "the object of science is not God but the world . . . (yet) God has created the world and thus the object of science." *Franz Rosenzweig: His Life and Thought,* ed. Nahum N. Glatzer (New York: Schocken Books, 1953), p. 210.

22. This is cited in the name of Israel ben Eliezer, the Besht (Ba'al Shem Tov), in Martin Buber, *Tales of the Hasidim: Early Masters* (New York: Schocken Paperback, 1961), p. 48.

23. BT Shabbat 88a.

24. I am grateful to Rabbi Yitzhak Greenberg of New York, from whom I learned a great deal concerning the theological significance of Purim.

25. Esther Rabbah 10:1.

26. See Rabbi Adin Steinsaltz's comment on this passage. Steinsaltz cites the opinion that lifting the mountain like a barrel hints at "the abundance of love that God brought upon Israel through the Exodus, the manna, etc, and that, therefore, they said: 'We shall do and listen.' " *Tractate Shabbat.* (Jerusalem: The Israel Institute for Talmudic Publications, vol. 3, 1983), p. 380.

27. My translation of *halakhah l' Moshe mi-Sinai* is purposely somewhat awkward, because this is a technical term connoting an ancient tradition having no source in the Torah. Whether it is to be considered as having Scriptural or rabbinic authority is, therefore, a subject of controversy among rabbinic jurists. In either case, it is quite reasonable, given its "origin in doubt" nature, that a "halakhah given to Moses at Sinai" would not be known to Moses. We may say, therefore, that he was reassured by Rabbi Akiva's exposition in this sense: that the entire tradition, in its most "imposed" *and* in its most innovative aspects, could be linked to his name and teaching.

## Conclusion

1. See Chapter 4, n. 22, herein.
2. For a discussion of this distinction, see Emil L. Fackenheim, "Man and his World in the Perspective of Judaism; Reflections in Expo 1967," *Judaism* 16(2):166–175 (Spring 1967).

# Acknowledgments

The author wishes to thank the following individuals and publishers for their kind permission to quote from the sources listed:

The estate of Martin Buber, for quotations from Martin Buber, *Eclipse of God* (New York: Harper Torchbooks, 1952).

Harcourt Brace Jovanovich, Inc., for quotations from Karl Mannheim, *Ideology and Utopia: An Introduction to the Sociology of Knowledge,* trans. Louis Wirth and Edward Shils (New York: Harcourt Brace, 1936).

Hebrew Publishing Company, for quotations from Walter Orenstein and Hertz Frankel, *Torah as Our Guide* (New York: Hebrew Publishing Company, 1960).

Macmillan Publishing Company, for reprinting the diagram from J. Milton Yinger, *The Scientific Study of Religion* (New York: Macmillan Publishing Company, 1970).

Drs. E. Rauch and B. Holtz, for quotations from Leonard Gardner, *Genesis: The Teacher's Guide,* ed. Louis Newman (New York: United Synagogue Book Service, 1966); Ruth Zielenziger, *Genesis: A New Teacher's Guide,* ed. Barry W. Holtz (New York: The Melton Center, The Jewish Theological Seminary of America, 1979); and Louis Newman, ed. *Genesis: The Student's Guide* (New York: United Synagogue Book Service, 1967).

Schocken Books (New York), for quotations from Martin Buber, *On Judaism* (New York: Schocken Books Inc., 1967).

Schocken Books (New York), for quotation from Franz Rosenzweig, "The Builders: Concerning the Law" from F. Rosenzweig, *On Jewish Learning,* ed. N.N. Glatzer (New York: Schocken Books, 1955).

Schocken Books (Tel Aviv), for quotations from Isaiah Leibowitz, *Yahadut, Am Yehudi U'Medinat Yisrael* (*Judaism, the Jewish People and the State of Israel*) (Jerusalem: Schocken, 1975).

The Youth and Hechalutz Department of the World Zionist Organization, for quotations from Samuel Bergman, *The Quality of Faith: Essays on Judaism and Morality,* trans. Yehudah Hanegbi (Jerusalem: The Youth and Hechalutz Department of the World Zionist Organization, 1970).

# Index

Note: Entries referring to entire chapters appear in **boldface** type.

Abraham, 234
Academic discussion, of religious education, 9–10
Aggadah, 103
  and halakhah, 103, 171–174
Agnon, S.Y., 180–181
Ahad Ha-am, 41, 55, 57, 65, 74, 257
Akiva (Rabbi), 109, 178–180, 269
Alienation, Berger's concept of, 219–220, 222
Allport, Gordon, 213
Alston, William P., 91–92
American Council for Judaism, 271
*Am Yisrael,* 100, 102. *See also Eretz Yisrael* and Israel.
Anti-theological arguments, against religion and religious education, 58–61
Ashkenazim, 72
Augustine, 208
Authority, versus autonomy, 80

Behavioral psychology, 229
Beilin, Harry, 246
Beliefs, articulation of, 68
Berger, Peter, 210–214, 219–220, 222
Bergman, Samuel Hugo, 153–154
Berkovits, Eliezer, 175
Bialik, Hayyim Nahman, 171

Bible, 56–57, 161–162, 245. *See also* Torah.
Binding of Isaac, 61
Biology, world view in, 52
Breuer, Isaac, 125, 136–137, 245, 249
Buber, Martin, 111–112, 116, 125, 151–153, 180, 245, 249, 259

Children, communication with, 235–238
  development of, 235–242
  religious education of, 21
*Chukim,* 143–145
Cohen, Jack, 125
Communication, with children, 235–238
Communities, religious, nature of, 97–98
Conservative Jews, 39–40, 270
Creation (story of), 162–163
Cultural arguments, against religion and religious education, 55–58
Cultural initiation, 210–215
  in normative-ideational educational theory, 32–34, 37–38
Culture, Jewish, religion and, 55–56, 72–76
  nature of, 211

Curriculum, effect of educational philosophy on, 253–256

Definitions, in religion, 85, 91–95
Deliberative-inductive educational theory, 10, 21–26, 36, 44–45, **48–63,** 64–68
Development, ethical, 240–241, 243–244
of personality, 238–242
Developmental model of education, 33, 231, 233
Dewey, John, 21–22, 241
Diaspora, 60, 66, 84
Dubnow, Simon, 56
Durkheim, Émile, 209–210, 213–214, 217–218, 238

Education, developmental model of, 33, 231, 233
disciplines of, world view in, 52–53
four elements of, 86–87
Lamm's models of, 33
imitation model of, 33
nature of, 79–83
philosophy of, effect of, on curriculum, 253–256
religious. *See* Religious education.
theology of. *See* Educational theology.
theory of. *See* Educational theory.
Educational arguments, against religion and religious education, 61–63
Educational theology, 106–107
explicit, **129–150**
and implicit, **108–126,** 132–133
implicit, **151–169**
in educational theory, 194–198
limits of, 193–194
Educational theory, deliberative-inductive, 10, 21–26, 36, 44–45, **48–63,** 64–68
normative-ideational. *See* Normative-ideational educational theory.
two models of, 16–25
Egan, Kieran, 248–249
Elkind, David, 235–237

Enlightenment, Philosophical, 68–70
*Eretz Yisrael,* 74–76, 101–103. *See also Am Yisrael* and Israel.
Erikson, Erik H., 240, 244
Ethical development, 240–241, 243–244
Explicit theology, 129–150
and implicit, **108–126,** 132–133
in religious education, 166, **207–227**
modernity and, 200–201

Fackenheim, Emil L., 68, 70, 259–260
Faith, 206
and religion, 29–30
Ferre, Frederick, 174
Fowler, James W., 242–243
Fox, Marvin, 125
Fox, Seymour, 22–23
Frankel, Hertz, 142
Freedom, 185–187
Freud, Sigmund, 69, 229, 238

Gellner, Ernest, 230
*Genesis: The Teacher's Guide,* and *Genesis: A New Teacher's Guide,* 159–164
Glock, C.Y., 97, 214
Goldman, Ronald, 245
Growth, in religious understanding, 245

Halakhah, 66, 109, 137. *See also* Normative-ideational religious education; Talmud.
and aggadah, 103, 171–174
Conservative Jews and, 39
Judaism and, 135
morality and, 154
religious crisis and, 76–78
secularism and, 60
Hallel, 129–131
Hegel, Georg Wilhelm Friedrich, 68
Herzog, Yaakov, 76
Heschel, Abraham Joshua, 109–110, 156–157, 171
Himmelfarb, Milton, 72
Hirst, Paul H., 18–19, 22

History, world view in, 52
Holocaust, 59, 109
  theological responses to, 77
Humanistic psychology, 16, 229–230

Ideals, in theological objectives, 41
  of behavior, 17–18
Individual, and society, 32
  "whole," in normative-ideational educational theory, 34–36, 38
Individuality, in normative-ideational educational theory, 28–32, 37–38
Indoctrination, religious education and, 79–80
Imitation model of education, 33
Implicit theology, **151–169**
  and explicit, **108–126**, 132–133
  in religious education, **228–249**
  modernity and, 200–201
Initiation, cultural, 210–215
  in normative-ideational educational theory, 32–34, 37–38
Isaac, Binding of, 161
Israel, 155–156. *See also Am Yisrael; Eretz Yisrael.*
  Jewish secularism and, 75–76
  religious education in, 60

Jewish Theological Seminary of America, 159
Jews, Ashkenazi, 72
  Conservative, 39–40, 270
  "good," models of, 54
  Orthodox. *See* Orthodox Jews.
  Reform. *See* Reform Jews.
  secular, 71
Judaism, halakhah in, 135
  versus aggadah, 171–174
  nature of, 72–76
  "problem" of, 47–50
  specificity of, 99–104
Jung, Carl, 69

Kant, Immanuel, 70, 208
Kaplan, Mordecai, 58, 71
Karelitz, Abraham Y., 169
Kaufmann, Yechezkel, 65–66

Klatzkin, Yaakov, 66
Knowledge, sociology of, 223–227
  of world, 80–81
Kohlberg, Lawrence, 238–239, 240–241, 243–244
Kook, Abraham Isaac, 77, 155–156, 169
Kushner, Harold S., 125

Labor and General Zionism, 6
Lamm, Zvi, 33, 138–139, 231
Learning, process of, 207–210. *See also* Development; Education.
Leibnitz, Gottfried Wilhelm, 229
Leibowitz, Isaiah, 133–136
Locke, John, 208

Maddon, Ward, 121
Mannheim, Karl, 224–226
Mark, Yudel, 57–58
Marx, Karl, 224–225
Meissner, William, 240
Melton Center, 159
Messianism, 59–61, 77, 100, 102
Midrash, 234
Mishnah, 181–182
*Mitzvah(vot)*, 135, 137, 148, 175–176, 180
Models and theories, in science and religion, 174–185
Modernity, affecting explicit and implicit theologians, 200–201
  affecting Jewish religion and education, 8–9
  norms and, **129 150**
Molding model of education, 33
Moore, T.W., 194–195
Morality, and halakhah, 154
Morris, Van Cleve, 185–186
Moses, 146, 269
Mossenson, Ben-Zion, 56

Nationalism, spiritual and natural, 65–66
Neo-behaviorism, 16
Noachide commandments, 90, 118, 183

Normative-ideational    educational
    theory, 10, 17–21, 25–26, **27–
    47**
    historical crisis of, 40–41
    individuality in, 28–32, 32–34,
        37–38
    religion and, 37–47
    underlying assumption of, 36–37
    "whole" person in, 34–36, 38
    world view in, 28–32, 37
Norms, and modernity, **129–150**
Novak, David, 172


Objectives, theological, 41
Orenstein, Walter, 142
Orthodox Jews, 39, 41, 84
    and Reform Jews, 3, 20, 102,
        270
    choice of school by, 30
    modern educational crisis and, 40
Orthodox Zionism, 6


Particularist approach, in under-
    standing religion, 88–91, 96–99
Paton, H.J., 52
Perry, Ralph Barton, 79–80
Personality, development of, 238–
    242
Peters, Richard, 208–209
Phenix, Philip H., 80, 95
Philosophical arguments, against re-
    ligion and religious education,
    52–55
Philosophical Enlightenment, 68–70
Philosophy, educational, effect of on
    curriculum, 253–256
    of religious education, **15–26**
Physics, world view in, 52
Piaget, Jean, 210, 218, 235–238
Plato, 207
Popper, Karl, 69
Prayer. *See under specific prayers,*
    e.g., Hallel; *Shema.*
Psychoanalytic theory, 229
Psychology, behavioral, 229
    humanistic, 16, 229–230
    in religious educational theory,
    **228–249**
Purim, 129–131, 267

Rackman, Emanuel, 115
Ramah camps, 7–8
Rashi, 207–208, 267
Readiness, for religious understand-
    ing, 245
Reform Jews, 39, 172, 271
    and Orthodox Jews, 3, 20, 102,
        270
    choice of school by, 30
    modern educational crisis and, 40
Religion, and Jewish culture, 55–56,
    72–76
    and faith, 29–30
    and religiosity, 152
    arguments against, anti-theologi-
        cal, 58–61
    cultural, 55–58
    educational, 61–63
    philosophical, 52–55
    crisis of, 76–79
    and halakhah, 76–78
    definitions in, 85, 91–95
    deliberative-inductive educational
        theory and, **48–63**
    developmental stages of, 242–243
    explicit and implicit, **108–126,**
        132–133
    Jewish. *See* Judaism.
    models and theories in, 174–185
    normative-ideational    educational
        theory and, 37–47
    particularist approach to, 88–91,
        96–99
    ultimacy in, 95–96
    understanding    of,    particularist
        and universalist approach to,
        88–91
Religious communities, nature of,
    97–98
Religious education, academic dis-
    cussion of, 9–10
    arguments against, anti-theologi-
        cal, 58–61
    cultural, 55–58
    educational, 61–63
    philosophical, 52–55
    contemporary distortions in, 251–
        253
    explicit, 166, **207–227**
    and implicit, 168
    socialization theories contrib-
        uting to, 213–217

Religious education
*(continued)*
  implicit, **228–249**
  in Israel, 60
  Jewish, elements of, **250–269**
    explicit and implicit, 257–269
    secular deliberation and, **48–63**
  malfunctioning of, 81
  modernity and, 8–9
  of children, 21
  philosophical schools of, **15–26**
  sociology and, 207–227
  theory of, **191–206**
    psychology in, **228–249**
  versus indoctrination, 79–80
  views of, 3–8
Religious experience, 88
Responsibility, 185–187
Richardson, Herbert W., 231–234
Rosenzweig, Franz, 53, 173–174

Sabbath, 163
Scheffler, Israel, 208, 229
Schoem, David, 46
School, selection of, by Orthodox Jews, 30
  by Reform Jews, 30
Schwab, Joseph J., 101
Science, impact of, on religion, 68–70
  models and theories in, 174–185
Secular deliberation, 64–68. *See also* Deliberative-inductive educational theory.
  Jewish education and, **48–63**
Secularism, and halakhah, 60
  and Israel, 75–76
Segal, Mordecai, 56
*Shema,* 109, 178–180
Sholl, Doug, 238
Society, and individual, 32
  nature of, 212
Sociology, of knowledge, 223–227
  religious education and, **207–227**
  theory in, limits of, 220–223
Soloveitchik, Aaron, 117
Soloveitchik, Joseph B., 116–118, 137–138, 213–214, 222–223
Sosevsky, Moshe Chaim, 244
*Stages of Faith,* 242
Stark, R., 97, 214
Strauss, Leo, 76

Talmud, 34, 56, 129–132. *See also* Halakhah.
Tanakh. *See* Bible; Torah.
Theologians, explicit versus implicit, 198–201, 202–206
  and their publics, 202–206
Theology, and depth theology, 156–157
  educational. *See* Educational theology.
  ideal objectives for, 41
  models and theories in, 174–185
  versus depth theology, 156–157
Theory(ies), and models, in science and religion, 174–185
  of religious education, **191–206**
    psychology in, **228–249**
*Three Myths of Transcendence,* 231–234
Torah, 89, 96, 102–103, 117, 140, 176, 207, 227. *See also* Bible.
  as "forced upon" Israelites, 266–269
  as God's word, 182
  as key Jewish concept, 100
  as teacher, 136, 138
  children's learning of, 216, 257–258
  in textbook, 142–147, 164
  Jewish denominations and, 30
*Torah as Our Guide,* 142–147, 164
Tradition, Jewish religious, key terms of, 100–104
Tyler, Ralph W., 18, 22

Ultimacy, in religion, 95–96
Universalist approach, in understanding religion, 88–91

Wach, Joachim, 88–89, 98
World view, in educational disciplines, 52–53
  in normative-ideational educational theory, 28–32, 37
Wurzburger, Walter S., 173

Yeshiva High Schools, 7–8
*Yiddishkeit,* 57–58
Yinger, J. Milton, 92–93

Zionism, 49, 74–75
  Labor and General, 6
  Orthodox, 6